To dear Pe[...]
lots of love,
Mother & Dad.

Xmas 2015
Adelaide

The Changi Book

EDITED BY LACHLAN GRANT

Published in association with the Australian War Memorial

NEWSOUTH

AUSTRALIAN
WAR MEMORIAL

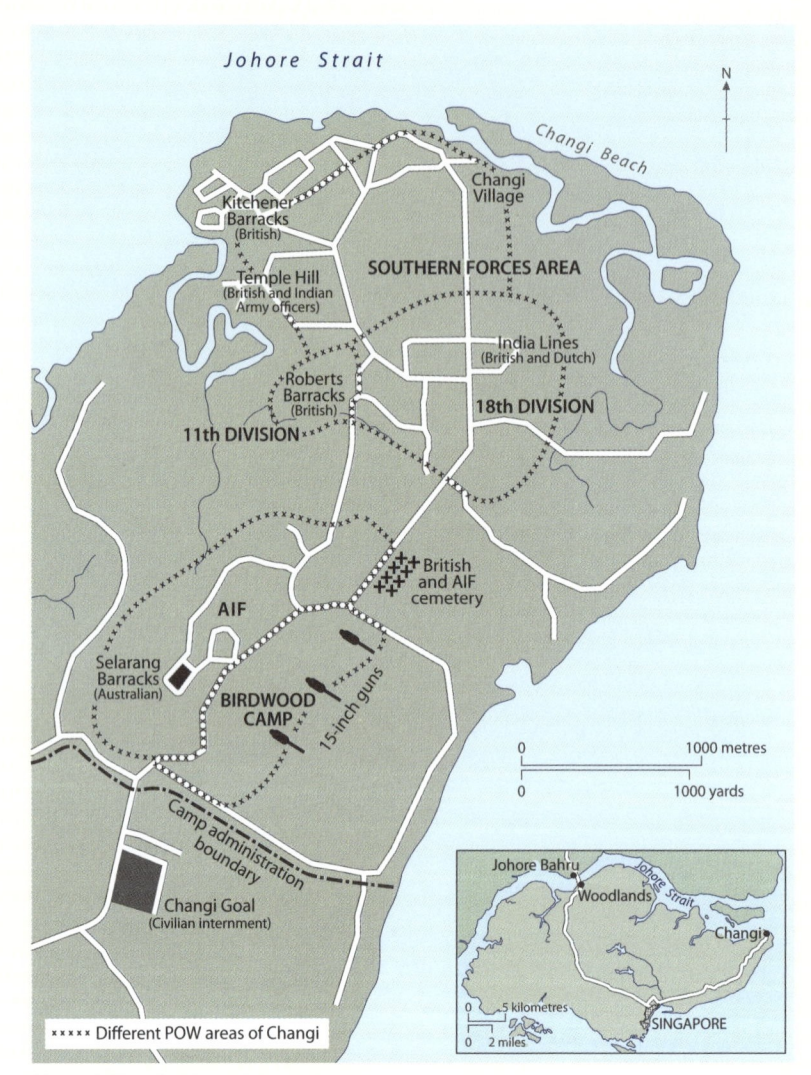

Map of Changi Keith Mitchell

Contents

Changi authors   6

Australian War Memorial contributors   9

LETTERS FROM THE PAST   11
Changi in myth, memory and history *Lachlan Grant*   13

CHANGI LIFE AND SOCIETY   29
The Changi backdrop *C. David Griffin*   30

The Barracks Square incident *Hector Chalmers*   80

Pay *Unknown author*   90

The black market *Unknown author*   94

Trading *Unknown author*   99

Books and prisoners *C. David Griffin*   103

Prisoner-of-war politics *Alick R. Downer*   115

The hidden radio *Patrick Matthews, A. 'Tommy' Thompson, Walter Beadman and Don Wall*   124

On with the motley: the Changi Concert Party *Unknown author*   134

The Panzer Division *Rex Bucknell*   156

Observations on accommodation *Unknown author*   164

Moving house *Unknown author*   177

Christmas in prison *Unknown author*   181

Contents

CHANGI INDUSTRIES 185

The tinkers of Selarang *Unknown author* 186
Workshop operations *Noel Hill* 189
Report on camp workshop *P.G. Miller* 194
Soap Factory *John Kemp* 196
Rubber Factory report *Robert Moffett* 200
Saving our soles as prisoners of war: rubber *Unknown author* 203
The AIF Seedling Nursery *Peter Maddern* 205
Pottery *Unknown author* 212
The broom-makers of Changi *Frederick Roche* 214
Artificial-limb-making *Arthur Purdon and S. Lad* 219

HEALTH AND SURVIVAL 225

The Vitamin Centre *Robert Morton* 226
Hygiene *Carl Gunther* 232
Skin disease among prisoners of war in Malaya *Burnett Clarke* 236
The Pathological Department *Unknown author* 244
Live to eat *Unknown author* 250
Food *Unknown author* 261
Swamps, fun and fever *Rodney Matthews* 268
The Mosquito Squad *Thomas Mitchell* 272
Dental *Unknown author* 275

Contents

WORK AND WORK PARTIES 279

Singapore working party *Charles Tracey* 280
The Changi Garden Party *H. Hutchance* 290
The AIF Forestry Company *E.J. Oraines* 301
2nd Echelon *Unknown author* 313
The work of the Australian Chaplains' Department *Unknown author* 318
Fishing from behind scratch *Jack Bennett* 326
The aerodrome at Changi Point *Stan Arneil* 332
The peace comes to X Party *Unknown author* 337

THOUGHTS OF HOME
Liberation and repatriation *Lachlan Grant* 340

Acknowledgments 342

Notes 343

Further reading 345

Index 346

Changi authors

STANLEY FOCH ARNEIL was born in Sydney in 1918 and grew up in the Blue Mountains. A sergeant in the 2/30th Battalion, after the war Arneil wrote several books, including a biography of 'Black Jack' Galleghan and his published wartime diary *One Man's War*, and dedicated his time to many causes, including church work, drug rehabilitation and the co-operative movement. He died in 1992. (NX54846)

WALTER STANLEY RANDWICK BEADMAN was born in Blackheath, New South Wales, in 1907 and served as a gunner in the 2/15th Field Regiment, Royal Australian Artillery. For his service and devotion to fellow prisoners of war in Thailand, Beadman was later awarded the British Empire Medal. Married and a father of eight children, Beadman was killed by his son in a family dispute in 1953. The son was later acquitted of murder when the court heard that he had struck his father with an axe in an attempt to save his sister's life after Beadman had returned home drunk and assaulted her. (NX31607)

JACK WILSON BENNETT, born in Orange, New South Wales, in 1906, served as a captain in the Australian Army Service Corps. He died in 1994. (NX19301)

REX STRAFFORD BUCKNELL was born in Suva, Fiji, on 30 September 1909 but later lived in Australia. He served as a major in the 2/10th Field Regiment, Royal Australian Artillery. He died in Brisbane in 1971. (QX6319)

HECTOR MACDONALD CHALMERS was born in Flixton, England, in 1904 and served as a lieutenant in the 8th Division Provost Company. Following the war he became involved in politics, running for the Queensland senate as a member of the Australian Labor Party, and attended the Third World Conference Against Atomic and Hydrogen Bombs in Tokyo in 1957. He died in Queensland in 1978. (NX57772)

DR BURNETT LESLIE WOODBURN CLARKE was born in Melbourne in 1897. As a medical student, Clarke served during the First World War in the Australian Army Medical Corps. He continued to serve in the army between the wars and later became a specialist in radiology. In the Second World War Clarke served as a major in the 2/13th Australian General Hospital. He died in 1974. His wartime diary was posthumously published as *Behind the Wire: The Clinical War Diary of Major Burnett Clarke* (1989). (QX22806)

SIR ALEXANDER RUSSELL (ALICK) DOWNER was born in North Adelaide in 1910, and served in Singapore as a gunner with the 8th Divisional Artillery. At Changi he took charge of the library, and taught law and politics to fellow prisoners. In 1949 he was elected to the House of Representatives as the Liberal–Country Party member for Angas. He was appointed Minister for Immigration in 1958 and joined Menzies' cabinet the following year. In 1963 Downer became Australian High Commissioner to London and received a knighthood in 1965. He left the post in 1972 and retained an active interest in politics until his death in 1981. His son, Alexander John Gosse Downer, also became a prominent politician and was the Commonwealth Minister for Foreign Affairs and Trade from 1996 to 2007.

SIR CHARLES DAVID GRIFFIN, born in Leura, New South Wales, in 1915, trained and worked as a lawyer before enlisting in the

AIF in 1940. In Malaya Griffin served as a sergeant with the 2/3rd Motor Ambulance Convoy. After the war Griffin returned to the legal profession, joined the Sydney City Council and later became Lord Mayor (he was awarded a knighthood in 1972). In 1947 he published *The Happiness Box*, a story he had written in Changi in 1942 for the children interned in Changi Gaol. Illustrated by Leslie Greener, *The Happiness Box* told the story of Winston the clever lizard, Martin the monkey, Wobbley the frog, and their search for the secret of happiness. Republished in 1990, *The Happiness Box* was later declared one of the 'national treasures' of the *Australia's Great Libraries* exhibition, and in recent years has been turned into a stage production. In 2002 Griffin also compiled and published *Changi Days*, a collection of poetry by prisoners in Changi. Griffin died in 2004, aged 88. (NX69235)

CARL ERNEST MITCHELMORE GUNTHER was born in Sydney in 1904. A graduate of the University of Sydney, specialising in tropical medicine, Gunther served as a major, first as a medical officer in New Guinea, before joining the 8th Division Headquarters in Malaya. Gunther published several studies on malarial control and other tropical diseases – one book was published in New York in 1944 while he was still a captive in Changi. He joined the New Guinea Volunteer Rifles in 1951. He died in 1976. (NX76596)

NOEL ARTHUR HILL was born in Sydney in 1906. Before the war he was a lecturer in engineering technology at the University of Sydney. Serving as a captain in the Australian Army Ordnance Corps, Hill was later Mentioned in Despatches for his services to fellow prisoners in Changi. He died in 1977. (NX70185)

H. HUTCHANCE was from the Melbourne suburb of Thornbury (he includes a postal address at the end of his essay). As there is no record of anyone named Hutchance serving in the Australian forces, this may have been a pen name. It is also possible he was a civilian, or served with the British forces, the Straits Settlements Volunteer Force, or the Federated Malay States Volunteer Force.

JOHN ERNEST KEMP, born in 1892, served in the First World War with the 6th Light Horse on Gallipoli and in the Middle East. He lied about his age to enlist in the Second World War, stating on his enlistment paper that he was 39 when he was ten years older. In the Second AIF, Kemp served as a private in the 2/4th Casualty Clearing Station. He died in 1970. (VX59807)

S. LAD is believed to be the pen name of an unknown Australian soldier of the 2/29th Battalion.

NORMAN PETERSON MADDERN was born around 1919 in Adelaide and served as captain with the 2/40th Battalion as part of Sparrow Force in Timor. In 1947 he was made a Member of the Order of the British Empire for his 'highly meritorious service' while a prisoner of war in Changi. After the war he continued to serve in the military, eventually being made lieutenant colonel and general staff officer at the Directorate of Military Intelligence in Canberra. He passed away on Anzac Day 1964. (NX34934)

PATRICK JAMES MATTHEWS was born in Adelaide in 1922. He served with the 2/10th Field Company Engineers, and at Changi was deeply involved with the procurement and concealment of radios. In 1947 he was Mentioned in Despatches for services rendered while in Japanese hands. (VX20825)

RODNEY GORDON MATTHEWS was born in Adelaide's inner south in October 1912. He served in Malaya with the Australian Mobile Bacterial Laboratory. After the war he worked as an agricultural-horticultural journalist with the Melbourne *Herald*. He and his wife, pioneering doctor Ida Bell Matthews, adopted four children. Matthews was said to have suffered ill-health from his prisoner days, and died in 1978. (VX38929)

P.G. MILLER was a British soldier who served as a warrant officer with the appointment of Artificer Sergeant Major in the Royal Army Ordnance Corps of the British 18th Division.

THOMAS WALTER MITCHELL was born in 1906 on his family's grazing property, Towong Hill station, near Corryong in Victoria. A champion skier and multiple gold medallist, Mitchell founded the Australian National Ski Federation, and also captained the Australian skiing team. He was a captain in the 2/22nd Battalion and survived work on the Burma–Thailand Railway, and after the war he built a chapel on his property in memory of his lost comrades. Mitchell wrote several books and also made contributions to the official history of the Second World War. He served as state member for Benambra for 29 years, including terms as attorney-general and solicitor-general. He and his wife, author Elyne Mitchell, become the first people to cross the Australian Alps in a motor vehicle. He died in Melbourne in 1984. (VX43577)

ROBERT NIXON MOFFETT was sent to Singapore in 1928 on the Royal Navy yacht *Sea Belle II*. He lived and worked there as an engineer with the Straits Steamship Company before being captured by the Japanese. In various prison camps he served as a civilian attached to the Straits Settlements Volunteer Force, and was imprisoned with the prisoners of war at Changi. After the war he returned to the SSC as stores superintendent in Telok Ayer, and worked there until 1961. He died the following year.

ROBERT CECIL MORTON was born in Bundaberg, Queensland, in 1913. During the Second World War he served with the 2/9th Field Ambulance. He died in 1986. (QX22744)

E.J. ORAINES is believed to have been the pen name of an unknown Australian, British or Dutch soldier imprisoned at Changi during the war.

ARTHUR HENRY MASON PURDON was born in Sydney in 1900. He served in the First World War and in the interim years worked as a health inspector. Joining up again in 1941, Purdon served as warrant officer with the 2/30th Battalion. On 16 January 1942 the battalion was attacked near Gemas. During the withdrawal Purdon remained behind to ensure the evacuation of the wounded, risking heavy, close-range enemy fire. He also led daily ration parties to the forward-most troops, succeeding despite heavy shelling. After the war he was awarded the Distinguished Conduct Medal for his actions, citing his 'exceptional courage and devotion to duty'. (NX67447)

FREDERIC CHARLES ROCHE was born in 1901 in Sydney. A boundary rider before the war, he enlisted in 1940 and served as a bombardier in the 2/10th Field Regiment. In 1947 he was Mentioned in Despatches for services rendered while a prisoner of war of the Japanese. He died in 1982. (QX9721)

A. 'TOMMY' THOMPSON's identity is unclear. He may have been one of the eight A. Thompsons with the AIF in Changi. However, since we know his friend Don Wall called him 'Tommy', it is possible he was a British soldier.

CHARLES PATRICK TRACEY was born in the Sydney suburb of Hurstville in 1908 and commanded the 2/26th Australian Infantry Battalion in Malaya. After the war he was Mentioned in Despatches. There is little information available now on Tracey's postwar life, and he died aged 66 in 1974. (NX70508)

DONALD WALL was born in Bombala, New South Wales, in January 1920, and served as a private with the 2/20th Australian Infantry Battalion. He endured eight months working on the Burma–Thailand Railway, and was later Mentioned in Despatches for his role in constructing a hidden radio at Changi. Some years after the war he published *Singapore and Beyond*, which detailed his own and his comrades' experiences as prisoners of the Japanese. He published several more books, including *Sandakan: The Last March*, which led to the establishment of the Sandakan Memorial Foundation. In 1995 he was awarded the Order of Australia in recognition of his contribution to Australian military history. (NX36620)

Editor's note

Some of the language used by the authors of the original essays might be considered racist or offensive, but is included here for the purpose of representing past attitudes and outlooks. Such views do not necessarily reflect those of the editor or of the Australian War Memorial.

Australian War Memorial contributors

KATE ARIOTTI completed a PhD at the University of Queensland and joined the Australian War Memorial's Military History Section in 2014. Her research explores the impact of wartime imprisonment on Australians during the First World War, specifically those affected by captivity in Turkey, and she has longstanding interests in the legacy of captivity for returned prisoners of war. In 2015 she was appointed lecturer in Australian history at the University of Newcastle.

CRAIG BLANCH joined the Australian War Memorial in 2007. In 2010 he was involved in the redevelopment of the Hall of Valour and continues to work closely with the Memorial's Victoria Cross and George Cross collection. He is currently an assistant curator with the Military Heraldry and Technology section.

EMMA CAMPBELL is Manager of *Wartime*, the official magazine of the Australian War Memorial. A journalist for almost ten years, Emma has a Bachelor of Arts (Communications) from Charles Sturt University. She came to the Memorial in 2006, joining the Military History Section in 2011.

CHRIS GODDARD is a curator in the Memorial's Military Heraldry and Technology section. He has worked with this collection for more than 20 years and knows many of the fascinating stories behind its vast holdings. He has curated a number of the Memorial's travelling exhibitions, including *Australia Under Attack 1942–43* and *Out in the Cold: Australia's Involvement in the Korean War*.

LACHLAN GRANT joined the Australian War Memorial in 2011 as a historian in the Military History Section. Previously, he worked as a lecturer at Monash University, where he completed his PhD in 2010. He has published widely on the Second World War and on the prisoner-of-war experience, and his first book, *Australian Soldiers in Asia–Pacific in World War II*, was published in 2014. He is also a Visiting Fellow at the Strategic and Defence Studies Centre at the Australian National University.

VICK GWYN joined the Australian War Memorial in 2010 as an assistant curator in the Photographs section, where she has researched and worked closely with the Aspinall collection. Vick has also undertaken Memorial assignments in Australia as an oral historian and photographer.

LENORE HEATH commenced work at the Australian War Memorial in 2004 following careers in teaching and librarianship. Her role as assistant curator in the Photographs section encompasses collection development, research and documentation. She has written articles for the Memorial's *Wartime* magazine and other publications.

WARWICK HEYWOOD has been curator of art at the Australian War Memorial for more than eight years. He has played a key role in enhancing the Memorial's collection of modernist art and the development and exhibition of its contemporary official war art scheme. He curated the Second World War art exhibition *Reality in Flames*, and is the author of numerous publications and articles related to the Memorial's art collection.

ELENI HOLLOWAY is an assistant curator with the Memorial's Military Heraldry and Technology section. She joined the Australian

War Memorial in 2012. Previously, she worked at the Anzac Memorial, and was a volunteer at the Sydney Jewish Museum and the NSW Office of Veterans' Affairs. She is currently completing a Master of Studies in History and Museums and Collections.

KARL JAMES is a senior historian in the Memorial's Military History Section. He completed his PhD at the University of Wollongong in 2005 and has published widely on Australia's involvement in the Second World War. Karl is also a Visiting Fellow at the Strategic and Defence Studies Centre at the Australian National University. His first book, *The Hard Slog: Australians in the Bougainville Campaign, 1944–45*, was published in 2012.

KERRY NEALE is an acting curator in the Memorial's Military Heraldry and Technology section. She has worked at the Memorial in various roles since 2004 and is completing a PhD in History at the University of New South Wales, Canberra, focusing on First World War facial wounds and disfigured soldiers.

GARTH O'CONNELL joined the Australian War Memorial in 1996 as a volunteer when studying Cultural Heritage Management at the University of Canberra. Made permanent after his graduation in 1999, he is a curator within the Military Heraldry and Technology section. As a soldier he has deployed on Australian peacekeeping operations and to Malaysia and Singapore with Rifle Company Butterworth in 2002–03.

JANE PEEK is a curator in the Military Heraldry and Technology section of the Australian War Memorial. Among the many significant items across the Memorial's collection that she has worked with closely for more than 30 years are the Changi quilts.

LUCY ROBERTSON was selected as a 2013 Australian War Memorial Summer Vacation Scholar, and her published report focused on military discipline in Changi. She has completed a Master of Liberal Arts (Museums and Collections) at the Australian National University, and has a Bachelor of Arts (History) from the University of Adelaide.

Letters from the past

Reunion at Changi, by Harold Abbott, 1945. An ex-prisoner (foreground, left) tells a newly arrived soldier about the gaol.
ART23949

12

Changi in myth, memory and history
LACHLAN GRANT

The most lasting memory of the fall of Singapore was the terrific silence following the cease fire order. The din of firing, bombs falling and exploding and the general noises of war, had become normal to us. When it suddenly ceased, the silence seemed to hurt. One felt as though he were alone in a secluded forest glade with all the bird sounds and noises muted.[1]

Since 1923 Singapore had been identified as the keystone of British Empire defence planning in Asia. The so-called 'Singapore strategy' dictated that if a threat developed in Asia a fleet could be sent from Britain to the new naval base in Singapore within three months. British propagandists proclaimed Singapore an 'impregnable fortress', but at the outbreak of war in the Pacific the military resources required for the defence of the Malay Peninsula had not been adequately provided. With Britain's best and most modern arms and equipment committed in Europe for the war against Germany and Italy, the defenders of Malaya were forced to make do with inadequate aircraft.

The Japanese landed on the Malay Peninsula on 8 December 1941 (the same day as the attack on Pearl Harbor, 7 December on the opposite side of the International Date Line). The 22nd and 27th Brigades of the 8th Division of the Australian Imperial Force (AIF), based in the southern Malayan province of Johore, first encountered the Japanese in mid-January. The Australians had some successes, notably the 2/30th Battalion's ambush at Gemenceh (near Gemas) on 14 January 1942, and the destruction of eight enemy tanks at Bakri by the 2/4th Anti-Tank Regiment and 2/29th Battalion. But Japanese forces were mobile, they had air support (and controlled the sea following the sinking of HMS *Prince of Wales* and *Repulse*), and they aggressively attacked and pushed through the ill-prepared line of defenders, often outflanking them. This caused panic and confusion among senior commanders, and resulted in a series of withdrawals down the peninsula. The last British Empire troops were evacuated across the causeway from Malaya to Singapore on 31 January.

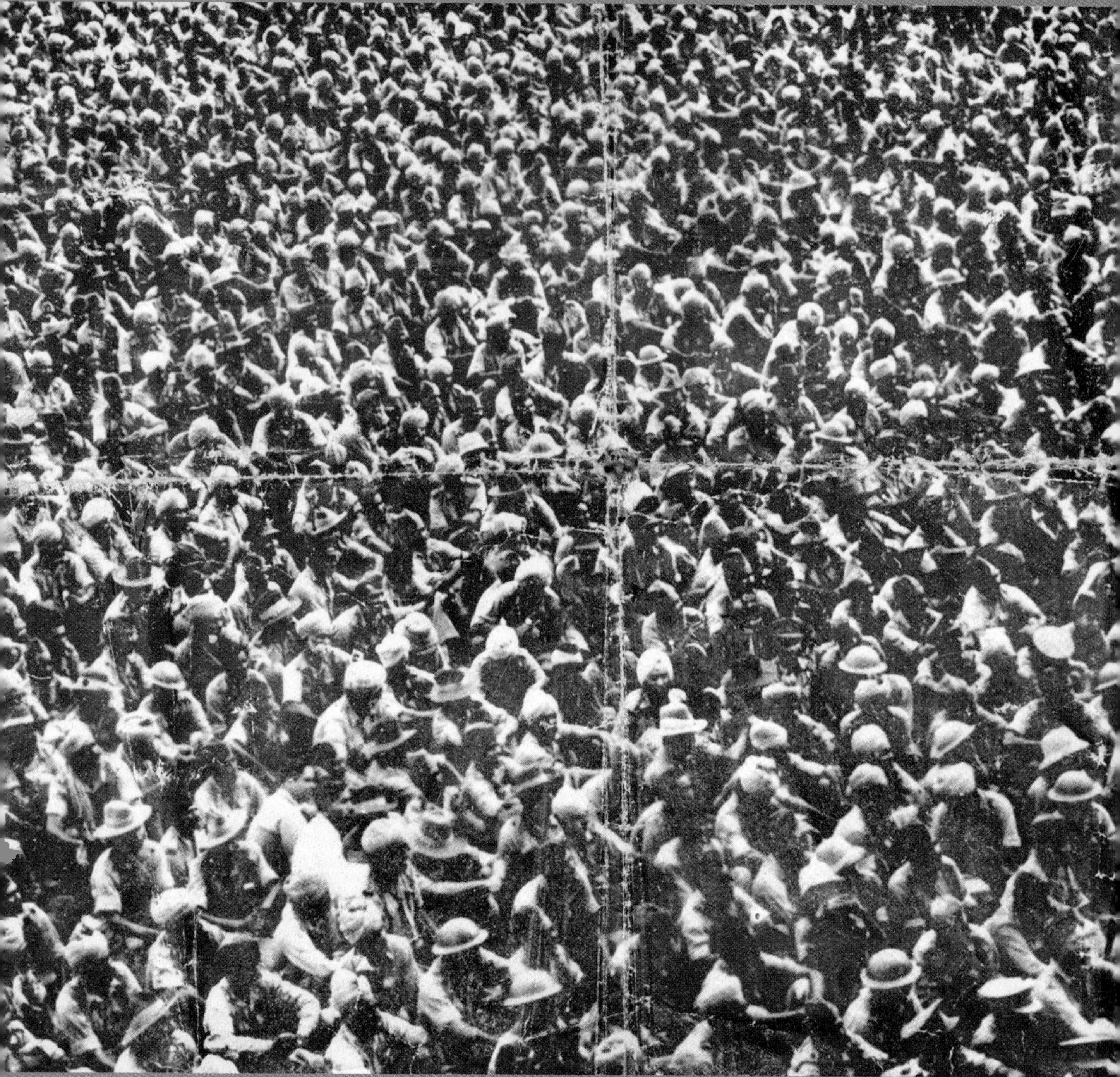

CHANGI IN MYTH, MEMORY AND HISTORY

The battle for Singapore commenced on the night of 8/9 February when the Japanese landed on the north-west of the island. Here they faced the Australian 22nd and 27th Brigades, the first of the British Empire troops to meet the attack. The fighting was fierce, but by 15 February the Allied forces had lost control of the island's reservoirs. That day Lieutenant General Arthur Percival, Commander of the British Empire forces in Malaya, accepted the Japanese demand for unconditional surrender.[2] Following the capitulation, Sergeant James Roxburgh of the 2/30th Battalion wrote in his diary: 'During the day we returned all our ammo, rifles, all arms and equipment and are now laying about the camp till we see what becomes of us'.[3]

> **We returned all our ammo, rifles, all arms and equipment**

AIF losses during the campaign were severe. Some battalions lost half their strength in the space of a few weeks. In one of the costliest campaigns for Australia in the Second World War, 1789 Australians were killed and 1306 were wounded. In a single week of fighting on Singapore Island more than 880 Australians were killed. It was one of the few campaigns in which the total dead exceeded the number of wounded.[4] At the stroke of a pen, 130 000 British troops, including 15 000 members of the 8th Division, became prisoners of war.

Many myths persist about the wartime experiences of prisoners of the Japanese. The view of Changi as a prisoner 'hell', expressed within many popular historical works and often

A Japanese photograph showing some of the thousands of British and Commonwealth troops captured at the fall of Singapore.
134903

15

repeated within the media, is an interpretation derived from knowledge of the horrific conditions on the Burma–Thailand Railway. But prisoners of war across Asia faced quite different conditions in each camp depending on local circumstances and the attitudes of the camp commanders. In Burma and Thailand, where the brutal enslavement of prisoners has become indelibly ingrained upon the Australian wartime narrative, more than 2800 Australians (almost 22 per cent) died constructing the railway. In some work parties in Thailand, as many as 30 per cent of Australian prisoners did not survive. While conditions in camps across Japan were better, at Naoetsu 20 per cent of the 300 Australians who entered that camp died. More than 70 per cent of the Australians captured on the island of Ambon died in captivity. At Sandakan in Borneo only six prisoners survived of the 2500 Australians and Britons transported there from Singapore. At sea, 1800 Australian prisoners of war and civilian internees lost their lives when the ships in which they were transported were sunk by Allied submarines. This included all 1054 captives aboard the *Monte-video Maru*, which was sunk on 1 July 1942. In total, of the 22 000 Australians to become prisoners of the Japanese, one-third died in captivity.[5]

Of the estimated 87 000 Allied prisoners who passed through Changi prisoner-of-war camp, 850 died there.[6] Those who remained in the camp were in many ways the lucky ones. After the experience of camps in Burma and Thailand, some prisoners considered Changi to be more 'like heaven'.[7]

RIGHT A cartoon from George Sprod's magazine *Smoke-oh*, published in Changi.
3DRL/5040.002

An illustration from cartoonist George Sprod's scrapbook. In the tropics of Malaya it did not take long for the jungle to reclaim traces of the battlefield.
3DRL/5040.001

WHILE UNDERTAKING research in the Australian War Memorial's archive in early 2012 I came across a collection labelled '8 Div. Papers'. I had expected a large file of official documents and reports on the Malayan campaign, but the collection turned out to contain 11 folders of 51 mostly handwritten essays about various aspects of life in the

They sent him far away
They shouted "Hip Hooray!"

— But look at him today! —

Changi prisoner-of-war camp. They were written on the backs of Singapore prison records from the 1930s or on paper handmade in Changi. Essay subjects included anecdotes on camp life, various forms of work and industry, health, hygiene, and food. Intrigued, I looked deeper into the institutional records to discover that these were essays for a proposed Changi book. In fact, reference was made to the proposed publication in Stan Arneil's *One Man's War* (his original diary is held in the Australian War Memorial's collection): 'One day we received news of a short story competition', Arneil wrote, 'for a proposed publication called "Changi Papers", after the war, of course.'[8] The Changi book, however, was never published.

The collection of essays provides a narrative of life in the Changi prisoner-of-war camp written by those who were there, while they were there. Some essays reinforce the tendency in Australian prisoner-of-war writing to emphasise the traits synonymous with the Anzac legend. Others, however, offer complex accounts that challenge popular myths and misconceptions. That they were contributions for a proposed Changi book tells us that these were stories prisoners wanted to tell, stories they wanted the public to know and that they wanted Changi to be remembered by. Significantly, it is a collection offering not a single narrative but rather multiple viewpoints that reveal for the reader the complexities of life for a prisoner of war.

Contrary to some representations of prisoners of war, those interned at Changi did not necessarily perceive themselves as passive victims. Rather, in many cases they regarded themselves as agents of their own fate and fortune. In dire circumstances these men made the best of their lot and of the society and community that was created in the camp. Their stories tell of inventiveness regarding food and food production, and display a keen awareness of the right nutritional and vitamin intake required to supplement the failings of a captive's diet. They detail measures taken to implement and improve health, hygiene, medicine, hospitals and housing. They speak of organised education and of the concert halls that attracted up to 1000 spectators daily; of camp politics and the formation of political groups; of the establishment of industries, trades and markets; and of civic institutions such as the library and the university. And there are stories of the various workshops and industries that were established to maintain the camp. During working hours Changi was a hive of activity, every prisoner with his own job to do. Colourful anecdotes paint a rich picture of Changi life, from how news and rumours spread within the camp to the more insidious tales of the black market, theft and the darker aspects of camp life.

They regarded themselves as agents of their own fate

There are also aspects of Changi these essays do not tell. Despite known divisions in

Sergeant Griffin's flyer advertising the Changi prisoner-of-war literary competition, entries for which were collected for a proposed publication of 'Changi papers'.
AWM54 554/11/33

```
AIF - SECOND LITERARY CONTEST

1.  Success of the first AIF Literary Contest has encouraged a second
    contest in an extended form.  Entries are called for from:-
        (a)  All ranks AIF, including working parties whenever possible
        (b)  All ranks in Selarang Area.
2.  Contest is divided into the following Sections:-
    Section I    Essay - set subject; "How Changi will influence our ethical
                 outlook"          (Not more than 2000 words)
    Section II   Short Story - any setting.  (Not more than 2500 words)
    Section III  Adventures in the Campaign, or as a POW (Up to 2500 words)
    Section IV   Verse - (a) Serious. (b) Humorous.     (Any length)
    Section V    Theatre - Plays, sketches, dramatic material (Any length)
3.  Judging Committee will include an experienced journalist, a book-
    reviewer and a Lecturer in English.
4.  Prizes will consist of certificates signed by Commander AIF.
    First, Second and Third Prizes will be awarded in each Section.
    The Judges, however, reserve the     right to withold awards if,
    in their opinion, entries do not reach a sufficient standard.
5.  Readings of winning entries will be made at public meetings.  An
    author may read his own entry, or delegate the task.
6.  It is hoped that, on release, a selection of entries in these
    contests will be published, together with other papers and talks
    written in Changi or Singapore.
7.  CLOSING DATE 31 OCT 42, AT EDUCATION CENTRE AIF
            IMPORTANT - Entries must NOT bear author's name.
                        Name & Unit must be on a separate
                        sheet which can be detached from the
                        manuscript.
```

the relationships between officers and Other Ranks, they contain few criticisms of officers. We know, too, that the desperate circumstances of captivity brought out the best and worst in people, but the focus of the prisoner-of-war authors here leans towards the finer aspects of the human character. In this sense, these essays are not out of character with the popular postwar memoirs by authors such as Russell Braddon and Rohan Rivett, which were written in the style of a *Boy's Own* adventure emphasising the virtues of the British character.[9] They are, therefore, a product of their time.

This unique collection of essays was compiled by Sergeant C. David Griffin and fellow members of the AIF Education Centre established in Changi: an officer, Captain Leslie Greener, and three sergeants; Griffin, Alick Downer and Anthony Newsom (the lawyer, the scholar, and the salesman, as Braddon described them[10]). In October 1942 Griffin organised a literary competition, inviting Australian and British prisoners to submit short stories.[11] The rules of the competition dictated that the authors remain anonymous. This may have been for security reasons: anonymity may well have been preferable for the author of a revealing essay on black-market activities, for example. It may also have been in part a measure to keep in the tradition of earlier AIF annuals such as *Active Service* and *Soldiering On*. However, Griffin also felt that anonymity might encourage those not practised or confident in their writing to come forward with submissions.[12] Despite this rule a number of the essays are signed by the authors.

> **Captivity brought out the best and worst in people**

On 14 October 1944 David Griffin was given formal approval by the camp's senior AIF officers to prepare a Changi publication. The purpose of the collection was to present 'in vivid and interesting form as many aspects as possible of POW life, without avoidance but without emphasis of the hardship angle, and bringing out the features of POW life which may not be apparent from official reports'.[13] The official war artist V. Murray Griffin, already contracted by the Memorial in 1941, was tasked with providing illustrations. Some of the essays were written while the men were in captivity; some were written in the days after the announcement of the Japanese surrender, or shortly following the liberation of the camp in September 1945. Not all the essays contain dates, but some were written as early as 1942, with the majority written between 1944 and 1945.

Shortly after returning to Australia, David Griffin sent the collection to John Treloar, then Director of the Australian War Memorial and head of the military history section of the army. *The Changi Memorial Book* (alternatively, *The Changi Book* or *8th Division*

Book) would be produced in the style of *The Anzac Book* and subsequent First and Second World War annuals. These Memorial publications had proved extremely popular. The 1941 Christmas annual, *Active Service*, had an original print run of 94 531 copies, the largest print order in Australia at that time, and 1944's *Jungle Warfare*, the most popular in the series, sold 230 407 copies in its first print.[14] The Memorial planned to publish the Changi book immediately following the respective publication of the 1945 AIF, RAN and RAAF Christmas annuals, but industrial action among printing firms led to a backlog, and subsequent limits were placed on Memorial publications. One way or another, with no prospect of publication until at least 1948, momentum was lost and the original proposal lapsed. Versions of some of the stories appeared in the *As You Were* series (the 1946–50 annuals), but the single Changi volume never eventuated.

Not all of the 51 essays in the collection have been included in this volume. Limitations on space have required editorial decisions that

This entry in the 8th Division's War Diary outlines plans for the suggested publication of a Changi book by the Australian War Memorial.
AWM52 1/5/19

LETTERS FROM THE PAST

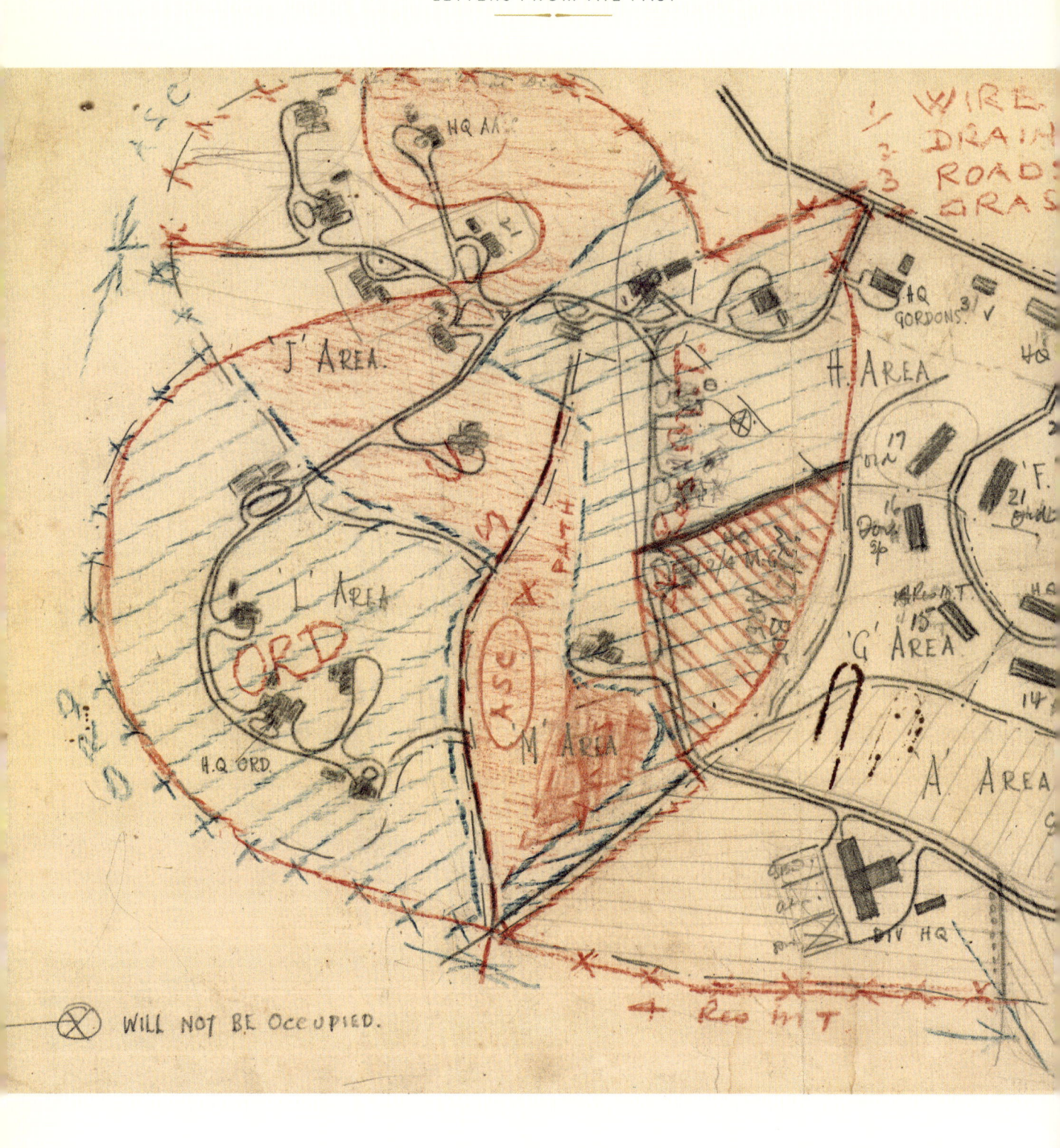

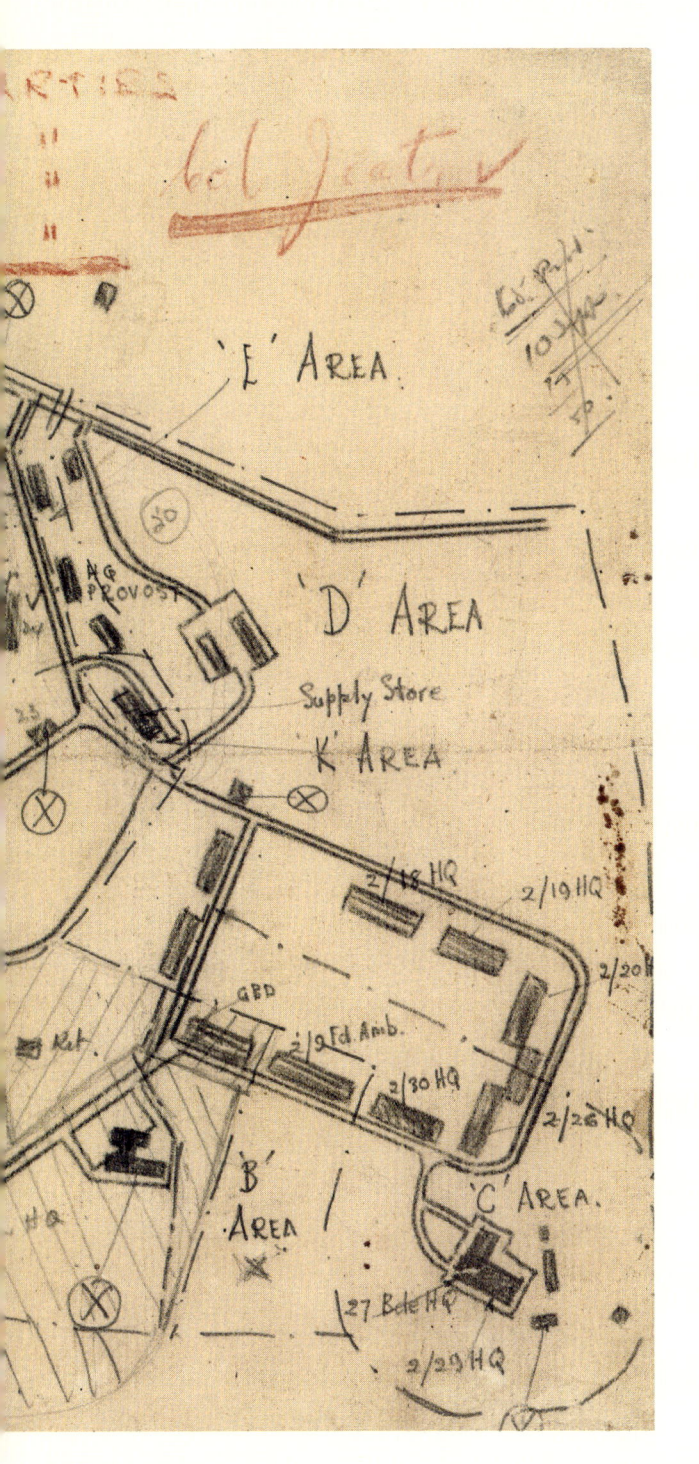

have ultimately shaped the final presentation. A few essays that dealt with experiences on the Burma–Thailand Railway – even though this horrific interlude was part of the narrative – were omitted to keep Changi the focus of the book. Other stories, which read more like myth than reality, were left out. One, about preparing a bath for a Japanese officer to just below boiling point (in order to scald the bather) has been claimed not only by prisoners from a variety of camps but also by prisoners of the Italians and Germans.

While the essays presented here focus solely on the Changi camp, many make reference to 'up-country' camps in Thailand. This acknowledgment of the unspoken horrors of the 'Railway' experience makes clear the authors' sombre awareness of the disparity between their circumstances at Changi and the more acute suffering of fellow prisoners elsewhere. Later on in their captivity a divide developed between the prisoners who had remained in Changi, working in industries supporting the camp, and those who had been drafted into work parties to work for the Japanese (such as those on the Burma–Thailand Railway).[15]

Map outlining the AIF area of Changi. Selarang Barracks Square is at the right of the map. Not shown are the Roberts Barracks (Hospital), Southern Forces, 11th Division and 18th Division areas, which were located further north, while Changi Gaol sat to the south.
AWM54 554/11/46

An AIF parade in Selarang Barracks Square in 1942 and (overleaf) Australian prisoners of war watching a performance by the Concert Party. These photographs, taken secretly by Kennedy Burnside, give a sense of the size of Changi camp.
P03821.029

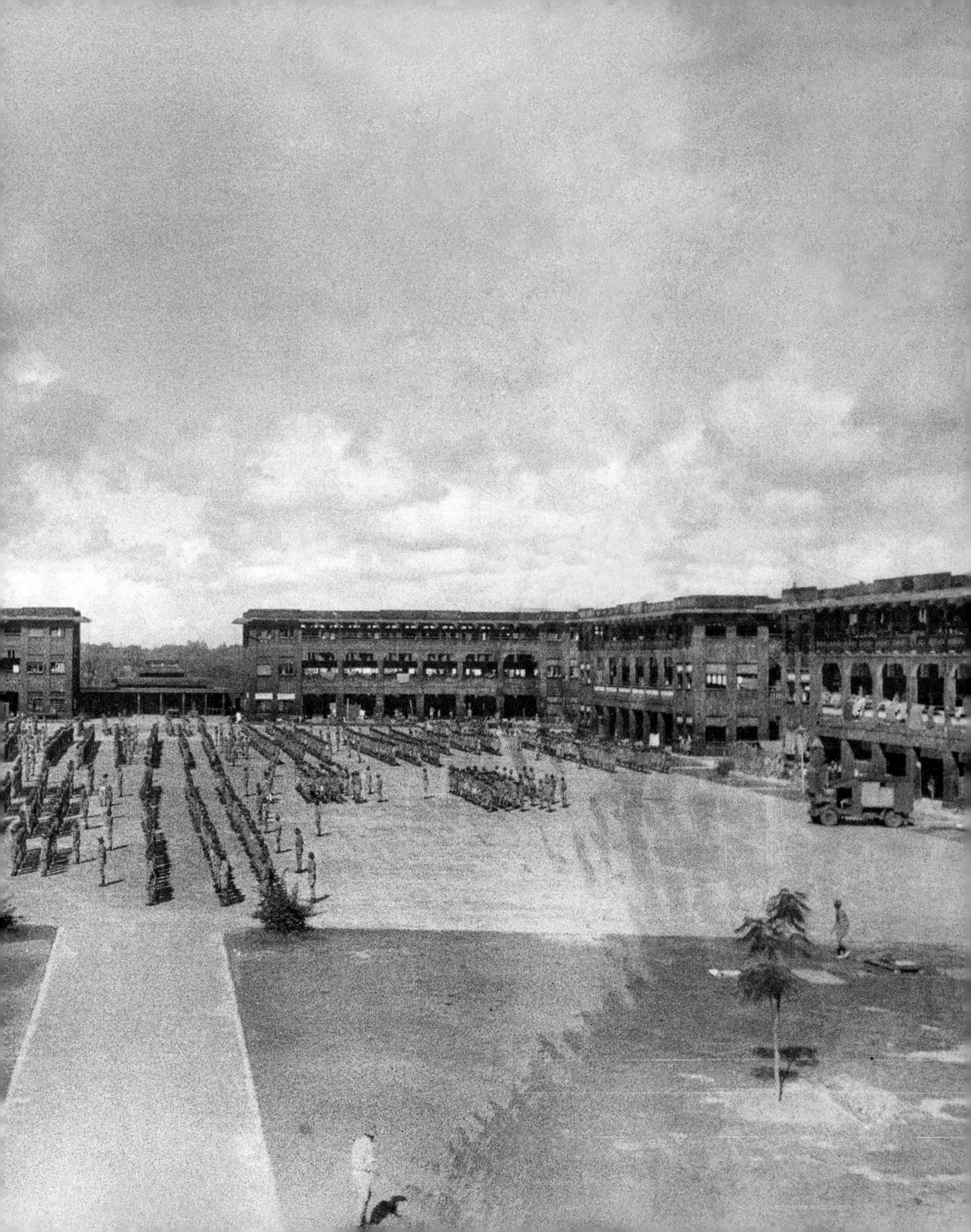

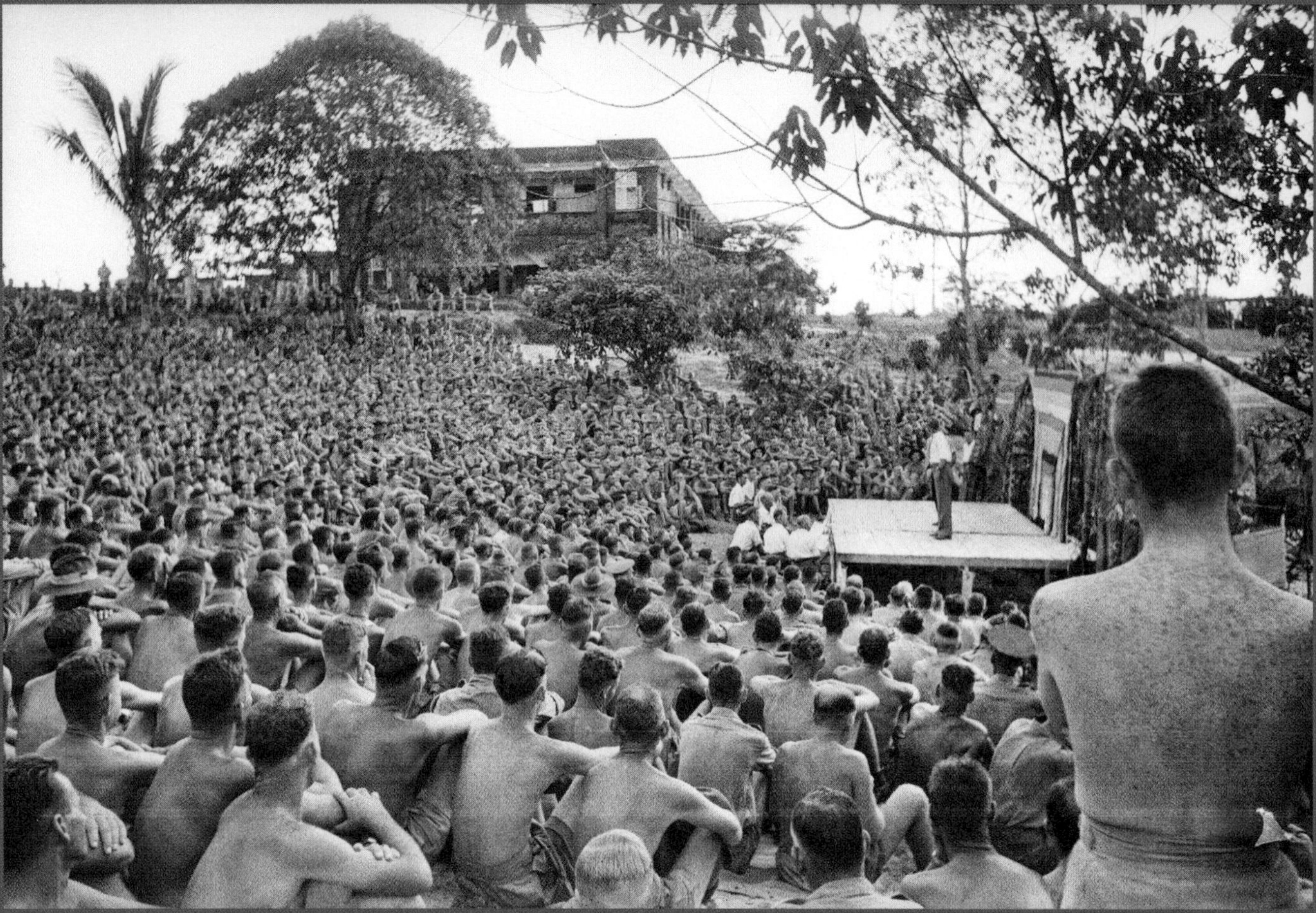

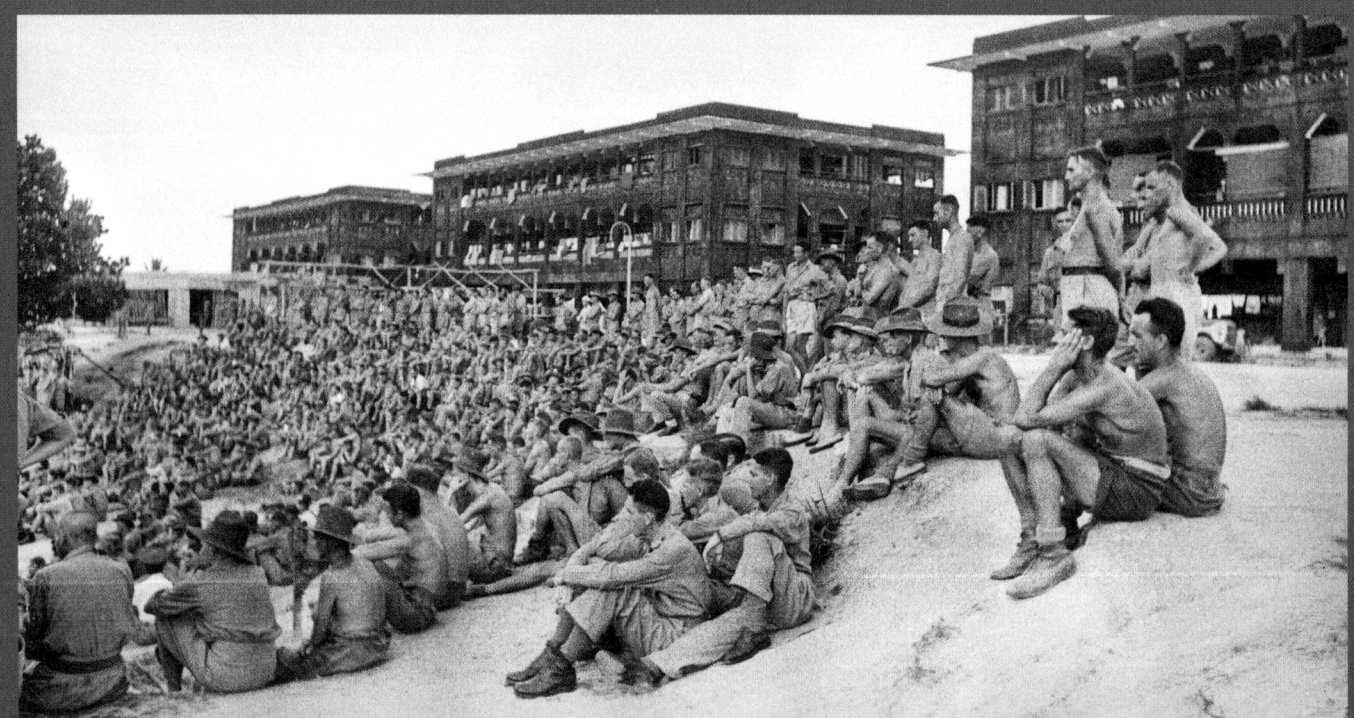

The essays have been left in their original form as much as possible. They have been changed only for consistency of style, and for the correction of the occasional error (such as dates or statistics based on the estimates by the author). On occasion, for lengthy essays, passages that were tangential to the crux of the story were cut. However, no words have been changed that might alter the meaning or tone of the original text.

Complementing the original essays written by the prisoners are short entries by Australian War Memorial historians and curators, included to help provide context, introduce key characters, or tell the remarkable stories behind unique collection items. Illustrating the book are many of Murray Griffin's drawings, a number of which were developed with the intention to illustrate the essays in this collection. The essays and the artworks have been combined here for the first time. Research into the Australian War Memorial's collections revealed many further objects, items and photographs that directly relate to stories being told in these papers, and these are included where possible. A number of the photographs that appear in this book have never before been published, and many of the objects have never been seen by the general public.

HISTORIANS HAVE NOTED that in their postwar writing, which emphasised the resilience, resourcefulness and sense of camaraderie among the captured men and women, prisoners of war forged a place as inheritors of the Anzac legend.[16] This has been seen by some historians as a concerted attempt to address the stigma that came with defeat. By laying down arms in surrender, it has been said that prisoners of war contradicted the traditional stereotype of the Anzac warrior.[17] Certainly, individual prisoners in Changi came to terms with their predicament in their own way. As prisoner John Nevell of the 2/10th Field Regiment reflected following the surrender:

> **There is great emphasis that they were always soldiers**

> It had never entered my head there should be such a thing as surrender. I never thought about being a prisoner. On the previous Wednesday we had all been told that we had to fight to the last man. Such discipline, through long training, does this to you … To hear that we had 'capitulated' left us dumbfounded.[18]

When the prisoners of war returned home a degree of ambivalence was directed towards them, and there was a sense within the community that they were different from other returning veterans. That their captors were of a race that in the attitudes of the era were considered inferior to those of British descent also cast a shadow. While some prisoners found accommodations with their past or simply moved on in life, for others the experience of captivity was a burden they carried for the rest of their lives. Still, hundreds of prisoners of war – including many of the authors in this collection – received military honours and awards in recognition of their efforts assisting fellow prisoners during years of captivity.

For those in Changi, working under AIF command for the benefit of the entire camp, there is a sense within these essays that they were active participants in shaping the best possible conditions for their survival. In their own writings there is great emphasis – very much as the AIF commander in Changi, Lieutenant Colonel Frederick 'Black Jack' Galleghan, had persistently drummed into them – that they were always soldiers. To be a soldier was to be disciplined, which corresponded to the maintenance of health and an increased chance of survival.

Much of the prisoner-of-war story has so far focused on the atrocities perpetuated and the places where conditions were worst, and while it is important to remember that 8000 prisoners of war died during their captivity, it should also be recognised that 14 000 Australian prisoners survived. The resourcefulness and ingenuity shown by the prisoners in Changi, as demonstrated in their writing, is a reflection that for those who lived through it, despite coming second-best in the battle for Malaya and Singapore, surviving captivity was ultimately regarded as a personal triumph.

A Japanese postcard depicting Percival's surrender to Yamashita at the Ford factory, 15 February 1942.
Garth O'Connell collection

Changi life and society

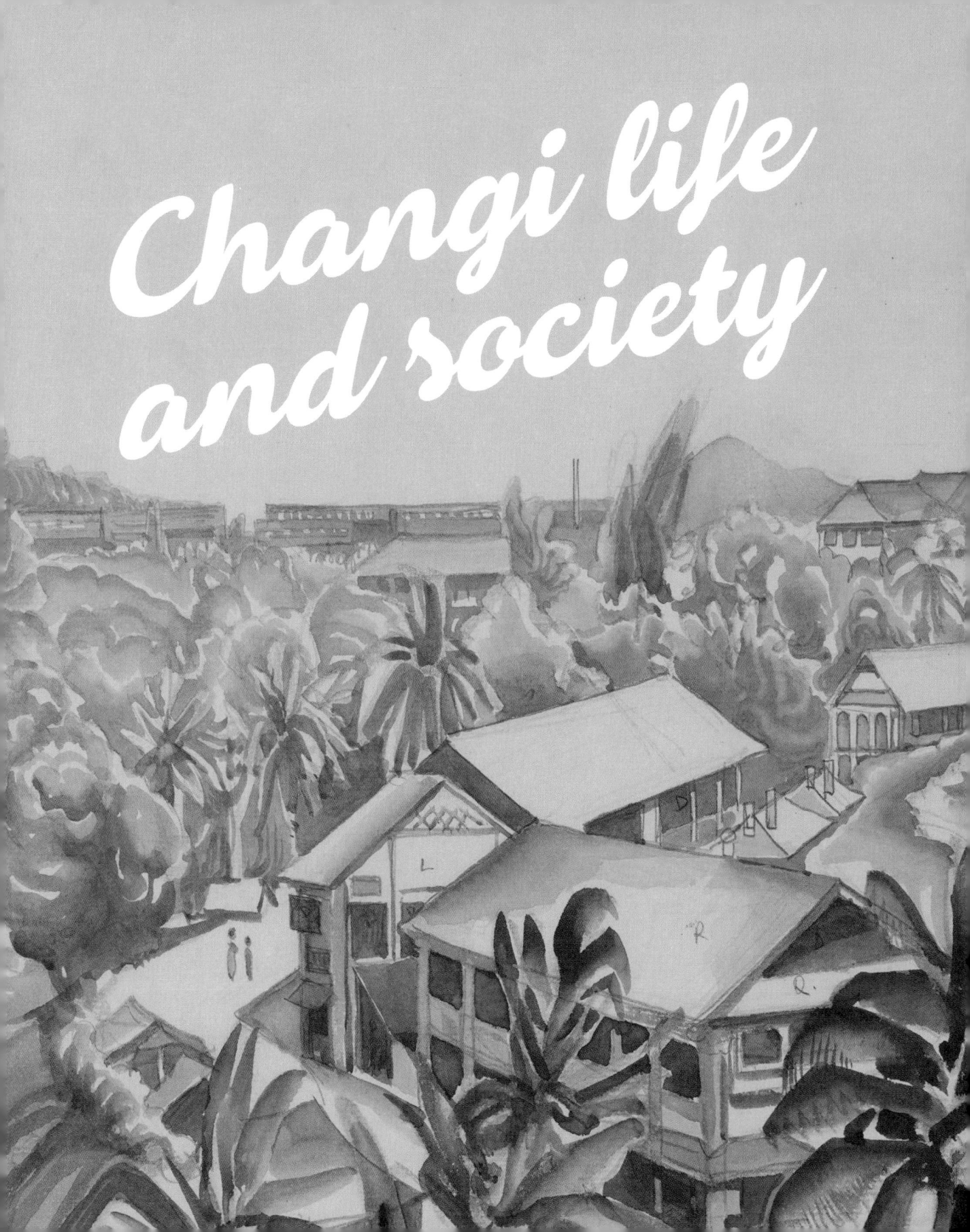

THE CHANGI BACKDROP
C. DAVID GRIFFIN

At 8.30 pm on Sunday 15 February 1942, firing ceased on the island of Singapore. The campaign of 69 days was over. Earlier in the afternoon Lieutenant General Percival had crossed the enemy lines and in the office of the Ford Motor Company had interviewed General Yamashita, his conqueror. There, according to a Japanese report, he had answered the thundering question, 'Do you surrender unconditionally?' with a quietly spoken, 'Yes.' So, to the world at large another British possession had fallen into enemy hands. The war must be won without Singapore; another hole must be taken up in the already shrinking Allied belt, that was all. What of the feelings of the 130 000 British, Australian and Indian troops upon whom the door to freedom had so swiftly and yet so finally been closed?

It is difficult to generalise on so sweeping a panorama as the secret thoughts of an army facing the unknown for the first time. There was, of course, dismay and astonishment, with an uncomfortable impression of guilt. There were mixed feelings, too, of having let Britain down and of being let down; of having fought well, of having fought badly; and overall of relief. The din, the shrieks of Singapore's death agonies, was at a stroke replaced by the blissful silence of evening. Too weary for self-analysis and reproach, the defenders of Singapore sank that night into sleep – beaten but too tired to think. Only occasional firing broke the stillness, only the red patches of old fires pricked the darkness of night. For the 8th Australian Division the war was over, but a different battle had begun, a battle from which years later they were to emerge triumphant. They had no weapons now, only those with which nature had provided them: resource, resolution, courage and unbreakable morale, and with these and these alone they won for their country a strange but glorious victory.

When dawn broke on the first morning of captivity the confusion of thoughts had begun to take more definite shape. The initial humiliation occurred early. It was ordered that each soldier, save for a small band appointed to act as local police, must divest himself of his arms. Even those to whom a service rifle had been nothing more than a penance, a useless article that must be occasionally cleaned, felt keenly this act of parting with his arms. It is the most final signal of defeat. Few there were who did not experience deep emotion as he threw his rifle and ammunition onto the ever growing pile which littered the *padang* [field] at Tanglin Barracks.

The Japanese occupation of the city, with the exception of the massacre at Alexandra Hospital, was well disciplined and well ordered. In a sense it was almost an anti-climax. Officers in cars and

THE CHANGI BACKDROP

troops on push bicycles began to appear, many of them girded with nothing more formidable than a Kodak camera. The wave of Asiatic barbarism, pillage, looting, fire and rape, so universally expected, did not on those first days take place. Singapore was apparently not to be a second Nanking.

This exemplary conduct did not escape the Australians' notice. There were many expressions of grudging admiration: 'Maybe these little yellow b–s aren't so bad as they're painted,' and 'If we had taken this joint I'll bet we'd have been a damned sight worse.'

How soon the Japanese were to reverse these good opinions! Here the stage was set for a magnificent gesture by this little-known people, a gesture which may have won them world esteem and established their country as a civilised and enlightened power. However, this was not to be. Drunk with success, oblivious to everything save the certainty of victory, Japan threw away its opportunity. By their vicious brutality, their studied cruelty and indifference to all that civilised nations hold dear in life, they hurled to the winds all the moral fruits of their campaigns. The prisoners saw the Japanese as they really were and to their lives' end their loathing for this wicked race will never die. This was no hastily gained impression springing from the natural resentment of the captured towards their captors. The troops commenced their captivity with open

For the 8th Australian Division the war was over

minds, hoping for fair play but preparing for hardships. Yet they were totally unprepared for what was to follow; starvation, beatings and indifferences to life and suffering amounting to the mass murder of tens of thousands of helpless victims – threats which hang like a dark and undispersing shadow over every phase of prison life. In the camps … were theatres, sports meetings, cafés and political clubs, all the evidence of normal life, but beneath the gaiety and behind the make-believe lay the ever-present threat of Japanese callousness and the knowledge that life itself depended on the whim of a nation of irresponsibles. 'Dangerous children', one prisoner has aptly named them: quick to rage and thoughtless of its consequences in victory; obsequious in defeat. Herein lies the true menace of Japan.

On the day following capitulation the prisoners were absorbed with one topic: what would become of them in the immediate future? … From the web of speculation and surmise one threat emerged which was shortly to be converted into certainty. All captured British troops were to occupy the barracks at Changi, where they would be administered by their own officers … And in spite of the bitterness of the men towards their officers resulting from the different standards of living and additional privileges – a bitterness which cannot be disguised if any true picture of Changi is to be gained – it must be fairly conceded that the presence of the officers was for everyone of the greatest importance, otherwise this largely demoralised army would

The Sook Ching massacres

Lachlan Grant
Australian War Memorial

THE STORY OF CHANGI and the fall of Singapore is a shared international history. As well as Australians there were other nationalities, including Britons, Americans, Dutch and a small number of New Zealanders who were prisoners of war at Changi. Apart from these Western prisoners, a majority of the 130 000 captured at Singapore were Indian soldiers. There were also some local Malaysian and Chinese soldiers captured. Of the 55 000 Indian prisoners, some 40 000 joined the pro-Japanese Indian National Army while 15 000 remained loyal to Britain and continued as prisoners of war.

Australian and British audiences or visitors to Singapore may not be aware that the worst atrocity committed in Singapore during the period of the Japanese occupation was not the treatment of Allied prisoners but the massacre of local Chinese civilians by the Japanese. The Japanese occupation of Singapore was a brutal period. Japan had been waging an imperialist war in China since 1937 and, as an extension of this, when conquests were made in south-east Asia the Japanese purged local Chinese communities in an attempt to rid the area of anti-Japanese elements. In Singapore all male Chinese had to report to screening centres. In the months following the British surrender the Japanese killed up to 25 000 local Chinese men in a series of massacres known as *Sook Ching* in Singapore. Perhaps as many were murdered in later mass killings throughout the Malayan Peninsula. Australian prisoners were witness to these atrocities. Following massacres at Changi beach on 20 February 1942 and at Tanah Merah Besar on 22 February, Australian prisoners were given the grisly task of burying the dead. In the days and months that followed, prisoners in work parties across Singapore wrote in their diaries of the massacres; some spoke of decapitated heads on poles lining roads or of witnessing the torturing of local Chinese.[1]

undoubtedly have galled into utter chaos. The sight of generals and other senior officers in camp gave to the whole organisation an impression of stability from which sprang discipline. And discipline for a prisoner is an essential concomitant of life. The task of rebuilding morale, of setting and establishing new sanctions for the fulfilment of commands, was enormous. But these things were done by precept and by example, and to those who did it each man of Changi owes his freedom. 'You are still soldiers,' they were told, day after day until they believed it. 'You are not coolies, but Australians. Whatever happens, never forget that.' Very few did.

> **'You are still soldiers,' they were told, day after day.**

Changi Barracks lies on an undulating spur of land at the extreme north-eastern tip of the island, approximately 16 miles from the city of Singapore. To the south are the emerald waters of the South China Sea, to the north the narrow Straits of Johore, with the wild tangle of the Johore jungle stretching away to the skyline beyond.

The site was more or less familiar to most Australians. Some had camped there before the war and the remainder had seen it from the decks of troopships as they slipped up the straits. It was remembered as a scattered collection of cream-coloured buildings picturesquely set among palms and pleasant lawns hedged with bright flowering bougainvillea. From the ship, the villas on these gentle hills gave a promise of a cool and comfortable life.

'Are those small places barracks?' asked an incredulous voice. 'Hell, they don't half do things in style here.'

At 2 pm on 17 February the march to the concentration camp began. Although entirely overshadowed by the famous Thailand march, this first weary tramp will not easily be forgotten by those who took part in it. The amount of kit carried by each man was a matter of individual choice. But, whatever he took, he knew these would be his only possessions in the world. Clothes, food, bedding, or boots; what should it be? The final choices were infinite in their variety. Some of them were comical and extraordinary. One man jettisoned almost everything to make room for a solid ten-pound block of polished brass. This treasure he not only took to Changi but also clung to throughout the horrific days of the march in Thailand. When asked on his death-bed in Burma why he had not thrown away this valueless millstone he replied with pathetic simplicity: 'Stuff like this is hard to come by back home.'

On the advice of headquarters the majority had destroyed their private belongings, photographs, letters, diaries, believing that the Japanese would confiscate these and use them for propaganda. Warnings were issued of a systematic search and the possible death penalty for men caught with cameras, compasses and bundles of stolen money. Accordingly, most of these precious articles were abandoned. How many regrets and heart

These photographs of the 15-inch naval guns at Changi were taken secretly by George Aspinall. The guns had been disabled by British engineers to prevent them from being used by the Japanese.

burnings have there been since? The Japanese carried out no search; indeed it would have been possible to wear the crown jewels of the Sultan of Johore on that march to Changi.

On the contrary, the enemy seemed overawed by this army of Britishers whom, for the first time in history, they were called upon to direct. Occasionally, the more courageous Japanese descended on the columns and snatched wristlet watches. These were meekly given. The snickersnee of the Lord High Executioner seemed very close in those days. Sometimes the watches were returned on the command of Japanese officers who had forbidden looting. More often they were not.

The march began in reasonably good spirits. It takes more than the collapse of 'Britain's bastion in the Far East' to depress the British race … from that day was set the tone of cheerful optimism which was to sustain [the men] in the dark hours to come. The long columns wound through the city, picking their way through the bomb craters and debris and avoiding the puffed bodies of the dead surrounded with an ominous cloud of flies. The local population, displaying an irritating sense of realism, had been converted overnight to the Great East Asia Co-Prosperity Sphere, and houses lining the route were gay with Japanese flags and extravagant notices of welcome … it was felt that out of consideration for the vanquished these demonstrations of loyalty could well have been postponed.

However, despite the flags, the troops were not entirely forsaken. Chinese women, displaying a provoking contempt for the Japanese, frequently dashed out with cups of coffee for the rapidly tiring men. The strain of the campaign was beginning to tell. The buzz of chatter died down and heads were bent forward as the sun danced on the bitumen and clothes merged with bodies in a sticky mass of sweat. As the day wore on more and more men dropped by the roadside. That infinite weariness which only soldiers know had sapped their last ounces of energy.

'Come on mate,' their friends urged them as they stumbled forward. 'The Nips will get you if you stay here.' Later, lorries came to gather up the exhausted. On future marches they would be left to die.

Late at night the march ended on arrival at Selarang Barracks, the site shortly afterwards chosen as the permanent camp for the Australians. The principal body of the British troops was to be accommodated in quarters some ¾ miles distant.

Selarang had, before the war, been occupied by the 2nd Battalion of the Gordon Highlanders; that is to say, about 900 men plus the wives and children of [the battalion's] married members. The first problem for Major General Cecil Callaghan, who commanded the 8th Division in its early captivity, was to house approximately 15 000 men in the same area. True, there was no shortage of land, but accommodation was grossly inadequate. By using every available square inch of shelter, lavatories, churches, and ammunition dumps, and by instituting a system whereby men slept in the open for half the night only, every man was eventually accommodated in some building. However, it was soon apparent to [even] the most battle-dazed prisoner that his future life would be anything but spacious. The housing problem was greatly aggravated by the absolute necessity of providing reasonable accommodation for the two Australian hospitals overflowing with their hundreds of wounded and dying men.

At capitulation the 10th Australian General Hospital had been operating in the Cathay Picture Theatre in Singapore and the 13th AGH at St. Joseph's Convent, some five miles from the city. The magnitude of the task of moving such an elaborate organisation as a bare hospital on a limited number of vehicles can scarcely be exaggerated. In addition to the wounded, many for whom the slightest motion of the bed caused agonising pain, there were the installations – hundreds of beds and bedding, X-ray equipment, pathological laboratories, operating theatres, dispensaries, and mountainous piles of vital medical stores. Australian ambulance units and motor transport companies, under the inspiring direction of Lieutenant Colonel Glyn White, carried out this movement with tireless efficiency; even so, much precious equipment had to be abandoned.

The magnitude of the task ... can scarcely be exaggerated

Nor did the buildings allotted to the hospital at Selarang simplify the movement; the 10th AGH had the Officers' Mess and the 13th AGH had one of the three-storied blocks facing the Barrack Square. Before the war the mess housed about 15 unmarried officers, and the barrack building one company of infantry. As prison hospitals they provided accommodation for over 2000 patients.

The work of tending the sick and wounded in these makeshift hospitals, bereft as they were of water supply, sewerage system and lighting, called for the utmost endurance from medical staff and patients alike. Indeed, throughout the whole imprisonment the Australian medical organisation was superb. Strong language, certainly, but moderate on the lips of all those who, year in and year out, came to regard the doctor as the most important person in camp.

Scarcely had the last bed been slung into position when the hospitals were ordered to move again. The Japanese had selected Roberts Barracks, an island of buildings lying midway between Selarang and the British area, as a permanent hospital block. Here [the hospitals] remained unmolested until August 1943 when once again they were returned to their starting point in the square.

To establish a new camp anywhere, as every soldier knows, is a herculean task, even when the camp has been lately prepared for occupants who are equipped with all tools and essential gear. On the occupation of Selarang the Australians had none of these things. The bombing had destroyed the whole range of public utilities and had littered the area with

Prisoners transport bedding and supplies on a converted army jeep to Roberts Barracks, Changi. This photograph was taken secretly by Major John Rosson, and the camera and negatives were kept hidden from the Japanese throughout his internment.
P04485.070

debris of demolished buildings. There were no kitchens, no showers, no means of transport, nothing save a collection of buildings and bungalows stained an ugly black, and sundry pieces of elaborately useless furniture. Moreover, the only labourers available were men exhausted by warfare, stunned by defeat and appalled by the prospect of captivity.

For every man in camp aching for rest and longing only for sleep those opening days were a succession of shocks interrupted with orders and counter orders in bewildering confusion. There was no time to ponder on the even greater problem: the personal adjustment to the violent changes of this new and terrible life.

For AIF Headquarters, which even behind the wire had retained its imposing name, the problem was twofold: discipline had to be preserved and a huge programme of public works launched. Field kitchens were built from scraps of galvanised iron, in which the few available stores were installed. Water points were established at several wells – or *tongs*, as they were invariably called, after the Malay word for 'water dipper'. At first it seemed strange to be one of 1000 naked men moving forward in a slow queue towards a few pints of water. But this strangeness was all too soon eclipsed by others and was quickly forgotten.

Owing to the absence of a regular water supply and the dense concentration of men, the camp hygiene officer, Major C.E.M. Gunther, was faced with a problem worthy of his own abundant powers. As soon as the work

37

of constructing latrines was placed under his firm and masterly direction he lost no time in solving it with ruthless vigour.

There were in Changi a small number of augurs used in peacetime by Chinese labourers for digging post holes. These clumsy affairs were operated within a straddled tripod of steel poles. To rotate the augur a team of men trudged in a narrow circle about the central pole. The similarity of this procedure with pictures of slaves labouring for the early Egyptians was inescapable. A few shifts on the augur and the prisoners were fully alive to their condition. As with everything else in Changi there was an acute shortage of augurs, so squads were forced to work in relays all day and all night. Thus arose the first 'boreholes', a word which rapidly became the most common in all the prisoners' vocabulary. In meant, literally, 'latrines', later 'all rumours of news'.

In addition to these arduous camp fatigues the Japanese lost no time in calling for working parties for cleaning debris in Singapore. The officers in charge of these parties … were obliged to make unwilling men work for the enemy and were responsible for such work being carried out. As the months wore on, to be on a working party seemed as natural as watching a test match, but in the early days everyone felt himself disgraced. To be in charge of a party loading bombs for the possible destruction of Australia, and to be forced to urge half-mutinous men to greater speed under a threat of repercussions to the whole party – this was the common experience of junior officers. By the end of the incarceration, however, both officers and men had evolved a perfect working-party technique, the sole object of which was to accomplish nothing. Working parties, like rice and starvation, were simply things which had to be accepted as part of a prisoner's lot.

…

Another job which made exacting demands on camp labour in the first hectic weeks was perhaps the most ironical of all – the erection of the barbed-wire fence closing the road to freedom. The Japanese, probably owing to the shortage of wire and the extent of the concentration area, dispensed with the high fences familiar to European prisoners and ordered the erection of a simple concertina wire. This was no more than a token fence – to pass through it was not difficult. The Straits of Johore and the isolation of Singapore were the real obstacles to escape, obstacles so effective that of the 45 000 prisoners in Changi there is no record of a single successful escape attempt.

The wiring parties worked hard and completed the perimeter within the time allowed. The Japanese were pleased and astonished. As a reward, Lieutenant Okasaki, the camp commandant, allowed the importation of 50 stoves from Singapore. The apparent munificence of this gesture, however, is somewhat marred by the knowledge that the cooking equipment … was ridiculously inadequate.

Other parties were less pleasant, such as for the burial of scores of Chinese who had been machine-gunned on the beach where

These views were taken from the water tower at Selarang by George Aspinall. The tower was actually out of bounds.

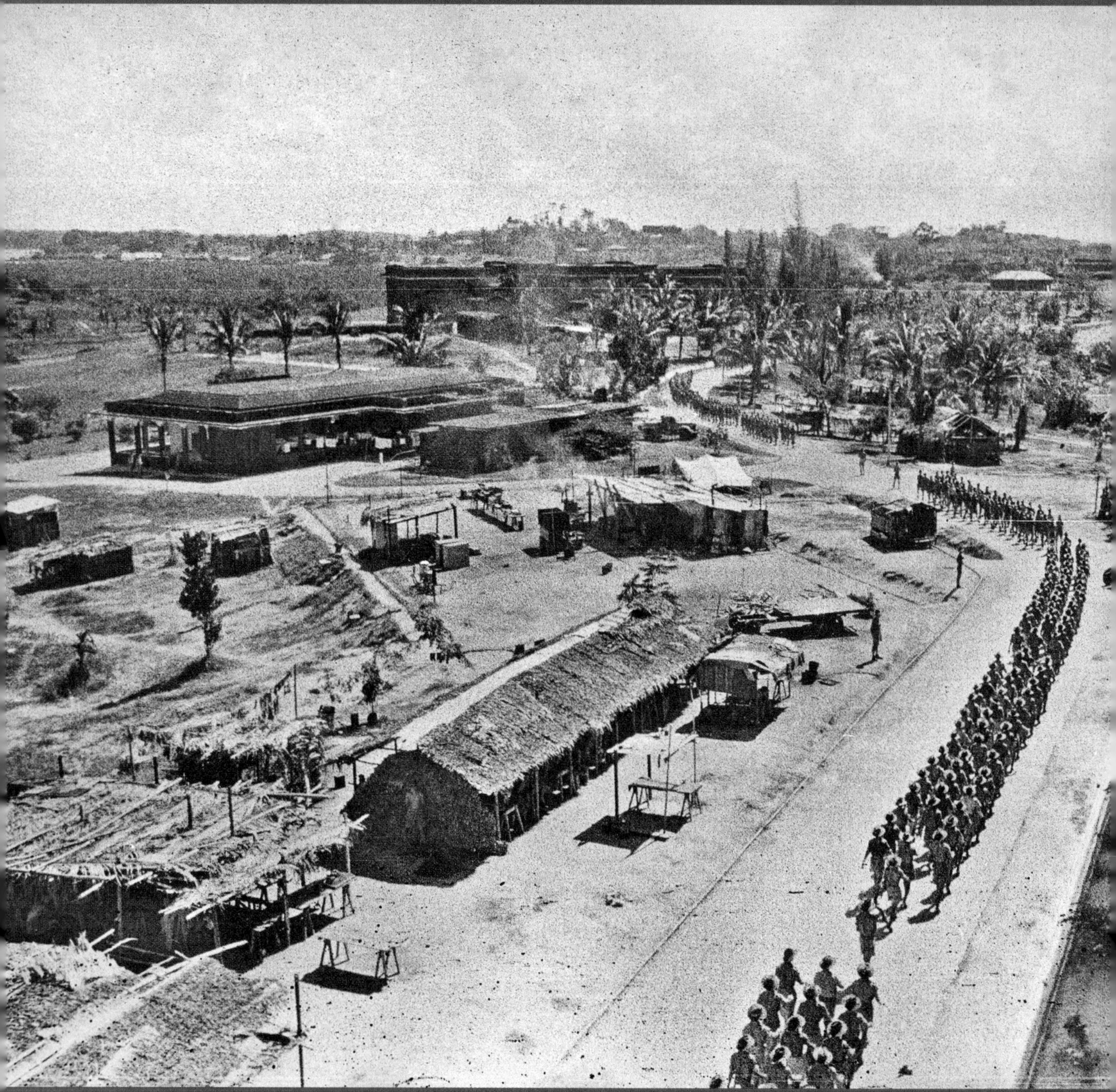

THE CHANGI BACKDROP

A parade in Selarang Barracks. Note the Changi 'trailer' parked on the right. This photograph was taken in secret by Kennedy Burnside.
P03821.056

subsequently the camp drew its salt water and staged swimming races. Parties for the recovery of identity discs and burial of men who had been killed in the campaign, parties to clean the Singapore sewer, parties to work waist-deep in decaying offal, seething with putrefaction, parties to do work too nauseating to mention – while Japanese guards beat the sick or weary about the head. Slaves they were by occupation but by temperament they were still always free men. The Japanese shrieked, screamed, kicked and bullied in an effort to secure complete submission and hangdog obedience. But they failed, and to the last the Australian spirit of proud defiance remained unbroken.

With every prisoner of war the importance of food overshadows all other considerations. That food is the focal point of existence is seldom realised in [affluent] countries such as Australia. The ready availability of such basic commodities as bread, butter and potatoes and meat places them in the same category as air and water. But from the moment when the prisoner feels the first gnawing hunger pangs his attitude undergoes a profound change. Food and everything connected with it rapidly becomes an obsession. The whole universe revolves about a tin plate, and the thought of eggs and oranges are dearer and remoter visions than the golden apples of the Hesperides.

Having fallen into the clutches of an Asiatic power, every man was reconciled to a diet of rice and fish. During the first days of captivity, however, disorganisation in Singapore was such that no rice was delivered to the camp. Accordingly, the quartermasters had to utilise the small amount of regular army rations which by devious and ingenious means had been carried into camp. These were issued in minute quantities and were consumed at one gulp by ravenous men. This store, apart from a reserve maintained for the sick and wounded, was rapidly exhausted.

So it was that the first truckloads of rice were greeted with enthusiasm. Here at last was something which would take the hunger pangs away. Rice would give you 'the bulk'. Never mind the palate, 'the bulk' was the thing. Thus from the start all food fell into two classes: 'the bulk' and that which was 'tasty'. There were no alternatives; soldiers are as conservative in their language as in their preferences.

As the unloading parties staggered under the weighty sacks the onlookers conjured up pictures of gargantuan feasts. Memories of fine white rice cooked by expert Chinese and served at delicious curry tiffins flashed through many minds …

The dismay, the bitterness of disappointment, which followed the first efforts of army cooks to cope with rice defy description. It appeared on the plate as a tight ball of greyish gelatinous substance, nauseating in its lack of flavour and utterly repulsive. The fish – when it came, which was not often – proclaimed its arrival by an overpowering stench and massed squadrons of flies. To gaze on a sack of rotting shrimps moving slowly under the impulse of a million maggots was a poor prelude to the meals which followed, meals which were nothing but a series of gastronomic disasters. Constipation of astonishing duration was the immediate result of this unnatural diet, only to be replaced as the years wore on by an almost universally chronic diarrhoea.

Prisoners of the Japanese are probably the most food-conscious body of people in the world, and soon the function of the alimentary tract was one of the chief topics of conversation in the camp. Such will-of-the-wisps as vitamins, proteins and carbohydrates rapidly became household words. A bullock driver from the Northern Territory would often be heard discussing the B1 content of rice polishings with a racing tout to the accompaniment of sage comments by an erstwhile undertaker's clerk. It was not surprising, since variations in the diet produced sudden and unpleasant effects on one and all. Thus a drop in vitamin B made the legs ache and lips go bluish. Too little protein and these same legs collapsed unexpectedly. Too much carbohydrate and the body swelled into the unrecognisable corpulence of beriberi.

However, although the food brought into the camp remained atrocious until Japan was beaten, the cooking improved steadily until, by release, an amazing standard of imaginative preparation had been attained. The average army cook in Australia, accustomed as he is to the ruination of first-class commodities, would have hung his head in shame at the apparent sumptuousness of a Changi dinner prepared from food unfit for dogs. If the watchword in Changi was 'resources' it may well have been inscribed in the letters of gold above the tumbledown cookhouses from which such miracles of inventiveness emerged. Changi was super-critical of its cooks, but their ultimate efforts rose above criticism.

Every man was reconciled to a diet of rice and fish

In any collection of 15 000 men there will always be found a number of adventurous spirits who are prepared to risk death for reasonable reward. Such men were not wanting in the 8th Division. It was soon discovered that Chinese and Malays living in *kampongs* [villages] near the camp had large supplies of tinned goods for sale. The Japanese had announced that any prisoner found outside the wire would be shot. There was no reason to disbelieve this order. Accordingly, those who slipped through the wire to found the black market, one of the most famous of all Changi institutions, took their lives in their hands.

In one of the valleys there was a weak spot in the fence adjacent to a stormwater pipe passing beneath Changi Road. It was here that the black-market operators laid the foundations of their fortune and brought into camp the precious food that saved so many lives. Prices were high and profits enormous but the risks were great. Three dollars (about 9/-) would buy one tin of milk or bully beef and cigarettes were a dollar for ten, but those who complained so vociferously of their usurious charges did so from the security of their beds.

The number of black marketeers – or 'traders', as they were called – grew rapidly when it was found that the threatened shootings did not take place. The majority of men caught trading were sentenced to one or two days in the 'tennis court' … a novel punishment invented by the local Japanese guards. Within its wire surrounds offenders languished without food or water for the period stated. But this was taken in good part by the troops and the confiscation of the swag was reckoned the greater misfortune …

The sudden change of diet and environment was soon to have its effect on health. In addition to which the overcrowding, the lack of water closets and the general decline in morale made the outbreak of an epidemic a certainty. The onset was not long delayed.

Roberts Hospital was barely established when the dreaded sickness came. Dysentery, the scourge of armies down through the centuries, swept through the camp. Australians, who were not accustomed to associating the common house fly with death, at first paid little attention to the orders of the medical authorities. Borehole seats were left open, hands were not washed, since there was no water, and scraps of rubbish were allowed to rot in garbage tins. As a result, Selarang, which had once scarcely boasted a fly (in common with the rest of hygienic Malaya) shortly became a breeding ground …

After cholera – which until the Thailand disaster had not been encountered – dysentery must rank as one of the [prisoner of war's]

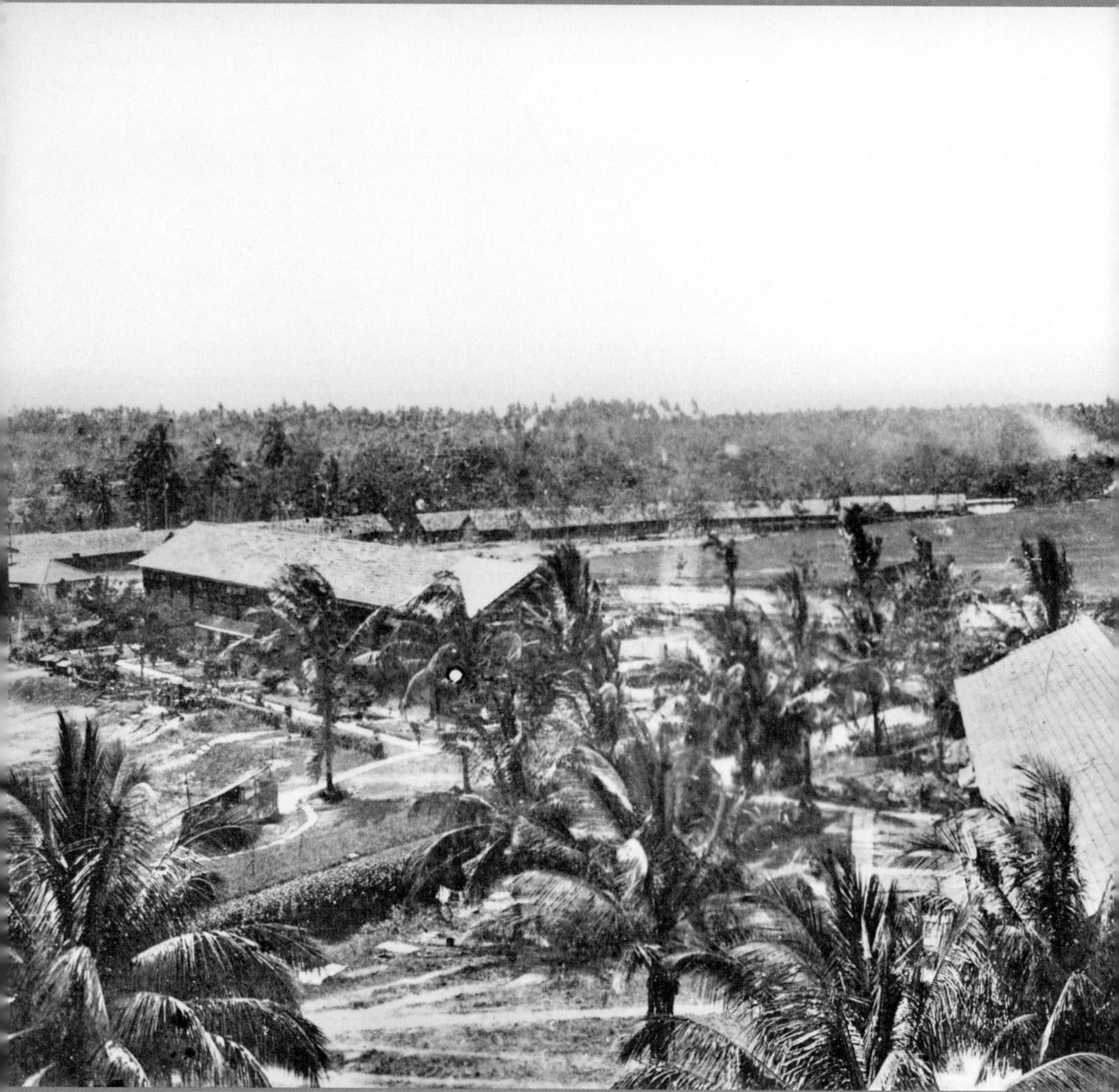

THE CHANGI BACKDROP

most devastating diseases. The pain, the fever, the sensation of life actually ebbing away, is one which will never be forgotten by the thousands who were stricken. The hospital, despite valiant efforts, was swamped with patients for whom, owing to lack of drugs, the doctors could do little. It was not until later that M&B693 [sulphanilamide], the saviour of Changi, was used to combat the disease. Scenes in the dysentery ward at the height of the attack beggar description, and the entry of Florence Nightingale complete with lamp would have surprised no one. Yet such scenes, disgusting as they appeared then, sank into nothingness when stood beside the memories of cholera in the death camps of Thailand. The dysentery epidemic passed, leaving the camp thankful and exhausted. And though the price was paid in lives the experience was not wholly wasteful: it emphasised more potently than a hundred routine orders how precarious is a prisoner's life, how vital his hygiene and … the amenities which the civilian sick so habitually take for granted.

Of all periods of a prisoner of war's day the hours between the evening meal and bedtime were the most tedious. For the philosophical and better educated among them this was a welcome time of rest when psychological adjustments could be made, but for the wide mass of the troops, unequipped for abstract speculation, these hours were dreary. The absence of any form of electrical lighting was universally depressing. Crouched about the spluttering ends of candles, the more energetic

A view from the water tower at Selarang, photographed secretly by George Aspinall.
P02569.125

Selarang AIF area.
Murray Griffin, 1943.
ART26512

played cards, but for the rest there was only conversation … Since there was no food worthy of the name and no authentic news whatsoever, conversation on these points was unproductive of anything except argument. Some form of distraction was imperative if spirits were to be maintained. Thus arose the concert parties, modest amateur affairs to begin with but [later] a powerful theatre movement.

Despite the difficulty of transport an extraordinary number of musical instruments had been carried into captivity. They ranged from fiddles strung with signal wire – which later were playing Brahms and Beethoven concerts to orchestral accompaniment – to trombones and weighty piano accordions. Possessors of these treasures clubbed together and with singers and raconteurs constituted themselves unit entertainers. These groups in turn supplied their best talents to the brigade parties. Every night thousands flocked to the open-air stages to laugh an hour away. To witness one of these performances, however unskilled, was to come away refreshed and proud to be a member of a body whose humour was unsullied by adversity.

While these impromptu entertainers were drawing record houses, the AIF Concert Party was busily reforming. This was a group of professional and amateur actors and singers who had toured Australian camps before the war. Now, with additional members, they opened with light variety entertainment for the prisoners. The importance of their work and its instantaneous effect on morale, reaching as it did to the very heart of every man within the camp, can be appreciated only by those who sat week after week, month after month, year after year, through their improving performances. They were an inspiration and a constant reminder that freedom, however remote, would one day come. With laughter, with tears, they rounded off the harsh corners of prison life and kept alive the precious sparks of humanity without which no man can long endure.

> **Distraction was imperative if spirits were to be maintained**

Only four days after capitulation the Australian education scheme was launched. Its purpose was to fit men for the postwar world and to lesson boredom with interest in study. Instructors were readily obtainable and a comprehensive syllabus was drawn up. There was scarcely a single branch of knowledge, theoretical or practical, for which classes were not provided. Every man not engaged on regular duty was obliged to enrol in at least one subject, and the resulting huge classes were competently handled by the Education Centre staff.

The education scheme was a far-sighted plan, and if it had been allowed to function as its originator, Brigadier H.A. Taylor, had planned, its benefits to the camp community would have been great. Unfortunately, many factors detracted from its ultimate success: the irregularity of working parties, the lack of enthusiasm on the part of some commanding officers and the inherent mental laziness of the troops themselves. Yet there were many who attended lectures under the casuarina trees, and for these men the Education Centre and its pleasant library helped to restore the mental balance so badly shaken by captivity and defeat.

As already mentioned, the military organisation of the division was resumed in the concentration camp as though capitulation were a detail which might occur to any combatant force. This was a blow to some troops, who loudly proclaimed that prisoners of war were no longer subject to the commands of their superior officers. But to the more thoughtful this policy appeared as a master stroke. The life of every man depended on his and his neighbour's discipline. To maintain it almost any measure was justified, as the events of later years were to prove so conclusively.

This studied oblivion to the fact of defeat had some amusing consequences. The entrances to the camp were picqueted by Australian guards who were inspected daily and who paid similar compliments to Australian and Japanese officers. The gates also bore patriotic emblems and mottoes: 'He who laughs last laughs best' on the British gate and 'One day we will recall with pleasure all these things' [on the Australian] – both approved by a Japanese interpreter a trifle uncertain of his classics.

…

The most impressive military display took place each evening in the Selarang Barracks Square. Shortly before seven o'clock Australian battalions and regiments marched to the square … [accompanied by] a drum-and-fifes band. Here, after a ceremonial inspection, all stood to attention awaiting the Sergeant Major's order: 'Buglers: sound retreat.'

Through the gathering dusk came the rising and falling of the call, sighing away into echoes while all who heard were quiet. And the palms, it seemed, catching the atmosphere, stopped their rustling and stood still. 'Playing at soldiers,' the troops called it, but a game worth playing by men who lived defeated, yet unwilling to admit defeat.

Early in April a curious event took place which illustrates the then unbalanced state of mind of the camp … Changi at this time was a rumour-monger's paradise. The abrupt cessation of war news came as a severe psychological shock, as keenly felt as the cessation of food. The mind was as hungry as the body and no particle of information, no matter what the source, was overlooked. Everything was repeated, everything distorted and everything half-believed … Australia, so the story went, had arranged with Japan for the return of the 8th Division in exchange for bales of wool. The first consignment of prisoners would leave Changi on 14 May en route for Lorenzo Marquis, a neutral port.

Like a Sumatran gale the rumour raged through the camp, gathering as it went sufficient circumstantial evidence to convince the full bench of the Commonwealth High Court. Men by the thousands believed it; bet their pay-books, their wives, their rights to return

THE CHANGI BACKDROP

A view from Selarang Barracks Square. Murray Griffin, 1943.
ART26511

home, on it. Captains believed it, majors were enthusiastic and colonels were known to be positive of it. British troops in adjoining areas threw insults at the Australians for being parties to so dishonourable an agreement, denounced as it had been by Winston Churchill himself. The senior chaplain preached a warning sermon about it, denouncing the story as complete fiction. The warning was ignored: the padre was simply ordered by division to keep down spirits for fear of mutiny.

The greatest anxiety was the lack of news from home

Naturally, there were cynics … The camp's reaction was to pity them. And many a cynic must have had some inward qualm when, miraculously, the Japanese issued orders for an overseas party of 3000 Australians to leave camp …

[On 14 May 1942] 'A' Force left, crammed aboard motor trucks, for death and slavery in Burma to the accompaniment of cheers, coo-ees and cries of 'Have one in the pub for me,' and 'Tell Mum I'm coming on the next draft.' Beatty's Rumour had served its purpose.

Other working parties followed, [leaving] in quick succession for Borneo, for islands nearby and for coolie labour in the vicinity of Singapore. To the handful who remained in Selarang, the camp was quiet and pleasantly free from disturbance. The greatest anxiety was the lack of news from home and the growing suspicion that the Japanese were not prepared to send casualty lists of prisoners. The thought of mothers and wives, tortured by anxiety, waiting for news of the living and the dead, added the fresh touch of bitterness to the prisoners' already well-nigh insupportable life.

Within the first week of captivity the Australian casualty lists had been prepared. The echelon organisation, like so many of the other services, continued its normal activities and detailed nominal rolls were handed to the Japanese. These rolls had in their closely typed columns the power to set half-a-million anxious hearts at rest. They were never sent … The victors of Greater East Asia could not be troubled with such trifles.

Prisoners of war expect ill treatment; they know that they are a completely useless force, unable to assist their own country and unwanted by the foe, and that the exigencies of war make difficult and impossible much that would normally be done for their greater security and comfort. The Japanese may endeavour to justify, on these grounds, many aspects of their treatment. But their refusal to allow communication with home … a duty which would have cost them nothing, must always be ranked as one of their most diabolical acts …

In three and a half years the men in Changi were permitted to write only five postcards of 24 words each, and [the luckier ones] received and replied to random radio messages. The first postcards were not permitted until four months after [the Allied] surrender and took a further five months to be delivered. The first incoming mail, one of the most

THE CHANGI BACKDROP

memorable days of all, was not received in Changi until March 1943 – that is, a year and a month after the great silence had come down. Small wonder that the letters were taken by shaking hands and that they were read hours, sometimes days after delivery by men unable to nerve themselves to tear the envelope and learn the worst.

The lack of mail, the refusal to repatriate limbless and wounded men and the generally obstructive attitude toward any form of Red Cross relief were the aspects of Japanese unpleasantness which the prisoners found most exasperating. For this they can never be forgiven.

In August 1942 orders arrived from Tokyo that all officers above the rank of lieutenant colonel were to proceed to Japan. Accordingly, Major General Callaghan was obliged to relinquish his command of the Australians, and Lieutenant Colonel Frederick Galleghan was recalled from a working camp in Singapore to command all remaining Australian troops on the island. This position he retained until relief came on 5 September 1945.

…

Towards the middle of the first year in captivity conditions in Changi began to improve. In May the Japanese announced that henceforth prisoners would be paid on a sliding scale. A private soldier labouring from dawn to dusk was valued at 10 cents per day. This princely sum was later increased to 35 cents a day to keep pace with inflation, which had sent peanuts up to 68 dollars a pound. Six months' hard labour for one pound of peanuts are novel conditions for Australian workmen. There were no trade unions in Changi.

Following the [announcement of payment] a canteen was opened, well stocked with

A postcard home, restricted to 24 words.
PR01123.003

'Black Jack' Galleghan: hero of Changi

Karl James
Australian War Memorial

FEW AUSTRALIAN commanders were more colourful or controversial than Lieutenant Colonel Frederick 'Black Jack' Galleghan. A strict disciplinarian, he was abrasive and could be arrogant and tactless. By his own admission he was 'pugnacious'.[2] 'Being a commander demands hardness,' he was once heard to say.[3] Yet Galleghan also inspired loyalty and formed strong friendships.

Born in 1897, as a teenager Galleghan served in the cadets, where was he commissioned as a second lieutenant. In January 1916 he enlisted as a private in the AIF and was soon promoted to sergeant, serving in the 34th Battalion. On the Western Front he was seriously wounded during the battle of Messines in June 1917 and again in the Somme offensive in August 1918. He forever carried a bullet fragment in his left shoulder and his back was scarred from shrapnel.[4] He soldiered on during the interwar period and by 1932 was a lieutenant colonel commanding a battalion in the Militia.

When the Second World War broke out in September 1939, despite his seniority and experience, Galleghan was initially passed over for a command in the Second AIF. He was told frankly that he would not fit in.[5] After extensive lobbying, in October 1940 Galleghan was appointed to raise the 8th Division's 2/30th Battalion. He pushed his new battalion hard, and some soldiers even mutinied before they left Australia. Galleghan likely drove rather than inspired his men. Yet the 2/30th Battalion was one of the best battalions in Malaya.[6] Its ambush of an advancing Japanese column at Gemas on 14 January 1942 was one of the few AIF highpoints of that campaign.

In captivity Galleghan applied the same high standards of discipline and strictness when he assumed command of the AIF in Malaya. He also became the deputy camp commandant of Changi to Colonel E.B. Holmes. Galleghan saw an adherence to discipline as paramount to maintaining control and cohesion amongst the troops. 'Discipline', he reported afterwards, 'saved many men from the illogical temper and brutality of the Japanese'. It 'kept morale high and avoided any tendency to drift into a mob of prisoners instead of a formed body of soldiers'.[7] When told there were not enough razor blades for the men to shave, for example, Galleghan replied: 'Make razors'. He was known to berate both Australian and Japanese soldiers for a slackly turned-out appearance.[8]

Galleghan's approach was not without controversy or criticism. In January 1943 he clashed with Lieutenant Colonel Edward 'Weary' Dunlop for not providing greater support to Dunlop's party as it moved through Changi en route to the

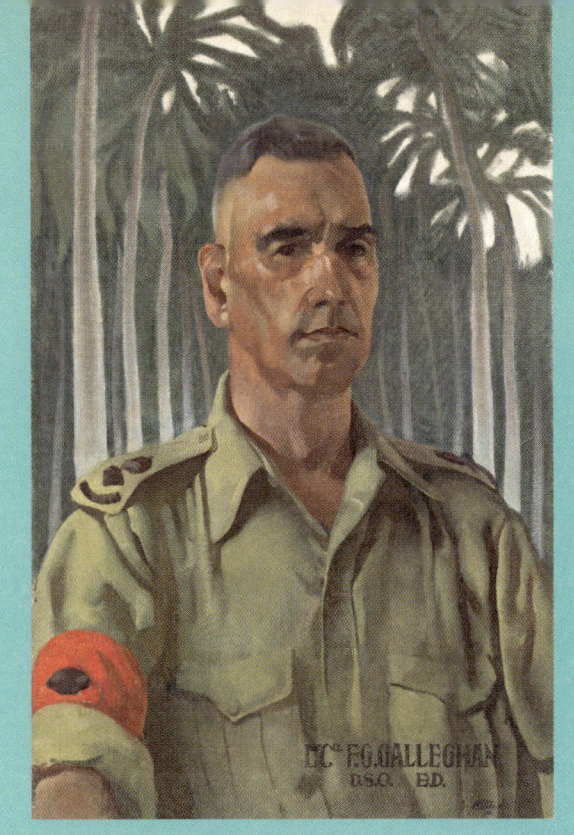

Murray Griffin's portrait of Galleghan, 1945.
ART26547

Galleghan (right) with Colonel E.B. Holmes in Singapore on 20 September 1945. During his captivity Galleghan's weight dropped from 95 to 57 kilograms.
AWM 117117

Burma–Thailand Railway. Dunlop was disgusted at all the 'well-shod and clothed people' in Changi, while his party was not issued with new shoes or clothes and left Changi in 'the same sorry plight' in which it had arrived.[9] Yet even Galleghan cracked when the emaciated survivors of F Force returned to Changi from the railway in December 1943. 'Where are the rest, Major?' Galleghan asked. The reply: 'They're all here, sir'. It is said that Galleghan was moved to tears.[10]

At war's end Galleghan was repatriated to Australia, where he was informed he had been promoted to brigadier. He resumed duty with the Commonwealth Investigation Service and spent 1948–49 in Germany as the head of the Australian Military Mission. He worked tirelessly to assist his former soldiers but adamantly rejected any association with ex-prisoner-of-war organisations. Galleghan instead preferred that emphasis was placed on the 2/30th Battalion's fighting record. He received many honours and awards, including a knighthood in 1969. On Galleghan's death in 1971 he was described as the 'hero of Changi'.[11]

The measure of Galleghan's own success is best reflected in his farewell message to the AIF troops in Changi in September 1945: 'You finish your prisoner period as disciplined soldiers whom the Jap could not break – that is an achievement I have always hoped for, and it has been realised only by the united efforts of you all'.[12]

CHANGI LIFE AND SOCIETY

Australian tinned food and local fruit and vegetables. Yeast centres (for vitamin B), grass soup factories (for thyamin), rubber factories, artificial limb factories – factories of all kinds gradually came into being. Attractive churches were erected complete with altar cloths and locally made stained-glass windows, and extensive vegetable gardens were laid out. In a word, Changi had become an almost self-supporting town complete with sports fields and supper parties, with a bevy of camp gossips ready to pass on the latest tit bit concerning Colonel X's new trousers or the scandal of Lieutenant Y and the stolen pair of fowls. A new vocabulary was invented and the slang became universal … Swearing remained, though diminished; the familiar words being repeated rather to give punctuation than to add emphasis …

In July 1942 the first official radio news bulletins were issued. At once the camp lost that air of remoteness which had characterised the opening months. To be in touch with the outside world and to be able to follow the progress of the war was the greatest benefit ever conferred on the prisoners. The daily reading of 'the screed' or 'the canary' was the moment for which everyone waited. Without the radio in Changi, especially after Italy's surrender, when even the *Syonan Shimbun* (the Japanese-controlled Singapore newspaper) was forbidden, life would have been appalling. The radio made a unique contribution to morale, and to Major Bostey and his staff, who were prepared to risk their lives to provide this service, the camp must forever be grateful.

Tents and wooden huts surrounding Roberts Hospital. This photograph was taken secretly by Major John Rosson.
P04485.027

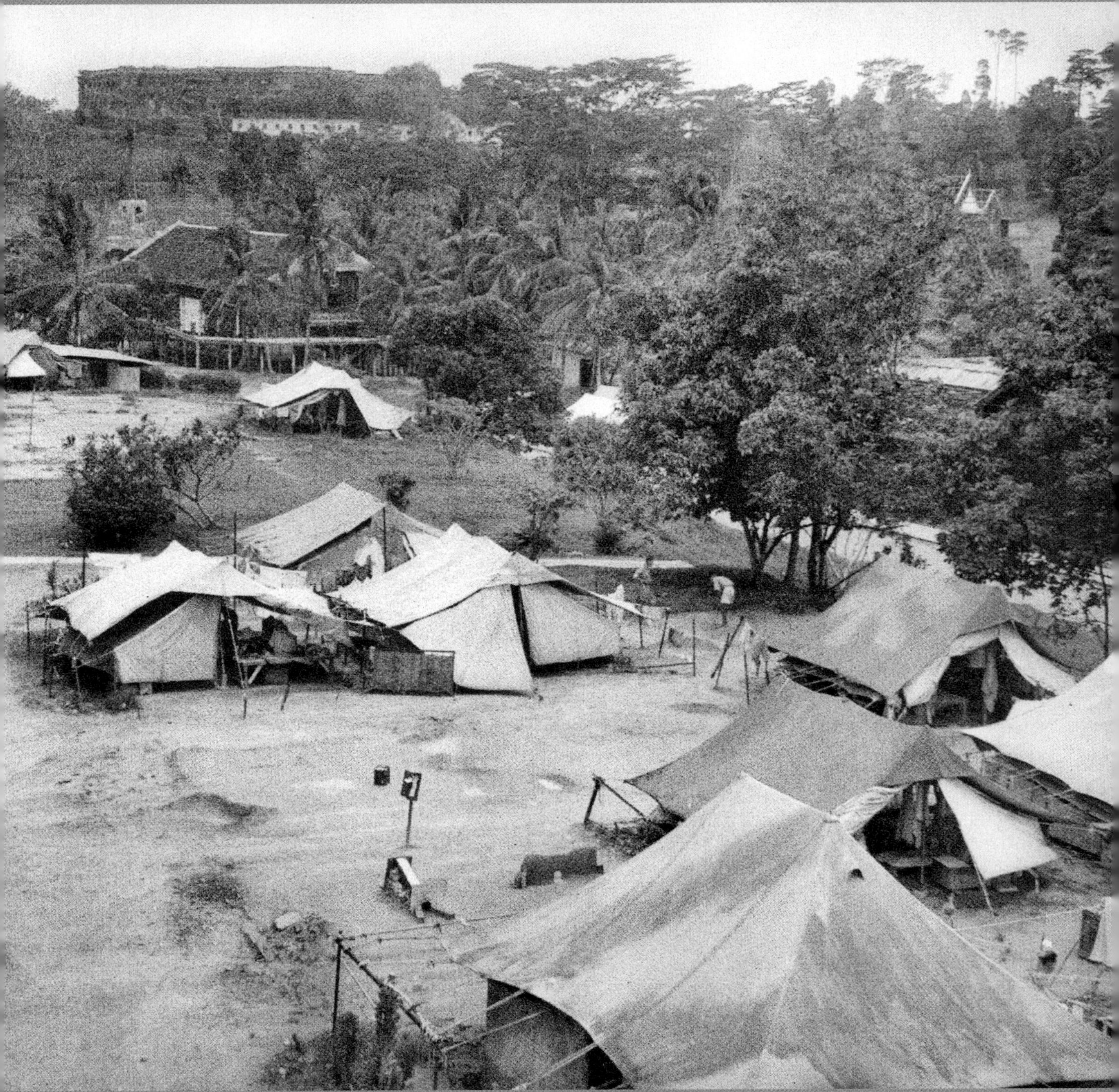

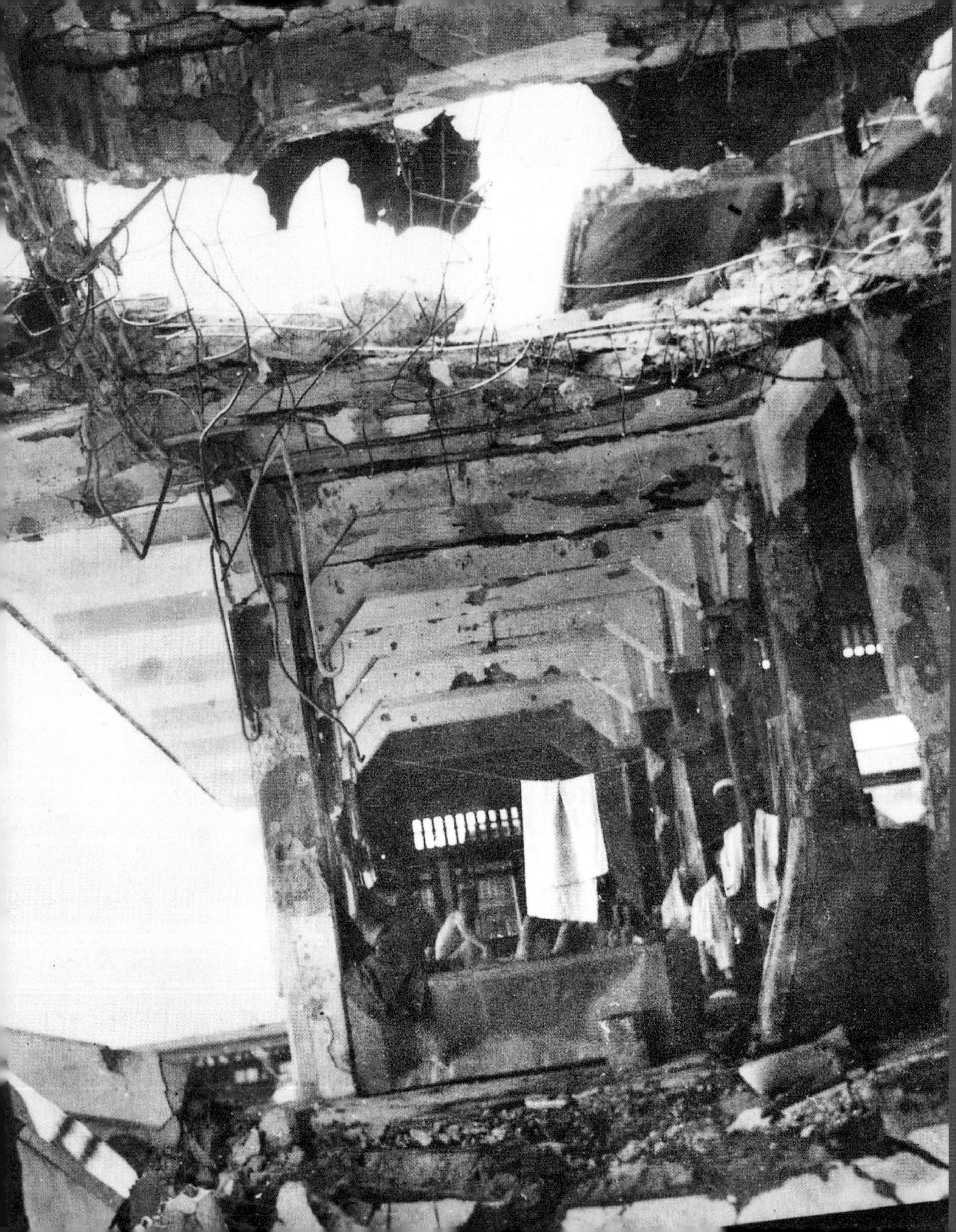

LEFT Some of the bomb damage done to Selarang Barracks during the battle of Singapore.
P00077.016

ABOVE A George Aspinall photo showing members of F Force assembling before their departure from Changi in April 1943 for the Burma–Thailand Railway.
P02569.170

The departure of F Force from Changi. Almost one in three of these men would not survive their time on the railway. From the Aspinall collection.
P02569.173 / P02569.172

On the third day of September 1942 the pleasant tedium of this life was dramatically interrupted. The 'Non-Escape Declaration' had arrived from Japan. This document was worded as follows: 'I, the undersigned, hereby solemnly swear on my honour that under no circumstances will I attempt to escape.' All prisoners were ordered to sign it.

Immediately on receipt of this order Galleghan accompanied senior British officers to the Japanese Conference House and bluntly told the Japanese that neither they nor the troops under their command would sign any such document. It was the first occasion in which the prisoners as a corporate body had refused to obey a Japanese order and troops were worried that coercion of some kind would immediately follow. For several hours the camp waited expectantly for the outburst of Japanese wrath. It was not long delayed.

> **When release came 72 hours later the force had won**

On the morning of the anniversary of the European war, all men were called on a dawn muster parade. Here, commanding officers read them the Imperial Japanese Army's decree: by six o'clock that night all British and Australian troops – except those in Roberts Hospital – were to move to the Selarang Barracks Square, where they were to remain for an indefinite period. Men who had attempted weeks before to escape were to be shot. The troops were asked to remain … to uphold the honour of the British Empire and obey orders.

Before the sun was fully up the amazing pilgrimage had begun, and by nightfall the last man had squeezed himself into the area. Thus 17 000 people found themselves living on a flat asphalt surface some 260 yards long and 155 yards broad, bounded on three sides by high concrete buildings. The only water came from one miserable well, the only food that which had been carried …

When release came 72 hours later the force had won, and the esprit de corps remained with it until long after the imprisonment was over. The Japanese had their bits of paper, but the prisoners had their pride.

At Christmas the majority of the Singapore parties returned to Changi – not, as might be imagined, to be united for the festive season but because they had completed the Japanese war memorial at Bukit Timah … The new year brought with it rumours of big movements to Thailand and French Indochina, and on 14 March 1943 D Force left Changi for 'up country'.

…

As with all departures, there was a full measure of suppressed emotion, more so since friends were leaving for the unknown, perhaps to freedom, perhaps to death. Nowhere did the awful uncertainty of prison life assert itself more positively than on the Barracks Square when the last handshakes were being given and 'good lucks' exchanged.

The knowledge that in Thailand were such luxuries as eggs and bananas sent the men of D Force away smiling and rubbing their stomachs in pleasurable anticipation. Those remaining began to be envious and discontented. After the comparative interest of work in Singapore the routine of Changi was a bore. Accordingly, the announcement of another huge working party for the north set the camp buzzing with excitement, especially since Headquarters, after conferences with the Japanese, was able to announce that this party was being sent to a comfortable rest camp. The Japanese were apparently concerned with the deteriorating health of the prisoners on the island, where food was now scarce, and were taking their first humanitarian action. To be going 'up country' was immediately the vogue.

...

There was a rush to be included in the Australian contingent of F Force under the command of Lieutenant Colonel Kappe. The party was assembled with great pomp, and cheery farewell suppers were held throughout the camp. Sick men who had been in bed for weeks struggled to their feet. One British unit conducted a qualification test – if a man could walk 100 yards up a slope without fainting he was eligible for the party. There were still the cynical who had their doubts; it seemed too good to be true.

'Better the devil you know,' they growled. 'Changi will do me.'

Camp Headquarters was suspicious. A party being sent by rail for no better purpose than to grow fat amid the plentiful groves of Thailand was scarcely consistent with Japanese policy. As the departure date came closer, repeated conferences were held, with General Arimura's representatives asking for confirmation of instructions in view of the camp's decision to send sick men. To all questions they received bland smiles and further assurances. Only at the eleventh hour did the Japanese admit apologetically that, owing to a shortage of transport, there may be a little marching in Thailand – perhaps a few kilometres – but that all gear would be taken by lorry.

At 4 am on 18 April 1943, soaked by a torrential downpour, F Force left the Barracks Square on the fateful journey that was destined to shock the world. They left with pianos, with books, with entertainers, with furniture … Japanese bestiality, cruelty and deceit are bywords in Australia today but in F Force and all that it stood for these qualities reached their apotheosis. Language does not exist to describe the tortures and agonies of the jungle march, the hideous deaths in the cholera camps, the insane brutality of the Japanese delighting in the spectacle of this barbaric murder. The episode will forever live in history for its horror, but for Australia let it be remembered for the achievement of those men of our country who faced death and the lowest depths of human suffering with the courage, the faith and the resolution of a great people. Morale, that intangible and wonderful thing, kept men alive when all hope of life was gone. It was heroism of a new and different sort which brought them back, grotesque skeletons though they were, eaten by ulcers, grey with disease, but smiling still.

After F Force, other up-country parties followed in quick succession until Changi was reduced to a few thousand, whereupon the remainder settled down to a fairly placid existence. Cafés were opened, local gardening rose in popularity and a great wave of poultry breeding engulfed the camp, dotting the landscape with hen coops and netting. Officers of the Indian Army, whose appearance and explosive speech so often exceeded the music hall's most outrageous efforts, were habitually seen clad in tattered shorts calling wooingly to a flock of surprised ducks, or discussing angrily the latest order appropriating rice slops to the hospital poultry farm. It was another twist of irony that while thousands were dying in Thailand the Changi prisoners were enjoying their greatest comfort.

Changi camp, in addition to providing asylum for the Singapore prisoners, was also used as a staging camp for the many thousands being shipped from the Netherlands Indies to countries further north. British and Australian troops arrived from Java, Sumatra and Timor, stayed a few weeks, then moved on leaving their sick behind them. Early in 1943 the first Dutch prisoners marched into Changi. These were later to come in their tens of thousands, native troops mostly, with oriental habits but with many full-blooded Hollanders among them. By degrees Changi lost its exclusively British flavour and on release was noisily cosmopolitan.

As 1943 wore on rumours of an epidemic in Thailand reached camp and the dispatch of a special medical party caused some disquiet. But as nothing was known officially these rumours were not treated seriously … a few days before Christmas, when the news of the tragedy came, it came with the stunning effect of a thunderclap from a cloudless sky.

'Have you heard about the Thailand parties?' People raced from building to building spreading the terrible news. 'Cholera has got them – nearly all wiped them out.'

The camp reeled and for a moment stood quiet, remembering those who had gone ten months before and wondering. Meals were left untouched and attendances at theatres fell away to nothing. All had friends in the party and to prisoners friends are the dearest things on earth – as yet there was no definite information beyond the fact that thousands of those friends would never be seen again. The story seemed almost unbelievable until the first truckloads began to arrive, crammed with their cargoes of human wreckage. Men so thin that they had lost human form, some in tatters, others naked, fell or were carried to waiting stretchers. Limbless men, dying men whose skins were puckered with blue scars, exposed legs and arms, or scarred with the most hideous of sights – gangrenous tropical ulcers.

The episode will forever live in history for its horror

'You should have seen us a month ago,' said the more healthy offhandedly. 'These boys have been on meat and eggs for four weeks. Up to then they were in pretty poor shape.' The Changi-ites by contrast felt themselves the most fortunate of beings and guilty to be the possessors of the few comforts remaining to them. At once, the camp's scanty resources were mobilised. Clothes, food, eggs and books were given individually and by groups, several units donating entire meals to the sick. There was a fine co-operative spirit in the camp that sober Christmas.

Even the Japanese, whose studied indifference to the welfare of the prisoners had undergone no change, declared that they were

"—The kids have got whooping-cough, the old stallion's dead, the crops have failed, the champion milker's fallen down the well and the cat's had kittens — gee, I'm glad I'm over here away from all the trouble."

A cartoon from George Sprod's *Smoke-oh*.
3DRL/5040.001

shocked by what they saw. But apart from excusing these derelicts from work they did nothing: the end of the war was still a long way off.

Once again the camp was thrown back on its own resources. The rehabilitation of the survivors from Thailand was a slow process, but that it was accomplished at all was a signal victory for the medical staff and administration alike. Gradually, the emaciated frames filled out and the hollow eyes brightened with some of the sparkle of life. The men still talked about Thailand – they will continue to talk about it until old age silences their tongues – but the horror had begun to fade as nightmares do when the sun rises on a new and better day.

A few months before the return of the Thailand parties the Japanese announced that work was to begin forthwith in the vicinity of Changi village. A large aerodrome was to be constructed with the help of prison labour. This was war work, so the Japanese, whose conscience was occasionally twinged by infringements of the Geneva conventions, declared that it would be known as a 'ground-levelling party' … to the camp it was always 'the drome', and to be a 'dromie' ranked as the greatest of misfortunes. Work continued on the aerodrome without interruption until, in May 1945, this grandiose undertaking was completed.

The drome was a Changi institution and was less acutely resented than other work because it was realised that one day it would be a British possession. As they pushed the endless trolleys of sand over the scorching surface the troops would rhapsodise on the future.

'I may bring the wife and kids here by airliner when the blue is over,' they would say, and '"What did you do in the Great War, Daddy?" – built a bleeding aerodrome, that's what.'

At liberation they cheered as they stood on the rooftops of the prison and watched the four-engine bombers of Britain sink onto the runway.

'Always knew she'd come in useful one day,' they said. The drome had been worth it after all.

The first months of 1944 were spent peacefully enough. With three good theatres running nightly and with a great variety of lectures, societies and clubs, no man had a legitimate excuse for boredom. The representatives of the YMCA, who had chosen to stay with the troops in their captivity rather than depart when the opportunity offered, arranged entertainments with enthusiasm. In their picturesque attap huts – surely the first of their kind behind barbed wire – were held concerts, lectures and evenings of recorded music. They worked hard at what was often a thankless task and were rewarded by earning for their organisation a reputation not easily forgotten.

In April it was announced that Major General Saito would take over command from the easygoing General Arimura. Changes in Japanese administration were of vital interest to prisoners since treatment varied considerably with different commanders. The only settled

63

Civilian internees: women in Changi

Lucy Robertson
Australian War Memorial

ON THE HOT AND HUMID afternoon of 8 March 1942, 457 civilian women and girls marched into Changi Gaol. The long march from their temporary camp at Katong had taken hours and they were exhausted. Yet as the gates closed behind them the last sound from their lips was the rousing chorus to 'There'll Always Be an England'. They would not know freedom for the next three and a half years.

While Changi is often associated with the male prisoner-of-war experience, few are as aware of Changi as a female internment camp. Yet when Singapore fell the Western civilian population included 388 women and 69 girls.[13] They had either not been able to obtain a shipping berth before the invasion or had made a conscious decision to stay in Singapore. The tragic sinking of the *Vyner Brooke* on 13 February certainly revealed the dangers of evacuation.

The Japanese ordered all Western civilians to be interned in Changi Gaol. The prisoner-of-war camps (also known collectively as 'Changi') were located further east on the same peninsula. The prison possessed an efficient sewerage system with flushing toilets, but had been designed to hold 600 prisoners, and the Japanese ordered all of the 2400 Western civilians to squeeze themselves inside its walls. The civilians were segregated into two sections – the women and children occupied one half of the prison, while the men were squeezed into the other half behind wire fences.

Helen Beck, an interned British housewife, wrote one of the most interesting accounts of life in Changi Gaol. Her essay 'Internment (from a woman's personal viewpoint)' describes in rich detail the women's living conditions. Each concrete prison cell was shared, often between two or three women. Soon after she arrived in Changi Beck 'managed to "scrounge" an empty milk-box, an unfinished piece of furniture which served admirably as bench or table, and a pot of red paint, with which I decorated the milk-box and a certain panel of wood, destined to screen a little of the hideous realism of that cell'.[14]

Despite the women's starvation, sickness and overcrowding, they ran the gaol efficiently. The women established a constitution for how the internment camp would be administered, and democratically elected a commandant and executive committee. Interned nurses and school teachers quickly organised a makeshift hospital and school for the children. Beck wrote: 'work comprised the daily cleaning of one's cell, washing of personal clothing and crockery, making and mending, and occasional duties in the way of cleaning corridors and emptying dustbins'. She volunteered in the women's hospital during the early days of internment, but on losing 2½ stone

The 'Japanese' quilt – one of three made by female internees at Changi.
RELAWM32526

in a bout of dysentery she became too weak for the task.

The women distracted themselves from their grim reality through creative forms of entertainment. Freddy Bloom, an interned American journalist, published the weekly women's newsletter *POW WOW* from April 1942 to October 1943. It reveals the variety of ways the women entertained themselves – performances and plays, arts and crafts, a Girl Guides unit, and lectures on topics from French to birth control.

On 7 May 1944 the civilian internees were transferred from Changi Gaol to the former military barracks at Sime Road, and the Japanese ordered the prisoners of war to move into the gaol. The conditions at Sime Road were little better than those in the prison – the women had access to a garden at last, but the barracks were overcrowded and leaked during storms.

Written records from the female internment camp are rare, owing to the Japanese rules against keeping diaries and the mould-breeding humidity, but material relics still remain. In closing her account, Helen wrote:

> To those who would learn a woman's point of view about internment, I would recommend a close inspection of the embroidered patches in the hospital quilts worked for the Red Cross. That sprig of heather, those snow-capped peaks, a miniature flower garden in full bloom, and the brave gesture or motto traced in coloured thread – these reveal, more clearly than any essay, the secrets of the heart.

65

policy from Tokyo appeared to be: work the prisoners, starve the prisoners, and inoculate the prisoners every six months. Within these broad limits the local commandant could give full rein to his own idiosyncrasy.

On taking over the camp the procedure was as follows: a huge parade was called on some playing field or barracks square. After interminable delays, the official party would drive up in expensive American cars flying coloured flags: blue for prison officers, red for field ranks and finally the general with a pale fluttering yellow. The parade was called to attention and saluted en bloc. The general then mounted a dais and bawled at the troops a short speech. This was immediately repeated in a high-pitched voice by an interpreter in a language bearing some resemblance to Japanese but having nothing in common with English.

As declarations of policy, these pronouncements were as inaccurate as most Japanese information. For example, Major General Shimpei Fukuye's 'I think I will be kind and generous to you,' was promptly followed by the Barracks Square incident and its bloodthirsty executions. General Saito, having kept the parade waiting four hours, was less encouraging. 'I am Saito,' he said aggressively. 'I do not intend to change anything unless it needs changing.' Ten days later he ordered the entire camp to leave Selarang and move to Changi Gaol.

The gaol was a landmark familiar to all prisoners. It lay about a mile distant in the direction of Singapore and its grey-white walls and angular buildings rose threateningly above the intervening palms. Here were languishing the civilian internees – men, women and children – for no greater crime than being present at the capture of the city. The knowledge that the children would be leaving the gaol lessened considerably the prisoners' regrets at having entered it. Soldiers as a body are soft-hearted.

Imagine the movement of an Australian country town

The move to the gaol was one of the camp's major achievements. A preliminary survey revealed that even Japanese methods could not compress the population of Selarang within the four walls of the prison itself. A hutted camp must also be established. Some new attap huts the Japanese undertook to supply but most of the required buildings had to be transported from Selarang.

An attap hut is an oblong structure of wood standing upon concrete supports. It owes its name to the palm fronds with which the sharply pitched roof is made. The last thing expected of an attap hut is that it should be moved …

To appreciate the magnitude of the task … it is necessary to imagine the movement of an Australian country town the size of Goulburn to a new location. Movement, not only of its population and its furniture but also of its buildings, tools, water pipes, wire, kitchens, hospitals, forges, power stations, workshops, diet centres and theatres was all to be accomplished by hand. The time allowed for this tremendous operation was one month. Such an order was quite impossible [but it was] nevertheless carried out. The camp had learnt much in its first two years of imprisonment.

On the night of 1 May 1944 an impressive fleet of 'trailers' was drawn up in Barracks Square. There was nothing more intimately associated with life in Changi than the trailer. Save for the bedridden there cannot have been one man, from colonel to private, who had not pulled one of those cumbersome vehicles. They were constructed by stripping the bodies from abandoned motor cars and trucks and substituting a wooden platform in place thereof. A stout rope or wire hawser was tied to the front axle, and to this were attached, at regular intervals, wooden poles, each pole giving pulling space for four men. Trailers were of three classifications: light (the chassis of a ten-horsepower car), medium, and heavy (the massive steel bones of a Harrington lorry), and the trailer teams varied accordingly between 16 and 40 men. A fourth type of two-wheeled machine known euphemistically as a 'handcart' was without doubt the most distasteful means of transport ever devised. Uphill they were immovable and downhill they buffeted the hapless men in the shafts with the malignancy of a Japanese sentry.

The spectacle of a heavy trailer fully loaded, preceded by a phalanx of brown and sweat-streaked backs, the rhythmic crunch of 80 feet and the bored nonchalance of the helmeted guard riding, like a potentate, on top of the load is perhaps the most striking memory of Changi. Wherever there was movement there

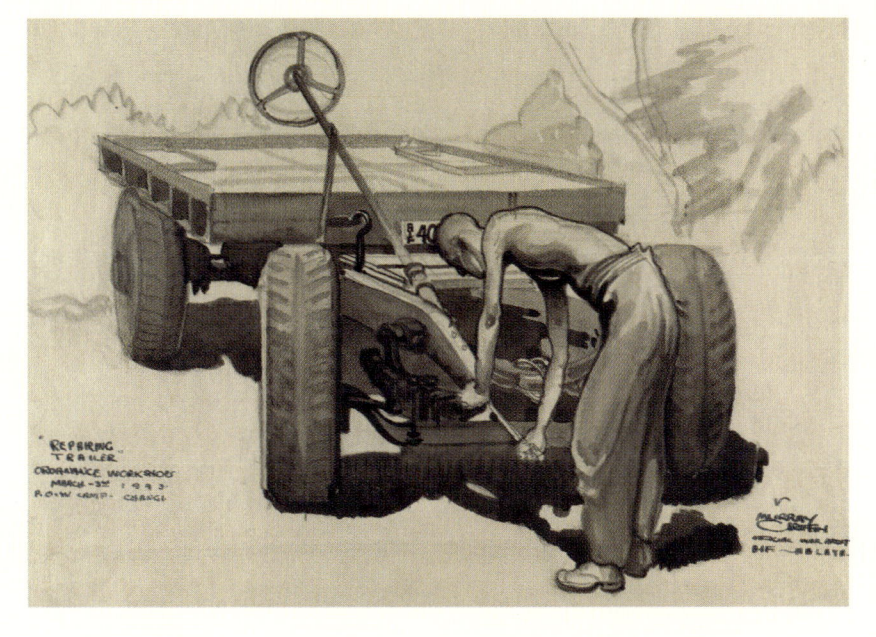

A Murray Griffin illustration of a trailer, a Changi icon.
ART26490

CHANGI LIFE AND SOCIETY

From His Majesty's Prison at Changi, this lion head door handle was souvenired by Private James Tracey.
REL33632

The key to Cell Block G, souvenired by Gunner Peter Hindley of the 2/15th Field Regiment.
REL/21826

were trailers. Rations were collected on them, saltwater was carried from the sea on them, the sick went to hospital on them, the dead went to the cemetery on them … And trailers took their toll of lives. Skids at high speeds doing downhill runs, capsizes and collisions killed men who had escaped the 101 other menaces of death. Some trips were long, six miles each way, returning with three tons of wood. By the end of the day legs ached, heads were dizzy with exhaustion and eyes were smarting with sweat. 'All together, wop it into her,' came the cry again and again, and the 'horses', apart from resentful muttering, had no breath left for a stinging Australian repartee.

...

As gaols go His Majesty's Prison at Changi is a fine specimen. It is dominated by a square tower from which a solemn-tongued clock sounds the passage of the hours. The whole vast structure from its high double walls to the flogging cells deep in its heart is built exclusively of two substances: concrete and steel. There is no wood whatsoever, nothing soft, nothing yielding. The prison is the embodiment of hard masculinity resembling in its endless corridors, its bars and grills, the hold of some enormous ship, dark and forbidding. Once inside, the world of trees and flowers, of faint breezes and pleasant vistas, is gone, it seems, forever. The din is constant – a whirring hum to which the prisoners added their own cacophony. The chopping of weeds (referred to by the picturesque Japanese inaccuracy 'vegetables'), the banging of food containers, the crackling of oxy-welders and the clanging of forges, the shouts, and the rattle of clogs all blended into an outlandish discord. Only in the courtyards, oases in this dynamo of ceaseless activity, did the ears catch the note of silence and the eyes a glimpse of sun and sky.

The gaol was built for 600 Asiatic and 50 European criminals. When relieving parachutists arrived in August 1945 they found in it no fewer than 5170 prisoners of war. Such was the Japanese conception of housing.

…

… in two weeks there sprang up from the rubble and rubbish a little township complete with suburbs and named streets. Thus in Lavender Street ([named for] the most notorious brothel centre in Singapore) lived the camp administrations while senior British officers reclined in deck chairs on the shaded pavement of the Boulevarde des Invalides.

The hospital conditions were at the outset very bad indeed. Apart from the very ill no patients had beds. Touching shoulder to shoulder they lay in their rags on the raised platforms on each side of the huts, whose floors were the uneven ground. By night a few dim bulbs served only to intensify the gloom. The hospital, even to prisoners with standards so drastically reduced, was unwholesome and sordid in the extreme.

Representation to the Japanese for better treatment of the sick was useless. If a man were ill he could not work, therefore he was better dead … on a man falling ill, his rations were reduced to a level which would have made recovery extremely difficult.

The new inhabitants of the gaol camp were now tested, tried and experienced prisoners of war. Initiative and resource had become part of every man's natural equipment. Those who lacked these advantages had long ago fallen by the wayside, as the growing rows of crosses in the two cemeteries bore witness. Before long the gaol area was restored and soon gardens and grass plots gave to this collection of hutments an air of neat suburbia. Britishers refuse to live permanently in squalor and whether in Thailand or elsewhere there were always men prepared to devote their scanty leisure to 'making the place look a bit like home'.

Life in the gaol settled down to a routine of monotony, work and hunger. Owing to a change in camp administration in July 1945 the officers no longer exercised a direct disciplinary control over the men. Except in the hospital, discipline was administered by warrant officers, who were responsible to the Representative Officer, Lieutenant Colonel Newey, Straits Settlements Volunteer Force.

The camp was administered by a body of four officers of whom the Australian representative was Major A. Thompson. In addition to his multifarious duties Major Thompson was entirely responsible for the camp quartering from May 1944 until release. His organisation of the various clothing ration, cooking and food distribution services and his foresight in

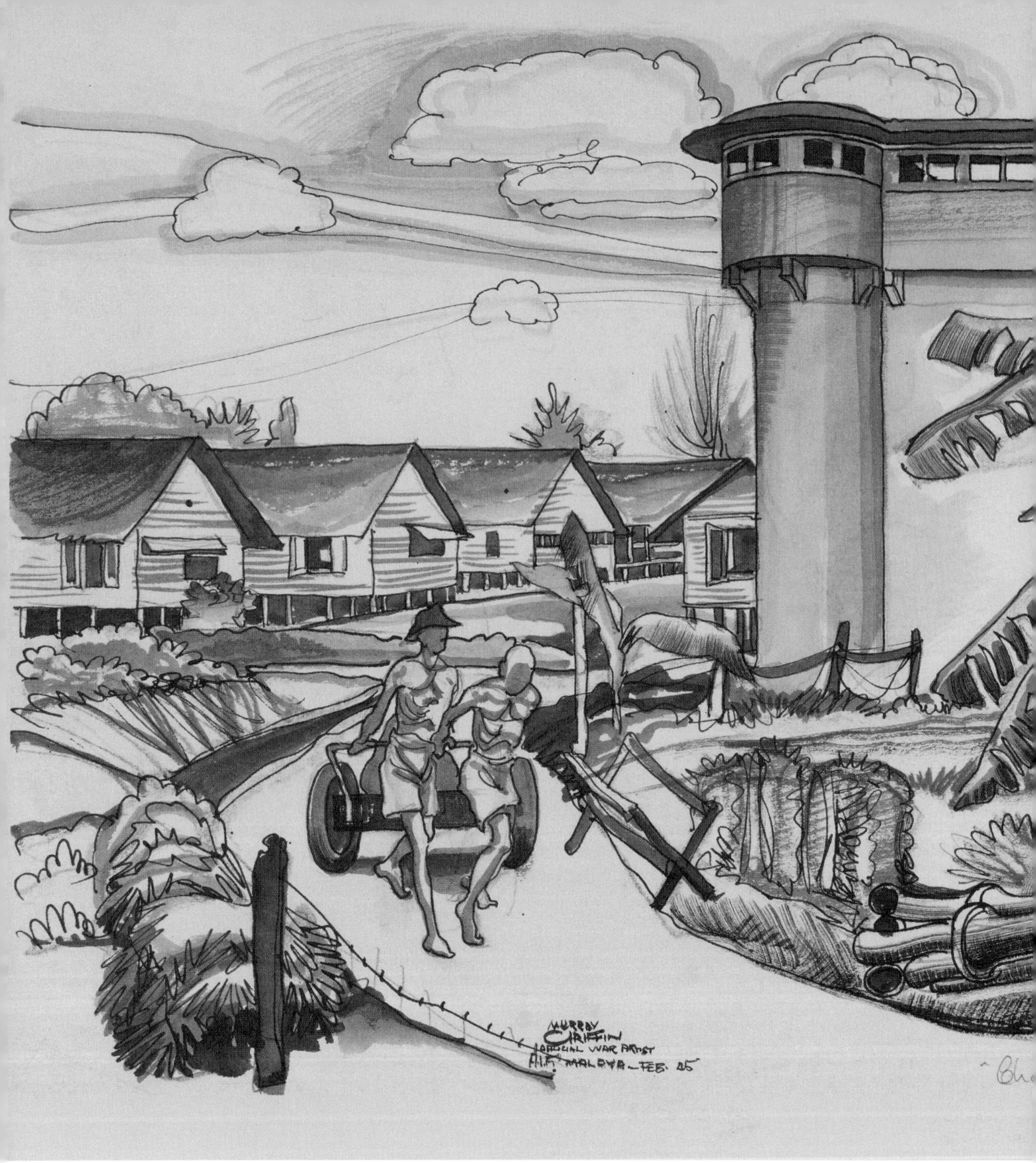
MURRAY
GRIFFIN
OFFICIAL WAR ARTIST
A.I.F. MALAYA – FEB. 45

THE CHANGI BACKDROP

Murray Griffin's views of Changi Gaol and surrounding camp, 1945.
ART26463

providing for a final siege which happily never came about were beyond praise. The gaol, in the opinion of inmates and newcomers alike, was extremely well run.

The good news from Europe towards the latter half of 1944 succeeded in reviving spirits at an otherwise difficult time. When a man has been slaving for years as a coolie beneath the equatorial sun; when he is drenched by icy rain and marches home after night has fallen, shivering and with no change of clothes; when

Former officers' quarters, here a hospital ward for officers. Murray Griffin, 1945.
ART26459

71

his bed is at best a concrete slab or a bug-infested grating; when his meal is cold and only half-fills a mess tin; when the air he breathes is foul with exhalations of unwashed bodies; when the future seems as distant as the past there are times when even the stoutest heart is bordering on despair.

Only the news can alter it. Only the cannons in remote Europe can blast away the crushing walls and rip up the wire forever.

'What's in the canary today?' they ask as they stumble up the iron stairs to the cells.

Mostly there is a shrug: 'Nothing, just the usual stuff.' So another 24 hours must pass. 'Never mind – it will end one day.'

And they believe it. Faith is the victory; this was never lost, not when the Germans were at the gates of Alexandria and Stalingrad was ablaze. 'Wait till we get cracking.' This was the slogan which sustained them through the years.

Early in the last year of the war the air raids began on Singapore. These and the portentous announcements from South East Asia Command convinced both prisoners and Japanese that an attack on Malaya was impending. No one was surprised, therefore, when the enemy called for a series of large working parties to dig tunnels and defence works on the island and in Johore. Thus the 'X Parties' left camp. Despite the dangerous nature of the work … the X Parties were reasonably popular. The Japanese promised extra rations. To starving men there are no other considerations.

These promises of more food, as with all Japanese promises of improved conditions, were at most only partially fulfilled. In some camps extra rations were provided for a few weeks; in others they were worse than the meagre issues at Changi.

For the five months preceding the Japanese surrender men were fed according to the work performed by them. Men on 'heavy duty' had three issues of rice a day; 'light duty' two issues; and 'no duty' two small issues. The heavy-duty ration for a full ten-hour working day amounted to 277 grams of rice while the 'no duties' were expected to survive on 177 grams. Sometimes there was a dessertspoon of dried fish and a trace of sugar. The only protection against beriberi was the leaves produced in tons by the camp gardens. These were served nightly in boiling water under the soubriquet of 'Changi', 'shadow', or 'jungle' stew. But without them the camp would have been prostrate.

…

The months following Germany's defeat were a depressing anti-climax. The expected attack on Malaya was apparently being delayed for no better purpose than to exacerbate the feelings of already outraged prisoners of war. Impolite nicknames were bestowed upon the supreme commander and the camp was restive. When Lieutenant Muira … complained that the prisoners were too arrogant he probably meant that at long last they were becoming impatient. The years in captivity with their unremitting physical and

Old Songs Resung...

There's something about a soldier —
There's something about a soldier —
There's something about a soldier that is fine, fine, fine—

A ditty and cartoon from George Sprod's *Smoke-oh* magazine, published in Changi.
3DRL/5040.001

He may be a great, big colonel —

He may be a sergeant major —

He may be a simple private of the line, line, line, —

There's something about his bearing—

There's something in what he's wearing

There's something about his buttons all a-shine, shine, shine—
For—

— A MILITARY CHEST
SEEMS TO SUIT THE LADIES BEST
THERE'S SOMETHING ABOUT A SOLDIER THAT IS FINE! —
FINE! — FINE!

nervous strain had begun to tell. The war had ceased to be a death struggle and had become a giant manoeuvre. To the optimists the big attack was always coming 'next week' and to the pessimists 'next year'. When Churchill promised speedy action he was toasted in hot water; when he warned that the war may be long he was hotly condemned. In truth the camp had lost its judgement.

Then came the night of 10 August 1945. It was moonless and bright with stars. The news of the past days had been encouraging but few allowed themselves the treat of optimism. As the buglers in the tower pumped out the Japanese call of 'Lights out', most men lowered themselves onto whatever served them as beds and turned their thoughts to the meals of the morrow. Save for the scraping of clogs and the muffled reports of slammed borehole lids all was quiet. It was the 1272nd night in prison, destined to be the hour for which the prisoners and the world were waiting.

Shortly after midnight the official and pirate radio operators had their greatest moment. Crouched in the darkness beside their faintly glowing machines they heard from London the breathtaking news. Japan had accepted the Potsdam terms.

The penalty for wireless operating was death. The only safeguard was secrecy. Yet who could rest all night with this stupendous fact bursting within him?

Out of their cells they came, dark shadows slipping along the corridors. 'Wake up!' Sleepers felt themselves shaken as the words were hissed in their ears …

'The news – it's all over son, Japan is out. Down at home they are going mad and God knows everything.'

'It's right is it, absolutely right?' Everyone had been caught by rumours. 'Heard it myself. The Nips are going for the Parker. You're free, Digger. Think of it: free.' … There were few who slept in the gaol that night.

Next morning life went on. The news was too big, too stunning for instant assimilation. Only after many days did the full realisation take root. Enough to know that the shades of misery were receding, that life would start again new and glorious, that they were alive and free. The war was over.

Time now to look back on the dreadful past, to assess the losses and the gains. The years of waste, of unremitting, unprofitable toil – these were gone forever, gone with the thousands whose lives had been squandered by a brutal foe. But for the living, Changi had its lessons which all had learnt: the appreciation of essential values, toleration towards fellow men and confidence for the future.

So the steel gates were opened and there was liberty.

Resolution, courageous independence and undying humour had won it. And above these things, shining its encouragement, was the undimmed star of faith. Faith in victory, which was theirs at last.

August–September 1945

THIS SIMPLE TEAK TABLE at which the negotiations between Generals Percival and Yamashita took place is a poignant physical reminder of one of the darkest chapters in the history of not only Australia and Britain but also the region. The fates of thousands of Indian, Malaysian, Singaporean, British and Australian lives were played out on this table.

The surrender table has global significance; it tells an important Australian story within the larger story of the war. With this surrender came massive military, social and political changes in the Asia–Pacific region and around the world. Japanese occupation was a catalyst for independence, and the nations of Malaysia and Singapore, born in the postwar era, emerged from the events that unfolded on this teak table.

If not for the initiative of one man, Andrew John 'Jack' Balsillie, the table may never have been saved for posterity. Balsillie was serving in the Australian Army in Malaya during the Malayan Emergency. On one journey to Singapore in February 1961 he was reading a *Reveille* article on the 2/30th Battalion's ambush on Imperial Japanese troops at Gemencheh Bridge in Johore. He realised that he was on that very same Gemas–Tampin road through which hundreds of Japanese Army troops had cycled 19 years before.

The Singapore surrender table

Garth O'Connell
Australian War Memorial

With his trusty copy of *Reveille* in hand, and with a picture of the bridge from the article, he and his driver pulled over. Inspecting the side of the road, he found several Australian relics from the ambush. These discoveries sparked an interest that was to see him become a modern-day Charles Bean, as he collected from the battlefields of Malaya, Singapore and South Vietnam objects that became some of the most significant in the Australian War Memorial's collection.

In mid-1961, during another trip to Singapore, Balsillie visited the Old Ford Factory on the Bukit–Timah Road. A staff member who had been there since the war identified the table as the one at which Percival signed the surrender in 1942 – it was still inside the company boardroom. The room still had the original linoleum floor on which handwritten markings from the Japanese indicated where each representative was to sit.

Balsillie asked if the factory would be happy to either sell or donate the table to the Australian War Memorial as a relic of Australia's involvement in the failed Malayan campaign. At first, the representatives at Ford were reluctant to part with the table, and Balsillie left his contact details in the hope that they would change their minds. Almost three years later, on 30 April 1964, Ford contacted Balsillie and agreed to donate the table and linoleum flooring to the Memorial. With the exception of a short period of gallery redevelopment in 1998, the table has been on permanent display in the Memorial's Second World War Galleries for almost 50 years.

Two replica tables were later built and are now displayed in Singapore at the Memories at Old Ford Factory museum at Bukit Timah, and at the Surrender Chambers museum at the popular tourist destination of Sentosa Island (formerly Blakang Mati), where a prisoner-of-war camp was once located.

The table on which the surrender of Singapore was signed on 15 February 1942 is an object symbolic of an act that transformed so many lives forever. It is held in great reverence and respect by visitors to the Australian War Memorial.
RELAWM32783

THE BARRACKS SQUARE INCIDENT
HECTOR CHALMERS

At the end of August 1942, in accordance with the instructions of the Imperial Japanese Army (IJA), the senior officers – British and Australian – of the Changi prisoner-of-war camp gave all the troops under their command the 'opportunity' of signing a so-called non-escape form – supplied already printed by the Japanese – promising 'on their honour' not to attempt escape. As a body the troops refused, and the Japanese were advised of this.

On the night of 1 September, Colonel Holmes, who was commander of all troops in the Changi area, was warned by the Japanese Headquarters that a continued refusal to sign would be regarded as a direct refusal to obey a regulation which the Imperial Japanese Army considered necessary, and that, if necessary, 'measures of severity' would be instituted. All prisoners who persisted in this attitude of defiance were ordered, if they had not signed by noon on 2 September, to be concentrated in the Selarang Barracks Square by not later than 1800 hours on that day, but in the meantime they were to be given another chance to repent. The deadline came and the form was still unsigned. Colonel Holmes gave the order for the move [to Selarang].

The great trek started shortly after midday, and in a short time the roads were one intricate mass of moving humanity. The British troops came from what was known as Southern Area, and from Changi village … then the AIF from Selarang itself joined the ever-thickening stream, while odds and sods straggled in, apparently from nowhere in particular.

All these thousands of men appeared, carrying, drawing or pushing their belongings, manually and on every conceivable kind of transport. Trailers were piled high … with goods of all sorts. They swayed along unsteadily, like camels in the desert. Push-bikes were loaded till you could hardly see them; even lawnmowers had been pressed into service …

All through the afternoon the seemingly endless undulating serpent of men poured itself into the square. Joking, laughing, they moved on through the hot afternoon, ignoring the Indian and Japanese guards who stood, helpless and gaping, by the side of the road; they might not have existed for all the notice the troops took of them. By 1800 hours that night every man had moved in; the impossible had been achieved. The whole movement had been a triumph of determination.

Sixteen thousand men were crammed into an area measuring 155 by 261 yards. Think of it! Five square yards per man for all purposes: cooking, washing, sleeping, stores, latrine facilities; all had to be accommodated within that space. One thousand men were allotted to each of six buildings designed originally to hold 150. More than 10 000 others occupied tents and hastily erected tarpaulin shelters in the square. All those men in less than ten acres! No latrine facilities were available and there was only one water tap!

Think of it! Five square yards per man for all purposes

Continuous shifts of men, under the direction of Major Carl Gunther, toiled through the night cracking the hard asphalt so that other men might dig into the clay below the surface of the square. Latrines were the first essential – dysentery was already threatening to become a menace. Instructions were to dig, and dig deep; 25 feet deep, three feet wide and 25 long …

Members of the 2/13th Australian General Hospital standing amid makeshift tents in Selarang during the Barracks Square incident.
P01344.012

Morning dawned on this human ant heap of tired and almost worn-out men, but already signs of their industry were obvious. Debris from the excavations was piling into a mound, higher and higher. Quickly this hill – as it soon came to be – acquired the name of Mount Gunther, or Latrine Hill. Fifty yards away kitchens were established … they shouldn't have been so close, we knew that, but there was nowhere else to put them. We christened those rows and rows of blazing, boiling Soyer stoves 'Hardacre Avenue', after the popular AIF signals officer who was in charge of them.

82

THE BARRACKS SQUARE INCIDENT

Hospital tents were quickly erected – there was great need of them – and the sick were soon being admitted. Before long AIF Headquarters was functioning almost as normal, and runners were flying here and there … Strange things began to appear; boxes of ducklings saw the light of day; full-grown ducks quacked their disapproval of the whole business … A herd of goats browsed contentedly on the grass which fringed the surrounding road … Amazing chaps, those soldiers! In the few short hours at their disposal they had apparently shifted everything of value, including the kitchen sink.

> **The three main problems were food, water, and sickness**

The three main problems were food, water, and sickness. As part of the 'measures of severity' our captors had denied the prisoners the right to have any food other than that which they could carry with them. Fresh meat did arrive by some strange mistake, but the trucks were turned and sent back before eager hands could be laid on the contents. Rebels couldn't have fresh meat! Fortunately, our AIF supply depot came to the rescue and produced the reserve rations they had tucked away in anticipation of some such emergency; our past criticisms of this policy of storing up reserves vanished in a moment, and after we had tasted the lunch – our best since capitulation – we were satisfied that some far-sighted person had been at work to have made so adequate a provision as this.

LEFT AND OVERLEAF
The conditions facing the prisoners of war during the Barracks Square incident at Selarang.
042303

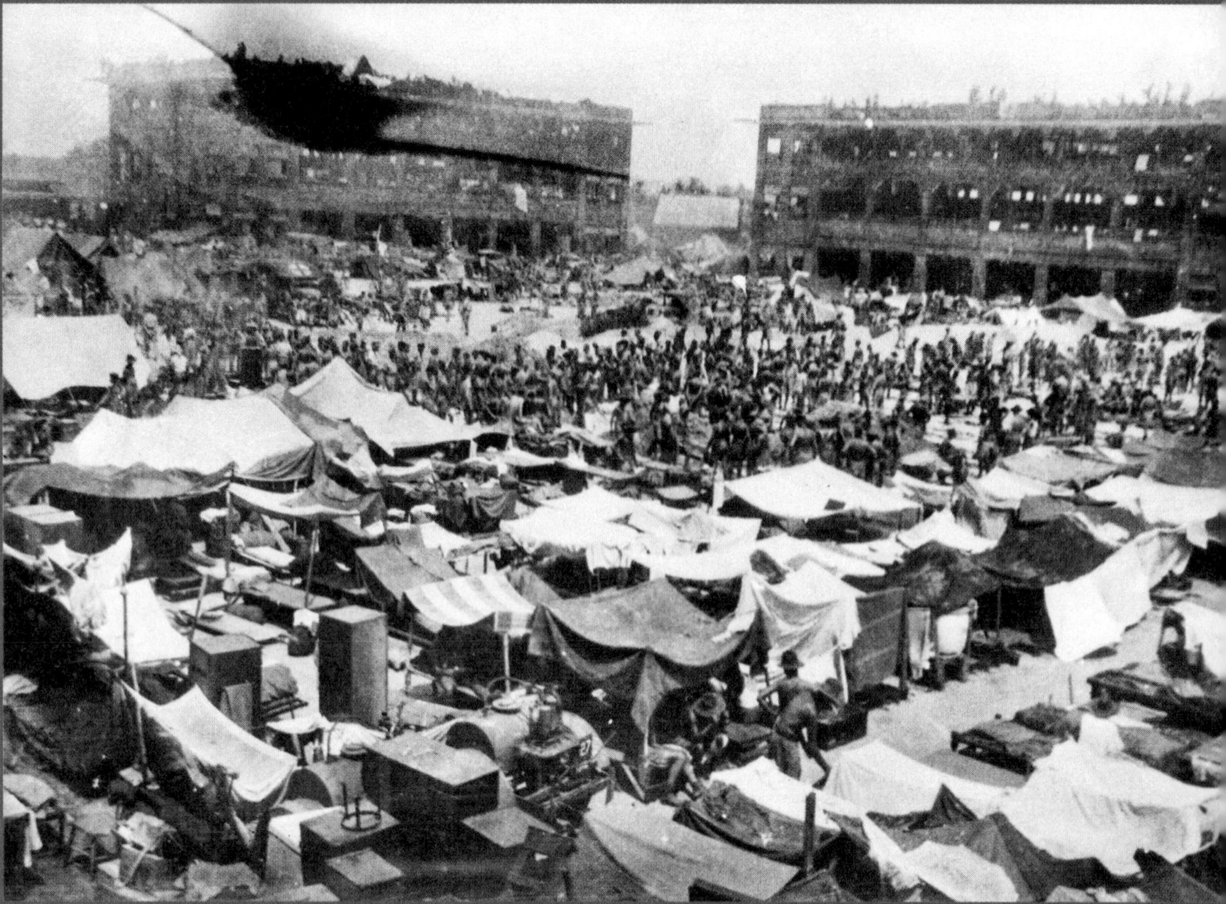

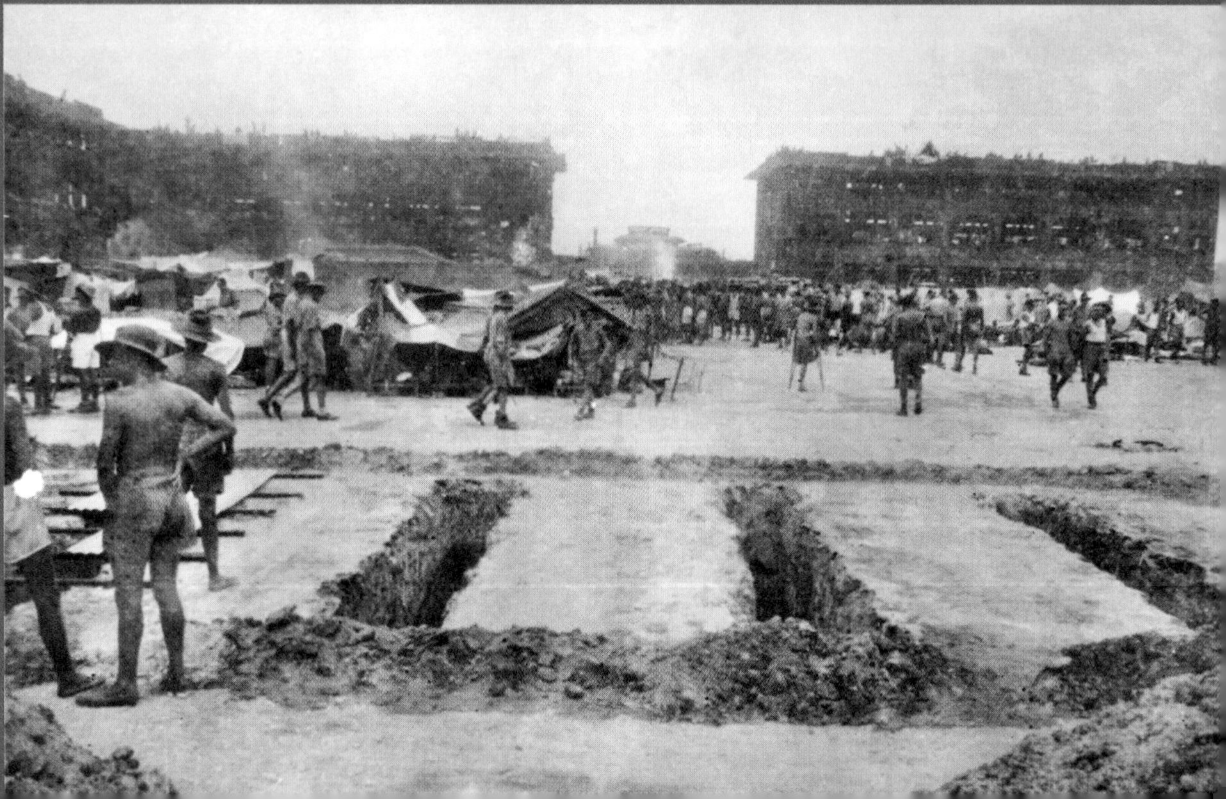

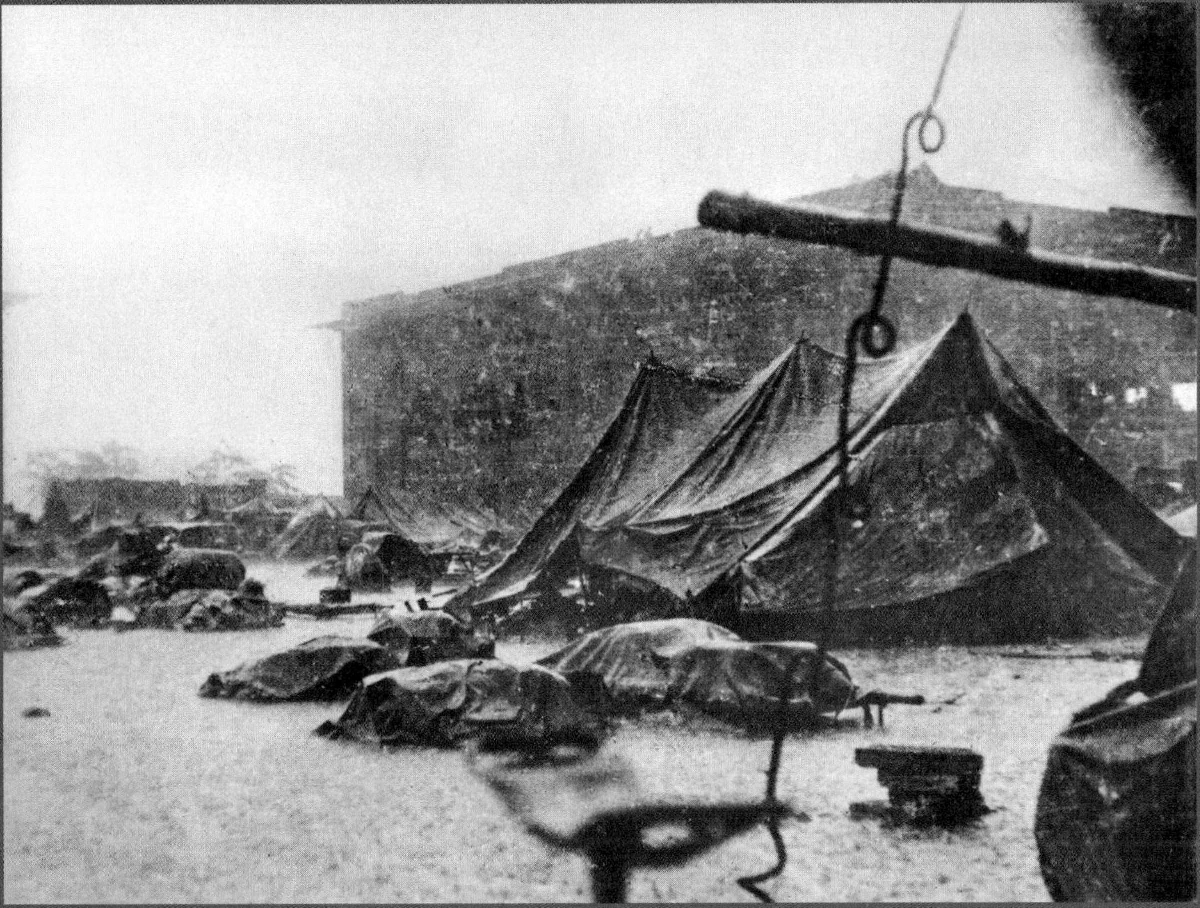

P00603.028

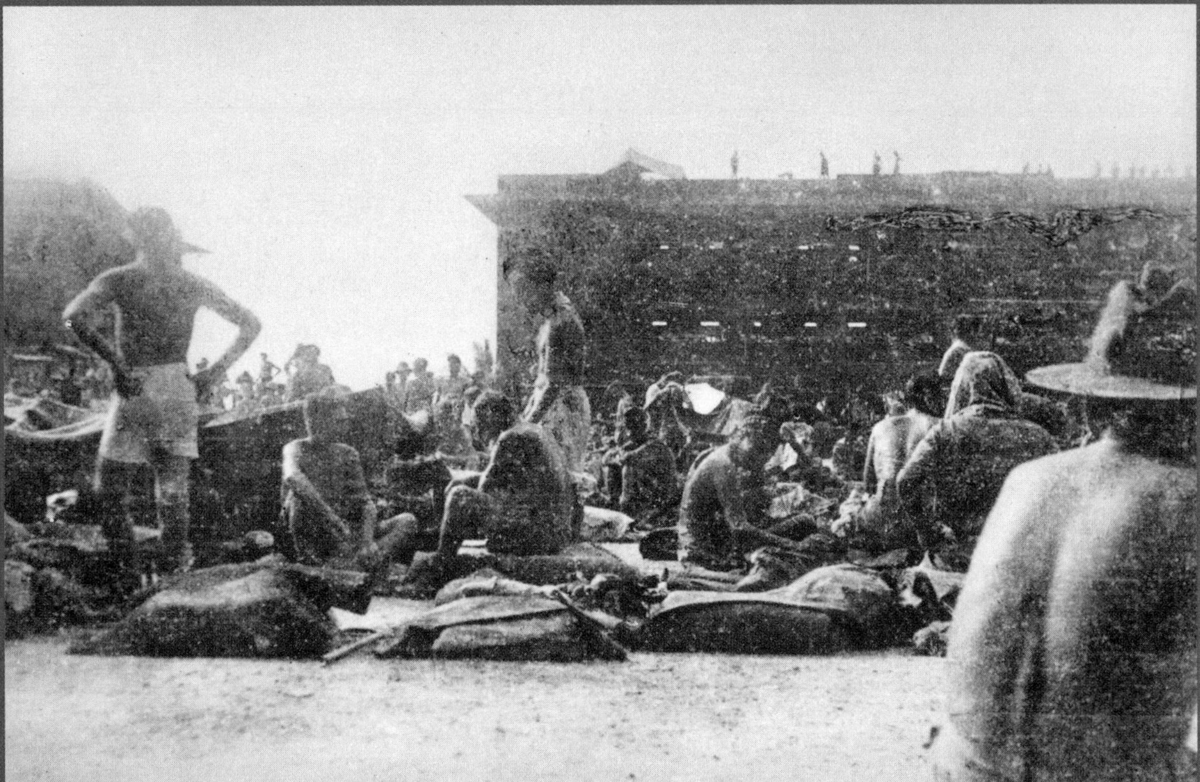

P00603.031

CHANGI LIFE AND SOCIETY

There was only one water point in the area. Plenty of others outside, but between them and the prisoners Japanese and Indian sentries patrolled the way, and woe to any unfortunate who set foot on the road. Yet, in the darkness of the night, and in between the marching sentries, our Engineers slipped across that no man's land …

Sickness was something about which [our commanders] could do little. Everything possible was done to minimise its incidence, but medical opinion was that existence under such conditions as ours would, within a few days, 'result in the outbreak of an epidemic, and the most serious consequences would ensue … with inevitable death to many'. The various commanders, with Holmes and Galleghan, were in constant touch with the Japanese, seeking some formula that would satisfy all parties; and soon it was obvious that the prisoners were not the only worried people in Changi.

On the day that the troops marched into the square Galleghan, in a moving announcement, stated that two Australians who had been recaptured after an escape from one of the Singapore working parties … and two English lads, also escapees – had been shot by order of Major General Fukuye, the Japanese Commander of Prisoners of War, as an object lesson to the rest of the prisoners.

But even with the sadness and gloom that lay heavily on the imprisoned men after that horrible deed, the situation was not without its lighter moments. Odd highlights of humour began to filter through. Everybody, except the main participant, for instance, saw the humourous side of things when an English colonel made a miscalculation and fell into the clinging, odiferous depths of an unguarded latrine trench. The language he used wasn't taught in the best schools, but it was imitated far and wide by the admiring AIF for many days to come …

Each night brought its inevitable impromptu concert. Thousands of men sat on the heights of Mount Gunther, and thousands of voices bellowed 'Daisy, Daisy' into the night air. All the songs which have brought solace to the hearts of men. All the refrains of peace and war. Songs that Empire men have ever sung in their darkest hours. Tender songs. Heartbreaking songs. Songs of memory and songs which couldn't have been sung anywhere else without police interference. And then – solemnly, grandly – 'God Save the King' …

Night brought its inevitable impromptu concert

The troops had been praying that it wouldn't rain, but it did, and when they saw and felt it their prayers changed to shouts of joy. Within a moment the better part of 16 000 men, mother naked, were scampering about the square with buckets and pieces of soap. Soon they were standing like animated statuary, under every cascading stream that fell from the folds of the tarpaulin shelters or overhead gutters, in lathered ecstasy.

The spirit of the men was magnificent through the whole period, despite the fact

An officer signs the 'no escape' form.
P00603.025

that armed guards patrolled every inch of the roadway, and that machine-guns menaced them from every angle. They just couldn't be kept down … Wherever you went, you could hear officers of all ranks saying, 'The men, the men, they're wonderful! Not a groan from any of them.' Why, there wasn't even a growl from the cooks, and everyone knows what army cooks are. In spite of the difficulties they had to put up with, the cooks still managed to prepare special meals for the sick in hospital. They were all magnificent – and didn't know it.

Then came the climax. On 4 September the IJA issued a new order … all prisoners of war [were] to sign the non-escape form. A threat was added that if this order was not obeyed the entire outside hospital, comprising about 2000 wounded and sick men, would be pushed into the square under the same conditions as ourselves. That, of course, ended things.

Galleghan, in his address to the troops, said: 'Your honour, like mine, is a personal thing. No one can *order* you to do a thing on your honour, or to refrain from doing that thing. Remember this, and further, remember the date of this Japanese order … Now in accordance with these Japanese instructions, I *order* you to sign this form.' During the day the form was signed by all troops, and the victory was won – but by whom?

On 5 September all the guards were withdrawn and the troops marched back to their lines. I still think most of them would have laughed if you had called them heroes!

This Australian Army-issue water bottle contains a false bottom in which photographic negatives of the Barracks Square incident and conditions on the Burma–Thailand Railway were safely hidden. It was brought home from Changi by Corporal John Little.
RELAWM20448

George Aspinall's secret camera

Vick Gwyn
Australian War Memorial

THE PHOTOGRAPHS HELD in the Australian War Memorial's George Aspinall collection serve as both a record of the conditions faced by prisoners at Changi and an example of the ingenuity and perserverance they displayed. Aged 17, Aspinall enlisted in the Australian Army in July 1941 and was posted to the 2/30th Battalion. He arrived in Singapore on 15 August, bringing with him a Kodak Six-20 camera that his uncle had bought him before he left Australia.

In Changi Aspinall continued to take photographs in secret, at great risk to himself and his fellow prisoners, carrying his folding camera in a hidden belt. Using developing chemicals and photographic material scrounged at Singapore docks while with a working party early in his captivity, he improvised a rudimentary developing process that allowed him to continue photographing life as a prisoner of war long after his commercial camera film supplies were depleted. While at Changi he documented his day-to-day life and the activities of other prisoners.

Perhaps the most recognisable photographs from the Aspinall collection are those documenting the infamous Selarang Barracks Square incident and, later, the conditions on the Burma–Thailand Railway. Returning from Thailand in 1943 and fearing searches by the *kenpeitai* (Japanese police), Aspinall destroyed his camera before reaching Changi.

Towards the end of the war Aspinall's photographs were buried, along with other material, in a latrine borehole at Changi. Later, prosecutors used several of these images, including the Selarang Barracks photographs, in war crimes trials. Those photos were never returned, but the remainder were restored to Aspinall, and 108 nitrate negatives relating to his service have survived to the present day.

Nearly 40 years later his story became well known through the publication of Tim Bowden's *The Changi Photographer* in 1984.[1] Today, the photographs stand as iconic images of the prisoner-of-war experience and hold a significant place in the Australian War Memorial's collection.

LEFT Aspinall's camera captured some of the worst conditions that prisoners faced. These members of F Force, standing outside the Sonkurai camp hospital in Thailand in 1943, were considered by the Japanese to be fit to work.
P02569.192

PAY

UNKNOWN AUTHOR

'Have you heard that the Nips are going to pay us?'
This statement, made in May 1942, eventually proved to be one of the
very few rumours [around Changi] that came true. We were not particularly
optimistic … as our earliest dealing with the IJA in connection with money
matters had turned out very much to our disadvantage …

Very shortly after our arrival in camp the IJA had informed the prisoner-of-war administration that 'local purchase' facilities (the purchase of foodstuffs and other commodities in Singapore) would be afforded the camp, provided public funds were available. A conference of all services was held and it was decided that the whole of the public money available should be declared and an attempt made to obtain certain items urgently required. The AIF had $47 000 [Malayan] which had been called in from all units and this was eventually given to an IJA officer who stated that the cash was being handed over for safe custody. From that day to this, repeated requests for the use of the money have met with the same answer by each Japanese officer who has been approached: 'The officer who collected the money cannot be traced.' Whether the Japanese government will honour the receipt held for this cash is something to be found out.

With the memory of this incident in mind it is not to be wondered that we regarded as a rumour the statement that we were to receive pay. However, in June 1942 the Japs apparently considered that the efforts made by prisoners in rebuilding 'Syonan' [as the Japanese renamed Singapore] were worthy of some more tangible reward than the rice, hibiscus leaves, and water that were being issued as rations at that time, and in consequence Singapore working parties commenced to be paid. The following month the prisoner-of-war garrison at Changi (including hospital patients and all unfits) … received their first pay [in Japanese occupation currency].

Whether the Japs desired to show exactly what they thought of the white race or whether they considered it was all we were worth has not been discovered – probably a little of both – but the hard facts were that we received about ¼ of the amount received by the lowest Asiatic menial [worker]. Officers earned 25 cents per day, NCOs 15 cents, and the private who did all the manual work and took most of the bashings earned the magnificent sum of 10 cents per day … After camp administration had deducted contributions amounting to nine days' pay per month there was scarcely anything left, but the fact remained that everyone now had some money to spend as and how they pleased. At this time canteens were opened, and even though prices

"Well, men — It looks as if we'll all have to tighten our belts a bit —"

Officers were paid more than Other Ranks, giving them more purchasing power, a situation mocked in this cartoon by Sprod.
3DRL/5040.002

Prisoners were paid by the Japanese for their work. These bank notes are examples of the occupation currency introduced in Malaya and Singapore by the Japanese.

of all commodities had risen 100 per cent since February the men were at least able to keep themselves in smokes.

In September 1942 the IJA instituted an officers' pay scheme which was closely followed by the cessation of pay to hospital patients. The officers received varying rates according to rank but all were charged $60 per month for board and lodging, and after paying all ranks of captain and above $30 and lieutenants $25 per month, the remainder was banked. This latter amount was apparently intended to cover the charge of re-clothing us and paying our boat fares home when Japan won the war.

It is an interesting point to know that as the cost of commodities rose, so the Jap charge for board and lodging was reduced, until in March 1944 the charge was only $27 per month.

Perhaps the greatest instance of Japanese pay wizardry occurred in March 1943 when they decided for reasons known only to themselves to pay holders of original Red Cross Certificates a special rate of pay. Under this scheme, which affected neither officers nor Ordinary Ranks, who had either lost or had never been issued with original cards, various NCO ranks received higher rates of pay than officers. Thus a warrant officer holding a certificate received, or at least signed for, $70 per month cash, whilst his colonel, commanding a 1200-bed hospital, received $30 per month. It is needless to say that this state of affairs did not exist very long …

From the inception of the officers' pay scheme the officers, although signing Japanese pay sheets for the full amount of cash, never actually received their full pay; the IJA scale of rations was such that to keep the force in anything like a healthy state it was essential that additional foodstuffs be purchased. The medical authorities, therefore, decided that the cash amount of additional food necessary to maintain the health of the camp was deducted from the total amount of cash received …

Despite rapidly increasing prices it was over two years before the Japs increased the rates of pay to Ordinary Ranks, and in this time prices had risen ten to 20 times that when pay was first introduced. Even when the new rates of pay became operative, they were only twice as high as the previous rates.

As previously stated, hospital patients and no-duty personnel, amounting to some 500 to 800 men, did not receive pay from the Japs, but camp schemes were instituted whereby everyone in camp received at least 5 cents per day. In order that this might be accomplished, it was necessary to make deductions from Ordinary Ranks as well as officers, and consequently no one ever received the full amount paid by the Japs. However, it is to the credit of all prisoners that, apart from the ever-present perpetual grumbler and troublemaker – and these formed a very small minority – the various schemes of pay distribution … always met with the approval of the ranks.

THE BLACK MARKET
UNKNOWN AUTHOR

Restricted purchasing always creates a demand for illegally purchased goods. On arrival in Changi the troops found themselves with money to spend, and the threat of a death penalty for spending it. This was irksome to the many with empty stomachs and a few dollars of accumulated pay. It was worse for those who had acquired tens of thousands of dollars from the abandoned safes and cash boxes of Singapore. Some avenue of expenditure had to be found.

There were several difficulties. There was no certainty the British currency would be accepted by the natives: they were on the other side of the wire, and the Japanese guards were vigilant and fond of shooting. Still, to a born black marketer, these are but the risks of normal business against which may be set profit – enormous profit – with lightening returns.

The name of the first soldier to slip through the wire will never be known, yet it deserves to be recorded since [in doing so] he founded one of the most elaborate and, in a sense, valuable of all Changi services.

Early black-market operators worked in small syndicates: a financier who advanced the initial capital; a man who went out with a kit bag and returned with the goods; and a third who remained in camp taking orders and generally attending to the sales department.

Down a slope adjacent to the Selarang Barracks Square was a pleasant grove of coconut palms, and bordering the palms was the wire, with the main Changi–Singapore road beyond. Operators would cross the wire singly or in groups of two or three, sink into the long grass and wait for the whistle signal of 'all clear' given by the sales manager from the grove. Then one quick dash across the road into the welcome cover of the rubber trees. From here the going was easy until Changi village was reached. The village was constantly patrolled by Japanese guards so transactions had to be carried out with the utmost speed.

…

Back now through the undergrowth to the camp … The coconut grove is now thronged with people jostling about the salesman, anxious to spend their precious dollars to the best advantage. The officers have removed their badges of rank, since the black market is contrary to orders.

'Milk four-fifty,' shouts the salesman after whispered confidences with the operators. The bargain hunters are so ravenous that most of the tins are censured on the spot, but others carry off cigarettes and tins inside bulging shirts. The [Australian guards] posted to prevent this menace do well. They are given cigarettes and the sergeant perhaps a tin of bully beef to 'keep him sweet'.

The black market rapidly grew in scope and enterprise. The coconut grove was abandoned in favour of the road – the vicinity of what was later the canteen. Here, in open defiance of the authorities, many of whom were seen nightly spending their money with the rest, trade flourished. Stalls were built and in improvised braziers sweetened coconut was brewed for 10 cents a cup. Bread rolls were imported and a placard would proclaim – 'Cheese roll, milk cocoa and cigarette $1.50.' Thousands of dollars were spent and, long before the moon rose, every stall was sold out. The operators were building up fortunes. Nobody cared so long as the goods were delivered. When a man is starving he is prepared to pay and do almost anything to get food.

Two months after the imprisonment began, the Japanese agreed to send into camp some of the kit bags and officers' trunks which had been stored in Singapore at the outbreak of the war. A team of men were sent to the city, and, in due course, the kit bags arrived. They were transported by trailer from the camp gate to a building in the square. This was the signal for one of the most discreditable Changi incidents.

As the trailer proceeded up the long hill to the square, members of the black market lay in waiting. It was a simple matter for one of the trailer team to whip off a kit bag unobserved by the officer in charge of the party. The other men in the trailer, while often disapproving strongly of this disgraceful 'racket', did nothing to prevent it. The same night vendors would be offering soap, razor blades and clothes for sale. One man even bought his own wallet on the black market, complete with photographs of his wife and children. The authorities had accurately foreseen the evils of the market, but by this time were powerless to supress it.

With no additional money coming into camp it was not long before the black market reached saturation point, all funds being concentrated in the hands of relatively few operators. In order to revive the flow of spending, some system of money re-distribution had to be devised. Operators accordingly announced that they were prepared to accept securities in exchange for dollars. The rates were exorbitant; as little as 50 cents being offered for one pound sterling (the pre-war dollar being worth 2/11 Australian). At these rates a £9-tin of herrings cost £6 postwar. The most unusual rate, however, was 'one for one', and some less avaricious dealers were prepared to advance at the rate of four dollars to the pound. These philanthropists were frowned upon by the black-market kings and dire threats were issued against them for 'killing the market'.

The black market grew rapidly in scope and enterprise

When the pound notes were exhausted the operators fell back on cheques. They were usually only accepted from officers – the more senior, the better – but some of the men with sound civilian reputations were able to raise large amounts.

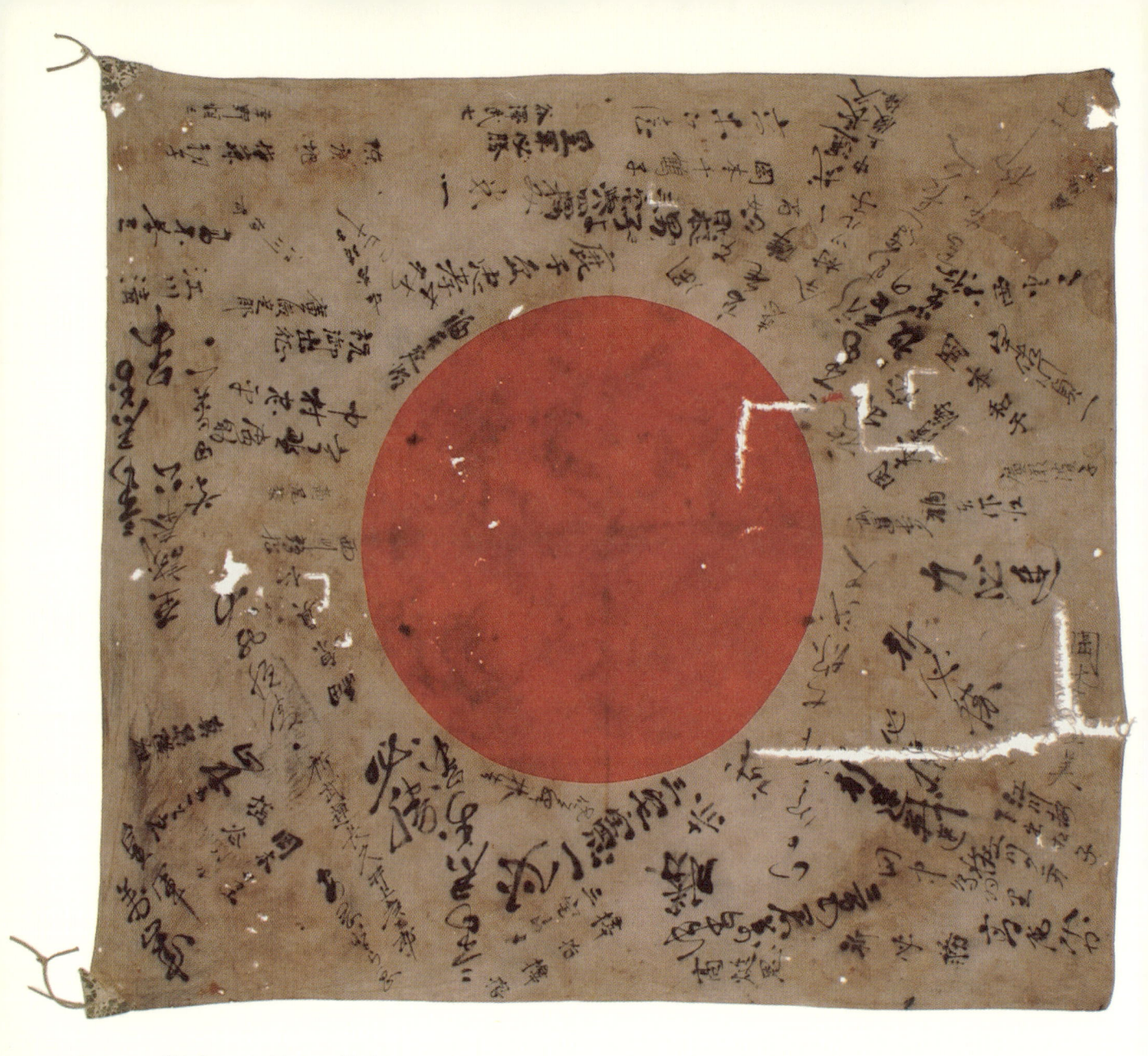

This flag containing good luck messages was carried by Japanese soldier Miyake Yoshio during the Malayan campaign. It came into the possession of an Australian soldier in January 1941 and was kept hidden in a 'Mae West' jacket he used as a pillow through his captivity in Changi.
REL/04411

The cashing of cheques, bonds, and other negotiable instruments continued without cessation until the war was over. Towards the end, the organisation was as elaborate as international banking, and rates for gold, silver, and other recognised securities were quoted weekly, always increasing to keep pace with the firm's inflation. At last, after three years of illegality, the black market was given semi-official status when the rep. officer in July 1945 proclaimed eight dollars to the pound as the maximum rate changeable.

The black market began solely as a buying organisation. However, it was in the field of selling that it fulfilled its more important role.

In 1942 the Japanese introduced their own Malayan currency. For a short time both currencies were accepted, but by the middle of the year British notes were no longer legal tender. Moreover, the camp was running short of funds, owing to the free spending of the early period.

It was soon discovered that the Japanese guards, from the general on downwards, were indulging in systematic profiteering and all appeared to have large sums of local currency which they were anxious to convert into goods. The prisoners, despite Japanese threats, had managed to smuggle a large amount of contraband into camp; cameras, compasses, binoculars, and similar equipment. To the average Japanese soldier these were irresistible. Sales began and good prices were paid: three or four hundred dollars for an average camera, with other articles on a similar scale.

The camp's greatest source of revenue was derived from wristlet watches, with fountain pens a few points behind. Sales of these articles proceeded at a far [steeper] pace than the hectic buying of tinned food. A reliable contact would first be made, usually a Korean guard or a Chinese coolie on the aerodrome or at Singapore. The black-market operator would meet his contact by night in some secluded spot within the camp. The goods were produced and, if handed over, a deposit was paid pending a valuation in Singapore. There were few instances of dishonesty since, for the contact, the maintenance of trade relations was of the utmost importance.

> **Guards were indulging in systematic profiteering**

As hunger increased, so did the activities of the black market, until by 1945 every article in camp, from gold teeth-fittings to camp-made mess containers, had a marketable value. When a man had sold all his possessions, including his scanty attire of Red Cross clothes, he turned his attention to the property of his neighbour. Theft became commonplace and to constrict it the camp administration issued a series of orders forbidding the taking of surplus articles on daily working parties. These decrees reached their peak in July 1945 when a man was prohibited from wearing a shirt out of the gaol by day, and by night was not permitted to leave the precinct unless he was wearing a shirt. The object of

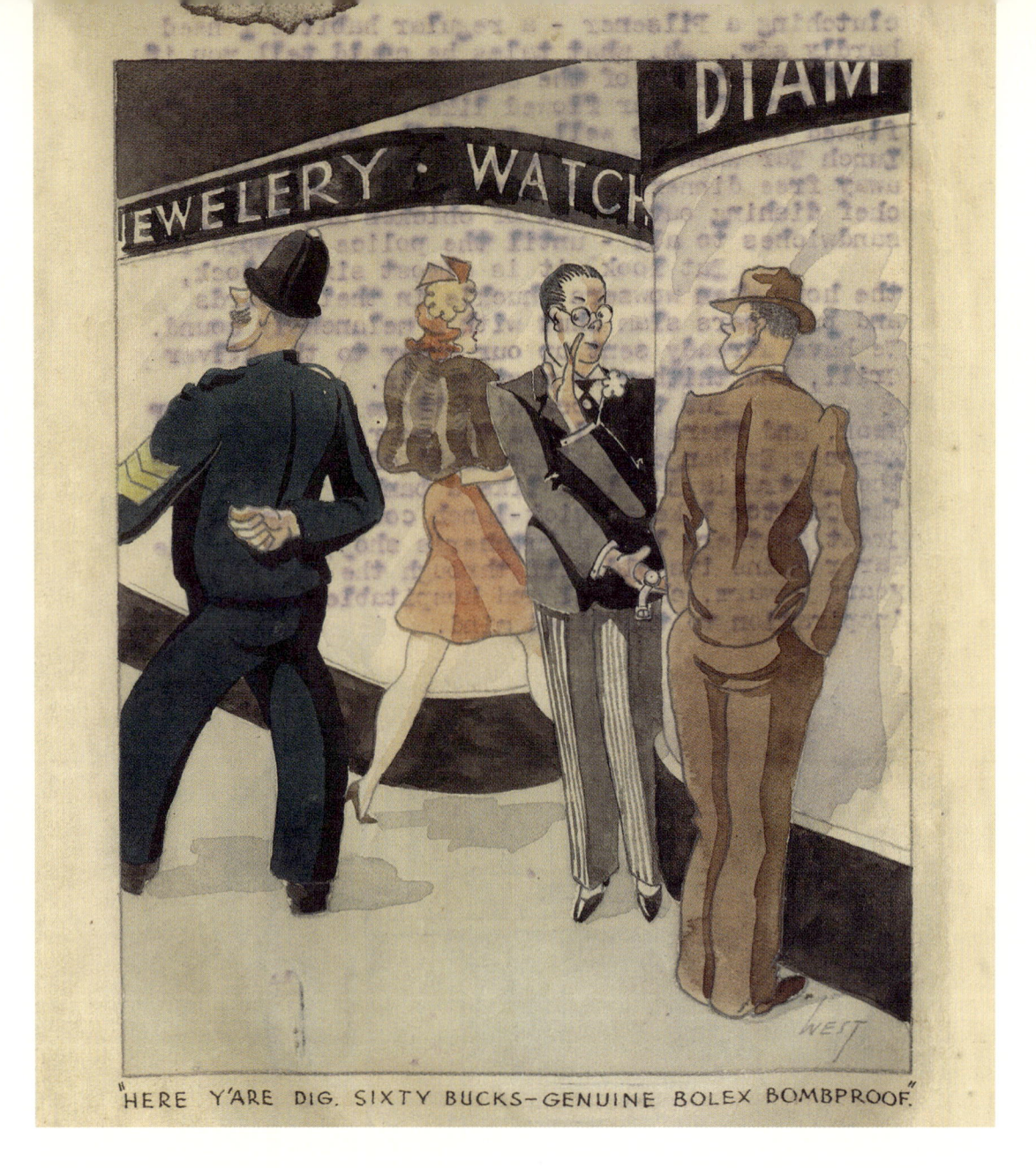

"HERE Y'ARE DIG. SIXTY BUCKS — GENUINE BOLEX BOMBPROOF."

this order was to ensure that shirts were not sold, and if they were sold that the sale would be detected.

Every man leaving camp was searched twice before he passed the gate and was searched again on his return at night. Means were thorough, but the prisoners were ingenious …

A cartoon from *Smoke-oh* magazine making light of Changi's black market.
3DRL/5040.001

98

TRADING

UNKNOWN AUTHOR

There was nothing which P Party would not attempt to take out of the camp to sell in Singapore. Without doubt the greatest achievement [of subterfuge in Changi] was that of the man who, in spite of two searches by the British Police and one of the Japanese Guard, walked straight out of the camp with a large typewriter.
(He then sold it in Singapore for $8,000.) This feat, however, must not blind one to the thousands of tools – spanners, pliers and wrenches – which were stolen from the Japanese workshops adjacent to the camp and then carried out strapped under armpits, in the smalls of backs, or in the crutches between men's legs: nor to dozens of electric motors, hundreds of rings, and thousands of watches which passed through unnoticed and returned home in the form of thousands of Japanese paper dollars.

Nor must it be imagined that, having escaped the various searches, all danger was passed – on the contrary, it had only begun. The Japanese had issued orders absolutely forbidding any contact with the native population, and yet it was with just these people that most of the trading was done. To contact them meant leaving the main working party, eluding numerous guards and then – in some hidden spot – making sufficiently violent signals to attract the attention of any passing Chinese, Indian or Malay.

Having at last lured one of these over to the hiding place an interminable wrangle conducted in an incredible mixture of Malay, Japanese and English would eventually clinch the deal. The trader then had to get back to his party unobserved.

Any slip at any time during this whole elaborate trading technique would inevitably lead to a terrific thrashing with the nearest available blunt instrument … it could just as easily mean incarceration in the dreaded Outram Road Gaol. No one who has not endeavoured casually to slip away from a group of 50 other men under the eyes of a maniacal little guard; to walk naturally with five or six pounds of iron-mongery firmly attached to one's genitalia by the strongest of all P Party weapons – the G string – can ever completely realise the nerve-wracking anxiety such trading involves. And yet, day in, day out, year in, year out, trading continued. Hundreds of thousands of dollars came into the camp (in one month $64 000 over and above the Japanese pay was spent in camp canteens alone) and enemy stores of electrical and mechanical parts steadily decreased. By the beginning of 1945 these activities had reached the stage of large combines, ruthless monopolies and organised sabotage.

CHANGI LIFE AND SOCIETY

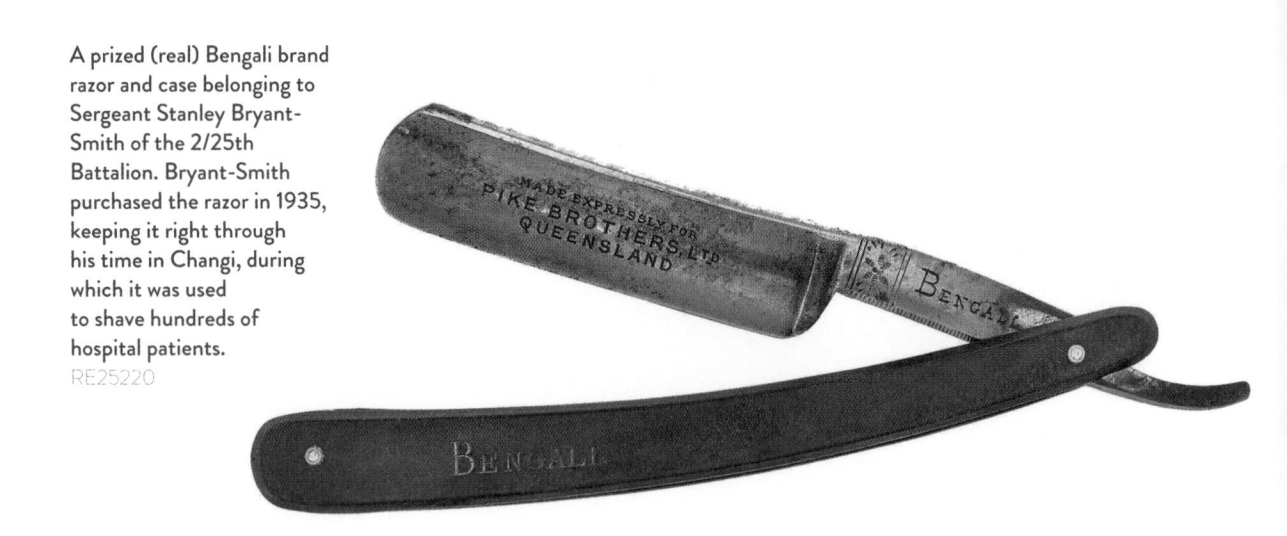

A prized (real) Bengali brand razor and case belonging to Sergeant Stanley Bryant-Smith of the 2/25th Battalion. Bryant-Smith purchased the razor in 1935, keeping it right through his time in Changi, during which it was used to shave hundreds of hospital patients.
RE25220

It is not fair, however, to pass over this subject without mentioning some of the earlier activities of Singapore working parties. For instance, the Bukit Timah pipeline, where an enterprising padre – having decided that the Japanese were the incarnation of evil and that robbing them was a legitimate phase of God's work – organised a highly successful petrol business with the Chinese outside the camp. One night he and his associates laid down hundreds of yards of one-inch piping out of the camp down into the scrub. During the day – whilst the men worked – he would wander round the barbed-wire fence collecting orders and money. That night the order … was poured merrily down the pipe within the camp and collected gravely by the Chinese with their tins at the other end. The Japanese petrol dump rapidly dwindled, the hospital fund swelled magnificently, [and] the padre's work continued. He was a brave man and a resourceful one – he died the following year in Burma.

Perhaps the most delightful instance of that most enjoyable of transactions – where the sale is carried out safely to the detriment of the Japanese – was the razor market.

Now the Japanese are an excessively vain race, and when they shave they like to shave everything – cheeks, chin, eyebrows and eyelids are carefully trimmed.

…

Dozens of Bengals were sold, as well as every other well-known brand of razor … the Japanese now regularly shaved themselves, whipping off beards and straggling ends of eyebrows and superfluous hairs on eyelids with wild enthusiasm – monkeys indeed, playing with their $70 Bengals … made in Changi Gaol by Australian engineers out of cross bars, car springs, old bayonets and broken swords, all stolen from the enemy.

TRADING

These beautiful examples of craftsmanship were hollow-ground, brilliantly polished, delicately inscribed and then encased in ebonite. Born imitators themselves, the Japanese were completely deceived by such masterpieces of imitation – to this day they imagine that they are shaving with 'Number One' German, English and American razors …

The same principle was faithfully observed by watch and fountain pen combines. The Japanese knew only two words in connection with watches – 'waterproof' and 'Rolex' – and one in connection with pens – 'Parker'. Consequently, in an extraordinarily short time, all sorts of very inferior watches found themselves encased in the gleaming carcasses of deceased and useless Rolex Oysters, whereupon they were sold for $2000, while a huge number of fountain pens suddenly acquired the magic letters 'Parker' on their barrels. Prices rocketed, the Japanese printed themselves some more money and prisoners of war bought themselves some more food. Criminal tendencies developed to a pitch of superlative efficiency, great daring, even greater unscrupulousness, infinite resource and irrepressible initiative. These poured into the crucible of Japanese slavery and, heated by the flame of Japanese brutality, fused together to form that strongest of all expressions of active resistance to Japanese subjection – trading in the black market. It was the greatest source of irritation to the enemy and of income to their prisoners. By it, many lived comfortably and few suffered a great deal; without it even more would have starved to death … Strictly ethical, it may not have been, but Changi owes much to its black market.

> **It was the greatest source of irritation to the enemy**

Buying and selling: the prisoner-of-war economy

Lachlan Grant
Australian War Memorial

THE PRISONER-OF-WAR CAMP economy was a microcosm of wider society. Social organisation and economic activities were essential in day-to-day camp activities. In theory, every prisoner received a roughly equal share of essentials, though officers were paid more than Other Ranks. It was through trade and the burgeoning black market, however, that a prisoner could increase his comfort and enhance his level of subsistence.

Fuelled by black-market trade, the scarcity and importance placed on certain materials caused massive inflation. In 1942 men on work parties in Singapore could buy tins of pineapple for 30 cents and bully beef for 35 cents. On their return to Changi, such items could fetch around $4 on the black market.[1] By the final year of captivity inflation was even worse. A pound of palm sugar, $1.80 per pound in April 1944, was selling for $16.17 per pound in 1945. *Blachang*, a type of shrimp paste effective in combatting beriberi, rose from $3.20 per pound in April 1944 to $14.40 per pound a year later.[2]

Individuals were quick to complain about the strict disciplinary measures introduced by senior Allied officers aimed at controlling black-market activities. The banning of trade, the ban on the issuing of IOU notes, restrictions on possession of certain items, and the regulation and registration of personal items such as watches were all seen as petty measures introduced by officers that interfered with prisoners' lives. Such measures appeared to lower ranks as insincere and hypocritical since prisoners of all ranks – officers included – were known to be involved and partake in black-market activities.

But the costs of inflation had an effect on the entire camp. If individuals were willing to pay higher prices, inflation caused by black-market activities inevitably meant that communal funds became stretched. The hospital fund had to pay higher prices for medicine and food and the entire camp's pooled resources could not be spread as far for the benefit of all prisoners. With this in mind, the disciplinary measures put in place by senior officers did have the wellbeing of all at heart.

BOOKS AND PRISONERS

C. DAVID GRIFFIN

The Australian Library at Changi was not floated, formed, or endowed; it emerged. Its evolution was gradual and its origin, as with all Changi institutions, was the surrender. It is fitting that our language allots three precious syllables for so momentous an event. 'Surrender' means the start of a new era, or as one of the early Changi song writers put it:

We all came through
So don't be blue
In nineteen-forty-two,
Let's give a cheer
For the brand new year
Of ONE – P – O – double U!

This spirit of cheerful optimism came later. In the first week, as the weary columns wound along the pleasant roads of Changi, there were few whose innermost hearts were not beset by the menace of the future and its terrible uncertainty. Fatigued to the uttermost pitch of exhaustion, anywhere, everywhere, they collapsed into sleep. Awaking they saw the bomb-scarred palms, the black building, the wreckage of one of the finest military establishments in the Empire that was to be their future home. They saw the men by their hundreds, a vast ant bed of khaki swarming with comings and goings. Then all too soon they were one of the ants and progress seemed more ordered.

In these nightmare days books were forgotten. There was so much to be done. Malicious powers devised hitherto unheard-of fatigues with which to plague the weary. Thus there were latrines to be dug (by day and night since there were insufficient augurs to go round), motor cars to be stripped of bodies and converted into trailers – no ex-prisoner will ever behold this familiar camping equipment without a shudder! – kitchens to be built and, most ironical of all, the erection of wire, the token barrier to freedom. Even so there were leisure hours, but these at first were filled with sleep or stunned contemplation of the new conditions of life, and later, when the first shock of defeat wore away, with endless discussion, speculation and rumour. Reading, for the majority of inexperienced prisoners, seemed too trivial. What thrill was there in the fanciful adventures of Two-Gun Dan when your own adventures were more exciting still? How could the more studious fix their attention on Plato or Freud when they themselves were in the centre of a psychological problem, the solution to which called for the last ounce of energy and determination?

But, fortunately, prisoners in unlimited captivity are still men, and man is adaptable, so before long the necessary re-adjustment was made. Gradually, life returned to a kind of perverted normality … Escape from an enemy

CHANGI LIFE AND SOCIETY

island some thousands of miles behind the front line did not appeal to many. Yet there were other escapes …

…

At the outset books were scarce. Of those who tramped the endless miles from Singapore, not many included in their scanty kit a select private library. The most enthusiastic reader called upon to decide between a book or a pair of trousers will choose the trousers. Accordingly, most men arrived in camp bookless. This deficiency was made up to some extent by those who came to prison by car, truck or ambulance. At least one resident of Malaya was driven thence by his chauffeur.

'Pergi Gaol, Syce!' says he, reclining on the cushions. And on arrival after the car has been packed:

'Tuan, when shall I call again?'

'When the New Order changeth, Syce, I will send for you'.

But he has brought books. So have the hospital patients, whose stretchers are piled high with miscellaneous reading matter; so have the men perched high on the overloaded transports rattling out to Changi.

On 19 February 1942 Brigadier Taylor had launched his education scheme under which every man was to have some form of intellectual activity, however slight. A small staff had been gathered together and these struggled to enrol what was left of the 8th Australian Division in classes ranging from Astronomy to Pig Breeding. On a shelf behind the enrolling desk reposed a handful of books collected at odd points about the camp. It was the nucleus of the library …

The first important influx of books, apart from those already mentioned, occurred when our captors decided to allow the salvaging of kitbags and trunks from the big dumps in Singapore. Any books found therein were put in a handcart – the bastard son of a four-wheeled trailer – and wheeled to the Education Centre … Here, such books as could be identified were returned to their owners and the remainder made available to the camp through the medium of a small reference library conducted by the Education Centre staff.

By degrees the stock of books increased. Outright gifts were made by some, while others were prepared to lend their books to the library as a fee for membership. In this way the lending principle became established. The turnover was limited to about ten volumes per day, the greater amount of book exchanges being carried on in the many individual unit libraries which had sprung up all over the camp. The Education Centre library was composed for the most part of works of reference, English literature, poetry, history, and economics, all of untold value to those faced with the difficult task of preparing lectures and classes under the education scheme.

Education was popular, since attendance at classes meant absence from fatigues. On the lawns beneath the casuarina trees the lecturers stood, surrounded by their sprawling pupils – attentive at the vortex, frankly somnolent on the outskirts. Then, just as Changi seemed about to stage a twentieth-century Renaissance, the whole edifice of learning crashed to the ground with the departure of the working parties for Singapore. Their pupils gone, the Education Centre retired to dignified seclusion at House 34 … The library accompanied them.

The range of books available in camp was astonishing

In August 1942 the trailers were loaded once again with bookcases and blackboards and the Education Centre returned to the Officers' Mess …

It was an ideal situation for a library. Large windows opened onto a verandah from which, beyond the *padang* and mangrove swamps, readers could watch the shipping moving up and down the Straits of Johore; old junks unchanged since the revelations of Marco Polo, fishing boats following, their white triangular sails and occasionally the sleek cruisers of the enemy picturesque and formidable reminders of freedom and the loss of it.

The return to the Officers' Mess, which in the meantime had become the AIF Convalescent Depot, was the signal for raising the library to official status. Headquarters announced that on production of a book in good repair membership could be obtained. Books came pouring in and exchanges mounted to 80 per day. Then at the end of 1942 the library suddenly leapt into prominence.

There were two contributing factors. Almost without warning the Singapore working parties, having completed their roads, Japanese shrines and systematic theft of the conquered city, returned en masse to Changi. With them came every conceivable article of utility and ornament; gramophones, pianos, women's dress, pictures, plate and – how the eyes of the stay-at-homes sparkled – books, books by the hundred. To these were added, early in the new year, some hundreds of volumes made available by our captors. They comprised the former stock in trade of the Green Circle Library, which was appropriated for the purpose …

Alarmed at the prospect of a rapid increase in membership, the staff applied for additional premises. A room in the middle of the building was cleared … and shelves were erected of sawn coconut palm …

Opening day was a memorable event. Publicity and the prospect of 'something decent to read' had formed up a crowd stretching in a serpentine queue halfway round the entire building. A sergeant major attached himself as controller of traffic, the librarians took a deep breath and the doors were flung open. That afternoon exchanges soared to the dizzy height of 500. At the end of the day the shelves showed all too clearly the ravages of the invading army of readers. It was new lamps for old, and there on the shelves lay the tattered bundles of sweat-soaked volumes: backless, coverless …

The library continued to conduct high-pressure business until in April and May 1943 the parties left for Thailand. Thinking they were bound for a rest camp, the force commander was anxious that there should be no lack of reading matter. A trunk of books was packed

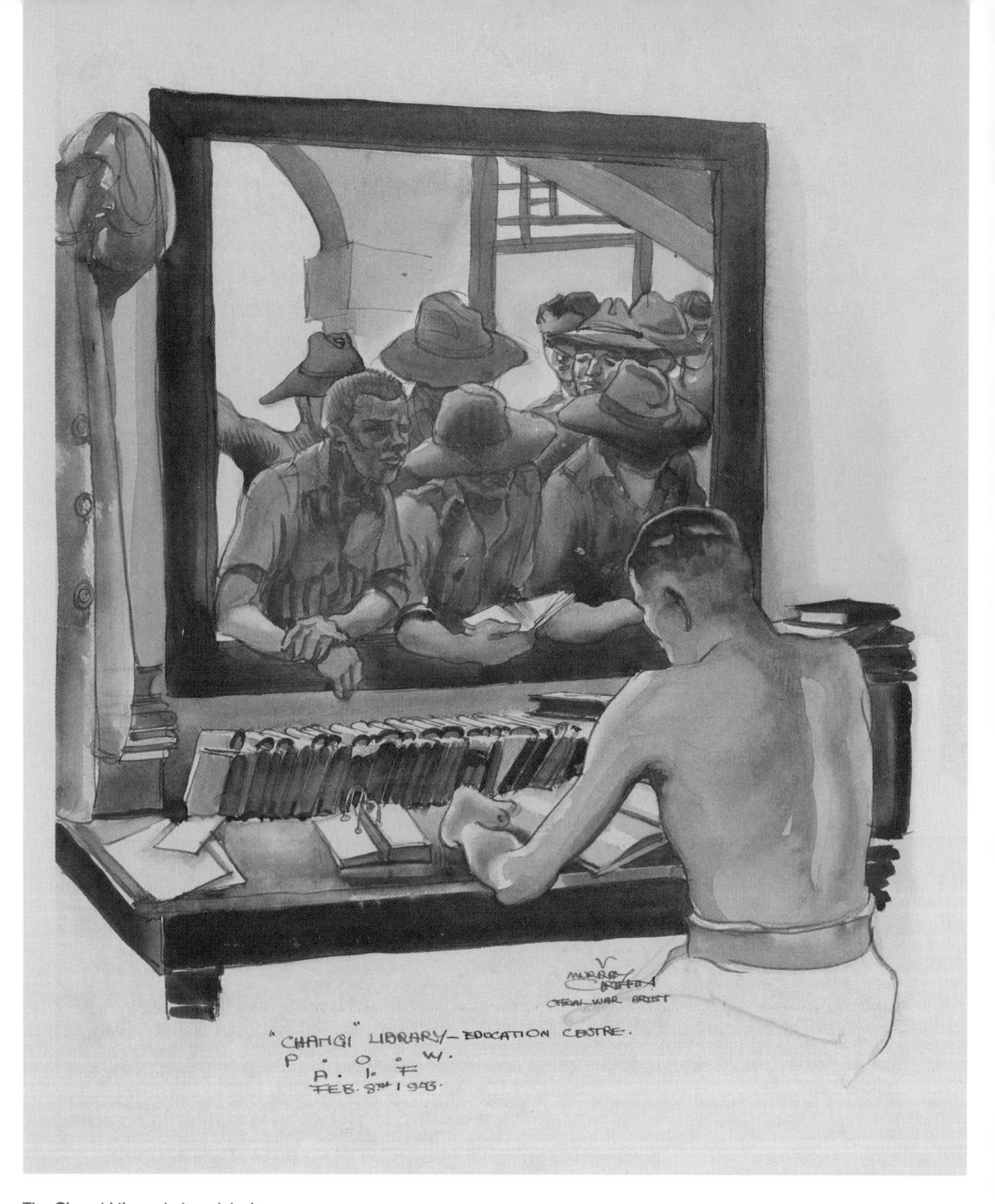

The Changi Library in its original
location. Murray Griffin, 1943.
ART26501

106

and included in the baggage. But the books, [as well as] many of the men for whom they were intended to pass some pleasant hours, were never seen again.

The camp was quiet when the Thailand parties had gone and the great flow of exchanges shrank to a trickle …

Life moved quietly enough for those remaining, until in May 1944 the mass movement of the prison city to Changi Gaol was ordered. At the same time a valuable shipment of books was received in camp from the International Red Cross. For the selection and quality of these books the YMCA, whose stamp they bore, must have full praise. To men who had seen nothing new for years, the sight and smell of the shiny volumes was a tonic and their contents a food. Prisoners live in a world of the sordid, the makeshift and the worn out, so that newness when it comes blows refreshingly from the past. It was wisely decided not to release these treasures until the move to the gaol was completed. Once there, the British and Australian libraries were to combine under a central control …

The room allocated to the Central Library was not inviting. At first glance it resembled a small hold deep in the recesses of a mighty ship. The air vibrated with a faint electric hum, while the walls were braced and pinioned by steel girders embodying in their very massiveness a sense of insupportable weight above. Light filtered down between grey concrete battlements, but when clouds covered the sun a single bulb fought an uneven struggle against the gloom. Into this cavern were crowded the shelves of books, the presses, tables, chairs, together with the beds and belongings of the librarians. This was the prisoners' library in Changi Gaol.

…

But in spite of hardships the crimeless prisoners had more liberty than their peacetime predecessors. And soon the hammers and chisels of the Royal Australian Engineers were busily at work, tearing down steel gratings and knocking in skylights so that on sunny mornings a shaft of light shone full on the librarian's desk and threw into prominence its solitary decoration – a small glass and china tree, made in Japan.

The range of books available in camp was astonishing. It was difficult to mention a single publication, from *The Golden Bough* to the latest thriller, that was not in someone's possession. Nor was the choice restricted to acknowledged works but included limited editions and private publications. One member of the AIF was actually presented with a copy of a book which he himself had written many years ago, and believed to be out of print. There never was a census taken, but one may assume that the total number of books far exceeded 20 000.

There was, however, one unfortunate deficiency: books dealing with Australia. In a camp where Englishmen, Dutchmen, Americans, Indians, French, Chinese, Malays, Russians and Italians were crowded together, the opportunity for salesmanship was unique. But the self-appointed ambassadors were handicapped by lack of attractive photographs and printed

Prisoners attend a lecture in Changi. George Sprod, 1942.

information. The library boasted but three publications of any value: *The Australian Handbook 1941*, *Australia To-day 1942*, and Arnold Haskell's *Waltzing Matilda*. The last-named was a most powerful agent in dispelling ignorance and misconceptions …

Towards the close of the imprisonment, membership of the library rose to about one in three of the population. It is safe, therefore, to arrive at certain conclusions concerning a prisoner's taste in reading matter. It must be admitted that these conclusions are most disappointing. The demand for well-written books was very small. Seven out of every ten declared that they could not be bothered with 'heavy stuff', even if they were in hospital, with unlimited opportunities for reading. Thus, books such as *The Duke* by Guedalla, *The Bridge of San Louis Rey*, and *Bliss*, by Katherine Mansfield, had long stretches on the shelves, men preferring to go away empty handed than attempt them. Yet, *Buffalo Bill's Life Story*, *The Key Above the Door* and indifferent American crime stories passed between eager hands as the very stuff of life. The novels of A.J. Cronin were in reasonable demand, for although 'heavy stuff' by definition they were at the same time 'good yarns'. Aldous Huxley and Evelyn Waugh were strongly condemned as 'bloody putrid'.

…

To the extent of inculcating in the minds of the working man a desire for better literature, it would appear from the evidence of Changi (a state of equal wealth and equal opportunity) that the system of education in force during the years prior to the war was but partially successful.

The care of books also left much to be desired. In spite of constant requests to handle books carefully, the rate of destruction was incredibly high. In many instances brand new books were reduced to tatters in less than a month. End papers were torn out and converted into cigarettes, covers were remorselessly bent back and pages were dog-eared. To complete the destruction, the average man habitually carried his book clamped under his dripping armpit and later expressed disgust and surprise at the greasy degeneration of his literature.

> **Each one was a precious drop in the life blood of the library**

The Library could not have functioned for more than a few months without some system of book repair. This was supplied by the AIF Bookbindery founded by Captain Greener in August 1942. As a result of his enterprise the Bookbindery was maintained by an ever-increasing staff until in the gaol Corporal Roberts of the 2/19th Battalion presided over a dozen workers. Notwithstanding the makeshift material, the re-bound books were stouter than when they first appeared from their original publishing house. Paste was frequently boiled rice, paper and cloth were anything that could be found, and thread was unravelled fire-hose sewn with locally made needles. Despite all obstacles, many hundreds of books were re-conditioned

CHANGI LIFE AND SOCIETY

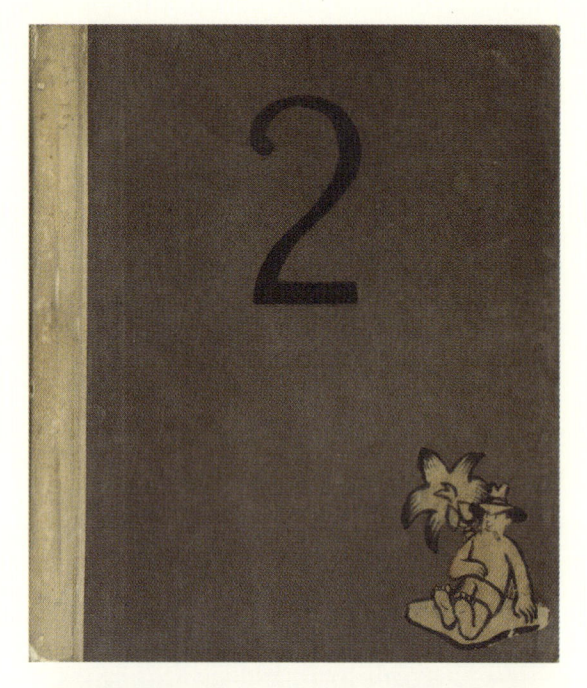

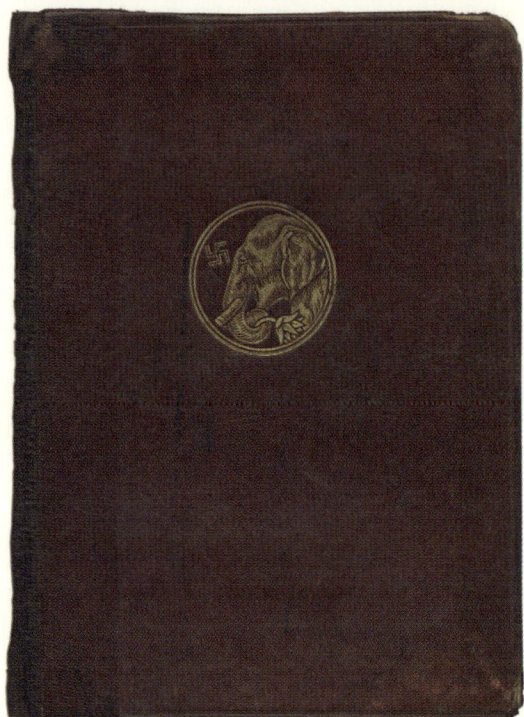

and each one was a precious drop in the life blood of the library.

The library was a Changi institution, and as such contributed to the maintenance of the high morale that was one of the outstanding features of imprisonment [there] … for most men the library at some time or another played its part and kept them going during the darkest hours. True, there were other amenities more spectacular and more useful – theatres for the eye, recorded music for the ear, and brushes for the teeth – but for the mind there was, and could only be, the library. For there on the shelves lay the dilapidated volumes with their contents of priceless words, memories of times past, hopes for the future; the one unpunishable, undetectable escape.

LEFT The Changi bookbindery used whatever was available to repair and maintain books. The volume below is bound in the cover a Kipling book. These scrapbooks belonged to cartoonist George Napier Sprod. In Changi he worked with British cartoonist Ronald Searle on *Exile* magazine before starting his own, *Smoke-oh*, which had a more Australian focus. Sprod later worked for *Punch* and the *Sydney Morning Herald*.
3DRL/3110

RIGHT The bookbinders at work in the Changi Library. Murray Griffin, 1944.
ART25062

MURRAY GRIFFIN
OFFICIAL WAR ARTIST
A.I.F. MALAYA
1944 - OCT.

LIST OF S.A. AND A.I.F. ACTIVITIES.
CHANGI LIFE AND SOCIETY, CIRCLES & CLUBS.

All activities at 2015 hrs unless otherwise stated.

EDUCATION.

SHORTHAND.
- Elementary. Mons & Fris. 'M' Office M.C.
- Advanced. Sats. " " "

TYPEWRITING. Sats. 'AQ' " "

SALESMANSHIP. Fris. 'AQ' " "

ADVERTISING. Mons. Billiards Room, Con. Depot.

BOOKKEEPING.
- Elementary. Thurs. - do -
- Advanced. Tues. SA Lending Libr.

BUILDING AND ALLIED TRADES.
Present Series "Ferro Concrete".
Weds. M.I. Tent.

AUTO ENGINEERING.
Mons & Thurs. BOD verandah.

SLIDE RULE. Fris. M.I. Tent.

HORTICULTURE. Weds. 'AQ' Office M.C. (at 20 00 hrs)

POULTRY KEEPING.
Weds. SA Lending Libr.

FRENCH.
- Grammar. Thurs. M.I. Tent.
- Elm.Conv. Mons. M.I. Tent.
- Adv.Conv. Tues. 'AQ' Office M.C.

LATIN (Officers).
Mons. Hut rear House 218.

ITALIAN. (Officers).
Mons & Fris. Vol Offrs Mess. at 1620 hrs.

MALAY.
On application to Welfare Offr. only.

GERMAN CONVERSATION. - do -

CHINESE (MANDARIN).
- Conv. Tues. M.I. Tent.
- Grammar. Thurs. 'M' Office M.C.
- Grammar. Sats. M.I. Tent.

ASTRONOMICAL NAVIGATION.
Vol. Offs. Mess.

PUBLIC SPEAKING.
Weds. YMCA Hut. 1600 hrs.

APPRECIATION OF PAINTING.
Fris. YMCA Hut, 1600 hrs.

ARCHITECTURE.
Tues. " "

MUSIC SYMPHONY CLASS.
Weds. Outside Education Centre Con. Depot. 2000 hrs.

17 March 44.

CHANGI GLEE SINGERS.
Mons & Fris. SA Lending Libr.

LITERARY CIRCLE.
Tues. Con. Depot.

TRAVELLERS CLUB.
Tues. Ch. of Scotland.

HORTICULTURAL SOCIETY.
Weds. 'AQ' Office, 2100 hrs.

FARMERS CLUB.
Sats. Sgts. Mess, Hospital Area.

PHOTOGRAPHY CIRCLE.
Weds. SA Reference Libr.

TOC H.
Thurs. SA Reference Libr.

YACHTING CLUB.
Fris. Ch. of Scotland.

TOWN PLANNING CIRCLE.
Weds. 'M' Office, M.C.

KNOW YOUR ENGLAND SERIES.
Mons. Thurs. As announced.
& Sats.

RIVER RESCUE.
Thurs. YMCA Hut.

CHANGI UNION BUSINESS BUREAU.
Mons. YMCA Hut.

PUBLIC SPEAKING & DEBATING.
Weds. YMCA Hut.

MUSIC.
- Light. Thurs. Outside Con. Depot.
- Classical. Sats. " " "

LEAGUES.
- Bridge. Secy. Capt. Allin. 'A' Mess.
- Chess. " Major Koe, 'F' Group.
- Darts. " Pte. Carr, R.S.D.

STARTING SHORTLY.
MODEL RAILWAYS.
SUSSEX YOKELS.
HIKERS & CYCLISTS.

Equitation Club

Major,
Welfare Officer, Southern Area

BOOKS AND PRISONERS

AIF Education Centre,
March 14 1943

PROGRAMME OF LECTURES ETC WEEK-ENDING 21 MARCH

Day	Time	Location	Event
Monday 15th	2000	Con Depot Hall	Popular Science Lecture II "Eight Hundred Million Years of Life" S/Sgt R Matthews.
Wednesday 16th	2000	Con Depot Hall	Economics Lecture VI - Dvr. Rodgers -
Thursday 17th	2000	Con Depot Hall	"Tennis Stroke Production & Experiences" Cpl Arthur Huxley.
	2000	Outside Ed Centre	Light Musical Programme
Saturday 19th	2000	" " "	Classical Programme
Sunday 20th	1445	" " "	Light Musical Programme.

Agricultural Programme

Day	Time	Topic
Monday	1430	Irrigation - WO Chisolm
	1530	Fruit Growing - Small Fruits - Lieut Pearsall
Tuesday	1430	Veterinary Lecture - Major V. Bartrum (will not be repeated)
	1530	Sheep & Wool - "Artificial Insemination" - Gnr V. Jelliman.
Wednesday	1430	Dairying - Farm Buildings etc - Pte D Powrie
	1530	General Farming - Lieut Tweedie
Thursday	1430	Repeat of Mondays Lecture
	1530	" " 22
Friday	1430	Sheep & Wool - Repeat of Tuesdays Lecture
	1530	To be arranged
Saturday	1430	Dairying - Dairy Hygiene - Pte D Powrie
	1530	General Farming - Lieut Tweedie

MALAY CLASSES
Cpl Hiley will re-commence his Malay classes on Tuesday at 1430 hours.

COST ACCOUNTING
Personnel who enrolled for these lectures should attend this Centre 1600 hours Friday 18th.

ELEMENTARY PHYSIOLOGY AND ANATOMY
WO H G Sanders of Con Depot Staff will commence a class in the above subject at 1430 hours on Monday 15th - those interested should attend Mess Room Building 51.

TIMBER & SAWMILLING INDUSTRY
It has been suggested, that with view to arranging a meeting of personnel engaged in the above or allied industries, names should be handed to Education Centre before Thursday 17th.

On 1 March 1942 Brigadier Taylor of the 22nd Brigade launched an education scheme that became known as 'Changi University'. Prisoners could undertake studies in law, engineering, science, medicine, social sciences, the arts and agriculture. As more prisoners were diverted from Changi on work parties the expertise and variety of courses decreased, as did the numbers of potential attendees, but lectures and classes continued to be run by the AIF Education Centre. At its peak in 1942, 9000 prisoners in Changi were enrolled.

ABOVE The Education Centre. Before Japanese demands for work parties made the program unsustainable, prisoners in Changi could study a range of topics. Murray Griffin, 1943.
ART26486

LEFT As well as holding literary contests, the AIF Education Centre also hosted craft and hobby fairs. This model ship was built with a small pocketknife and chisel by two Australian brothers-in-law, Privates William Barton and William Harrison of the Federated Malay States Volunteer Force. It took 18 months to complete.
REL/15884.001

PRISONER-OF-WAR POLITICS

ALICK R. DOWNER

Public apathy towards politics is a charge frequently levelled against English-speaking democracies. In an ordinary volunteer fighting force there is little opportunity for ascertaining political interest; indeed, the army deliberately frowns upon this, along with most other activities of the human mind. Amongst prisoners of war, however, it is impossible to enforce all forms of normal discipline over a protracted period. Once the stunning effect wears off of having passed from the none-too-benevolent despotism of their own commanders to the tyranny of a conqueror they inevitably recall their civilian lives and project themselves into future freedom.

This is what happened in Changi. Reflecting the attitude of their countrymen at home, men of the 8th Division on the whole were not politically minded. As they tramped the long 17 miles from Tanglin to Changi on 17 February 1942 they cursed British and Australian politicians for their failure to supply adequate support during the campaign. Thereafter they concerned themselves with the more practical problems of a prisoner's life. It was left to a small minority to display any real concern with public affairs.

The first stirrings of political life occurred in May 1942 when an energetic Queenslander propounded the necessity for forming a new postwar party throughout Australia. The idea met with some response from disillusioned troops, particularly as membership was to be confined to those who had served in the fighting forces, in munitions factories, and in other essential war industries. A skeleton organisation for each state was set up, regular meetings commenced in a rickety attap hut, and a strong appeal was made to abandon UAP, Country, or Labor prejudices. This embryo body was named the 'Services Party', and it might have developed … had it not been for the intervention of the IJA. The enemy was concerned about Australian working parties; by July all but eight members had been scattered in the slave camps of Burma, Borneo, and Singapore.

Coincident with the formation of the Services Party, less-ambitious schemes appeared. Several study groups sprang up, the most talented of which was that on 'Social Reconstruction'. Representatives of the Bar, the church, commerce, journalism, education, and the arts attended weekly gatherings on the lawn or veranda of the Education Centre. Papers were read and discussed, in quality often highly meritorious. The group worked closely to an agenda designed first to analyse the pre-war social and economic order, and then to synthesise from a common pool of knowledge plans for the building of a better world. It is not extravagant to say that for most members the early meetings of this group provided some of the best intellectual stimulus of 1942.

In August a different approach was made. Six months' captivity had emphasised what was only too apparent at home in the astonishing ignorance amongst officers and troops alike of public institutions and the machinery of government. In an attempt to correct this deficiency the Education Centre launched a series of lectures on the governments of Britain and Australia with allusion to the constitutions of the Great Powers. The response was surprising, starting with attendances of 50 or 60, and audiences rapidly swelled to between two and three hundred. The course was twice extended, lasting for over three months in all.

The interest aroused by these lectures evoked a demand in many quarters for further enlightenment. The new year, which many people thought would [bring] release, saw the formation of a study group on 'government'. Between January and March meetings took place every Tuesday in the Convalescent Depot, with average attendances of 50. The proceedings opened with an address, usually of three quarters of an hour's duration, with the remaining hour devoted to discussion. If prevailing opinion seemed somewhat conservative, at least every colour of the political rainbow was well in evidence. Graziers, lawyers, waterside workers, businessmen, communists, doctors, trade unionists, rubber planters, bank clerks and clergymen could agree only on their loyalty to the King, abomination of the Japanese, and a healthy aversion to the military mind.

The rightist tendencies of these political activities were not allowed to pass unchallenged.

In February 1943 socialists and sympathisers with the labour movement started to meet on Sunday evenings in an inner room in the sombre shadows of the detention barracks. At first their deliberations were shrouded in mystery – necessary, so the socialists claimed, in order not to engender hostility from AIF Headquarters. The right-wing dubbed this new society 'the Kremlin Club', a sobriquet which the more capitalistically inclined felt was truly warranted after having attended some of these provocative gatherings. But the discussions, though spirited, were always fairly conducted and the high quality of papers read and addresses given, followed by heated partisan clashes, infused the stagnant air of Changi with a refreshing blood of controversy that recalled for a few brief hours the real world beyond.

Unfortunately, left-wing premonitions as to Headquarters' reactions were not entirely groundless. Divisional officers received news of the Kremlin Club with raised eyebrows, and the promoters deemed it expedient to dissolve the association. To the believer, however, dissolution does not imply death. By the middle of 1943 the same spirits reappeared in an expanded and more catholic form. Under the banner of the YMCA they emerged as the 'Social and Economic Group'. With army apprehensions thus lulled, and the venues of meetings alternating between the easily observed Convalescent Depot lecture hall and the YMCA hut, capable speakers advanced ideas for the coming age. Lectures were delivered on such diverse subjects as socialism, the new capitalism, future immigration, and paying for the war. Discussion was invariably keen, critical, and at times constructive. The thoughts of all men were alive on a victorious future, never on the present, and seldom on the past. With such confident and vigorous morale, it is not surprising that the group persisted for ten months; it was only the move to Changi Gaol in May 1944 that brought these deliberations to a close.

Lectures and discussion groups on matters of state suggested experiment in the familiar device of a model parliament … The first session was opened on 26 June 1943 with as much ceremony as circumstances allowed. The Deputy Assistant Adjutant General played the role of governor-general with dignity. It was assumed that Labor had won the elections; accordingly, his speech bore ample evidence of His Majesty's Changi Ministers' determination to increase the powers of the Commonwealth parliament, extend education on uniform national lines, increase pensions, control all the transport services, and nationalise the banks. The chamber itself was arranged on traditional lines, with a Speaker, a Clerk of the House, government and opposition benches, bar, and galleries. Debates were regulated as far as Mr Speaker could remember in accordance with the rules of Australian parliamentary procedure. Tellers reported results of divisions, and only once had the Serjeant-at-Arms to exert physical force … So successful were these fortnightly meetings that after the move to the gaol they were resumed on a weekly basis, this time in confirmation with the British … animated debates took place throughout the latter months of 1944, and by February 1945 had reached such a crescendo that the camp authorities, with Cromwellian abruptness, abolished parliaments altogether.

The most worthwhile political venture in Changi has still to be told. The disastrous events of 1942 [had] convinced every man in the 8th Division of Australia's danger from lack of population. With a joint Anglo–Australian–Dutch camp, what opportunity could be more propitious for attracting suitable British and Allied settlers to Australia after the war? After 18 months' imprisonment, in default of the faintest suggestion of initiative along these lines from senior British and Australian officers, an immigration bureau was formed by the principal YMCA representative, two padres, and several Other Ranks. A committee was established composed of men of some standing in every state, a program of lectures published, and in December 1943 the campaign began. Weekly lectures were given in the YMCA … At the close of these meetings state representatives interviewed intending settlers, obtained from them all relevant particulars, and gave them whatever additional information could be collected.

From the start the committee emphasised that its aim was not to set up an immigration scheme of its own but rather to work in conjunction with the federal government's postwar plans. All data gathered from British and Dutch applicants would be forwarded to the Ministry of Immigration upon the AIF's return, backed by

CHANGI LIFE AND SOCIETY

the committee's personal recommendation as to the suitability of names submitted. Furthermore, whenever any Changi serviceman thus listed arrived in Australia, he would be met, looked after, and aided in employment by the state representatives concerned. Meetings of the bureau were well attended and, from December 1943 until May 1945, 85 men handed in their names. Sixty of these were British, ten were former British residents in Malaya, and 15 were Dutch. On the eve of release a British committee was formed to co-operate with the Australian committee from the English end.

If constructive work on Imperial lines was belated, still more so were attempts to improve foreign relations. Dutch troops had been quartered in Changi since the middle of 1942, but the predominance of the Eurasian element and language difficulties tended to isolate them from their Allies. At length, in May 1945, thanks to the enterprise of a handful of Australian and Dutch officers, the Australia–Netherlands Indies Society appeared. The object of this body was to improve cultural, political, and trade relations between the two countries after the war; and the foundations of an organisation were laid … Membership was by invitation, since the promoters strove to make the society as representative as possible of the various business, professional, and political interests of both sides. Lectures were given for three months every Monday evening, alternately on Australia and the Dutch East Indies, and the 70-odd members were able to exchange much useful information and prepare the way for future social and business contacts.

A survey of political life over three and a half years in a community such as Changi should end with some conclusions. Though the life of a prisoner was, in a sense, artificial, camp politicians were by no means dependent on uncertain memories. The libraries were well-stocked with the latest encyclopedias, standard works on economics, history, and constitutional law, and several political treatises as recent as 1941. Nor were the intelligentsia ignorant of the current events. Daily radio bulletins, though sketchy, at least enabled men to follow clearly the war's progress and plans mooted for world resettlement. Hence the ideas put forward were not simply those of a period that had already receded; on the contrary, they were strongly influenced by the changes going on without, changes which could be heard of, if not seen.

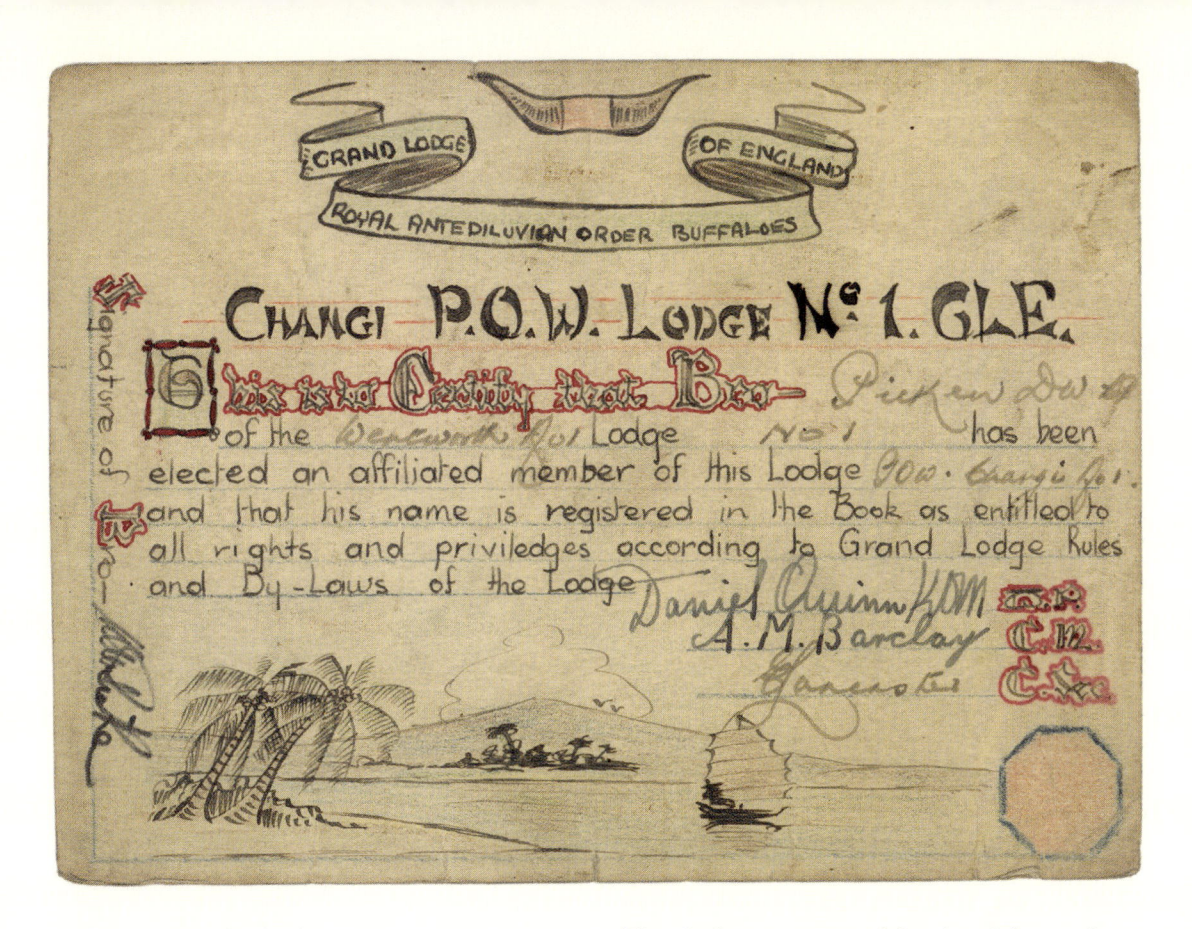

ABOVE AND LEFT Membership cards for the Changi chapter of the Royal Antediluvian Order of Buffaloes, a fraternal organisation that assists members, as well as their families, dependants and charitable organisations. A Buffalo Lodge was opened in Changi, and some 100 members from across Britain and Australia attended the first meeting, but by the end of the war there were just 34 members left in Changi for final handshakes and farewells.
PR0083

That faith in victory and freedom inherent in every Britisher resulted in all groups concentrating on the political and economic organisation of a future which most men believed to be never far away. No one, whether conservative or socialist, seemed satisfied with the pre-war social order; indeed, when it came to planning a new world, the dividing lines between right and left were often very thin. Prevailing opinion in the ranks was leftist, but seldom violently so. In affording men from all walks of life an opportunity to become friends and advance their views, the lectures, groups, and model parliaments served a useful purpose. Who will deny that the participants returned to Australia more enlightened, more tolerant, more sympathetic, and better citizens than if Changi had never been?

Murray Griffin: Changi official war artist

Warwick Heywood
Australian War Memorial

CONTINUING A TRADITION established in the First World War, 35 Australian official war artists were commissioned during the Second World War. Sent to document the 8th Division, (Vaughan) Murray Griffin arrived in Malaya in November 1941 and busily began his work. In February 1942 he was captured at the fall of Singapore, and spent the remainder of the war in Changi. He is the only artist in the history of the scheme to be captured and held as a prisoner of war.

Griffin's experience of internment differed from that of the typical soldier, in that he could continue his intended war work by chronicling Changi. He created more than 40 paintings and 150 drawings, and his capacity to work as an artist was aided by his official status as an officer, which also spared him from enforced labour gangs such as those sent to Burma and Thailand. Although the Japanese never actively prevented Griffin from his work, he began to hide his drawings and paintings during the last years of the war: a response to the growing atmosphere of desperation emerging within the prison.

Several months after his capture, Griffin recovered his paintbox from a storage depot where it had been left during the weeks of the Japanese invasion. When these supplies were depleted he relied on art materials 'scrounged' from outside the prison by various working parties, or created pigments and brushes from raw materials within the camp. From the outset he would paint on repurposed materials, including scraps of paper, which he often sealed with rice paste.

The first pictures Griffin made in Changi represented the events leading up to the fall of Singapore. The portrait of Lieutenant General Arthur Percival, who commanded the British and Commonwealth forces in Malaya, is one of many paintings and drawings of high-ranking officers completed during Griffin's first months of captivity. These are detailed and sensitive portraits, often made at the officer's request.

For the rest of the war Griffin's art recorded the ongoing hardships of prison life, dominated by a lack of food and resources, as well as by disease. A key theme in this body of work is the ingenuity and resilience of the interned Australians, to whom Griffin's art gave a 'feeling of eerie nobility'.[1]

Hospital Ward, Thailand Railway (1946) features Australian prisoners of war who were forced by the Japanese to build the Burma–Thailand Railway. It presents a hellish image of humans struggling to survive malnutrition and disease. Based on eyewitness reports by survivors who returned to Changi, this is one of many images through which the artist depicted the atrocious conditions.

On Griffith's return to Australia a nationwide exhibition of this art was quickly developed and

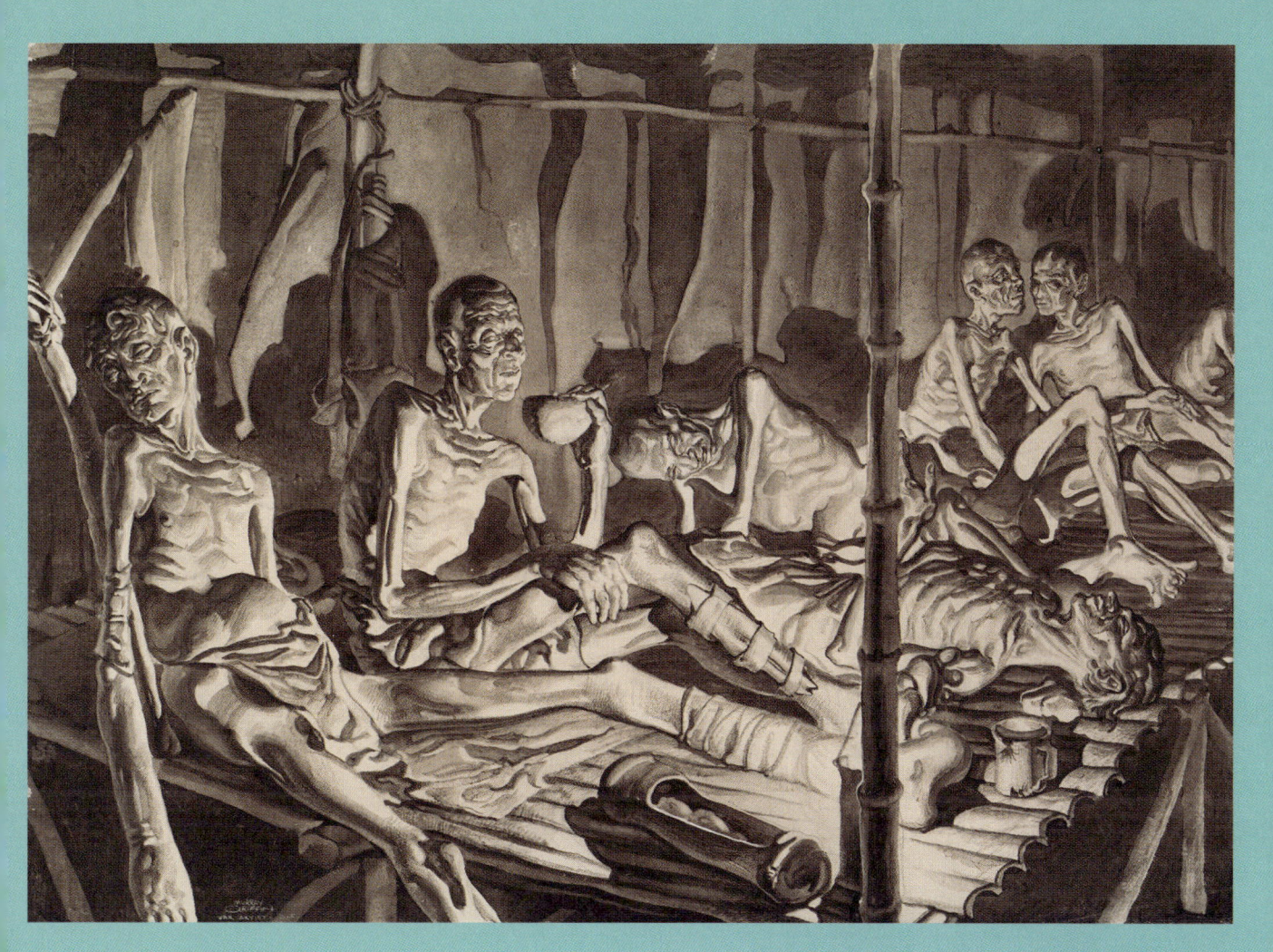

Murray Griffin, *Hospital Ward, Thailand Railway*, 1946
ART25104

RIGHT A postwar studio portrait of Murray Griffin. Griffin's work stands as an invaluable record of the Changi prisoner-of-war camp.
P04569.002

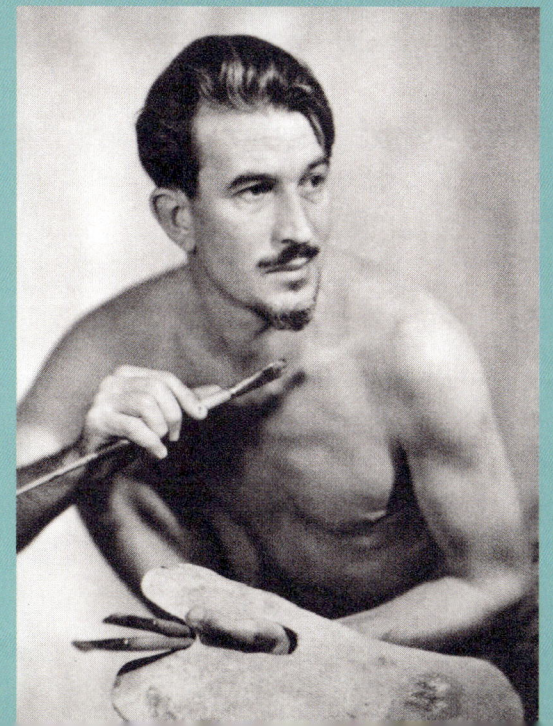

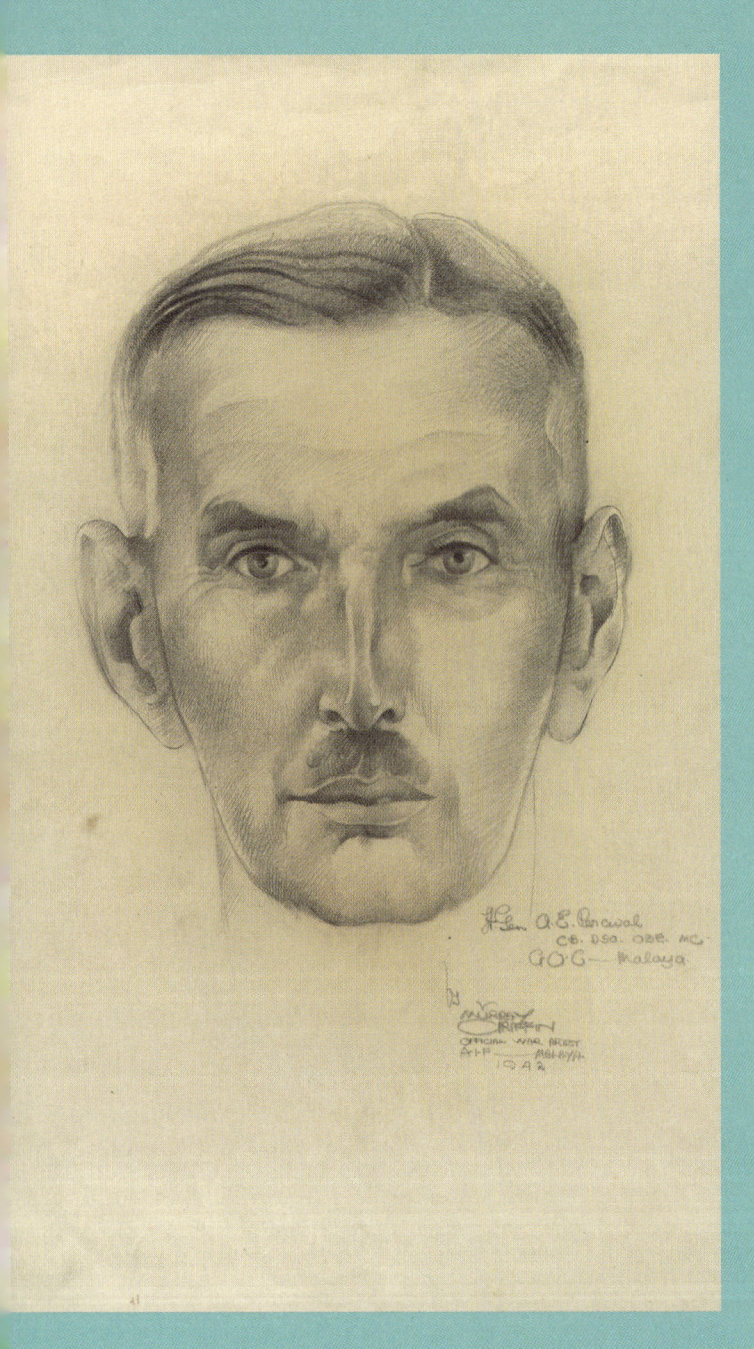

Murray Griffin, *Lieutenant General Arthur Percival*, 1942.
ART26420

toured throughout 1946 and 1947. Newspaper reviews of Griffin's exhibited work were varied and intense. In a scathing critique the *Sydney Morning Herald*'s art critic wrote that Griffin's work glamourised the wartime experiences of so many Australian prisoners: it was 'death, in fancy dress'.[2] Such views, however, appear to be in the minority. For another reviewer, Griffin's modern style provided 'a powerful and convincing record of war'.[3] His work was also celebrated as 'an enduring memorial' to the 8th Division.[4] The Brisbane *Courier-Mail* felt that 'from the misfortunes and misery of Malaya has come one of the finest, most dramatic pictorial records of the war'.[5]

When the exhibition opened in various cities across Australia, anticipation was immense. The suffering of the prisoners by this stage had been made well known, and many families had been touched by the incarceration of 22 000 Australians by the Japanese. Audiences came in their thousands. When the exhibition arrived at the National Gallery of South Australia in January 1947, Director Louis McCubbin – who in the First World War had, like Griffin, been an official war artist – reported that 17 000 people had seen the exhibition within the opening fortnight, including more than 3000 on a single weekday. In addition, the catalogue was sold out three times.[6]

Some visitors to the exhibition no doubt found the works confronting. One mother, whose son was a prisoner of war returned safely home, was so upset by the first set of pictures that she left, unable to look any more. 'I know now why he doesn't want to talk about it,' she said. Mostly, it seems visitors to Griffin's exhibition had a positive outlook. One ex-prisoner found the works an excellent impression of prisoner-of-war life, while a veteran from New Guinea thought them extremely sincere. Overwhelmingly, veterans – ex-prisoners and non-prisoners alike – believed Griffin's contribution to the national collection to be a permanent reminder to 'those people who like to shut their eyes to the realities' of war.[7]

For contemporary audiences Griffin's work stands out as an in-depth observation of the extremes of humanity and civilisation.

Murray Griffin, *25-pounders in Action at Gemas, 15 January 1942*, c. 1942.
ART24498

THE HIDDEN RADIO

PATRICK MATTHEWS, A. 'TOMMY' THOMPSON, WALTER BEADMAN AND DON WALL

The only prisoner ever to escape from Changi Gaol – which was designed along the same lines as Sing Sing – was a Chinaman. It was revealed that he achieved this miraculous feat with the aid of a coil of rope and his own incredible agility, but what shocked and amazed prison authorities was not so much that he had escaped … but that he had ever found a hiding place for that coil of rope. It was the subject of a written report full of vague disapproval and downright consternation. These were to be the new surroundings in which Changi must run its wireless.

This had been the scene of yet further atrocities when the Japanese, on unearthing a set operated by the civilian internees during their incarceration in the gaol, had brutally murdered an innocent woman as a warning to all against further radio activity [in fact, following the discovery of radios in Changi Gaol on 10 October 1943, 16 civilian internees were killed due to ill treatment].[1] Such was the mise en scène when General Saito concentrated all his prisoners in and around Changi Gaol.

The problem was solved in various ways. One set was concealed in the head of a stiff gardening broom, a second in the hollowed-out support of a makeshift bed, and the owner of a third – acting upon the principle that the most obvious is the least suspicious – simply hung his up on the wall in his kit-bag.

The broom set had an interesting history. It was operated every night for nine months, in a hut where there slept 60 men, without any of those 60 ever being aware of its existence. Its owner, Lieutenant Russell Wright, simply leaned the broom – which was used every day to sweep out the hut – against the wall by his bed. Then, as the lights went out (which they always did most conveniently just as a BBC session commenced) he inserted current lead and aerial, used a stethoscope as earphone and, lying blissfully on his side so that the earphone was concealed, listened in. Next morning he would pass on his information to Headquarters, and then – when [the news] was officially released that afternoon – would regularly be seen, eagerly and with an air of the most ingenuous surprise, drinking in the reader's every word. Changi operators, in their espionage-like occupation, were staggeringly thorough.

Yet another set was operated right in the heart of the gaol, underneath the boiler room. This provided the steam necessary to do all the cooking for five to six thousand men: it burned tons of wood a day. Underneath it was

THE HIDDEN RADIO

very hot indeed. Here three Australians and one Canadian had themselves locked in every night, and then, lying on their stomachs – there wasn't room for anything else – with only a small pinpoint of light to assist them, they worked their set. The boiler room, like all the rest of the hideouts inside the gaol, had one enormous drawback – there was no way out except the way they came in. To be discovered was to be captured: to be captured was to be shot. The wireless nevertheless continued to function for some time until, one disastrous night … which the roaring furnaces overhead now made unbearable, a stream of sweat falling from the barely visible head of the man who leaned over it dropped through the gloom into the heart of the set. The machine flared savagely, spat and then blew up. Their wireless was gone.

How to replace it – that was the problem. One might as well say replace the crown jewels of England … That night two dim figures slid into a drain which led out of the gaol underneath the outer wall, cut through with a hacksaw the iron bars which blocked it, and emerged into forbidden country. Silently, they made their way towards the barbed wire surrounding the camp, dropping motionless to the ground at the smallest sound, moving slowly but steadily … Through the first apron, under the centre fence and – 'Christ, what's that?' Both men froze: there they stood, black shadowy figures trapped by the fence and the second apron of wire as, approaching them with bayoneted rifle held grimly and purposefully, came a guard. Trapped without a hope of escape … the Jap came straight up toward them – trapped, trapped, trapped – and passed right on.

… like two ghosts they faded swiftly through the second apron out into the no man's land between the gaol and the aerodrome …

They walked swiftly now through the bush, across the wreckage of what had once been the camp's most profitable vegetable garden … and then – crossing a road – entered the aerodrome … Without faltering they made their way down the landing strips and towards the Japanese barracks … Easily eluding sentries, they marched boldly into the buildings, walked straight past long rooms full of sleeping Japanese and walked quietly up the corridors towards the storeroom. There was not a second to be lost; this was the door – and with a muffled curse the leading figure announced that the door was locked … Methodically and silently they unscrewed the hinges of the door and, lifting it out of its place, leaned it against the wall. Both men vanished inside.

Silently they unscrewed the hinges of the door …

They worked confidently according to a long-prepared and carefully rehearsed plan. Each knew what he had to get and in a matter of seconds there lay in the sugar bag they carried with them two wireless sets, 100-odd valves, and innumerable spare parts. They were ready to leave … without a second's warning, the sound hit their ears: footsteps.

125

With desperate speed they seized the door and replaced it: there was no time for escape, they must wait inside the store and hope for the best.

It seemed impossible that the approaching sentry could have failed to see their movement and – leaning against the door – they waited now in desperate anxiety. The footsteps came closer and closer, then halted: next second there was a mutter from the passageway outside and the door shook slightly as the guard gave it a tentative prod with his rifle butt. This was followed by a more determined shove with his shoulder – the two men inside returned the pressure with enthusiasm and the door remained firm. An animal grunt of extreme Japanese displeasure next greeted their straining ears and then – blessed sound – the crunch of retreating boots. Now was their chance – out and home.

But it was at this point that they were to show their greatest heroism and resource. To leave the door as it was, unhinged and leaning against the wall, was to leave unmistakable evidence of their presence and of their theft. Therefore – in spite of the fact that it was obvious that the guard who had just left them had gone for help – they calmly dropped their bag, replaced the door and screwed it up again. Then, with a last look round to see that all was as it had been when they arrived, they returned down the corridors, past the sleeping Japs and out into the concealing blanket of the night.

Theirs had been a desperate venture: to have been captured at any time would have meant certain execution … they would not even have had the assistance of our own Headquarters, for to acknowledge any complicity in their action would inevitably bring upon the whole camp the most savage of repercussions. Therefore, without hope of reward if they succeeded or sympathy if they failed, they were alone in the world …

They made their way quickly through the last patch of scrub and prepared for a final rush which would take them through the wire. But not ten yards had they advanced before that most terrifying of all sounds – the smack of a rifle bolt being shot home – told them all too clearly that they had been seen. The last stage, after all, was to be the most difficult.

The last stage, after all, was to be the most difficult

Crouching low, they ran and reached the wire … It clung passionately to their clothes, bit into their legs and arms with all the venom of an adder, clawed greedily at their bag and its precious contents and then suddenly grew vibrant with hisses and angry flashes – the guards were firing. Under this fusillade the two men worked desperately but systematically … they moved on, inch by inch. Another few feet, one foot more, one more layer of wire, and at last, miraculously, they were through. Dashing across the vegetable garden they rounded the corner of the gaol wall … And so up the drain they crawled and under the walls. They were back and once again the men inside the gaol had their wireless.

… the small band, now four Australians and a Canadian, quickly built themselves a magnificent set. Gone were the days of earphones made out of stethoscopes and bits stolen out of Japanese trucks and even General Saito's telephone: the time was past when they were compelled to magnetise their own steel and improvise their own parts – now they had a radio which would pick up not only all the major stations of England, Europe, India, America, and Australia but even a local mission station in South America magniloquently named 'The voice of the Andes'. The day of the complete and minutely detailed news screed had come to stay.

Prisoners of war in Changi now became a unique type of 'listener-in'. Being in constant receipt of Japanese propaganda as well as their own news, they developed a nicely balanced sense of cynicism which enabled them accurately to discriminate between the truth and the propaganda content of Allied communiques: realising that the end of the Japanese war depended ultimately upon the end of the European war, they followed the progress of the latter, village by village … Australians, moreover, were accustomed, and expected, to know which reading any new bill had reached in the House [of Representatives] just as much as what offensives had commenced in Europe or how plane production had increased in America. It is a very well-informed community indeed which – man for man – can, in a test of general information as to world affairs from 1942 to 1945, compete with the prisoners of war from Malaya.

News at this time was received at all hours of the night and passed on in typewritten screeds by a highly organised body of middlemen to all parts of the camp the following morning. These screeds were read, memorised and quickly passed on. In this way the camp knew at all times, within a few hours of its happening, the exact details of any important event. From the days when Lieutenant Takahashi had been pleased to tell his camp that Australians and Americans were starving and that the war would last for 20 years, Changi had passed to a period which was to culminate in their receipt of the [news of the] Japanese Emperor's decision to surrender, six minutes after it was broadcast to the world …

But the boiler room was too hot, both literally and metaphorically. The men who operated under it were losing weight and becoming nervy because of the impossible temperature, and they had had several extremely narrow escapes from detection in the recent past. They decided, therefore, first of all that they would work elsewhere and secondly that they would replace the officially provided protection squad with a privately organised and highly efficient 'cockatoo' system of their own.

Without further ado they moved their set, their gear, their beds and themselves into an old abandoned tool shed constructed since

CHANGI LIFE AND SOCIETY

their arrival in the gaol for the accommodation of borehole-digging equipment. This shed had a roof which leaked badly and was supported by four posts. They plugged up the holes in the roof and removed one of the posts: this was to be the new home of their wireless. Laboriously they hollowed it out and inserted their set: holes were made through the shell of wood into the cavity through which control knobs and wiring could be connected to the set; and these holes were themselves concealed during the day by two nails and a spike which were driven into them. From outside, the post seemed merely to be nailed to

RIGHT This wireless set was built in Changi in 1944 by Sapper Patrick Matthews from stolen Japanese aeroplane parts.
RELAWM31298

RIGHT Following liberation, prisoners pose with radio sets assembled in Changi from spare parts. Two of these wireless sets are now in the Australian War Memorial's collection. Sapper Patrick Matthews is front right. In May 1945 Matthews was found with electrical equipment stolen from the Japanese. Despite also stealing food and medical supplies for the hospital, he was sentenced by his own officers to 42 days' solitary confinement in the correction cells. This caused a rift between the men and officers of the AIF.
019328

RIGHT This radio receiver was constructed from scavenged spare parts by Signalman Sydney Slim in 1942. For his 'valuable service and devotion' in operating the radio and communicating the news across the camp Slim was awarded the British Empire Medal in 1946.
REL23204

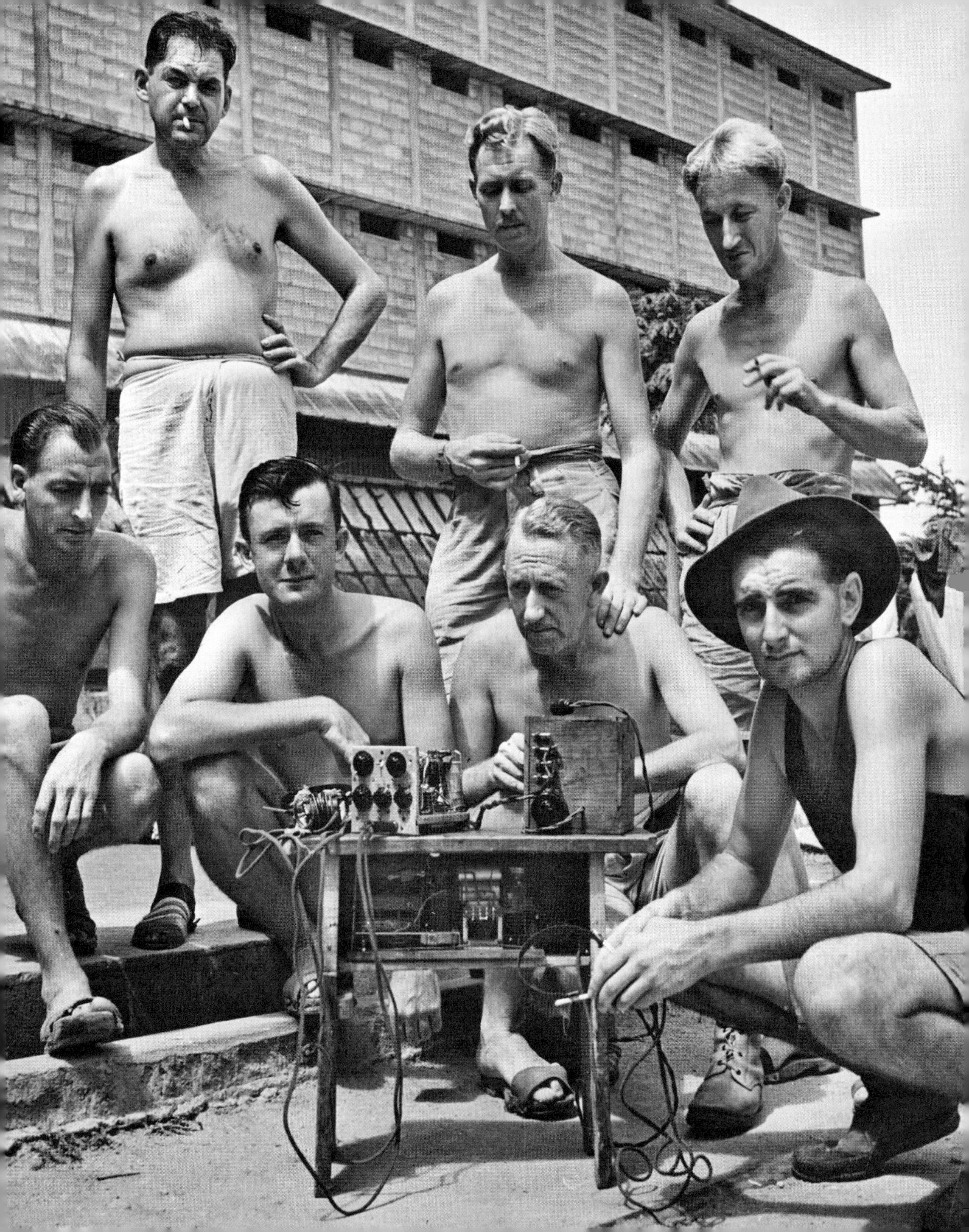

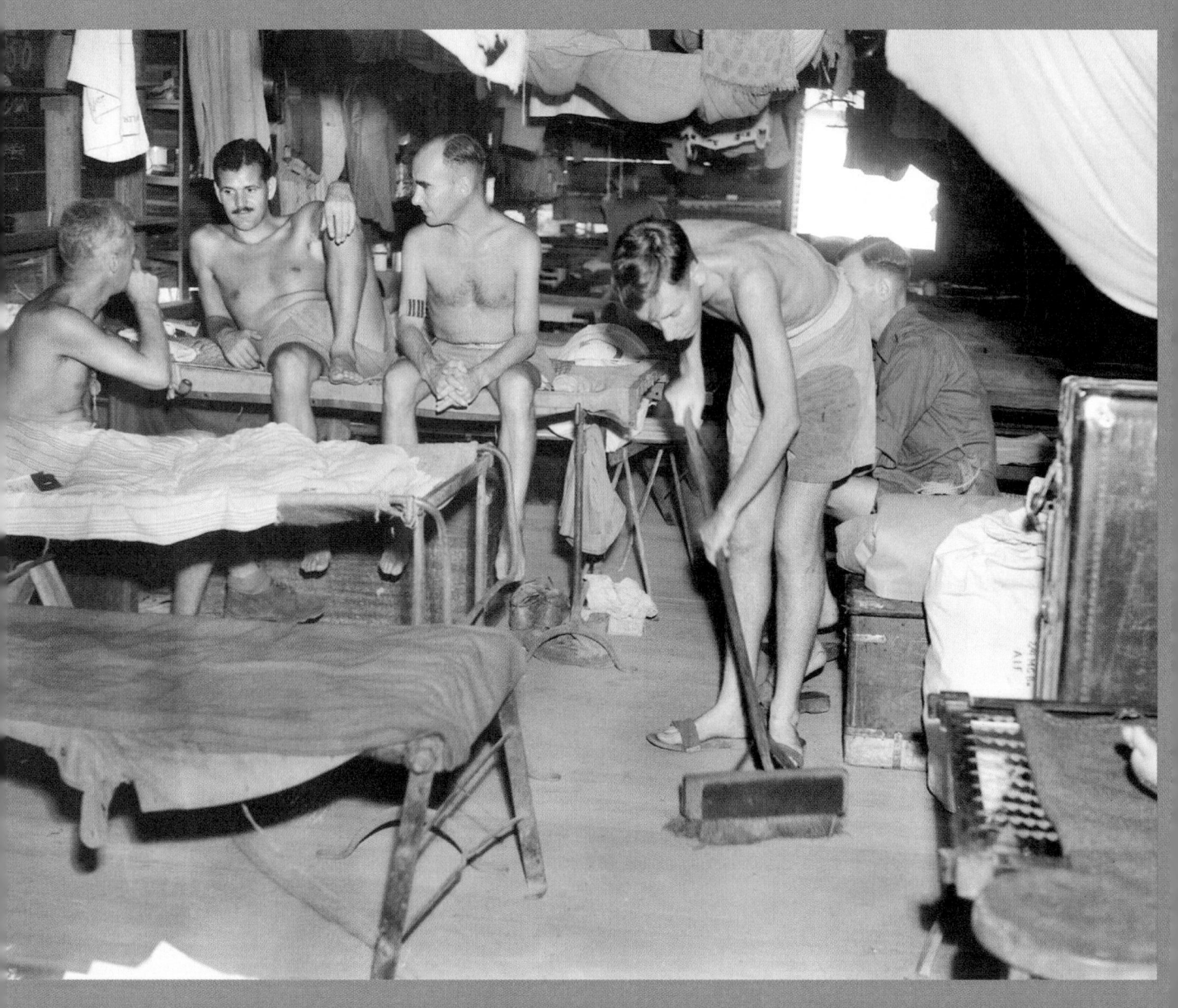

Another example of a hidden Changi radio. Lieutenant Wright of the Australian Army Ordnance Corps is seen sweeping the floor of his hut with a broom, inside of which is hidden a wireless.

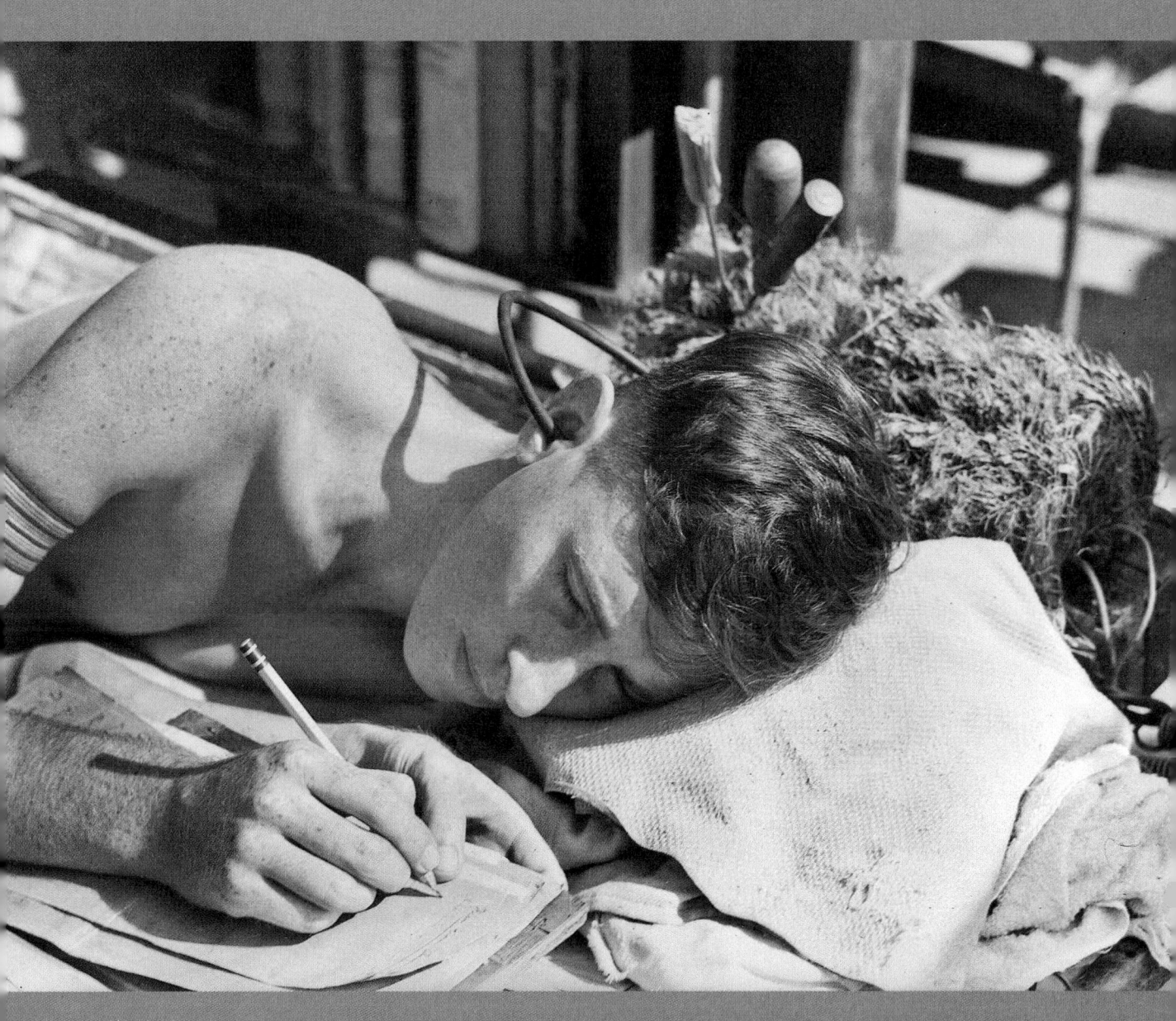

Wright demonstrates how he listened to his broom radio at night and wrote messages that were distributed to fellow prisoners.

a support, whilst from the spike there hung a hat. As a hiding place it was effective and safe.

The 'cockatoos' were well trained. Whenever the set was functioning they were at their posts. One stood at the main gate and passed word of any Japs approaching the gaol to another [lookout] 50 yards away at the entrance of a corridor. This corridor led down past the bookhouse, and at the bottom of it was an electric light switch controlling the current in that particular area. By this switch stood a third cockatoo who, on the sign from his colleague at the entrance, flicked the switch, thereby cutting off the current from the set for a second or two and those listening in at once knew that Japanese were in the area. Everything was quickly hidden and to hostile eyes the entire camp appeared to sleep.

In this way they made themselves completely safe: but they nevertheless adopted two further precautions. First of all they appointed a fourth cockatoo in their own courtyard; he, in the event of a surprise raid or one for which no warning had been received, was simply to start a fight to delay the Japs – if necessary with the Japanese themselves. [Secondly, they made] their set as portable as possible so that if their own area became the centre of too much attention they could easily move it.

This precaution was fortunate because the Japanese demand for all timber in the camp for use in tunnels seemed to threaten the existence of their own particular 'post'. Consequently, they sought another hiding place and eventually found it outside their shed. Here a hole was dug … A drill was evolved for the five men and they soon reduced the time needed to dismantle the set, put it in its waterproof case, drop the case in the hole, place the dirt-filled sack on top of the case and cover the lot with its layer of camouflage to a base two minutes from the time of the alarm being given at the main gaol gate. Since the walk from the gate to their shed took almost twice as long as that they felt themselves, at last, reasonably safe.

The small band of men resorted finally to an old cellar

… Driven almost frantic by false alarms and nervous strain, the small band of men … resorted finally to an old cellar underneath the gaol, 400 yards from the main gate. Here, working in a corner behind a rubbish heap of old boxes and back cloths – relics of the now idle playhouse – they worked every night, crouching over their set, barely visible in the gloom … as they listened and passed on what they heard and listened again. Always half-expecting the sudden harsh bellow of an invading patrol of Japanese – never wholly at ease … until one night they heard that the war was over and – after a moment's stupefied delight – realised that the news which they had obtained for so long at the risk of their lives was now theirs for the asking.

Wright displaying another radio set that he constructed, this one hidden within the legs of a table.

ON WITH THE MOTLEY: THE CHANGI CONCERT PARTY

UNKNOWN AUTHOR

The Concert Party … started with a small band, performing in the open air (to audiences of between three and four thousand) on a bare platform which had neither backdrop nor front curtain, without make-up or rehearsal, and managing nevertheless to provide regularly a few hours of escape for what must have been the world's most shattered army.

But the Concert Party did not rest here. It obtained for itself an old gymnasium and, having rapidly transformed this into a regular and respectable stage, announced the opening night. That theatre, however, was never to open: the Japanese, with that streak of vindictive perversity which was to cost their unfortunate guests so many gardens, buildings and camp fixtures during their term of purgatory … confiscated the newly built theatre for a guard room – into which, of course, they never at any time put guards! So the theatre was gone. The Australian reaction, however, was immediate. Within 24 hours every particle of the stage equipment had been removed and in October of 1942 a second theatre was completed in what had once been the garage of the Gordon Highlanders. This theatre seated thousands and was destined to be the greatest source of entertainment for Australians in Selarang – not to mention English, Dutch and American troops from other areas – for about 18 months.

The theatre created some of the earliest demands which were to result in that incredible display of resource and initiative so typical of prisoner-of-war life. Wigs were needed for female impersonators: they were produced – blonde, brunette and redhead; sophisticated and lifelike from the highly improbable raw materials of surgical hemp and the discarded sporrans of the excessively virile Scots. Make-up was non-existent and ersatz products, such as flesh tints made out of powdered clay and mosquito cream and eye shadow made out of chinograph pencils, were applied with vicious effects upon the faces of the artists until the pathology lab, in sympathy, went mad and produced results that Max Factor might have envied. Violin strings snapped merrily in the damp tropical heat and seemed to be irreplaceable – but not for long. Within a matter of days experiments had revealed that army signal wire … was almost as good as gut.

…

The Australians quickly revealed themselves as masters of vaudeville: it was in this sphere and in revue that they were to specialise for the entire period of the war, leaving drama and tragedy to other theatres in the camp, and it is for their vaudeville and revue that they will be

Prisoners attending a concert, as depicted by George Sprod, 1942.
ART29034

so long remembered. Topicalities were always their métier; respect for personalities was never their strong point, [and] the two qualities combined produced a brand of revue which was rich with humour and very much to the point. It was the perfect medium for mental escape.

It was typical of the Concert Party's entire career that, the Japanese having forbidden the singing of 'God Save the King', they promptly commenced every performance with a fortissimo rendition of 'Advance Australia Fair'.

…

The inevitable, of course, occurred. After very few shows every single gag known to every single artist, every act ever seen or produced all over the world, every source of ready-made humour and vaudeville entertainment (from the past program of the Tivoli to the militant purity of a book of sketches for Boy Scouts) had been exhausted. It was another case of wigs and make-up and violin strings – and the solution was the same. The Australians sat down and produced their own.

LEFT **Members of the Concert Party perform on a makeshift stage. Murray Griffin, 1942.**
ART24467

ABOVE **A scene from the pantomime *Dick Whittington*, written for Christmas 1943 by Australian prisoner Leslie Greener and produced by John Wood. Murray Griffin, 1943.**
ART24474

Thus began the era of original songs, original revues, and original slang – the era of men like Slim de Grey, [who] as a result of a strong difference of opinion between the Japanese and civilised peoples as to the minimum amount of vitamin B upon which one can continue to exist, had happy feet. He could not sit still during the day, nor could he sleep at night … But tho' his feet ached and small as his knowledge of musical theory was (his head was full of tunes), he then started his career as the camp's most talented composer. One would see him sitting on his bed, gently massaging the soles of his excruciating feet with a look in his eye so distant that it could only be measured in light years. Suddenly, he would shriek, 'Quick, get this down!' and he would burst into both melody and lyric of a brand new song. Whoever was nearest would scribble down the single notes of the singer's line: not to scribble them down was to lose the lot; Slim's feet were far too painful for sustained concentration, and having delivered himself of his inspiration he promptly forgot it.

…

Let it not be imagined, however, that the remainder of the party enjoyed riotous good health. Every one of them suffered one or other of the vast assortment of deficiency diseases provided by the IJA – mouths that were raw, eyes that could not read, rashes that would not heal and legs that were inclined suddenly to fold up – this was their lot. Nevertheless, they carried on every night. All of them became fully fledged not only as actors but also as playwrights and stage hands. Many wrote music: all lost weight under the ever-decreasing rations.

One result of this appalling loss of avoirdupois was a delightfully proportionate increase in the charms of female impersonators. Some of them developed figures of the most sylph-like nature, the proportions of which were pure Berlei; others managed at least to look not quite so aggressively masculine. John Wood, for example, fresh from a successful career on the stage in London and New York, appeared on some occasions as a hair-raising blonde, on others as a hot-blooded senorita, but at all times feminine. Enough credit can never be paid him for the fact that, by his superb acting, he educated Australian audiences – than whom none can be more demanding – from an attitude of ribald hilarity to one of grateful appreciation of feminine charms whenever he played a female role. It will never be forgotten by 10 000 faded, starved, half-dead prisoners of war that John Wood at the beginning of 1944 gave a performance as Judith in *Hay Fever* which competent critics have hailed as worthy of any of the great actresses who ever played Coward …

Australians produced a new show every fortnight

This triumph was all the more remarkable when one considers that in the early days of Changi it was necessary for a female impersonator to only set foot on the stage to be greeted by a blast of piercing whistles and remarks of a type which can only be described as biological, while by 1944 and 1945 it was possible to stage complete such episodes as the mountain love scene in Dodie Smith's *Autumn Crocus* to the accompaniment of the audience's death-like silence of sympathy and intense emotion.

Changi audiences presented – in retrospect – a remarkable phenomenon: a hard-bitten collection of cynical prisoners, ruthless racketeers and men whose one obsession was food becoming a community of regular theatre-goers, moreover who demanded good acting, good music, good scenery and good

ON WITH THE MOTLEY: THE CHANGI CONCERT PARTY

"First Night" — Changi Gaol Playhouse — 25.9.44

production ... It is an astonishing but nevertheless irrefutable fact that among almost all the prisoners of war for over three years there have been neither related nor invented any [performances] of dirty stories ...

Before such audiences and under such conditions 30-odd Australians produced a new show every fortnight, with new music and new scenery, new dialogue and complicated scores, and without a break for almost three years. It was a stupendous achievement.

A *Smoke-oh* magazine illustration of a well-attended performance
RC01887

CHANGI LIFE AND SOCIETY

With one revue running, another would be in rehearsal, a third would be drying on the innumerable pieces of dirty paper on which it was written and a fourth would be under discussion. The circle was unending, exhausting and vicious in the extreme: but never let it be imagined that anything about these productions was either slap-dash or amateurish. Camp magazines were ruthlessly critical of everything from stage effects to skill of production: Americans captured as late as the end of 1944 were staggered at the lavishness of it all and found no unpleasant contrasts with the products of Broadway and Hollywood on which they had so recently gazed; and the artists themselves strove constantly to perfect their technique and personality. Nothing was overlooked – they studied voice production, music theory, chord construction and character roles …

Thus the Concert Party became the instrument which relieved the camp of its boredom, provided it with its slang and – in times of extreme crisis – saved it from despair. When reports of the dead first came down to Changi from Thailand and Burma, when there was no one in the camp who had not lost two or three friends, when this devastating news was read out every night on parade, it was the theatre upon which fell the shocking task of lifting the camp, most of whom had just returned from the day's work in aerodrome construction, out of its bottomless pit of grief and horror. Themselves affected as much as anyone, [the actors] smoothed their make-up over haggard faces, transformed themselves into gorgeous blondes or toothless clowns, rehearsed their tag-lines with desperate energy and flung themselves before their public. Never had an audience responded less, for

LEFT The AIF theatre in the converted garage and workshop, whose wall shows bomb damage from the battle of Singapore. Murray Griffin, 1943.
ART26496

ABOVE Inside the AIF theatre, Changi. Murray Griffin, 1943.
ART26497

141

now it was not only the actors for whom it was a case of 'on with the motley', but every single man in the theatre. Nevertheless, artists sweated, came off into the wings to put on more make-up and hear who else had died, and then returned again to struggle with the audience ... No greater proof of their selfless service can be given than that in those shocking days of late 1943 the members of the Concert Party succeeded in making Changi laugh.

There was no quality so touchingly likeable in the prisoner-of-war psychology as the childish capacity of everyone for enjoying pantomimes. Each Christmas, without fail, thousands of haggard, misshapen, disillusioned men went galloping down to the theatre to see the pantomime and, unashamedly, to enjoy it. It is a comforting thought that even under the control of the Japanese men could enjoy such ingenuous humour and such nostalgic sentimentality – and come night after night to enjoy it again.

Their tastes, moreover, were well catered for. In 1942 the pantomime written was *Cinderella*; in 1943 *Dick Whittington*, slightly more lavish scenically and full of delightful De Grey–Tullipan music; and in 1944 *Twinkletoes*, whose sets were as lavish as anything to be seen in any city of the world, and whose music and costumes corresponded with the sets ...

It was a revue called *I'll Take You* which really initiated the era of lavish sets in Australian theatre productions. To the Concert Party were now attached scenic artists, stage managers, and stage directors, and the effects they achieved were magnificent. When one recollects that the same canvas, the same wood,

In 1942 the pantomime written was *Cinderella* ...

the same paint made out of different coloured clays were used for every single production over three and a half years; that nails had to be manufactured out of barbed wire and that wood had to be stolen ... one begins to realise the task which confronted the Concert Party. And yet still their shows appeared, polished, professional and consistently good for month after month ... It was all a triumph of initiative and the refusal to acknowledge defeat – a triumph which eventually the Japanese were themselves compelled to recognise, for, unable to entertain themselves, they began to arrive in droves at the camp shows. Nippon generals with obsequious retinues and large stomachs would arrive to revel in Coward's *Tonight at 8.30*, sending messages through interpreters that they had understood everything and enjoyed it very much – which was odd when one remembers some of the remarks which were directed at them from the stage ... [That] intellectual bullfrog General Saito insisted upon a little light relief by Piddington – the magician. Piddington gave a world-class performance with the Chinese rings and, the general having been duly mystified – and, if he only knew it, made publicly ridiculous by his brilliant artist – the show was allowed to go

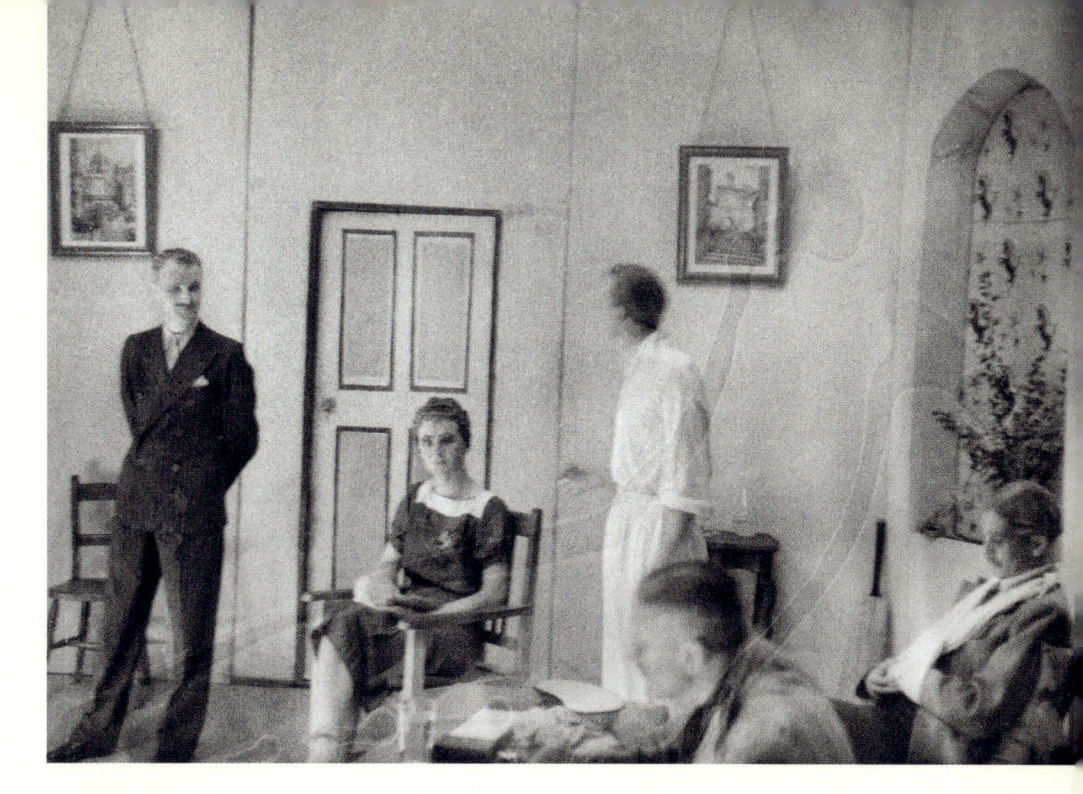

A play staged at Roberts Barracks, photographed in secret by Major John Rosson.
P04485.029

on. It became a commonplace statement by the guards and enemy garrison that the best show on the island was at Changi.

All this notwithstanding, an order was issued by the Imperial Japanese Army in March 1945 that all entertainment should cease. The order came as a result of a ballet performed in the last revue which our hosts interpreted as 'White Devils' propaganda' … The Concert Party was abruptly scattered to the four winds … and ceased to exist.

In spite of all requests the ban on entertainment continued until in July 1945 the order came through that the theatre was to be demolished – its timbers were needed for the innumerable tunnels and funk holes which prisoners of war were digging all over Singapore and Johore for what the Japanese fondly imaged was to be their defence of Malaya.

And so it was that the back drops, front curtains, tabs, and masks and wings, and all that complicated mechanism of pulleys and wires involved in a theatre where scenery is flown above-stage instead of stacked beneath it, was destroyed. The Concert Party had now irrevocably 'had it'. Even the return, a few weeks later, of its members from all over Malaya where they had been slaving to complete Japanese defences ever since March, could not re-establish it without a theatre to work in. And perhaps it was as well, for they were tired men and many of them were sick: they were just as much in need of entertainment as anyone else in the gaol – and now that the war was over it was pleasant to sit back and think of the past, and to smile comfortably (where for years now audiences had roared) at that infallible crack of the lugubrious 'Appy 'Arry's 'You'll Never Get Off the Island'.

Doug Peart

Slim De Grey

Ted Brightfield

John Wood

Mathers

Beattie

Harry Smith

V. Murray Griffin
Official War Artist
AIF Malaya

LEFT Men of the AIF Concert Party (Doug Peart, Slim de Grey, Fred Brightfield, John Wood, Doug Mathers, Eric Beattie, Harry Smith and Keith Stevens).
ART26495

RIGHT Men of the AIF Concert Party (Val Mack, Frazer Harvey, John Wood, Jack Smith, Frank Wood and Jack Geoghegan).
ART26494

CHANGI LIFE AND SOCIETY

CHANGI PRODUCTIONS

Dover Road, Milne	*Good Morning, Bill*	*The Admirable Dyeton*
Badger's Green	*Autumn Crocus*	*Pygmalion*
I Killed the Count	*A Murder Has Been Arranged*	*Tonight at 8.30*
Outward Bound	*Arms and the Man*	*A Bird in Hand*
Hay Fever	*Two Gentlemen of Soho*	*Jupiter Laughs*
Love on Dole	*On the Spot*	*Androcles and the Lion*
Lord Babs		*Rope*

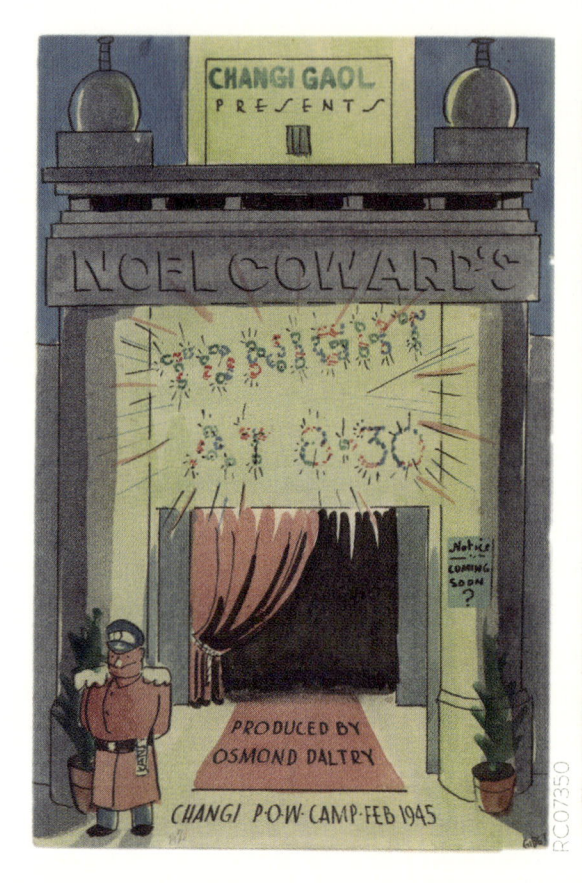

PAGES 146–53 The men produced their own theatre programs for each production. This sample of programs held in the Australian War Memorial's collection demonstrates the range of concerts, revues and plays staged at Changi.

THE PALLADIUM THEATRE Presents

HE CAME BACK

A Play In Three Acts By Cheeseborough

June 1943 — Changi POW Camp

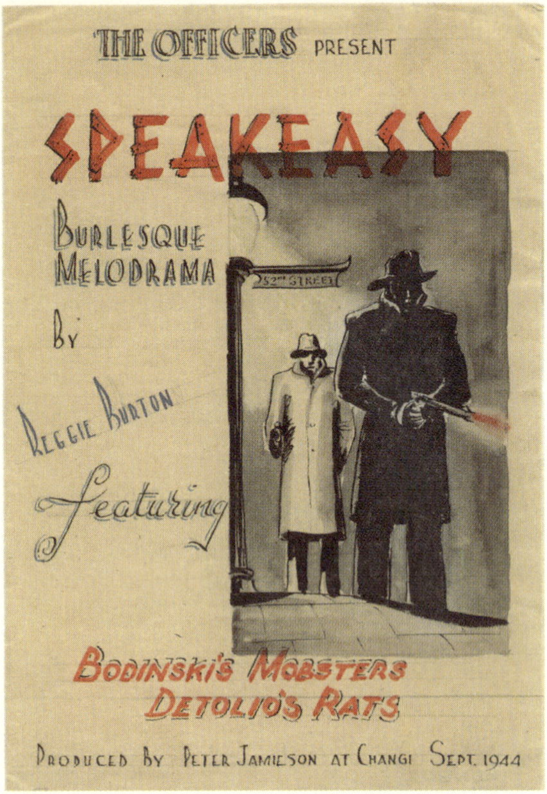

RC07344

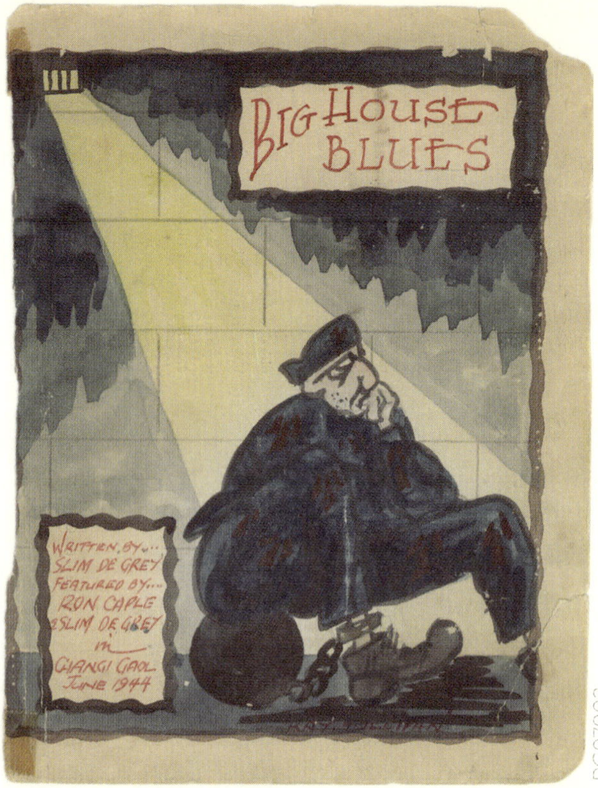

RC07003

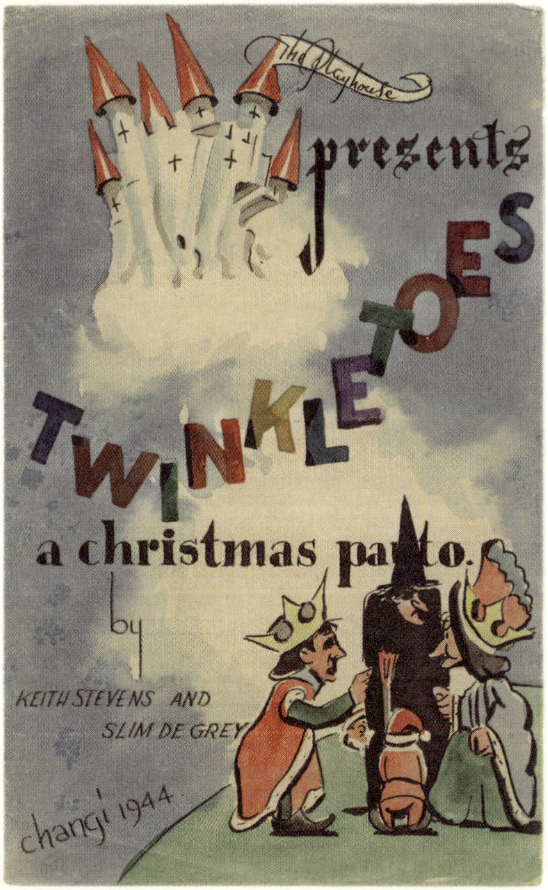

RC07351

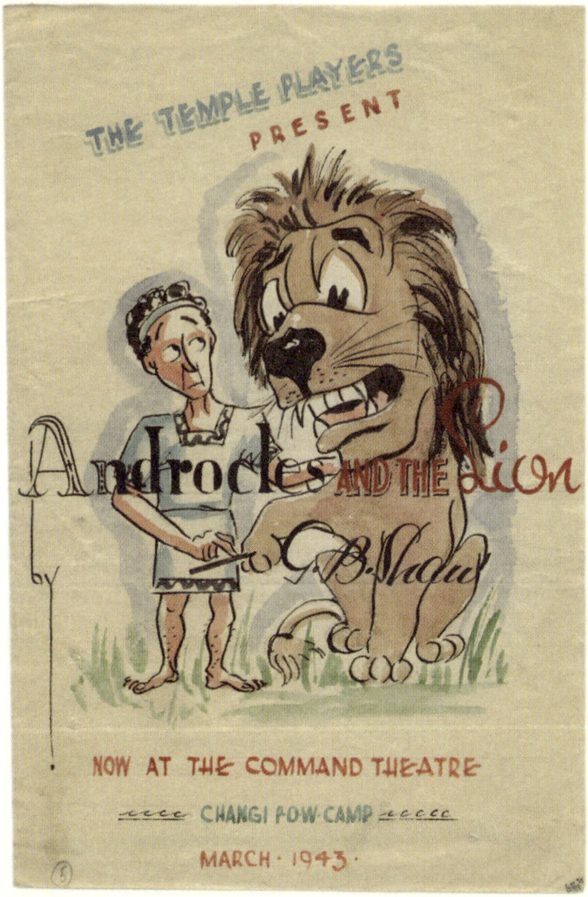

RC07304

THE A.I.F. CONCERT PARTY

presents

A NAUTICAL FARCE
WRITTEN BY SLIM DE GRAY
PRODUCED BY KEITH STEVENS

ALL AT SEA

MUSIC BY BILL MIDDLETON
AND THE AIF THEATRE ORCHESTRA

CHANGI POW CAMP   APRIL 1944

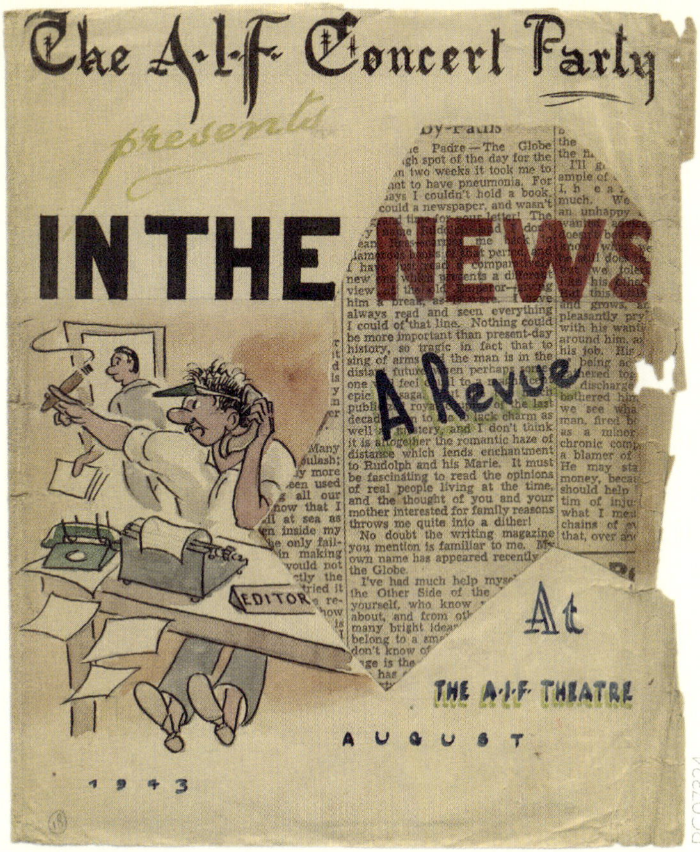

RC07324

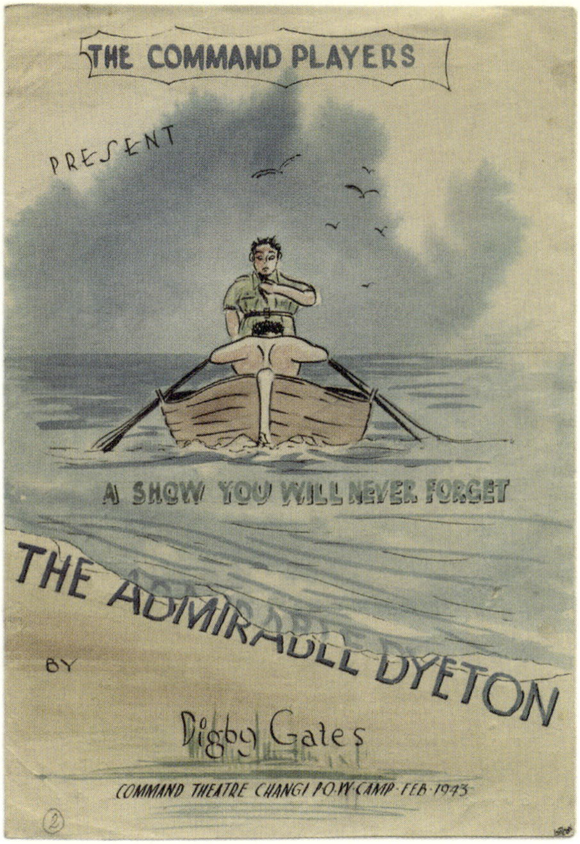

RC07301

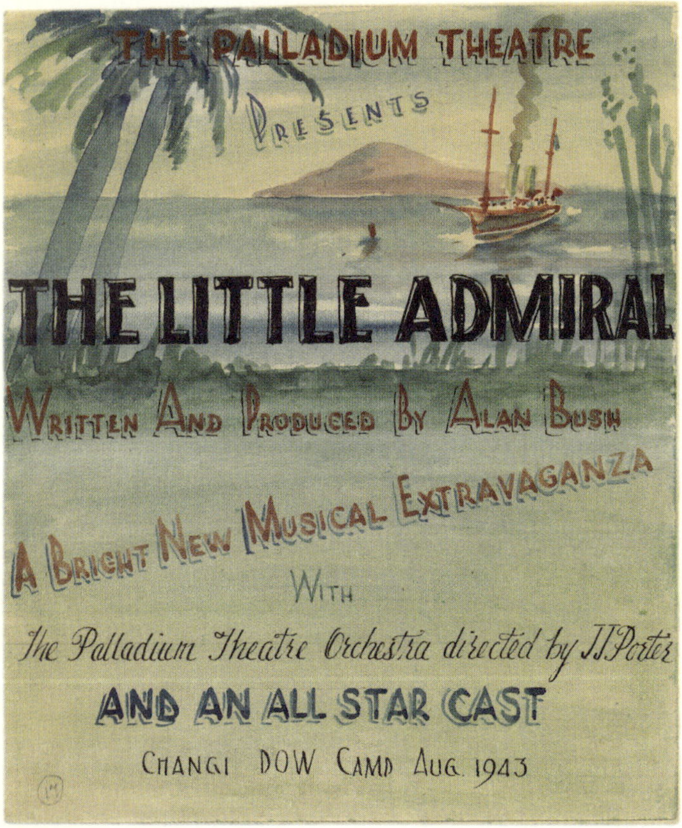

RC07327

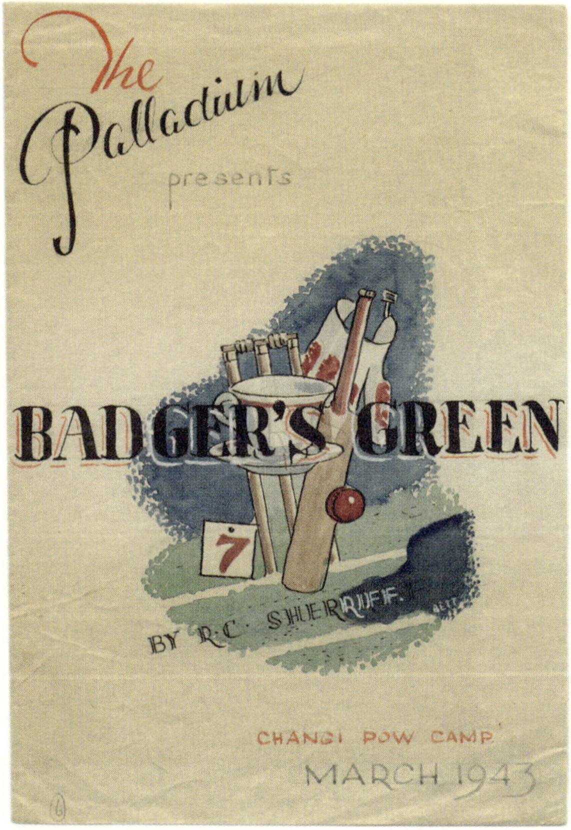

RC07307

jack wood presents

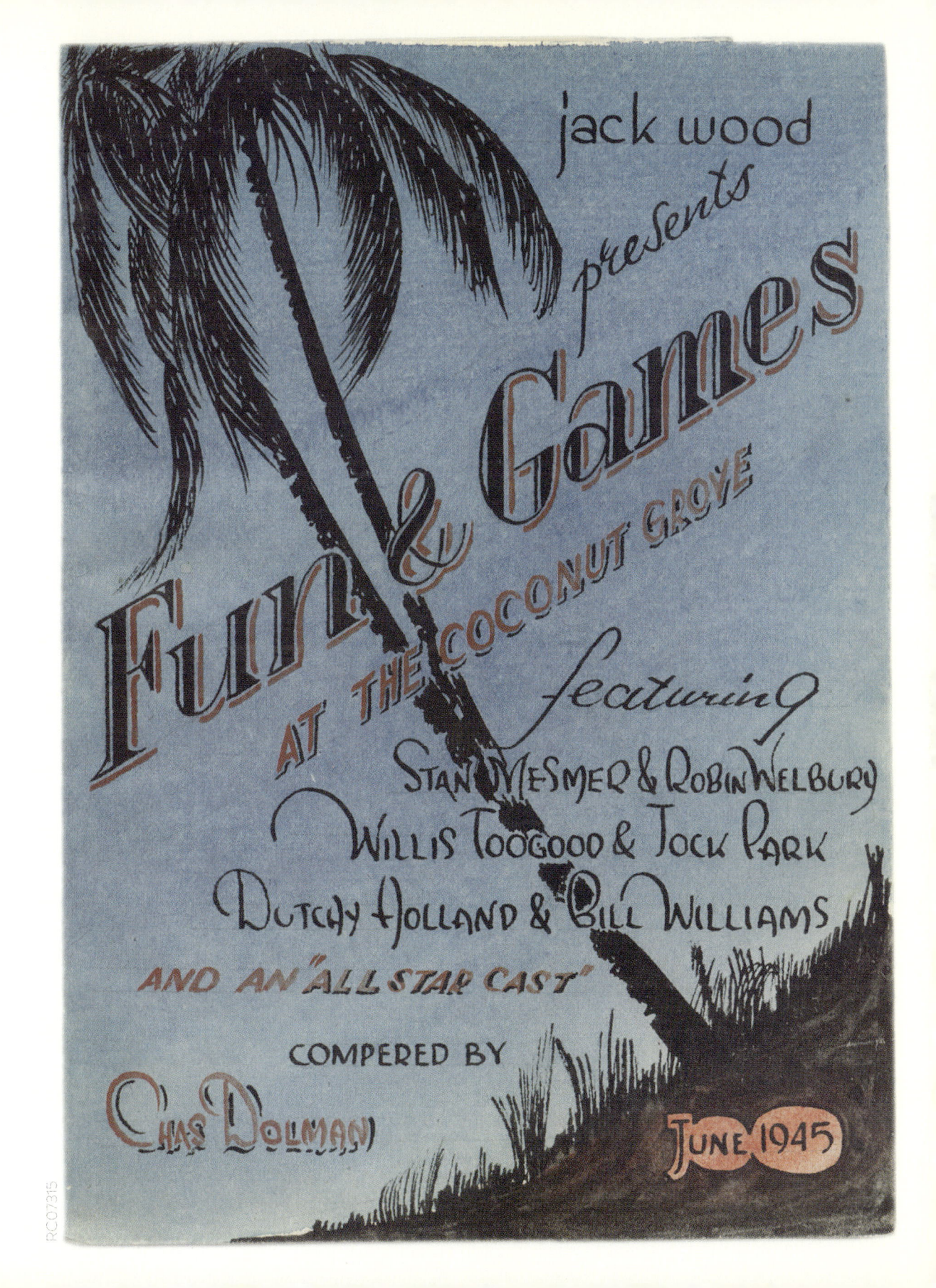

Fun & Games

at the Coconut Grove

featuring

Stan Mesmer & Robin Welbury

Willis Toogood & Jock Park

Dutchy Holland & Bill Williams

and an "All Star Cast"

COMPERED BY

Chas Dolman

June 1945

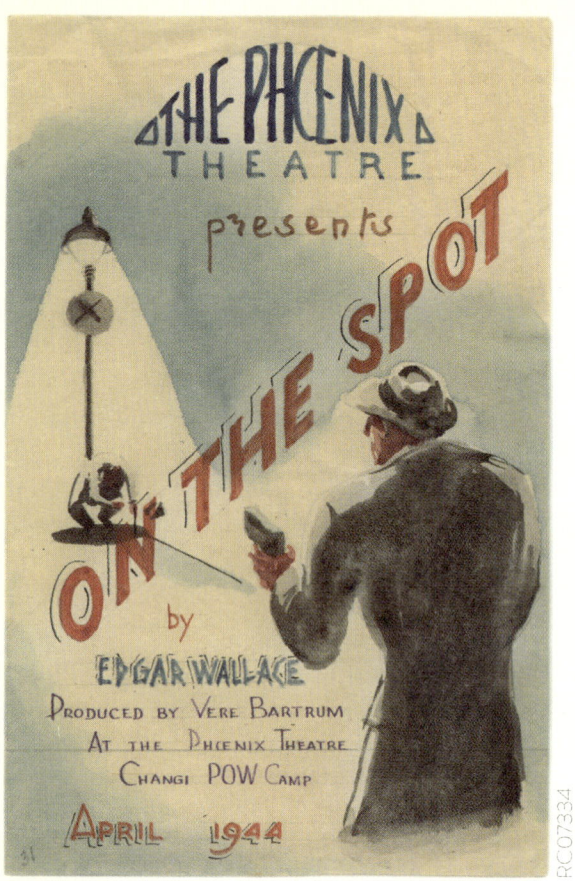

THE PHOENIX THEATRE presents ON THE SPOT
by EDGAR WALLACE
Produced by Vere Bartrum
At the Phoenix Theatre
Changi POW Camp
APRIL 1944

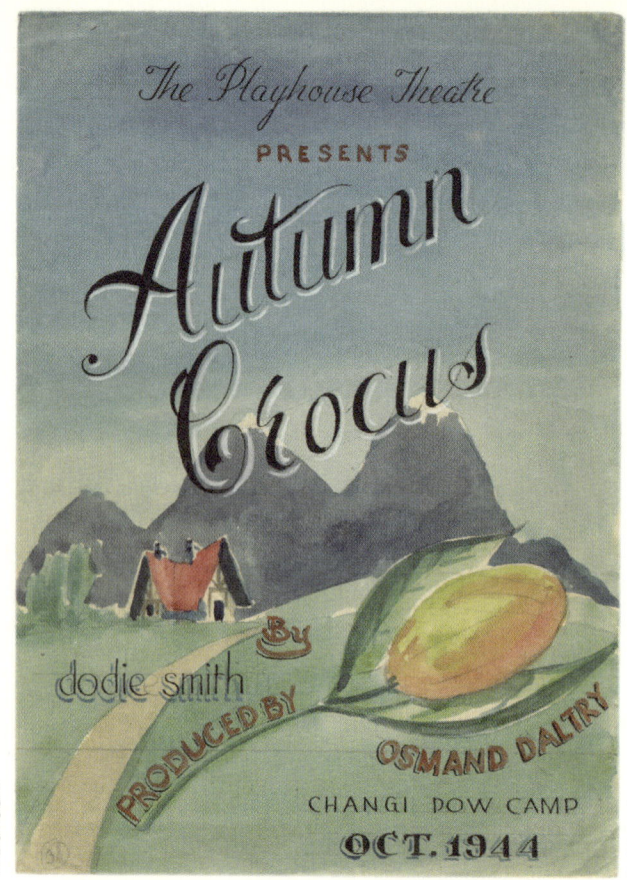

The Playhouse Theatre presents Autumn Crocus
by dodie smith
Produced by Osmand Daltry
CHANGI POW CAMP
OCT. 1944

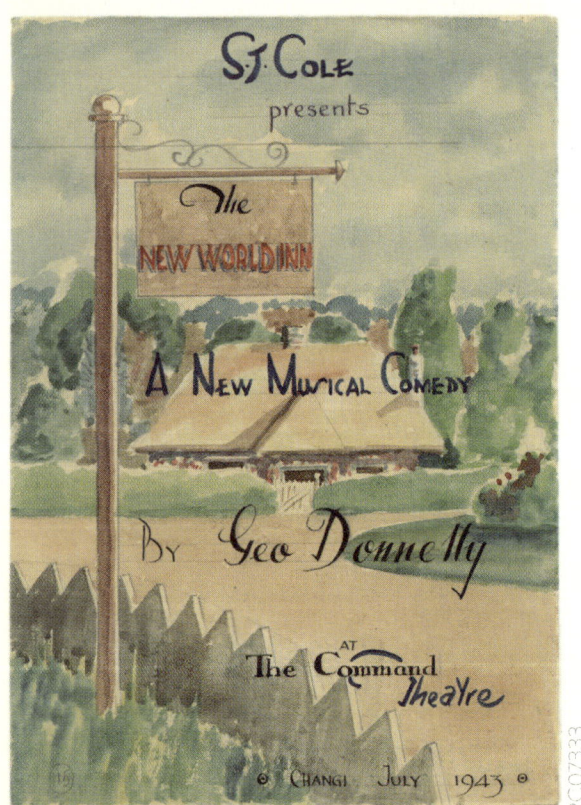

S.J. Cole presents The New World Inn
A New Musical Comedy
By Geo Donnelly
At The Command Theatre
Changi July 1943

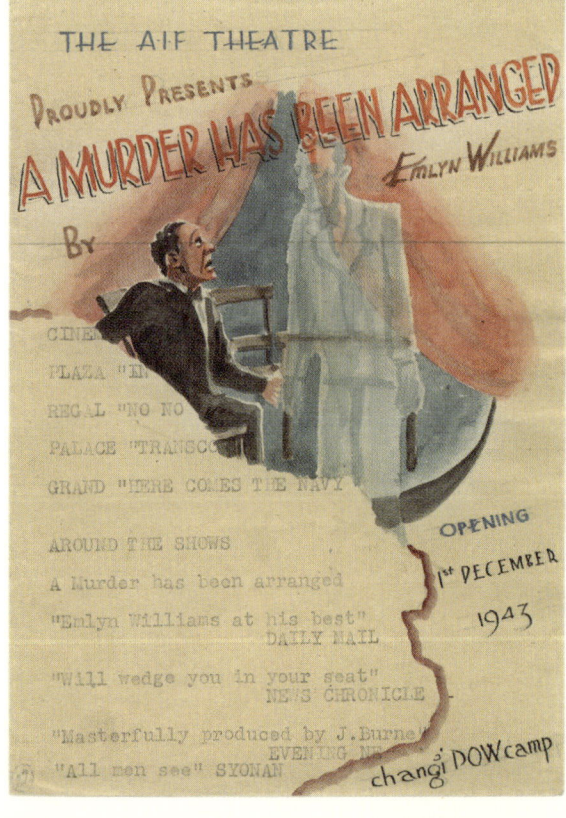

THE A.I.F. THEATRE Proudly Presents A MURDER HAS BEEN ARRANGED
by Emlyn Williams

CINE...
PLAZA "E..."
REGAL "NO NO..."
PALACE "TRANSC..."
GRAND "HERE COMES THE NAVY"

AROUND THE SHOWS
A Murder has been arranged
"Emlyn Williams at his best"
  DAILY MAIL
"Will wedge you in your seat"
  NEWS CHRONICLE
"Masterfully produced by J. Burne..."
  EVENING NE...
"All men see" SYONAN

OPENING 1st DECEMBER 1943
changi POW camp

THE SHOW GOES ON

PRESENTED BY SJ COLE

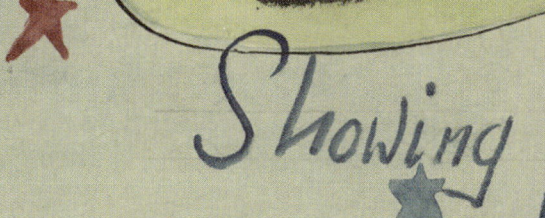

changi pow camp

Showing

AT THE COMMAND THEATRE

1943

THE DAY AFTER 15 000 Australian prisoners of war marched into Changi an Australian concert party had begun rehearsals of small individual acts, but soon a party of about 30 full-time performers was formed and moved into an open-sided steel-framed garage, which was gradually adapted as a theatre. The materials used to transform the garage, as well as those used for the costumes and musical instruments, were scrounged by prisoners on work parties outside the camp, and by small groups of men who went through the perimeter wire at night. Recognising the need for a piano, Keith 'Dizzy' Stevens, the party's 'female' comic who performed with a red-dyed mop on his head, led 11 men though the wire to a sailor's mess in the former British submarine base, 'liberated' the Robinson upright piano there, and hauled it back to camp, a distance of 1½ kilometres.

The piano proved ideal for the conditions in which it was kept and used as it was made by a Thai firm that specialised in producing instruments that adapted to extreme ranges of heat and humidity.

At the end of the war in 1945 a request made by the Concert Party to ship their beloved piano to Australia was refused. When the men declared they would not board the ship without it, the piano was finally loaded and lashed to the deck.

For many years it was lent to the Sussex Inlet Bowls Club in New South Wales before arriving in the foyer of the Sydney headquarters of the ex-prisoners-of-war association. As many as 31 former prisoners have signed the inside lid of the piano.

After the piano was donated to the Australian War Memorial in 2011 the Concert Party's original pianist, Jack Boardman, together with a singer, sax player and bass player from the Royal Military College band, gave a final performance on it, playing popular songs written in the camp.

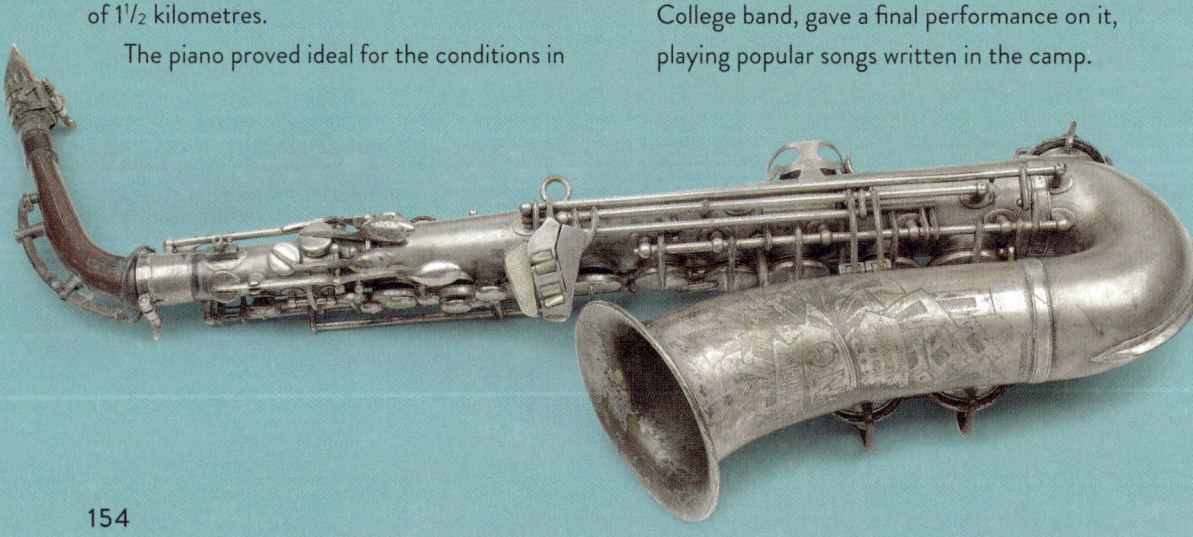

A 'liberated' piano becomes the life of the Concert Party

Jane Peek
Australian War Memorial

The Robinson upright piano is just one of the instruments belonging to the Changi Concert Party now held within the Australian War Memorial's collection.

155

THE PANZER DIVISION

REX BUCKNELL

With all the trials and anxieties that are a necessary part of the life of a prisoner of war, there is one thing for which those of us who have been permanently disabled can be thankful; that is that we have had to pass these first years of our incapacity away from the kindly and pampering influences of our families and friends. It has been a harsh treatment, but only by these means have we been able to reach a degree of independence and confidence in ourselves that could render us fit to take our place, with the minimum loss of time and the maximum amount of efficiency, in the working world upon our return to it.

There is not a man who has lost his right arm who cannot write as well with his left and do certain other work as efficiently as before, while to those who have lost a leg this has been an invaluable period of training in the use of his artificial limb. On behalf of the latter a tribute must be paid to the limb factory people who, with practically nothing to start from, managed to create an organisation for the work of which there can be nothing but praise …

We have been very fortunate in the fact that the Japs required us to administer ourselves, especially insofar as the medical side was concerned. Under that system all disabled men were brought together, and the natural result was a certain degree of rivalry in different accomplishments which had the best possible effect on the individual.

For the first few months, certainly, we were too fully occupied with the business of getting well to pay much attention to improving our capabilities; though even during this time, with the lack of ready-made cigarettes, the arm cases were forced to exercise their ingenuity in rolling their own with one hand. But by June or July the majority of the wounds had healed and the stage of convalescence had begun.

This took place in the No. 2 Convalescent Depot. There were approximately 35 limbless cases altogether, and the problem of providing employment for them for an unknown length of time could not be solved in a moment. However, the locality of the building allocated to the depot was ideal for its purpose. It was a broad, airy building with a semi-circular grass *padang* … in the front and two smaller grassed areas at the rear and on one side. In the early days these were mainly used for sitting out in the sun, but later came into their own as sports areas. Another [positive] was the location of the Education Centre and Library in the same building.

The administration … required that certain personnel be used as runners from one area to another and it was speedily found that arm cases could be profitably employed in this capacity. But this was a mere drop in the ocean. The number of runners required was small, as was the amount of running they had to do, and this could not be regarded as a solution to the problem. We turned in the direction of sport.

Golf was the first scheme that came to our minds … In a very short time we had accumulated a selection of golf clubs and some balls. The front *padang* was too small to make much of a golf course, but we smoothed a couple of spaces to make greens and sank a few holes.

The golf bug spread rapidly among both leg and arm patients; soon all the clubs were in use and the *padang* occupied for the greater part of the day. Men who had played before quickly adapted themselves to their new conditions, and many who had never played developed a keen interest in the game and soon became sufficiently adept that they should now be able to take their place on a public golf course without embarrassment. It might be mentioned here that the great advantage of this training was that, in the early stages, men were matched only against those with similar disability to their own and thus did not develop an inferiority complex right from the start. As they acquired greater proficiency so the field of competition was increased and many friends, sound in all limbs, were frequently invited for a hit. Learning to use the golf club with one hand is not so difficult as may at first be imagined. Certainly, the strength of the stroke and consequently the length of the shot is not so great as by using two hands, [but] using one hand only it is almost impossible to slice, which is probably the hardest vice for the average golfer to overcome.

The next activity that was tried with any amount of success was cricket. Unlike a golf club, however, a cricket bat is an unwieldy object with one hand and this form of sport was consequently adopted with more alacrity by the leg cases than by those with one arm. Also, about this time, artificial legs began to make their appearance, and with this assistance the leg cases rapidly gained superiority over the 'wingies'

Golf was the first scheme that came to our minds

[arm cases]. Still, the men with two legs were much more agile in the field, and in the several international matches played by the limbless of both the English and the Australian areas full consideration was given to both forms of disability when the teams were being selected.

Basketball and volleyball were also adopted with enthusiasm by the men, who were now becoming confident of their agility on artificial legs … [with] one leg only or … with one arm. Most of these games included fit men, and the limbless had the satisfaction of finding that they were able to take their place among them almost as easily as among those in their own condition.

But it was in tennis that they proved their ability to compete most ably with their more fortunate fellows. A tennis court which had fallen into disrepair was rebuilt entirely by the labour of the limbless. This entailed the chipping of grass and re-levelling as well as shifting the court a good three feet from its original position. Lines were marked in red clay which had been excavated from adjacent refuse pits. We had the original roller belonging to the court and a net was manufactured from odd pieces of netting, hessian and rope 'scrounged' from neighbouring dumps and buildings. We had no surrounding wire netting but its place was filled by fronds from coconut palms which were plaited and hung over barbed wire frames – there was no scarcity of barbed wire – supported on sticks, pickets and anything else that came to our hands. Racquets and balls were procured in the same manner as the golfing material and many pleasant and healthy hours resulted.

It may sound, from the foregoing, that we had only to decide to indulge ourselves in a sport and the materials were immediately forthcoming. But that was not so. Although there were many different articles of sporting gear at the commencement of the camp, it must be realised that these were irreplaceable when worn out, with the result that cricket bats were nailed together or tied with wire, balls were such that any self-respecting street Arab would be ashamed to play with, while tennis balls were used until every vestige of fabric was worn off them and the bare rubber cracked up under the strain.

The name of 'Panzer Division' was facetiously given

Another item of good came out of these sports: a few falls proved so painful to tender stumps that we decided that something would have to be done about it. A warrant officer attached to the Convalescent Depot who was familiar with ju-jitsu kindly gave his services, and before long those who were sufficiently strong to take the punishment had mastered the art of falling scientifically, as well as numerous other points of self-defence …

There were many other methods of employing ourselves usefully as time went on. Education played, probably, the biggest part. Many of those disabled, especially the younger ones who had joined the army almost from school, realised early that on their return home they would be subject to a degree of competition from fit men that their condition would aggravate considerably. Consequently, they very creditably determined to make the most of enforced inactivity by improving their existing qualifications … [We pay] tribute to those who organised such facilities for the energy they displayed in making the service as efficient as it eventually became, and also to those who so unselfishly gave up their time to teaching.

Among other modes of employment were cooking, fish-smoking, sandal-making, and librarianship [for] the leg cases and firewood-sawing, gardening, water-pumping, and barbering [for] the arm cases.

In addition to the above there was the regular parade every morning of the men who had lost a leg above the knee. This particular kind of amputation necessitated a longer artificial leg and one which was consequently much more difficult to wear. It was natural that these men should find walking with crutches much easier than using the artificial leg, and the

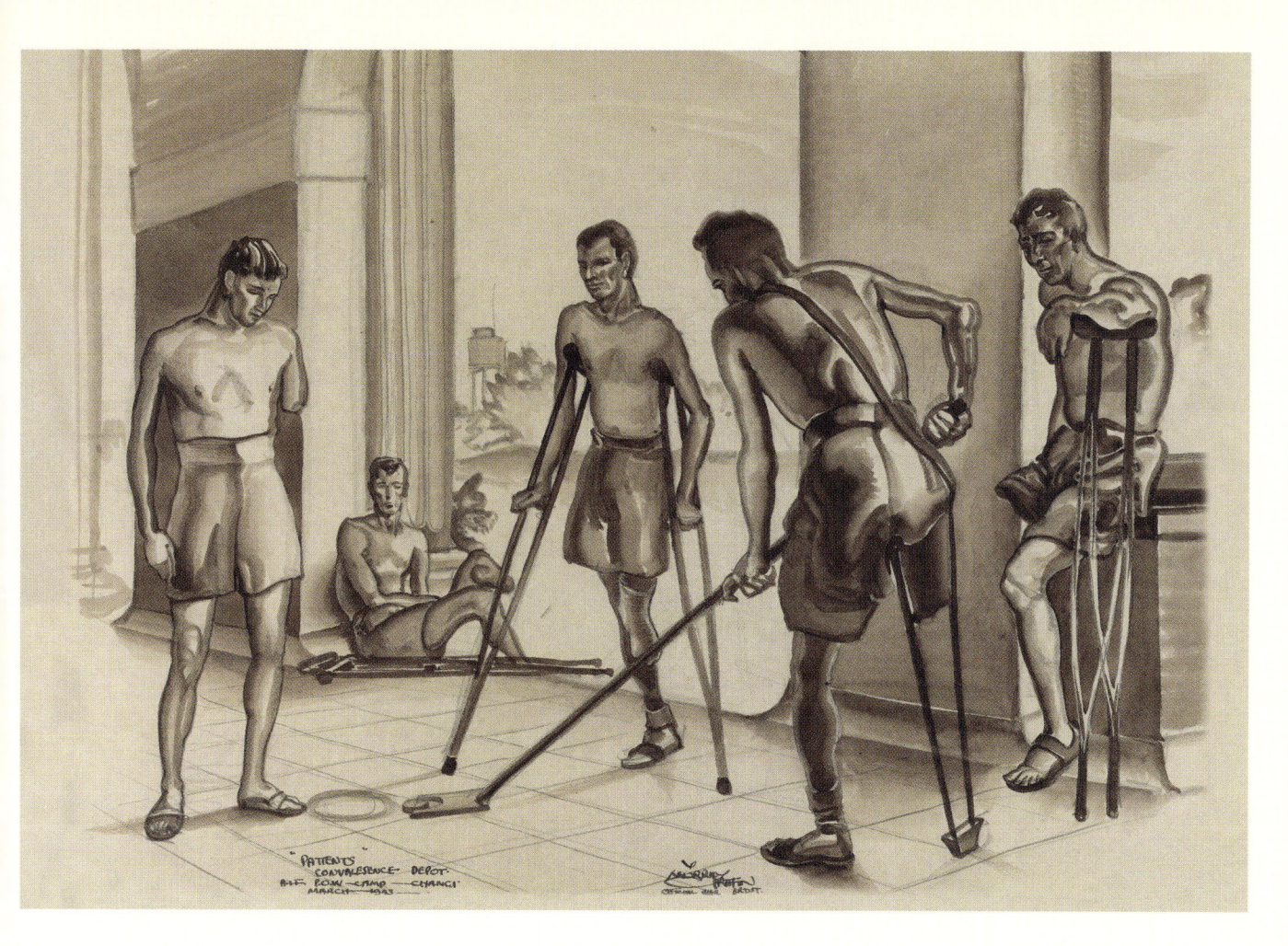

Men who required amputation undertook rehabilitation at the Convalescent Depot, and sport was an important part of their recovery. This drawing by Murray Griffin shows a game of deck golf.
ART25088

result was that they were inclined to overlook practising with the latter. To overcome this a parade was held every morning when all these fellows stalked mechanically along the road in front of the depot like so many robots. It was these in particular [to which] the name of the 'Panzer Division' was facetiously given [and] which afterwards came to include all those with artificial legs …

I have tried to emphasise, as far as possible, the spirit that has come to motivate all these men who in another society would be looked upon with pity and forbearance. During the last two years they have lived on terms as

CHANGI LIFE AND SOCIETY

This 2/15th Field Regiment flag was acquired in Changi by Sergeant Wilfred Bale following the liberation of the camp. When the repatriation ship *Highland Chief* entered Sydney Harbour its captain ordered that the ship be fully dressed in flags, allowing Bale and his fellow gunners to proudly unfurl their regimental flag as they steamed into port.
REL34237

nearly approaching equality with the fit men surrounding them as it was possible for them to get. In their own personal affairs they have looked out for themselves, washed their own clothes, darned their own socks – when they had any – and in many cases cooked extra for themselves under such difficulties as always attend illegal enterprises.

In short they have come to look upon themselves as efficient members of society, and it is in this light and not as ineffective cripples that they desire to be regarded by the world. To quote one of my one-armed comrades, 'I suppose nature gave us two arms from a desire for symmetry, but, since I have lost one, I cannot help thinking that it was meant only as a spare.'

The Australian Changi quilt

Jane Peek
Australian War Memorial

CONDITIONS FOR WOMEN and children during the first year of captivity at Changi were less harsh than they later became. Each year two women were chosen to administer their fellow internees, to liaise with the Japanese, and to organise activities to pass the time. The first of a series of concerts was performed in the presence of the male internees in May 1942. Sewing and craft work were encouraged both to provide practical items such as clothing and toys for the children and to boost morale by the creation of decorative items.

Ethel Mulvany, the Canadian-born wife of a British army medical officer who had become a prisoner of war, appointed herself the gaol's Red Cross representative. She successfully negotiated with the Japanese commandant to be allowed the use of an old Dodge truck once a month to drive into Singapore. Accompanied by an Australian internee, Norah Redfearn, she took items given to her by other internees and bartered or sold them for goods needed in the gaol, which included sewing fabric and threads.

A keen embroiderer, Mulvany conceived the idea of making a number of signature quilts that could eventually be passed outside the gaol to allow men to know that their wives and sweethearts were alive. She secured Japanese permission to do this by stating that one of the quilts was to be made for each of the Japanese, Australian and British Red Cross organisations for use by the wounded. Each woman who wanted to contribute a square was given a piece of white fabric, sourced from old sheets and flour bags, and asked to embroider an image that said 'something of herself', together with her name. From the evidence of some of the embroiderers it is likely that most of the women who made squares for the three signature quilts were patients in the part of the prison set aside as a hospital area.

Mulvany assembled the individual squares for the quilts with the help of two Dutch internees. The quilts dedicated to the Australian and Japanese wounded were displayed at a 'craft fair' held by the women in September 1942. It is not known when they were passed outside the gaol. At the end of the war they were given to Australian doctor Lieutenant Colonel Robert Webster, who took them home to Tasmania. Both were publicly exhibited there before the end of 1945. He then passed the quilt intended for the Australian Red Cross to the organisation's Melbourne headquarters, while his wife kept the Japanese quilt. Both quilts eventually came to the Australian War Memorial.

The work of at least six Australian women is represented on the Australian quilt: Dr Margaret Smallwood, Sheila Allan, Judy Good, Helen Loxton, Vera McIntyre and Eunice Austin-Hofer. Sheila Allan, aged 17 in 1942, was the daughter of an Australian engineer and Malay mother. Although she had not yet visited Australia she had been taught by her father to draw a map of the country, as shown on her square, from memory.

The Australian Changi quilt features 66 embroided patches, each of them signed by the maker or makers. At least six Australian women are represented on this quilt.
REL/14235

The women personalised and signed the quilt's squares.
REL/14235

163

OBSERVATIONS ON ACCOMMODATION

UNKNOWN AUTHOR

The Changi cantonment stands on undulating ground at the eastern tip of Singapore Island … Those [permanent buildings] at Selarang are highest of all above sea level and from many of them a good view is to be had of the Straits of Johore to the north and of the islands south and east of Singapore … first of all one remarks the seven rectangular three-storied barrack blocks which stand on three sides of the square. In these spacious concrete structures had lived the non-commissioned officers and men of the Gordons who were unmarried or separated from their wives. A short distance away, on the far side of a green valley, stand terraces of neat, two-storied houses, [once] comprising married quarters for some 50 soldiers and their families.

In addition to this living accommodation are substantial buildings which used to provide for regimental administration, education, and recreation. There are shops, store-houses and servants' quarters also (Asiatic servants were employed freely in Changi).

Accommodation intended for officers is at some little distance from the Barracks Square. The mess, a pretentious structure containing quarters for 14 officers, is nearest. Married officers' quarters, substantial masonry houses modern in style and appointments, dot the neighbouring hillsides.

In times of peace these must have been pleasant enough, each boasting a garden planted with hibiscus and other exotic shrubs and creepers, and many officers of my acquaintances have described them as varying upon the luxurious.

[Around 100 captured] officers and men of the AIF took up quarters in each house in that fateful February. Overcrowding on this scale was general throughout Selarang. Moreover, it was accompanied by complete disruption of services. No water flowed from the chromium-plated taps into the porcelain-enamelled baths and basins. Elaborate sanitary arrangements ceased to operate. Lights no longer appeared in the evening at the touch of a switch. There was almost no furniture. Only a fortunate few could enjoy the privilege of sleeping in a bed. Bad as such circumstances were to weary and disappointed troops, they were many times worse in the quarters occupied by the hospitals. It was not until August 1942 that electric light and anything like normal water services were restored in Selarang. Sanitation, in the civilised sense, was not restored, even in part, until the end of the year.

Upon the Engineers fell the multifarious tasks associated with restoration of the former

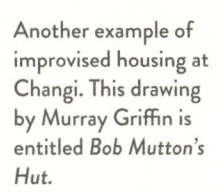

Another example of improvised housing at Changi. This drawing by Murray Griffin is entitled *Bob Mutton's Hut*.
ART 25060

accommodation and provision of additional facilities ... A number of buildings had been actually hit by bombs ... [and] many others had been partly unroofed by blast.

...

Permission was obtained from the Japanese to draw from dumps in Singapore such stores and material as necessary for the establishment of the camp, including hospitals ...

Day by day the stock of materials grew – timber, corrugated sheet iron, water pipes and fittings, nails, tools of all descriptions ... As material became available, repair work was put in hand.

...

Changes in accommodation began to happen shortly after concentration was complete. First, all the hospitals were concentrated in Roberts Barracks, about a mile north of Selarang. Then the AIF gave up Birdwood and Selarang camps to the surviving British personnel of 11th Indian Division. Then began the gradual exodus of Singapore and up-country working parties ... Each movement brought accommodation changes. 'Organisation, reorganisation, disorganisation!' cried the cynics as they unwillingly rolled up their few belongings and moved to other – successively less crowded but more adequately furnished – quarters.

The 2nd Convalescent Depot moved to the former Gordons' mess, where for 18 months Lieutenant Colonel Webster and his staff cared for the limbless, nursed those who were yet unfit to return to unit lines, and harboured the AIF Education Centre and library, destined to become foci of attention throughout Changi.

...

Ecclesiastical structures appeared, among them St Andrew's Church of England, which

LEFT Accommodation for the rank and file at Selarang. Compared to conditions in the gaol, prisoners would reflect on their time at the barracks as one of relative comfort. Photograph from the Aspinall collection.
P02569.128

RIGHT These officers' quarters in Selarang Barracks demonstrate some of the better living conditions in which prisoners were accommodated. This photograph was taken in 1942 by Kennedy Burnside.
P03821.033

Until the move to Changi Gaol in May 1944 the AIF was housed in and around the area of Selarang Barracks. The one vehicle that the AIF was allowed to keep for transporting the sick is visible in the foreground. This photograph was taken in secret by Kennedy Burnside.
P03821.020

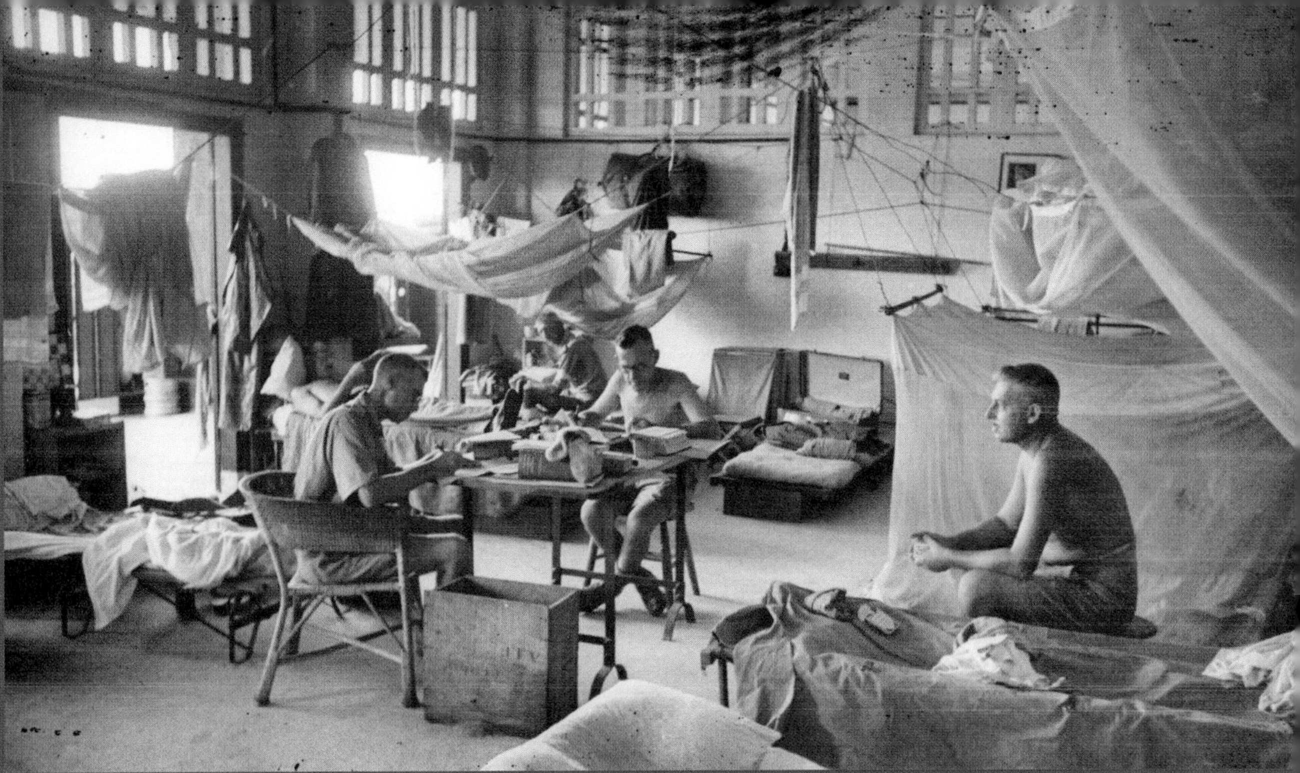

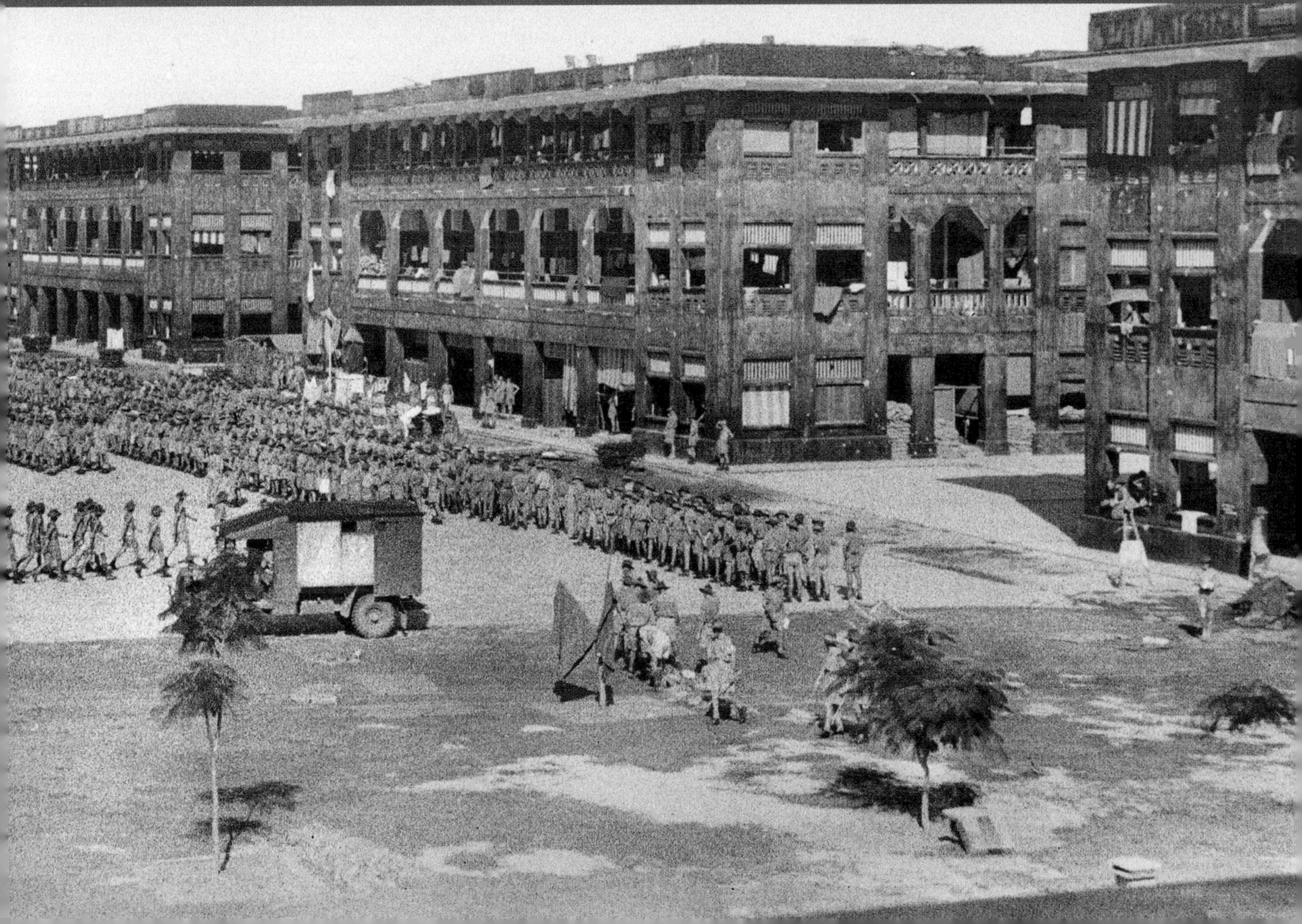

remained with its attap roof, convolvulus entwined walls and coloured east window, until the remnant of the camp moved to the Changi Gaol in May 1944 …

Towards the end of 1942 … the sappers were given their first opportunity to acquire that skill in transferring huts from A to B …

Some five attap-roofed huts in various stages of disrepair in the Roberts Barracks area, already four years old and ready for replacement by peacetime standards, were carefully dismantled and laboriously transported on trailers by AIF personnel to Selarang. Of the components thus acquired it was found possible to reconstruct, more or less completely, three huts. Our colleagues of the BEF similarly transferred a few more.

Scarcely had this activity died down when the Japanese announced their intention to erect new huts on the large *padang* which separated Birdwood and Selarang camps … many of us were given a first idea of Japanese bases of accommodation for soldiers. The labour for the project … was drawn from our midst. The materials were provided by Chinese merchants still in business in the co-prosperity sphere. Otherwise the matter was administered entirely by the Japanese. We found it interesting to compare their ideas on the subject of accommodation with our own … We were able to observe the differences in the common circumstances of locality, available material, and lack of urgency. The Japanese hut, unlike our own, had no wooden floor. Instead it had a corridor three metres wide running the full length, and on either side platforms two metres wide about knee-high. On these latter it was intended the soldiers should sleep or, in daytime, sit at their leisure. Again, whereas we used to reckon upon 32 soldiers being accommodated in a hut 96 feet long, the Japanese … expected that a [similar] hut … would house 60. The British hut, it must be admitted, was somewhat the narrower of the two.

To such accommodation, augmenting the original huts in Birdwood Camp, returned the remnants of F and H Forces. The demands for additions to and alterations of structures – cookhouses, clinics, and various other shelters appropriate to the circumstances – which followed this melancholy 'homecoming' were not entirely overcome before there set in the domestic alarms and excursions which heralded the evacuation of Selarang.

…

The magnitude of the construction program [following the move to Changi Gaol] – it was necessary to provide facilities for cooking, ablutions, lighting, and sanitation as well as housing – called for co-ordination of effort on the part of all. Thus one saw throughout the months of May and June gangs of workmen made up of British, Australians, New Zealanders, Dutch and Americans all toiling at the common task of setting up a new establishment …

With the pattern of the original Japanese huts before them, tradesmen started on the erection of 15 new ones, each 100 metres long … Seven multiple kitchens were erected;

Corporal S.K. Elliman of the 4th Australian Anti-Tank Regiment outside the hut he built for himself, in September 1942.

LEFT A Changi cell designed for two. This photograph was taken following the liberation to demonstrate the cramped conditions within the prison.
116463

RIGHT These overcrowded conditions faced prisoners of war housed in Changi Gaol.
043131

two of these were nearly 100 yards long! By the end of June the program was virtually complete. Other tasks were then undertaken: chapel sanctuaries, canteens, workshops, stores, libraries, and a variety of other structures were erected. The construction of a theatre stage and associated accommodation was put in hand.

If one considers the enterprise from the comprehensive viewpoint, one must take into account also the labour and ingenuity expended in activities such as the provision of running water at ablution points and kitchens, the laying on of electric light in the hutted camps, the transformation of the living room of a warder's quarters into a hospital operating theatre and a host of other things.

…

Up to 40 officers were accommodated in huts which, under British scales, would have housed 26 private soldiers. With the gaol the effect was most marked at night. The conditions within cells designed to house one Asiatic felon and actually occupied by four British soldiers may scarcely be imagined. Small wonder that most of the men elected to sleep out under the stars, and what good fortune that the Japanese did not see fit to forbid the practice.

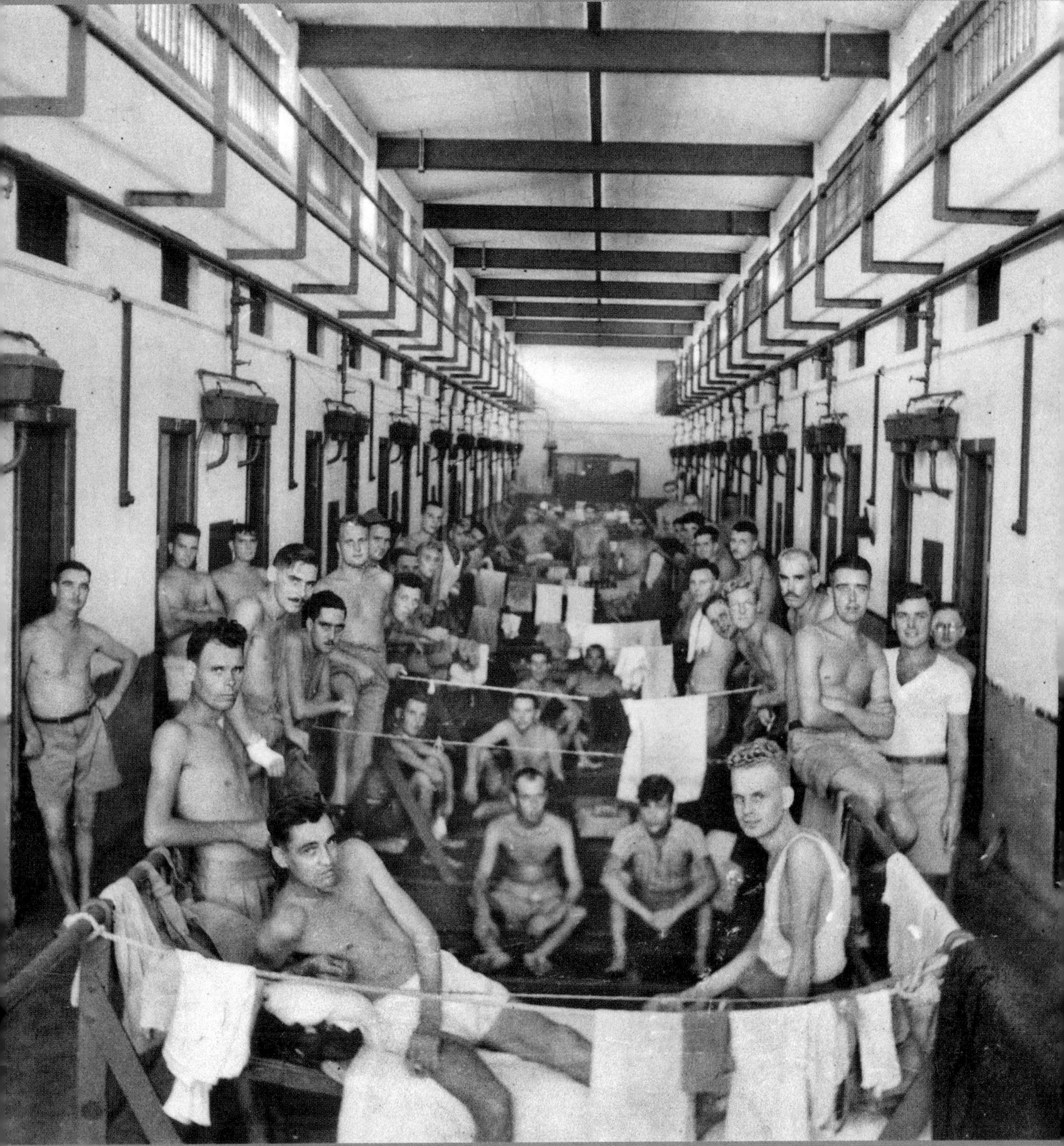

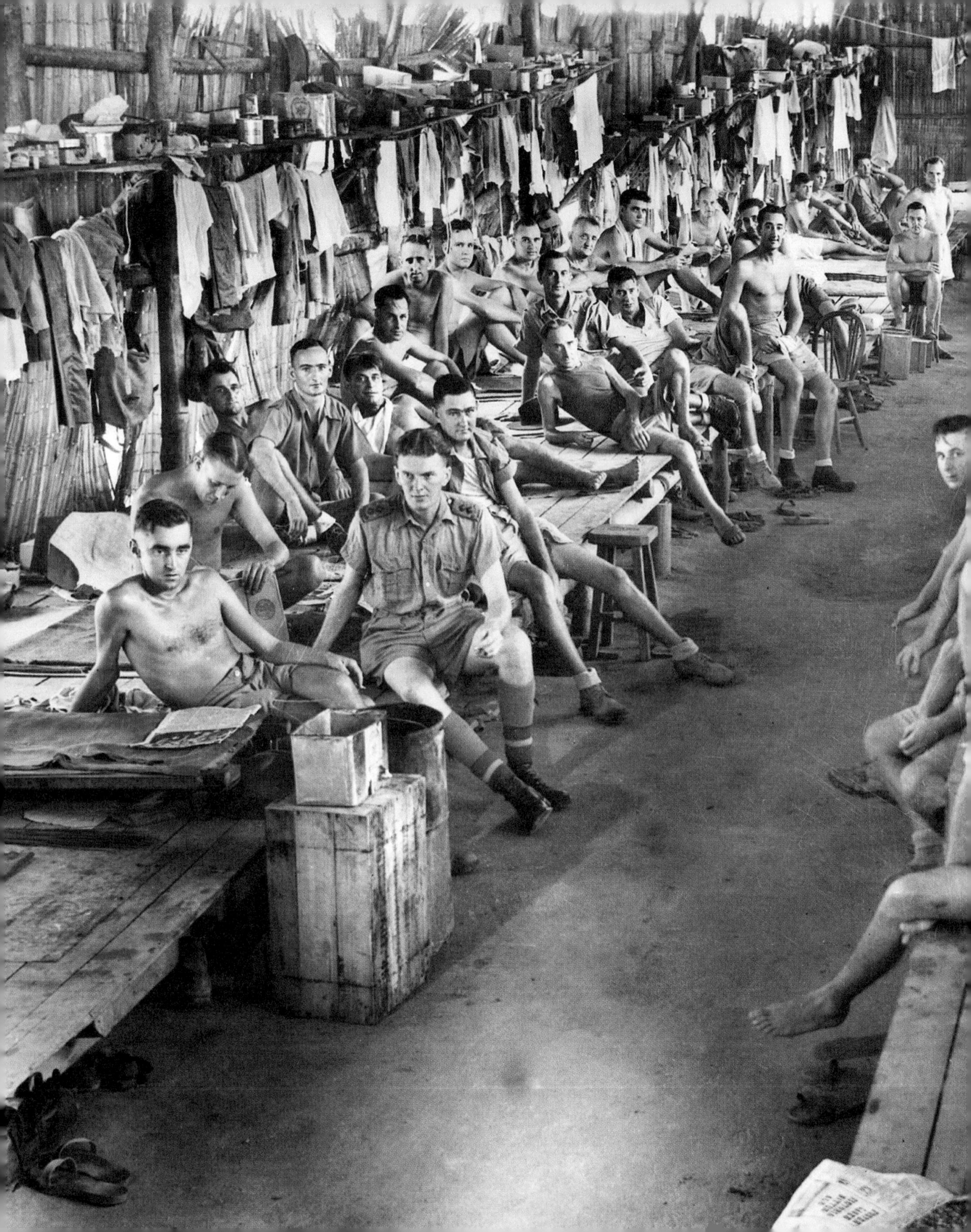

Members of the 2/29th Battalion in their attap hut at the rear of Changi Gaol following liberation.
117111

Changi's fluctuating population

Lachlan Grant
Australian War Memorial

AT WAR'S END, British military authorities estimated that 87 000 prisoners of war (mostly British, Australian, Dutch and American) had passed through Changi. Of this figure, some 850 prisoners had died, most from wounds received in battle or while convalescing following their return from hard labour on the Burma–Thailand Railway.

As the graph shows, from a peak of more than 45 000 in February 1942, the camp population fell as low as 5500 in mid-1943 after the departure of work forces to Burma, Thailand, Borneo, and Japan. Upon the return of some prisoners following the completion of the Burma–Thailand Railway the population increased again to around 10 000.[1]

These sketches of Changi Gaol from George Sprod's sketchbook include drawings by Corporal Richard Cochran.

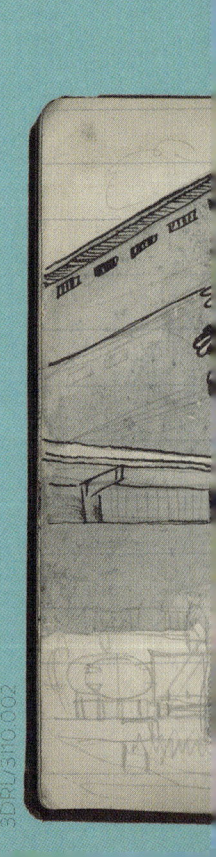

THE CLOCK-TOWER

"A" BLOCK

21-8-44

The Cookhouse   23-8-44

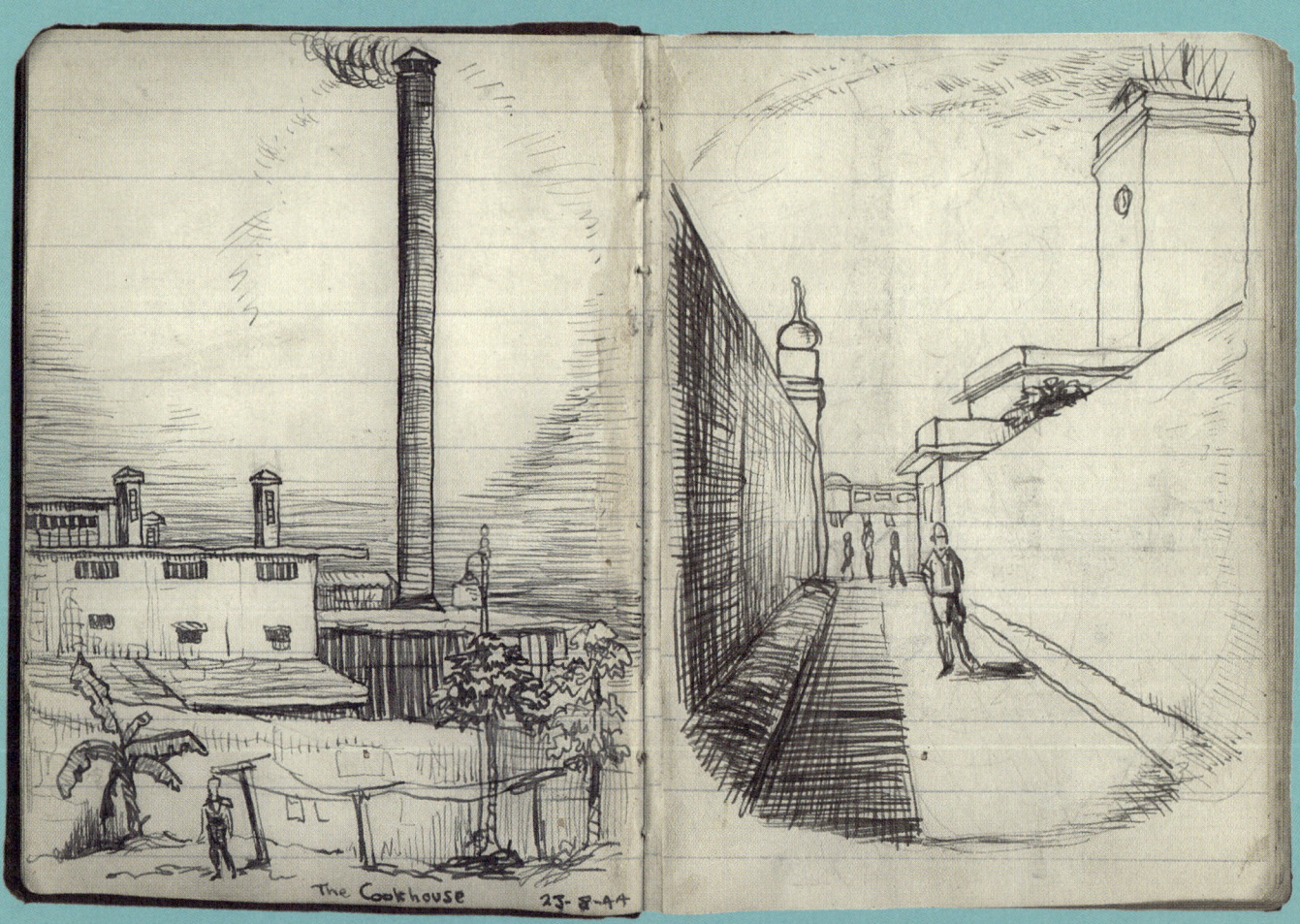

MOVING HOUSE

UNKNOWN AUTHOR

Nobody who has travelled even moderately in Malaya can have failed to become familiar with the ubiquitous attap hut. Every *kampong* numbers among its various structures a proportion, large or small, of these. Many are made up exclusively of them. These huts are, in fact, characteristic. A present-day architect might refer to them plausibly enough as 'functional'. They possess two highly desirable properties: they give a moderate degree of privacy for a small expenditure of time and effort; [and] they shed the heavy rains of the monsoons, yet do not unduly restrict natural ventilation. They receive their name from the material which constitutes their outer covering. An attap is a sheet of vegetable material consisting of a backbone made from the split stalk of a palm frond, and laced to it the flattened leaves of the nipa palm. It is usually between three and four feet long and nine inches or so wide. Three attaps are fastened to a light framework by means of split cane thongs.

…There are throughout Malaya many hundreds of such bungalows, with floors and sides of wood, covered with attap roofs having wide protecting eaves. In the hottest weather it is as pleasant inside one of these as in the shade of a leafy tree.

Small wonder that the appropriate authority, when the time came to augment existing military accommodation, chose a variation of the form as a solution to the problem. The army hut was built in various sizes; standardised, of course, to meet specific requirements. In some instances both sides and roof were attap-lined. Generally, however, the huts were constituted thus: a wooden floor rested upon brick or concrete pillars two or three feet high, wooden weatherboard sides surmounting this, and a simple attap roof, having ample eaves, protected the whole edifice. As members of the AIF in various camps, we were familiar with such accommodation. As prisoners of war we came to know it intimately …

Contraction of the prison camp area at Changi at length produced a situation in which … the question of moving some huts was first mooted.

Qualified Japanese consent having been given, the question became one for the Engineers. Clearly, the simplest method would have been to dismantle each hut piecemeal, transfer the material in convenient loads, and re-erect the huts in newly-chosen sites. But we had few fit tradesmen and we were warned that time was to be limited. Moreover, we had only a small number of tools; working parties proceeding overseas and up-country had all been fitted out with their anticipated requirements. Accordingly, it became necessary to devise a method whereby, using our available resources in personnel and tools, the greatest speed could be attained …

First of all, a few agile individuals climbed up among the roof timbers and released successive sheets of attap, thus dividing the roof into panels. Each of these panels was then released from the structure and allowed to slide down temporary skids to the ground; doors and window shutters were removed and the triangular roof frames taken down. The hut walls, framing and weatherboard in one, were then divided (after being marked) into convenient panels … Each panel was then lowered to the ground. The floor was similarly divided and partitioned. The floor supports, stout timbers of uniform size, were collected and finally the masonry stumps were dug up.

To move the dismantled components was a problem in itself. We had available a number of trailers … We found that up to 20 trailer-loads had to be moved to effect the transfer of one hut. The exact number depended upon the size

MOVING HOUSE

LEFT **The move to the Barracks Square in September 1942. Such scenes were repeated in May 1944 when the men transferred to Changi Gaol. Murray Griffin, 1942.**
ART25084

This rectangular sign made from an exposed X-ray plate adorned the cell door of civilian internees Eric Mekie, Jack Field and Ernest Hodgkin in Changi Gaol. Hodgkin had worked for the Colonial Medical Service at the Institute for Medical Research in Kuala Lumpur.
REL24941

of the hut and the nature of the route. Some hills could not be negotiated by trailer teams if the load exceeded a ton. It was a back-breaking and soul-searing task. One must remember that few men after nearly two years' imprisonment were fit for any but the lightest labour. Yet in the first phase of such movement five huts were transferred … In April and May 1944 about 60 others were similarly transferred … to the vicinity of the civil gaol … [assisted] by the loan of two old British lorries which the Japanese made available.

Re-erection brought its own especial problems. The markings on each component showed where it should go. But, after three years' occupation, few huts were in condition … [and] transportation had the effect of promoting further deterioration. Thus it rarely happened that a sufficient number of sound components were available when it became time to rebuild any one hut. This was overcome by substituting the better huts' components for others less well preserved. In local parlance, there was much 'cannibalisation'.

Moreover, although the tradesmen were at pains to recover every loose nail from the original structure, and although a search of the ground usually revealed a number of nails dropped by Asiatic tradesmen during the original construction, it was found that there were never enough to complete the re-erection of any hut … We made what we needed by cutting up coils of [barbed wire] … The wire was tough and the nails met our needs, albeit lacking heads of the orthodox sort.

Changi Gaol, as featured in George Sprod's *Smoke-oh* magazine, 1944.
3DRL/5040

Another difficulty which taxed us for a time was that which arose when we reached the stage of refixing the attap sections and patching up the cracks. We had no split cane, nor could we acquire any. Substitute was eventually found in some old electric fans, formerly installed in quarters but now out of service. Each of these contained a substantial quantity of thin insulated copper wire; enough, in fact, to enable us to reinstate two or three huts.

The move to the environs of the civil gaol gave nil to the need for additional tools. By this time we knew what items would be of most use and had the blacksmiths make them – half a dozen at a time. The most popular of such tools was an article which resembled, I was told, a burglar's jimmy, made of steel bar. Each end was flattened and split to form a claw, and one end was bent over in a half circle. With such a tool the practised carpenter could extract nails, dismantle roofs, separate wall sections, and on the other hand persuade similar components to fit again during the process of re-erection.

CHRISTMAS IN PRISON
UNKNOWN AUTHOR

Morale was a feature of imprisonment: the longer the term of the sentence the higher it became. It soared to its peak at Christmas. To the free man living with his family, surrounded by the pleasant amenities of modern life, Christmas must always be a season associated with handshakes, good wishes and the pleasure of giving and receiving. Good cheer is assisted by good food, good drink and a holiday from work. Contrast a prisoner's lot: he is faced with making Christmas – as he made so many other things – from nothing.

True, his church stands waiting with its altar loaded with temple flowers and the occasional crosses and candle sticks that were saved from the wreck of Singapore, with the padre, surplice clad, smiling a welcome at the gate. But for the rest there is nothing. No word has been received from families for perhaps over a year. The prisoner can only hope they are alive. He cannot put on fresh clothes for he has none. He cannot give a present to his friend since there is nothing to buy. He cannot receive.

In the kitchen the cooks are making heroic efforts to provide Christmas dinner. The meal is amazing but the food is the same. Rice always tastes much like rice, leaves much like leaves, sun-dried fish like sun-dried fish. The titles on the menu – Changi plum pudding with sweet sauce, mixed grill of vegetables with gravy, fish rissoles, tea with sugar – these do not deceive the diners. Yet they are happy and eat with gusto. The meal, the day, the camp; all has been blessed with the indefinable thing – the spirit of Christmas, a product of the human consciousness more potent, more real when divorced from its commercialisation and trappings.

…

After speculation comes preparation. If a bumper meal is to be served a campaign of saving must begin. Thus the sugar ration is cut down and the balance placed in the Christmas reserve. Similar action is taken with rice, oil and vegetables. Some messes call for a cash contribution in the hope of being able to buy from the canteen some garlic or *gula melaka* [palm sugar]. In 1944 a fresh pig was delivered to the camp … It was sold at $20 per pound – a sum equal to three months' wages …

The institution of Christmas cards was one of the most delightful aspects of a Changi Christmas. They ranged from simple greetings scrawled on an odd piece of paper to elaborate works of art, superior in inspiration and exertion to the majority of Christmas cards on sale in peacetime. The motifs of palms, prisons, Santa Claus and reindeer were the most usual. One showed a naked prisoner nailing his only article of clothing, a worn stocking, to the wall of his cell in Changi Gaol. The caption, 'Just in case. You never know,' expressed in a line the undying optimism that characterises the British race when faced with outrageous adversities.

> **They had faced hardship together and were alive**

The first Christmas was the most gay, with Red Cross supplies and a reasonable standard of health. Parties were given, calls made and the inevitable wishes for future prosperity exchanged. The Christmas of 1943 was altogether different. The battered remnants of the Thailand force limped into camp eaten by ulcers, crushed by the loss of thousands of their number, stunned by disaster. The camp rallied. Here was a set of people to whom something could be given, for they had nothing. Shirts, trousers and eggs were given – in some units even the precious dinner was presented to the skeletons peering round-eyed from their camp across the road.

Then came 1944; the best Christmas of all. At Changi Gaol the IJA made the minimum of concessions. Even the parties working on the aerodrome were forced to go to work – thus some were up at 5 am and others were not back in the camp until

CHRISTMAS IN PRISON

LEFT This cigarette box made from Japanese aircraft parts was a 1944 Christmas gift to Private John McGowan of the 2/9th Field Ambulance.
REL/17494

Following the move to Changi Gaol, staff worked round-the-clock at three large deep-fry cooking stoves. Drawing by Murray Griffin.
ART26493

9 pm. Yet the camp was determined to make it a special Christmas. They were prepared to make the effort. The working parties departed singing – an offence in the eyes of the IJA since it showed that the prisoners were not ashamed of the defeat … The meals were prodigious but the diarrhoea which followed took nothing from the day. There was not the gaiety of hysteria – the old optimism had gone – but a new and better optimism replaced it. That was the third Christmas; they had faced hardship together and were alive. They could and would stick it out … on Christmas Day the troops were unbeatable.

'You still got that tin of Johnson's?': a little scent of home

Chris Goddard
Australian War Memorial

WHEN CORPORAL ALBERT (Bertie) Webber was captured in February 1942 one of the personal items he managed to retain as he was marched into captivity at Changi was this small tin of Johnson's Baby Powder. Bertie Webber's feet suffered from the tropical climate and the powder helped bring relief.

Webber would end up in a work group toiling on the Burma–Thailand Railway, herded from camp to camp, suffering and enduring extreme privations. Throughout it all, he clung onto this tin, and it proved of paramount value, but not for his feet. Surrounded by illness and death, men would ask, 'Bertie, you still got that tin of Johnson's?' Webber would nod, produce the rust-speckled tin, unscrew the lid and hand it over. It would be passed from man to man, each one taking a long, lingering sniff of the fragrant powder that remained. They were smelling home, and it gave them a temporary escape from the reality of their hellish existence

When the war ended and he was free, Bertie Webber didn't toss the Johnson's – he brought it back home with him; it was that important. Seventy years on, the original printing and colour has almost completely faded from the exterior, but some of the original powder remains inside, still with that very same aroma which brought hope to the men at Changi.

This tin of Johnson's Baby Powder was an unlikely morale booster on the Burma–Thailand Railway.
REL48052

Changi industries

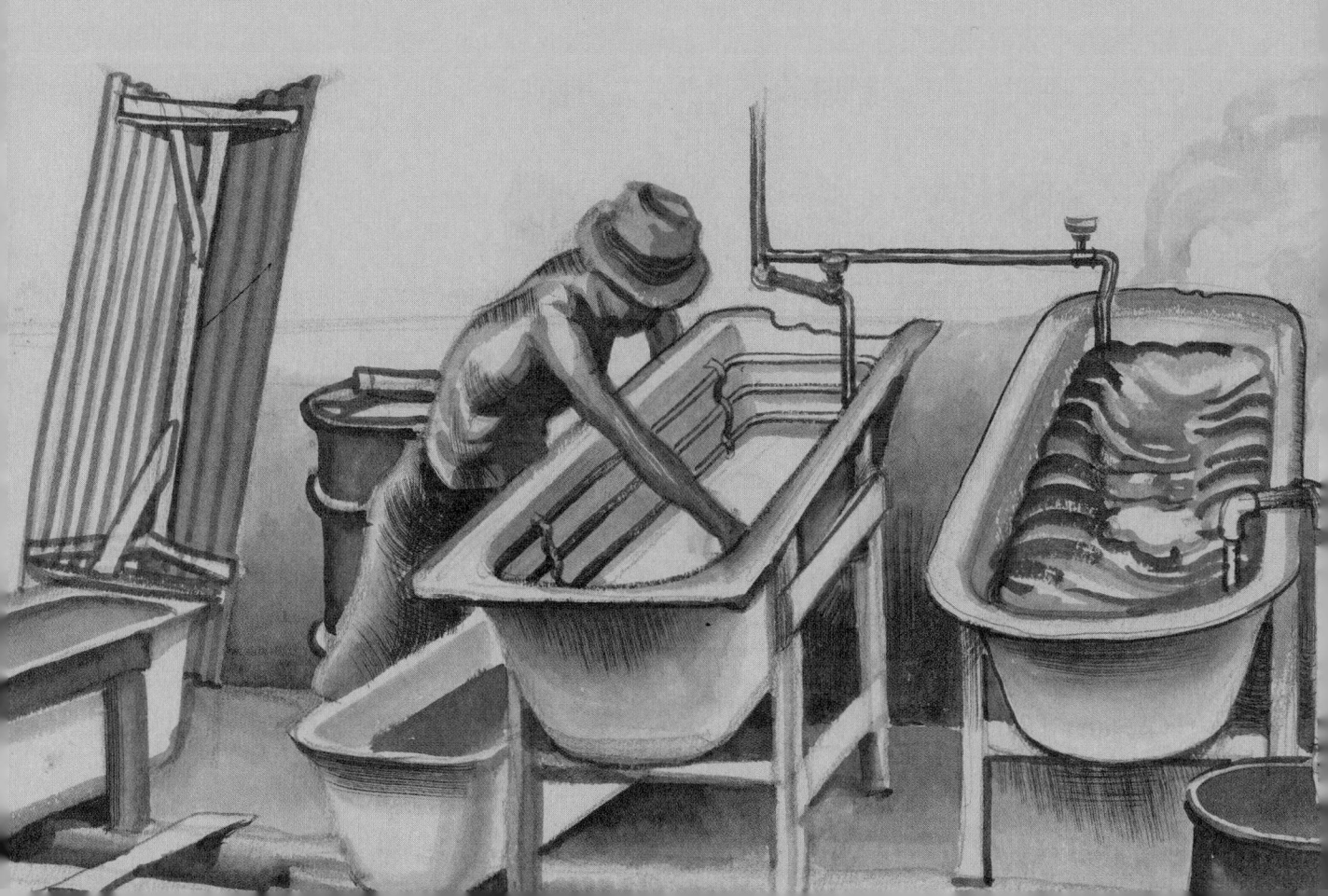

THE TINKERS OF SELARANG

UNKNOWN AUTHOR

When the AIF Malaya took up residence in Changi under the aegis of the IJA it brought with it an inadequacy of cooking pots. A few more such items were found in the quarters which the troops occupied. It is probable that no one gave heed to the question of prospective need a year hence. It might appear that the problem was not one for prisoners to solve, but rather for their captors. However, when after a few months the casualties among culinary utensils generally began to mount, it was also ascertained that little, if any, assistance was likely to be forthcoming from sources outside the camp. The tinsmiths who had access to tools and repair material busied themselves, but they soon proved unequal to the demands put upon them. Nor were culinary repairs the only problems of this sort now beginning to be felt.

Electric power became available in the camp area in August 1942, and in several minds the question of setting up an electric welding plant began to be turned over. Such a plant already existed, it is true, in the old Royal Engineers workshops in Changi. This establishment, however, was engaged almost exclusively in maintenance work on behalf of the Japanese, and was closely supervised by them. It seemed to offer slight prospect of being enlisted in service of the camp generally.

A start was made indirectly by the acquisition of a battery-charging set for operation in connection with the incoming electric supply. A petrol-electric charger had been used extensively to maintain a supply of charged batteries for hospitals and other purposes. It became more and more difficult, however, to acquire enough petrol to maintain this in service. The converter set was thus dictated by necessity. Here and there throughout the camp were found old dumps of defence equipment, dismantled and more or less unserviceable. Small foraging parties of active yet discriminating personnel were able to recover from these a great variety of useful stores. The components for our charger were acquired in this way. The motor was originally part of a potato peeler; the charging generator had formed part of the equipment of an expensive motor car. The two were coupled by means of a motor fan belt. In a short time this set proved inadequate for the work in hand … We discovered a larger generator and acquired a suitable motor and means for coupling the two and expanded the business.

With an eye to the future we took stock of other equipment of a similar sort. Then approval was given for domestic lighting on a restricted scale and our thoughts turned again to the idea of welding. As soon as time permitted – and routine matters occupied much of the day – a few stalwarts busied themselves dismantling a large petrol-electric set, formerly part of the emergency equipment of a hospital but stripped of a few essential components when we recovered it. From this the generator was separated, cleaned, dried out and tested. From the garrison swimming pool, now out of bounds, salvage in the shape of two electric motors and a switch-gear was obtained. The assembly of the various units in a satisfactory manner under conditions of considerable technical difficulty was accomplished in due course. The completed set comprised one of the swimming-pool motors coupled to the hospital generator, with the larger of the charging sets serving as an auxiliary 'exciter'.

The motor was originally part of a potato peeler

Tests were conducted with the impatience of fierce enthusiasm. We had no electrodes of the orthodox sort, no head-shields, nor other accessories normally considered essential in this occupation. Substitutes were made … However, success encouraged the welders from the first. Perhaps it was the rupture of following again a civil avocation that refused to acknowledge imperfection or worse. At any rate, in a short time the first tentative production was begun.

The current urgency related to the repair of Soyer stove insides. Made as they were of sheet steel, these utensils had begun to accumulate in the repair shops at an alarming rate. One of them was selected, the bottom cut out, the

A teapot and half-pint ladle made from steel taken from an old filing cabinet.
RELAWM33841 /
RELAWM33848

sides trimmed until sound metal was revealed and a new bottom welded in. The trial of this makeshift proved the possibility of success, and from then the welding set scarcely ceased to hum in its characteristic minor key. The supply of steel sheet was soon exhausted, so steel lockers provided originally to house the individual clothing and effects of the British garrison were broken up and converted, first into new bottoms for cooking pots and later into complete vessels and even complete Soyer stoves … mess tins were made by the score, pint mugs by the hundred; no creations of elegance, these, but serviceable items satisfying only the criterion that some people earnestly desired to possess them, having nothing better.

The current urgency related to the repair of Soyer stove[s]

… there grew up a general repair and minor construction service. It was this which brought about the need for a second welding set. For certain tasks the quality of the best work that the welders could turn out was inadequate. This we felt was due to the local pattern electrode we had to use. Repeated tests of wire available in the camp had shown that the springy material from which barbed-wire 'concertinas' were made gave the best results. Then one day we 'acquired' some regular manufactured electrodes. By this time orders were being executed for units and formations outside the AIF, and our sphere of exploitation widened accordingly.

After taking stock of available resources it was decided that as the possession of manufactured electrodes would enable us to use an alternating current welder it would be better to attempt one of these … In this we were probably influenced by the fact that our medical service directorate had placed an order for a transformer for operating an arc lamp in the local skin clinic. After examining the stock of coils and wire available, the decision to construct a dual-purpose transformer was arrived at. The windings were quickly laid on, but it was first necessary to un-strand, anneal and insulate some heavy copper conductor. For insulation we used flannelette bandage damaged by fire and unsuitable for medical use … A suitable tank was welded up with the aid of our original apparatus and in due course the transformer was installed and immersed in oil. It was soon in service in a dual capacity.

The capabilities of the installation were now sufficient to meet all reasonable needs, and it continued to be operated when the whole of the prison camp's workshops were amalgamated, and especially after the move of the prisoners to Changi Gaol … a peak of production in excess of a thousand articles per month was attained.

By now the work had acquired routine status. The hands which had directed the first faltering steps and the minds whose ingenuity overcame the inevitable difficulties were already busy in other fields.

WORKSHOP OPERATIONS
NOEL HILL

The Ordnance Workshop was taken over in the last quarter of 1942 by Captain N.H. Hill. Owing to the fact that most of the healthy personnel were in Singapore on working parties, the only operatives were unfit and the shop was regarded as an educational and instructional institution. The area of operations consisted of a single garage and the driveway. Operations consisted of repair of trailers, cycles and small fitting jobs, including the manufacture of sextants for enthusiastic navigators.

While on this location the workshop was raided by the IJA, who stopped operations, locked the garage, and declared that they would remove the tools the next day. All keys fitted the workshop lock, so useful tools were removed immediately … and work proceeded in a different locality without loss of continuity. The IJA seized what was to be a future lathe – geared head, saddle, tool rest, tailstock and chucks. It was only after a good quarter of an hour's protest and definite declaration that the pieces constituted a rice grinder that the potential lathe was released.

…

Particularly heavy demands were made for repair of cooking gear, and the workshop expanded. The number of personnel increased to 25 and the entire lower floor of a house was occupied. The main job was the re-bottoming of dixies, and in all some 400 were completed in the next few months. Materials used were panelling from trucks and cars (the dixie owner specified a 'Ford' or 'Chev.' bottom when requesting repair), hydrochloric acid from the medical branch and solder from where it could be got or made. If there was no solder, then bearing metal was used. Heavier gear … was repaired by bolting or riveting on plates …

Progress was made in overcoming the workshop's main difficulty – lack of tools.

A lathe … was constructed from salvaged head and tailstack, saddle and tool rest. This considerably enlarged workshop scope. Lathe work … consisted of hinges for artificial limbs, manufacture of pieces for woodwind instruments, repair of rice crushers, manufacture of cases and moulds for cricket and baseballs, winding of transformers, and manufacture of baseball bats. The lathe was driven by a one-horsepower motor, the transmission being truck fan belts.

The cycle and lawnmower repair shop was run as a branch of the main shop. Cycle repairs were mostly repairs to tubes, covers and brakes. New parts could rarely be obtained, and when obtainable were exorbitant in price. Patching solution was generally unobtainable and a technique was developed whereby fresh latex, readily obtainable from local trees, could be used. Covers were repaired with latex and canvas, substitute brake shoes made from the heads of truck tyres …

The construction of a grinding head from a motor and materials obtained locally further extended workshop activities and permitted the manufacture of various knives, chisels, shaping tools, rubber tappers' knives (for the Rubber Factory) and the like.

Construction of an electric welding set further widened the scope of the workshop and permitted the manufacture of such articles as cooking containers and artificial limbs, and aided in the construction of a grass-crushing plant for which there was great demand from medical services.

On movement to Changi Gaol, workshops were consolidated under the control of Captain Hill, with A.S.M. Miller of 18th Division second in charge.

…

Twenty-two trailers were necessary to move workshop equipment …

…

The workshop found its new home in the garages surrounding the gaol courtyard. After a certain amount of juggling to ensure that neither the blacksmith's nor the tinsmith's shops should be adjacent to the workrooms of Camp Control, the workshop settled down to work.

Personnel came from various units in the AIF, English Army, Royal Netherlands Forces, RN, RAF and RNZAF, and numbered 52.

Organisation was under the sections:

1. General shop
2. Sheet metal and welding
3. Blacksmiths
4. Carpenters
5. Nailmakers
6. Watchmakers
7. Typewriter repair shop
8. Trailer repair shop
9. Cycle repair shop
10. Brush factory
11. Needle manufacture

Demands from the outset were heavy. The reasons for this were threefold:

1. The departure of the hospital to Kranji without sufficient workshop facilities.
2. The arrival of parties from Burma without cooking gear.
3. Conditions in the gaol differing from those at Selarang.

… Such orders as the following were completed:

11 000 identity discs
400 watering cans and garden containers
400 wedges for garden tools
2000 mess tins
1000 mugs
200 food measures
500 spoons
5 centumweight of nails from one inch to six inches in length.

The demand for toothbrushes – 700 per week – necessitated the construction and installation of a small electric drill and the manufacture of jugs for the production of handles.

WORKSHOP OPERATIONS

This razor was made in Changi by Tom Russell as a birthday gift for his friend Sapper Ronald Lee. It is engraved on one side, 'To Ron from Todd', and on the reverse, 'Singapore 1944'. The black wooden handle is made from the back of an electricity box and it comes with a custom-made presentation box.
REL/11809

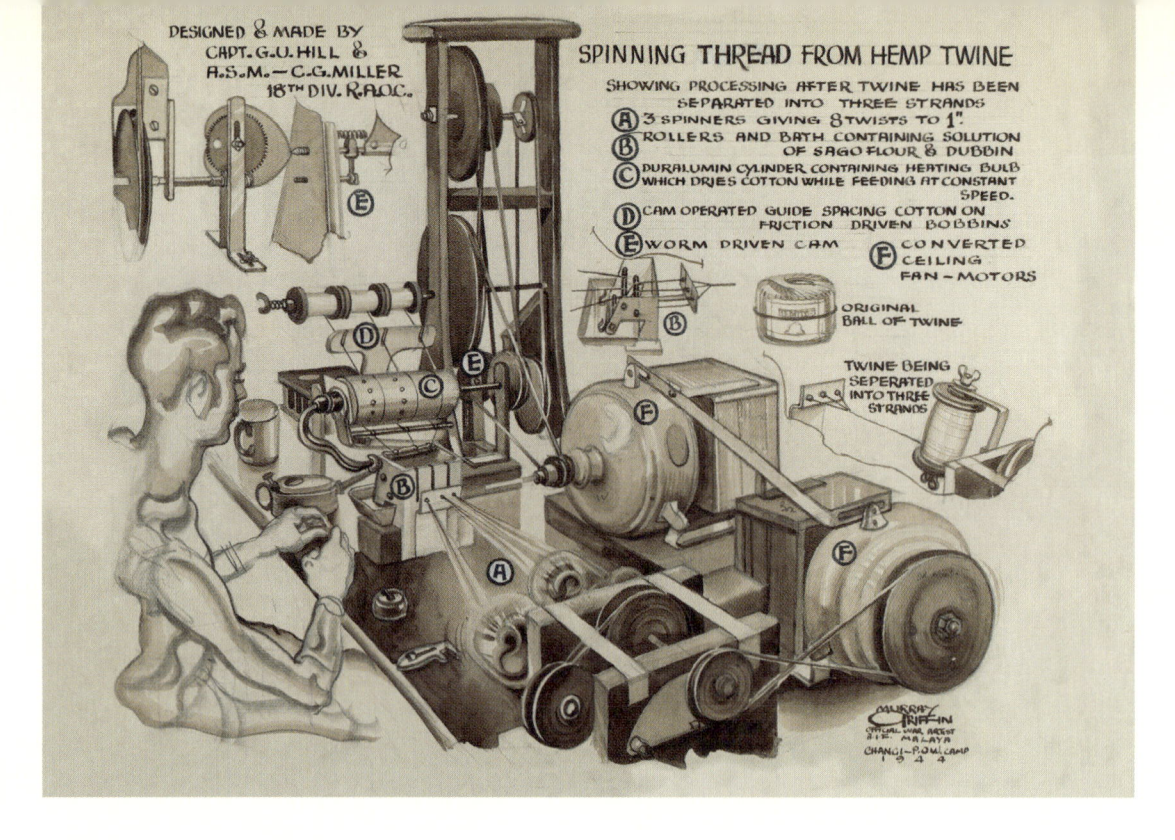

Sewing-machine needle manufacture deserves special mention. The raw material consisted of spring wire. The eye and grooves were punched after softening, straightening and cutting. Pointing and shaping were done on a fine wheel. The needle was then hardened and tempered, the result being quite as effective as the commercial article.

Unofficial jobs or 'foreign orders' were terms given to the production of things like cigarette lighters and lighter attachments. Lighter wheels were made by flattening – by hot forging – rollers from bearings, drilling and trucing the discs, then cutting and tempering. This yielded a better job than the original wheel.

Later, when the supply of safety-razor blades lagged behind, the demand and the price rose sharply and the great era of open blade razor manufacture came into being. These were made from all types of steel: bayonet, car springs, knife, and, when the supply was unearthed, tools. The number ran into hundreds. Infinite care and patience were exercised in the hollow grinding, polishing and toning. The handle, generally made of Bakelite composition board, was frequently highly ornamented and the blade had the owner's name etched on it.

The work was first class; a man's razor was his pride, and it is suspected that the commercially minded made the art some small source of revenue. In general the result could be compared readily with the commercial article.

Always in demand and the cause of many a secret conference between blacksmith and fitter was the coconut grater, generally of the serrated tooth, scraping type. The output of these must have been around the thousand mark.

WORKSHOP OPERATIONS

LEFT The spinning of thread from hemp twine. Murray Griffin, 1944.
ART26455

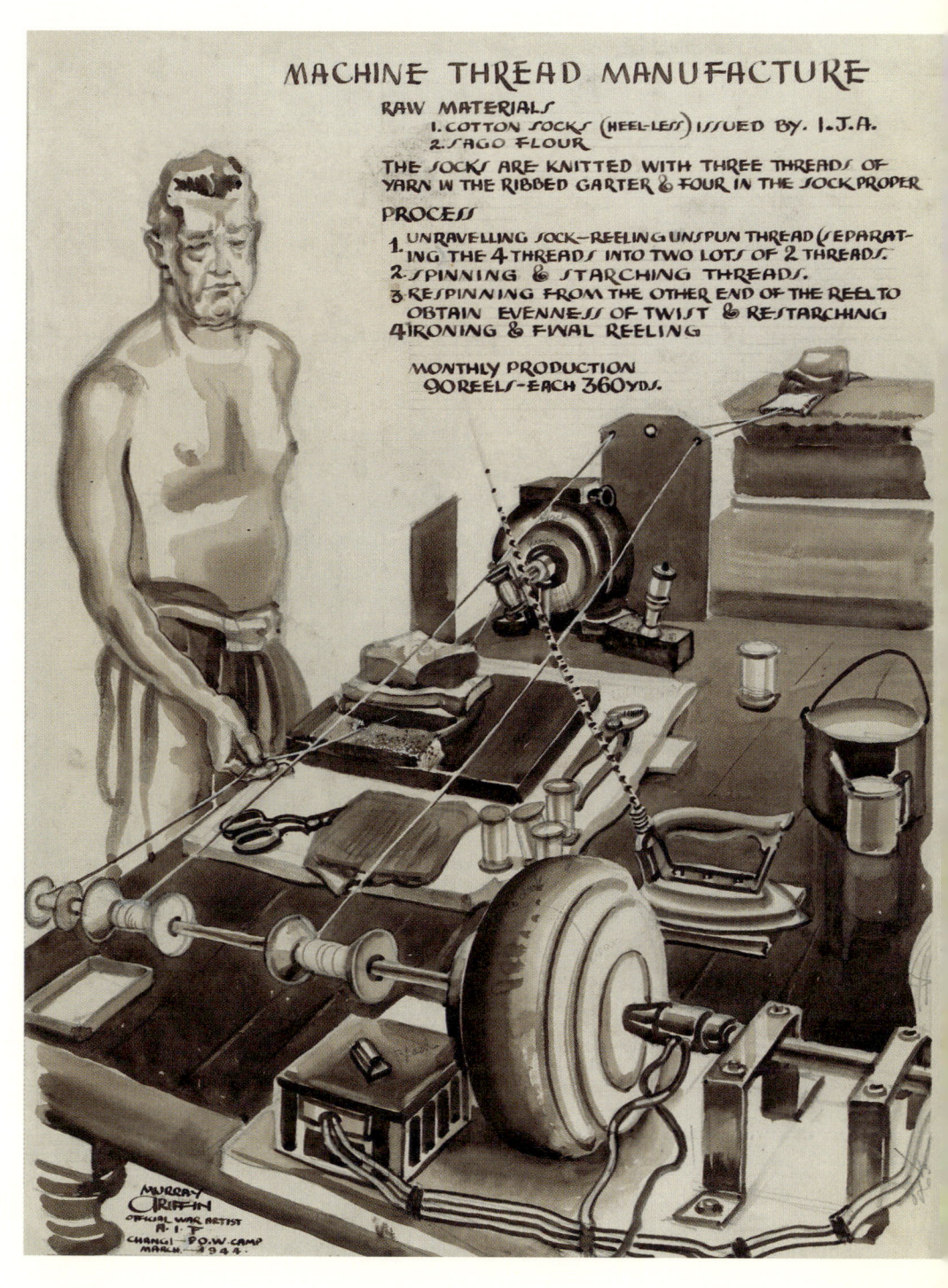

RIGHT The manufacture of machine thread. Murray Griffin, 1944.
ART25079

MACHINE THREAD MANUFACTURE

RAW MATERIALS
1. COTTON SOCKS (HEEL-LESS) ISSUED BY I.J.A.
2. SAGO FLOUR

THE SOCKS ARE KNITTED WITH THREE THREADS OF YARN IN THE RIBBED GARTER & FOUR IN THE SOCK PROPER

PROCESS
1. UNRAVELLING SOCK — REELING UNSPUN THREAD (SEPARATING THE 4 THREADS INTO TWO LOTS OF 2 THREADS.
2. SPINNING & STARCHING THREADS.
3. RESPINNING FROM THE OTHER END OF THE REEL TO OBTAIN EVENNESS OF TWIST & RESTARCHING
4. IRONING & FINAL REELING

MONTHLY PRODUCTION
90 REELS — EACH 360 YDS.

193

REPORT ON CAMP WORKSHOP
P.G. MILLER

In May 1944, on the occasion of moving to Changi Gaol, all workshops were combined to form one central workshop for the whole camp. It may safely be stated that everybody in the camp (including Kranji Hospital) was dependent to some extent on the efforts of camp workshops for cooking utensils, mess gear (new and repaired), wedges and axes for wood-splitting, machine needles for clothing repairs, toe and waist plates for boot repairs, all types of *changkols* [spiked garden hoes], rakes, and pitchforks, watering cans for gardening, latex cups and sprouts, rubber-tapping knives, shears and buffing machines for production of rubber shoes, pulp mills and steam chests for paper-making, razors and scissors for group barbers' use, equipment for soap-making, electric drives for mincers, tin openers, rice steamers, paddles, ladles, baking trays, *kualis* [Malayan woks], fly nets, and a variety of items and utensils for kitchen use.

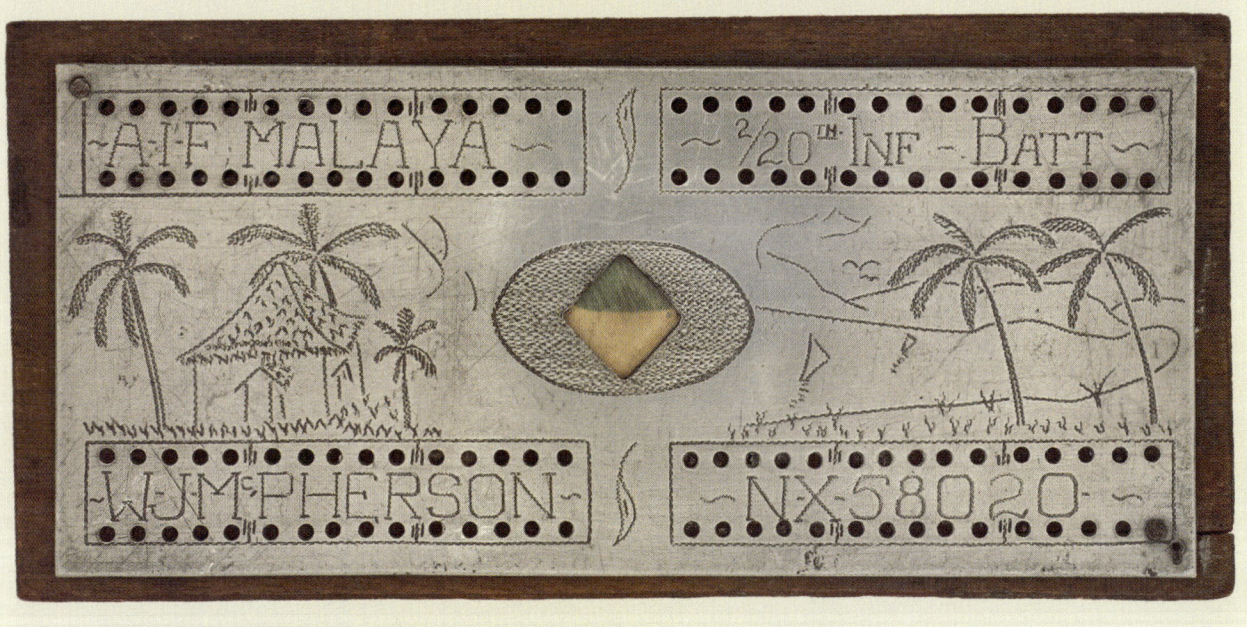

This cribbage board was made in Changi for Signalman William McPherson of the 2/20th Battalion.
REL29050

REPORT ON CAMP WORKSHOP

It is pointed out that practically the whole of our vast output was manufactured from scrap material with homemade tools. About 700 soldiers' lockers were dismantled and used for all sheet metal work: water cans, mess containers, Soyer stoves, cycle spokes for needles, cycle frames for oil-burning equipment, taps, motorcar springs for razors, kitchen knives, scissors, tapping knives, old rails for axe heads, half-axle shafts for wedges, old chassis frames, and iron for the framework of machines.

All solder and flux for the repair of thousands of mugs, mess tins, bowls, buckets and similar items had to be scrounged by men on working parties outside in return for a special favour such as a stainless mess tin … Both welding plants were camp-made, approximately 85 per cent of all welding being done with Dannert wire with the barbs removed.

The above, together with an assortment of items too comprehensive to give in detail, amount to a total of 40 477 articles manufactured … [and from] the Camp Repair Shop … gear, equipment and personal belongings (mess tins 1659; mugs 1965) totalling 20 099 articles were put in order … [as well as maintenance on] all typewriters, grass-extract machines, bean and rice crushers, scales and weighing machines, trailers, handcarts, and cycles.

2 July 1945

Below are a few items manufactured and repaired from 1 July 1944 to 30 June 1945.	
Containers, 14-gallon	15
Containers, ten-gallon	53
Containers, eight-gallon	7
Containers, six-gallon	407
Containers, four-gallon	2
Containers, three-gallon	392
Containers (assorted)	123
Swill bins	61
Rat traps	104
Pastry cutters etc.	147
Bread tins	15
'Smoke here's' [Ash trays]	105
Needles (machine)	1184
Needles (assorted)	313
Dartboards	12
Draughtboards	113
Darts (sets of three)	170
Container lids	349
Mess tins	2321
Mugs	2172
Spoons	458
Water cans	462
Urine buckets	443
Ladles and measures	736
Baking trays and dishes	221
Sieves and strainers	36
Kuali lids	15
Kualis	6
Latex cups and spouts	400
Boot heel plates	136
Boot heel waists	4000
Chess sets	44
Draught sets	118
Domino sets	116

SOAP FACTORY

JOHN KEMP

The Japanese having failed to issue their unfortunate prisoners with either washing soap or shaving soap for some considerable time, or with the money to buy it for themselves in sufficiently large quantities, Changi decided to make its own.

All the equipment used was made by the prisoners themselves out of scrap materials for which not even the Japanese had any use. Not only was soap produced but also tooth powder, milk of magnesia, fertiliser and paper … Old steel boxes, ashes, salt water, palm oil, odd bits of piping, a few decrepit bathtubs and some grass, and Changi had enough to provide for itself. For those who find this difficult to believe – there was so much about these men's lives which is difficult to believe – here is how it was done. It is perhaps the supreme example of their resource and ingenuity during their captivity.

The factory opened in August 1944, the plant having been built out of camp resources by the engineering staff. The primary product was bar soap for issue to troops, and the process used is as follows:

Wood-ash from all camp cookhouses is extracted with water whereby soluble potassium carbonate is leached out, together with other potassium salts. This is carried out in a counter-current extraction battery consisting of a series of enamel long-baths. The fresh ash is put into the baths containing the strongest solution, thereby enriching it still further, and is shifted daily from bath to bath in the opposite direction to the fluid contents, which is also shifted daily. Thus, pure water passes in at one end of the battery and emerges as strong potassium carbonate solution, whilst in the opposite direction fresh ash passes in and is taken out as exhausted ash and used on gardens for its calcium and magnesium contents.

The potassium carbonate solution is then pumped into a long-bath fitted with steam beating coils, where it is boiled with lime in order to convert it into potassium hydroxide, the end point of the reaction being determined by laboratory tests. After settling, the clear liquor is pumped into a further steam-heated enamel bath, where it is concentrated to about 20 per cent strength so that, upon cooling, crystals of potassium sulphate settle out and can be used as fertiliser, leaving a purified solution of potassium hydroxide. The calcium carbonate formed in the causticising reaction is removed for use as fertiliser.

The potash solution has been used for many purposes during the year ending August 1945: manufacture of soap; anticoagulant for rubber latex (used in the Camp Rubber Factory); de-greasing fluid (used in kitchens and workshops); manufacture of milk of magnesia from sea water; and manufacture of paper from lalang grass. In the course of the year about 40 tons of wood-ash was treated, yielding about five tons of strong potash solution.

For the manufacture of soap, the analysed potash solution is measured out and pumped into a 200-gallon steam-heated soap-boiler containing the weighed amount of palm oil. The mixture rapidly thickens as the potassium soap forms, and when the reaction is complete, judged by laboratory tests, common salt is added to convert the potassium soap to hard sodium soap. The latter rises to the top of the mass, and the underlying glycerine layer is run off before re-melting the soap and pumping into two quarter-ton moulds. After two or three days' setting, the moulds are opened and the two quarter-ton blocks are cut into bars …

From August 1944 until July 1945 production of bar soap totalled 33 000 pounds.

In producing bulk shaving soap for the unit barbers, the hard-grained sodium soap is taken out of the boiler before re-melting, and superfatted to 20 per cent palm oil before being cast into 20-pound blocks ready for cutting … from January to July 1945 production was 320 pounds.

In December 1944 the manufacture of tooth powder from exhausted wood-ash was begun. The ash from the final bath in the extraction battery is stirred with water and pumped into an apparatus consisting of a series of weirs, whereby the fine particles pass

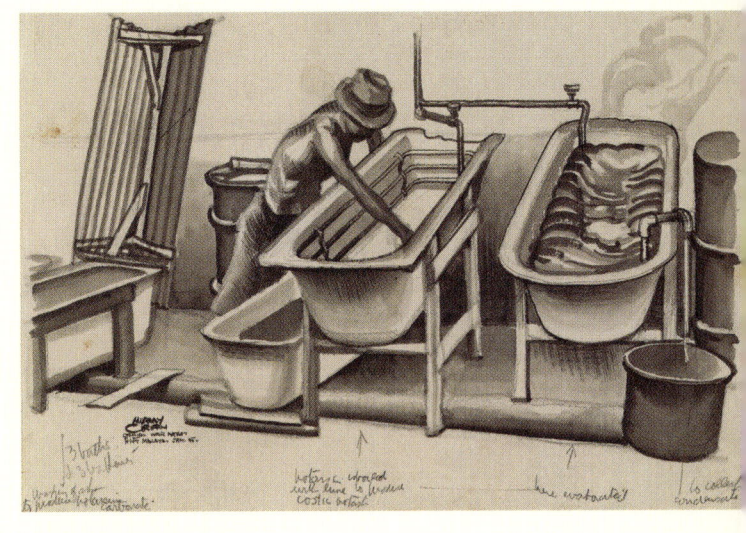

A prisoner carries out one of the three stages of soap making in Changi.
ART26518

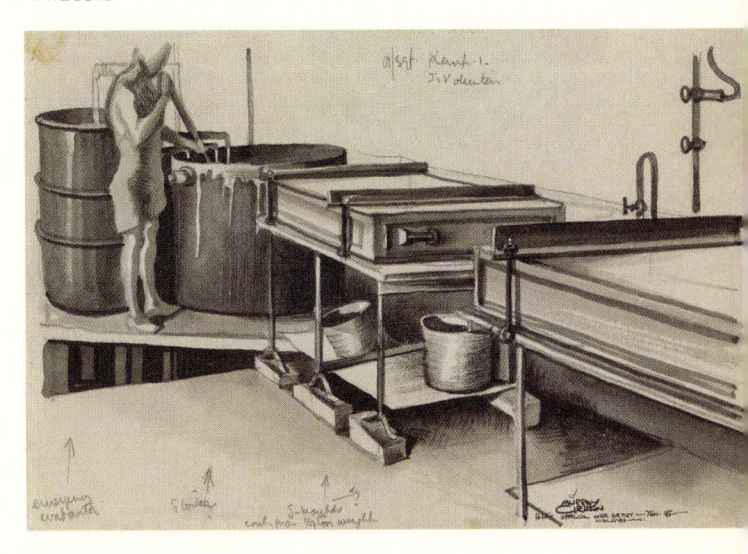

The later stages of soap production. On the left the boiling of the mixture and stirring, while on the right can be seen two moulds for the soap to cool and set.
ART26519

over and are collected in an enamel bath, while the coarse, gritty particles are retained. The fine particles are washed until alkali content is below 0.025 per cent, settled out, and dried in trays before sieving into boxes for dispatch ... Production to date totals 1300 pounds.

In April 1945 the production of milk of magnesia was started. A measured amount of potassium hydroxide solution is added to seawater, whereby white magnesium hydroxide is precipitated. The clear supernatant liquor is used in the kitchen for culinary purposes; the precipitate is removed and the liquid boiled in an enamel bath fitted with steam coils in order to sterilise and concentrate the milk of magnesia, the latter being subjected to analytical control so that the supply to the gaol dispensary is of standard strength. Up to August 1945 the production totalled 945 pounds.

Experiments were made in June 1945 on the production of lubricant grease by dispersion of calcium soaps in mineral oil. A non-corrosive lubricant grease was finally evolved.

In June 1945 experiments were begun on the manufacture of paper, and after working out the process and designing the necessary plant, production began in July. The original scheme was to use the waste treated grass from the Grass Extract Factory after removal of the B complex vitamins, but after the breakdown of the machinery in that factory, fresh lalang had to be used.

The lalang is cut up and boiled with strong potash solution for about six hours, so that non-cellulosic material is removed, and upon washing out raw cellulose remains. The alkali washings are all passed through the alkali batteries again in order to extract the potash. The raw cellulose is pulped

A summary of activities of the Soap Factory			
Item produced	Peak production rate	Period of operation	Total production
Potash solution	500 pounds per month	August 1944–45	5 tons
Bar soap	5000 pounds per month	August 1944 to July 1945	33 000 pounds
Shaving soap	80 pounds per month	January 1944 to July 1945	320 pounds
Tooth powder	200 pounds per month	December 1944 to August 1945	1300 pounds
Milk of magnesia	400 pounds per month	April 1945 to August 1945	945 pounds
Paper	500 sheets per day (six inches by eight inches)	July 1945 to August 1945	6000 sheets (six inches by eight inches)

SOAP FACTORY

in a ten-gallon rod-mill (Modern Repair Company Workshops) and the finished pulp is stored in tanks ready for paper manufacture. A measured amount of pulp is poured into a frame, having a wire mesh bottom upon which rests a rectangle of cotton netting, the frame being immersed in a vat of water. The water filters through, leaving on the netting a rectangle of cellulose, which is then transferred to a steam-heated surface for drying. Excess water is removed by a squeeze roller during heating, and when the cotton netting is pulled off a sheet of paper remains on the steam chest. The final process is that of rolling the sheets between high-pressure rollers before cutting to standard size of six inches by eight inches. Cardboard is also made here by the same process.

To date, 270 pounds of lalang have been treated, yielding 6000 sheets of standard size.

Bars of carbolic soap, (RELAWM27460, TOP) washing soap (RELAWM27461, BOTTOM) and toilet soap (RELAWM27459, LEFT) manufactured at the Changi Soap Factory.

199

RUBBER FACTORY REPORT

ROBERT MOFFETT

In the early days of our prisoner-of-war career ... a handful of volunteers got together with a view to repairing shoes ... [it] later proved to be the birth of one of the most essential and useful installations in the camp: namely, the Rubber Factory.

Having exhausted all supplies of repairing material, the staff got down to the possibilities of producing a composition sole manufactured from latex, laterite, chalk, granulated cork and cement. This was in time improved upon and the 'A' type shoes were manufactured. The shoes consisted of the composition sole with toe and ankle straps moulded into it. Some 2000 of these were issued to patients and orderlies and, being soft and pliable, were ideal for the wards, as most of the floors were of concrete.

In order to produce these shoes some sort of machinery was necessary for powdering the laterite. This was built up in the factory and comprised a wood frame on which was mounted a hand-operated ball-bearing roller operating against a back plate. Wooden moulds were also made in which to cast the soles. The moulded soles were then baked in an oven, and finally pressed in pressers made up from car jacks.

When the camp was moved to Changi Gaol the factory was rebuilt in a corner of the gaol garden. The staff planted creepers round the factory and in no time it was covered with a rich green foliage ...

A program of electrification of the factory machinery was embarked upon, including an electric drive for the grinder and emery wheel. The special electric mixer for mixing composition was designed by the Rubber Factory staff and produced by the camp workshops.

No fewer than 5800 of these composition soles were produced and 2880 pairs of shoes repaired in the last 15 months. A considerable number of canvas and rubber boots issued by the IJA were soon to find their way to the factory for repair. These were patched by the use of latex and scraps of cloth cuttings from the tailors, and a special mixture was used for sealing: 4250 pairs of these shoes were repaired in the last 15 months.

...

The IJA was approached with the object of supplying the factory with smoked rubber sheet. After considerable delay of haggling, it eventually produced a few bales, and in October 1944 the first 'B' type shoes were produced. However, before this stage was reached the necessary machinery for mass production had to be thought out – this was designed and drawn up by the Rubber Factory staff and produced from scrap metal and green lockers by the camp workshop. It comprised a multiple buffing machine

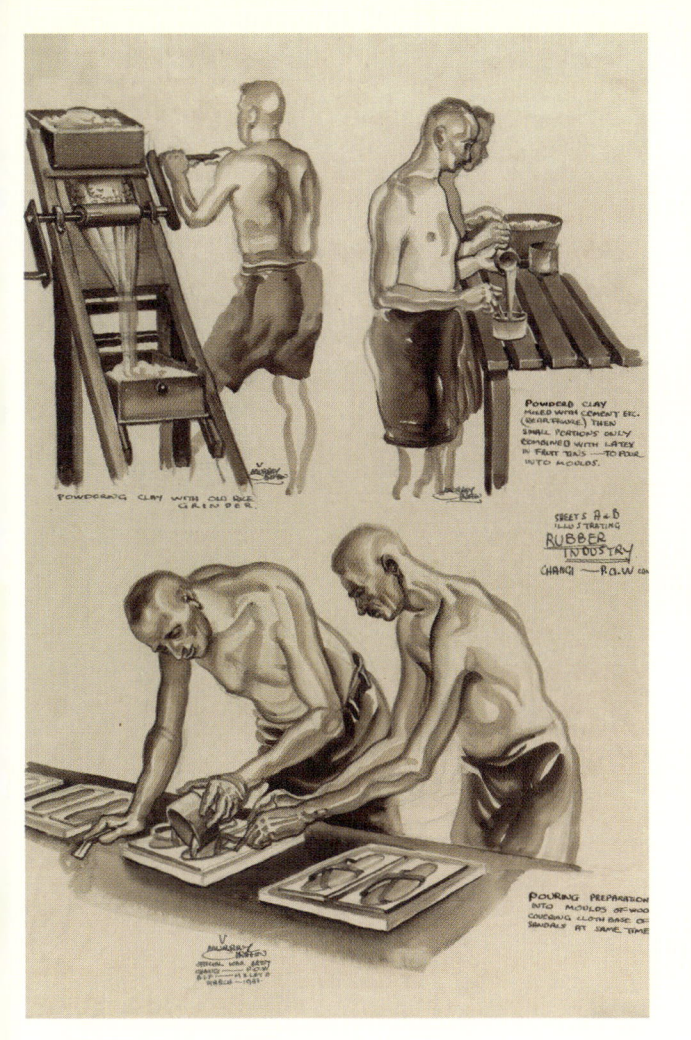

The steps to make rubber soles for footwear. Murray Griffin, 1943.
ART 25095 / ART 25096

with twin shafts driven by an electric motor through double pullies and belts, the whole being mounted on a steel frame. Each shaft carried two fractional buffing wheels and the peripheries of the wheels were serrated to fuse the rubber surfaces for the purposes of jointing the rubber soles and straps without the use of any adhesives. Various patterns were produced until finally the present type … [consisted] of two straps crosswise over the toes and one strap each for the heel and ankle. The improvement necessarily involved an increase in the use of rubber, but this was offset to a certain degree by a proportionate decrease in repairs: 8243 pairs of 'B' type shoes were produced, while 13 664 pairs were repaired.

CHANGI INDUSTRIES

An example of a raw latex sandal, one of 6000 pairs made in the Changi Rubber Factory. Note the resemblance to those in the illustration below.
RELAWM33843

BELOW Sandal-making. Murray Griffin, 1945.
ART25064

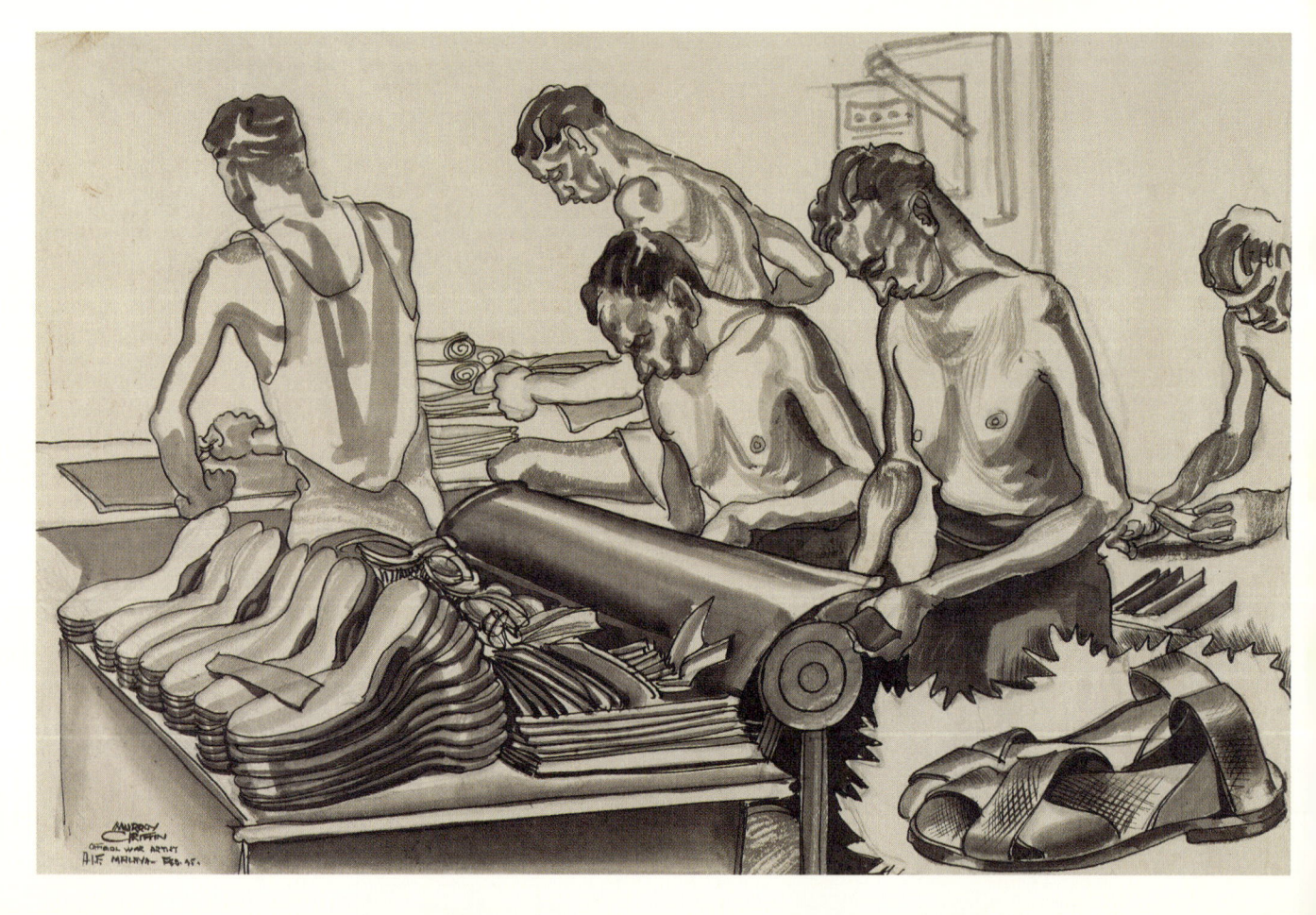

SAVING OUR SOLES AS PRISONERS OF WAR: RUBBER

UNKNOWN AUTHOR

We had been prisoners of war for some six months, and it was becoming increasingly evident that repair of footwear was to be a very serious problem.

The leather supplied by the IJA was hopelessly inadequate to effect even the most urgent repairs … The area had been scoured for rubber tyres and the considerable number which had been stripped and cut into soles provided temporary relief. The manufacture of tacks by the simple process of cutting suitable wire into half-inch lengths with a cold chisel provided the means of attaching soles to boots. However, the heavy work done by all fit men and incessant walking on trailer parties was taking a steady toll, and it was becoming a common sight to [see] the men wearing old boots just hanging together, or no footwear at all. The Red Cross issue of approximately one pair of boots per man was a godsend and provided a brief breathing space in which an attempt to tackle the problem from a new angle was made.

The new idea was the making of rubber soles out of latex from the rubber trees which were comparatively abundant in and around the camp. Numerous experiments were conducted … Eventually it was found that fresh latex would mix successfully with laterite. With the addition of a small quantity of cement it was found that by drying, pressing, and drying again in the sun a substance similar in consistency and hardness to a soft crepe rubber was produced. Tests over a period revealed that these soles, when stuck to boots or shoes by the application of a latex solution, not only stuck fast but also lasted some six weeks of normal wear.

On the strength of these experiments it was decided to open a factory for the manufacture of these rubber soles. Tappers, to tap the rubber trees and bring the latex to the factory each morning, were trained. Mixers were trained to mix the latex, laterite and cement in their exact quantities. A grinder for grinding the laterite to a fine powder was made and installed. A big double press for pressing the rubber in moulds and slabs was manufactured out of two car jacks and some heavy timber. Suitable moulds were manufactured and numerous small appurtenances, such as mixing bowls (old tins), and scraping knives of chrome (made from motorcar radiators) were made or 'scrounged', and within a few days the factory was ready to commence production.

Production proved quite up to expectations and the mixers became more and more expert in quick mixing to prevent coagulation. The proportions of latex, laterite and cement had to be adjusted day to day according to the humidity, and the nice judgement of the mixers became a matter of pride. Wet days were generally holidays due to no latex, but all was well

CHANGI INDUSTRIES

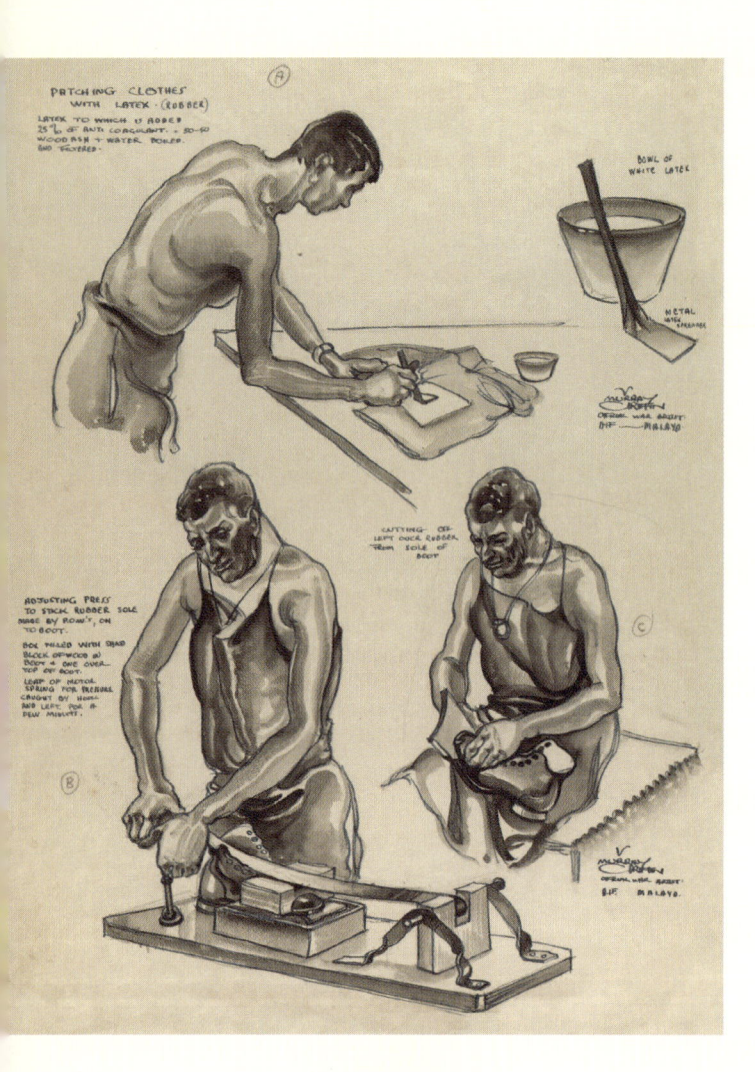

Rubber industry activities.
Murray Griffin, 1943.
ART26520

provided the rain did not come in the morning. Cleanliness around the factory and drying yard was an absolute essential as the smell of old latex was both most unpleasant to the staff and most attractive to flies.

The supply of latex and laterite offered no difficulty, but cement was a problem. Scientific pilfering of a few pounds each evening from a plant belonging to natives who were mending a malarial drain in the area provided a steady supply for some months. By this and other means the Rubber Factory managed to keep up a reasonable production and materially assist in keeping the men off the ground. Sandals for hospital and convalescent patients were also manufactured and proved a great boon. In addition to these two main objectives many small jobs were undertaken, such as repairs to canvas shoes, covering worn-out cricket balls with hard rubber, and repairs of any rubber articles.

The repair of shirts and shorts by the use of latex instead of cotton for attaching patches was also quite satisfactory and enabled the sewing machines in use to be used exclusively on more difficult repair jobs.

A pair of leather sandals made in Changi.
REL45624

THE AIF SEEDLING NURSERY
PETER MADDERN

Soon after their arrival in Changi it was obvious to many who were at the time subsisting on a practically unbroken diet of rice and 'jungle stew' prepared from the leaves of hibiscus hedges and edible grasses that some effort on their part was necessary to supplement the meagre food ration provided by the Japanese ...

Accordingly, some far-sighted officer set about placing under cultivation large tracts of ground between the Convalescent Depot and the Loyang Road. Others, their farming instincts sharpened by hunger, immediately followed suit, and in many parts of Selarang both officers and Other Ranks could be seen grimly swinging the unaccustomed *changkol*, determined to have sweet potatoes and Ceylon spinach growing where the lalang grass grew longest.

Two types of gardeners could be easily recognised by observing their activities: firstly, the professional and enthusiastic amateur gardeners of pre-war days; and secondly, the 'try anything once' gardeners who visualised several hours' hard work – but not too hard – digging and planting, thenceforth a life of

Officers tending a vegetable garden, September 1942.
P00077.021

ease and abundance with only daily cropping of their gardens to mar the halcyon days spent waiting for their release.

After the first six months there was ample evidence of the activities of the latter type in various parts of the camp – patches of furrowed, sunbaked ground, with perhaps several Ceylon spinach plants fighting a losing battle against drought and the sun. On the other hand the ex-professionals and enthusiastic amateurs, by dint of hard work and judicious use of the *Gardening Book for Malaya*, very shortly had flourishing gardens of Ceylon spinach, amaranth, sweet potatoes, beans, tapioca, yam beans and *brinjals* [eggplants], while some of the more successful could proudly display tomatoes and cucumbers.

The initial effort, unfortunately, had to be abandoned shortly after planting was completed owing to restrictions in the area allotted to the AIF. However, the No. 2 Convalescent Depot took over the area between the convalescent building and the perimeter wire running parallel to the Leyang Road, and finally had under cultivation an area which produced large quantities of food with which to supplement the rations of the patients in the depot.

Finally, almost every house in Selarang boasted a small garden, and continuous war was waged with *changkols*, chipping rakes and watering cans against conditions which would make a Victorian Mallee farmer tremble and grow pale. Wells were dug, storm drains tapped for irrigation purposes, and acres of lalang grass cut for compost. The competition for composting material waxed furious, as no artificial manure could be obtained, and to cut a hedge was immediately to draw a herd of hawkeyed gardeners with wheel barrows, handcarts and trailers, all anxious to save hedge-cutters the trouble of carting the waste material away.

The innumerable insect pests with which Malaya abounds caused a great deal of damage from time to time. Large brown and black beetles possessed of voracious appetites chewed the bark from the stems of Ceylon spinach, and their activities caused consternation and dismay in the ranks of the gardeners – until those who had grown cunning after many years of gardening in Malaya spread the good news that the dusting of the plants with white wood ash caused untold pain and suffering to the beetles, and was a good reason for them to direct their attentions to possibly less succulent, but certainly less gritty foods. The unfortunate Ceylon spinach was vulnerable to attack not only aboveground from the beetles but also underground by the eelworm. This interesting little nematode was responsible

> **Competition for composting material waxed furious**

Halt for midday rice.
Murray Griffin, 1944.
ART25093

MID-DAY RICE
LOG LOADING PARTY
CHANGI — P.O.W. CAMP

Murray Griffin
OFFICIAL WAR ARTIST

for the devastation of large areas and emerged victorious from any struggle, as no means of combating his effects could be found. Aphids on the beans, fruit fly and borers on the tomatoes, cucumbers and *brinjals*, and the homely slug and snail all took their toll on the produce, but gardeners returned undaunted to the attack with nicotine and derish root spray, while poultry owners rendered sterling service to the community at large in annihilating the slugs and snails.

Apart from organised unit and house gardens, numerous individual gardens were maintained by Other Ranks, who banded together in teams of three to six men, the fit men of the party doing the heavy work on their days off from working parties, and their unfit comrades doing the light maintenance and watering. The proceeds were cooked over fires at night, and many such fires could be seen twinkling through the palms, with shadowy figures crouched over them, waiting with watering mouths for the mess of potato tops, spinach, and perhaps the unconsumed portion of the current day's rice to be cooked. Indeed, a blackened billycan or cooking pot became an essential part of the equipment of almost every man, and after some time, when clothing became ragged and hats battered, Australians during a move resembled organised bands of 'sundowners', complete with 'bluey' and billycan.

Ceylon spinach, artichokes, and yams were grown

Frequent re-organisations and the consequent moves were the hardest blows the gardeners had to endure. Only too often, after weeks or even months of hard labour on their gardens, were gardeners informed that their unit had to move to a new section of the camp, resulting in the loss of the garden and weeks more of hard work before any produce could be obtained from gardens in the new area. The effects were sometimes mollified by the fact that there were gardens in the new area to be taken over, but normally they were in poor condition owing to too-close cropping during the few days before the move.

During November 1943 a survey of the food resources of the camp was carried out, and it was discovered that unit gardens were contributing monthly no less than 7000 pounds of vegetables to the rations – which, with a strength of approximately 1300 troops in Selarang, including the hospital, represented a worthwhile supplement to the small vegetable ration issued by the Japanese. By this time gardeners were far more efficient in their methods, and some splendid crops of Ceylon spinach, artichokes, and yams were grown. Unfortunately, insufficient men could be spared to develop fully the garden areas inside the camp, as the Japanese insisted on draining

AIF seedling nursery.
Murray Griffin, 1944.
ART26509

A.I.F
SEEDLING NURSERY
FOR UNIT GARDENS, CHANGI- APRIL 1944
V. MURRAY GRIFFIN
OFFICIAL WAR ARTIST
A.I.F
CHANGI — P.O.W. CAMP
1 9 4 4.

the camp of all but a few fit men to work on outside working parties.

Until January 1944 no organisation had existed for the coordination of unit gardens, or for the production or distribution of seeds and cuttings … The return of so many troops and the widespread gardening activities now called for an organisation not only to control the gardens but also to ensure that the whole area was developed to the fullest extent, and as a result the AIF Garden Scheme was launched.

The object of the Garden Scheme was to place all the available ground in the AIF under cultivation, using the better areas for the growing of leaf crops, beans, sweet potatoes and artichokes, and the areas of poorer soil to be planted with tapioca. In addition, papayas were to be planted throughout the whole area, along roads and between rows of tapioca … wherever there was room enough to accommodate a tree.

It was estimated that a minimum of 100 000 tapioca cuttings would be required, 30 000 papaya seedlings, and unlimited quantities of seeds, seedlings, and cuttings for leaf and root crops.

Areas within the camp were allotted to groups and units after the initial survey and work commenced on 3 March 1944. Lieutenant Colonel Galleghan evinced great interest in the scheme; not, however, because of any leanings towards horticulture on his part, as on being shown a newly planted tapioca cutting devoid of leaves, he tapped it smartly with his cane and said, 'Not much to eat on this one; what part of it do we eat, anyway?'

There was no shortage of labour, and … everyone engaged on duty inside the camp had to do one hour's gardening per day either in unit gardens or tapioca areas … Most progress was made by the Convalescent Depot, which had been allotted the side of the hill on which the depot was built to grow tapioca. Both staff and patients entered into the work with a will, armless and legless included – the latter wearing their 'Changi pattern' artificial limbs for a start, but later they could be seen leaping nimbly from terrace to terrace minus leg with a *changkol* or spade in hand.

The tapioca garden at the Convalescent Depot was surveyed by the survey class, terraced and planted, all within six weeks of starting.

As seeds and seedlings could not be purchased, it was obvious from the outset that a nursery would be required to produce the large quantities of plant material required. Accordingly, the AIF Nursery was formed … Two slab-sided attap-roofed huts surrounded by banana and coconut palms … terraced areas of tapioca, sweet potatoes, trellised Ceylon spinach and beans, and numerous seedling beds of papayas, Ceylon spinach, amaranth, chillies and lettuces constituted the nursery, about which the nursery staff toiled, wearing only breech clouts and burned to a deep brown by the tropic sun. Although the nursery was officially opened only on 3 March, by 31 March

1944 the following cuttings and seedlings had been distributed:

- 5000 Ceylon spinach seedlings
- 4000 Ceylon spinach cuttings
- 7000 red amaranth seedlings
- 150 chilli seedlings
- 2000 sweet potato cuttings.

In addition, some 20 000 papaya seeds had been planted … these were to have been issued when ten weeks old, and in the meantime gardeners were digging holes … and packing them with compost in anticipation of large-scale papaya planting when tapioca areas were completed.

The fact that large supplies of seedlings and cuttings were available gave in itself quite a fillip to gardening, and although it cannot be guaranteed that all seedlings were successfully brought to maturity, few were wasted because of a lack of enthusiasm.

As April 1944 drew to a close the end of the tapioca planting was in sight; everyone had worked with a will, and in addition to the fruits of their labour in some cases could proudly display blistered palms as evidence of their industry at the time …

During the last week in April the inevitable happened. News was received that Selarang was to be evacuated and all prisoners moved to the Changi Gaol by the end of May 1944. Within half an hour all gardening, apart from cropping, had ceased.

By the end of May the camp had moved, and Selarang was a scene of desolation and devastation. Not only had gardens been so closely cropped as to ruin them, but in many cases [were] wilfully destroyed – of the 60 000 tapioca cuttings planted some 20 000, six-weeks grown only, had been uprooted to obtain the minute tubers which were forming. Needless to say the damage had not been done by gardeners, most of whom had had at least one nocturnal battle with marauders … It was difficult for the gardeners to lose their patches after two years of work, but they had lost nothing by their labours and had gained not only the additional food for themselves and their comrades, but also a definite interest in life which those working for the Japanese outside the camp unfortunately lacked.

> **Some die-hards cultivated small patches … with good results**

In Changi Gaol few facilities were available for unit gardens, as the camp was extremely crowded, but some die-hards cultivated small patches intensively and with good results. Tucked away in odd corners, tipped only by occasional sunshine, their little gardens struggled against tremendous odds. Newer methods of gardening, however, including cultivation by urine, brought about a wondrous change. In the Australian end of the gaol these small gardens were consolidated, and in the months before release produced two additional pints of vegetable soup per week. 'Group stew rights', as they were called, were eagerly awaited by queues of starving men. The garden habit was a good one.

POTTERY

UNKNOWN AUTHOR

In August 1944 the medical authorities required suitably designed pots to collect toddy from the coconut palms for use with patients suffering from beriberi and other ailments. Suitable pots were unobtainable, and it was decided to endeavour to make them … Experiments were made and eventually a suitable clay for making pottery was found in one of the courtyards of the gaol itself. Then a pottery wheel was constructed and, from the meagre materials available, it was found possible to turn out on this wheel satisfactory pots for collecting the toddy.

An oven capable of efficiently baking the shaped clay had to be built, and … pottery was able to go into efficient production at the beginning of 1945, despite the many difficulties encountered. Experiments in glazing were continually being carried out, but the lack of suitable materials prevented a really satisfactory glaze being obtained. Other containers required by the camp were also made, including rubber-cups, ash trays, vases for the hospital, salt pods, drinking mugs, smoking pipes, seed trays and containers, and chalk.

Details of containers produced to date are set out hereunder:

Item	Amount produced
Toddy pots	105
Salt pots	78
Mugs	19
Vases	4
Rubber cups	256
Smoking pipes	700
Ash trays	79
Seed trays and containers	25
Hotplate bases	10
Crucibles	16
Containers (hospital)	16
Miscellaneous containers	16

Other miscellaneous items made for camp use included: chalk, jugs, lime, assorted trays for Sime Road Civil Internment Camp, and seed droppers.

22 August 1945

The camp potter at work. Murray Griffin, 1945.
ART25074

'God bless and protect': Jim Blondahl's pottery

Eleni Holloway
Australian War Memorial

JUST ONE of the wonders of Australian prisoner-of-war activities is that they were able to produce functional ceramic vessels within the confines of their camp. Suitable clay requires just enough grit or sand to give it strength, and the right amount of water for structure when throwing on a wheel. Equally, firing clay is a carefully coordinated and controlled process, as uneven temperatures in a kiln can cause pots to crack or explode. Despite these problems, prisoners produced a vast range of ceramic ware for their own use.

Private James (Jim) Blondahl of the 2/18th Battalion learned pottery as a hobby. As a prisoner Jim made these two mugs on a foot-operated pottery wheel constructed from found materials. The clay for the mugs was sourced from two distinct clay pits within the camp; the darker one of higher iron content. He also experimented with different shapes for handles made from slabs of clay: one rounded, the other square.

Jim worked as a head assistant at a large general store before enlisting with the Second AIF on 14 May 1941. He travelled more than 560 kilometres from rural Nyngan to sign up at Paddington, New South Wales. At the time he was 34, married with two children.

In Changi in December 1944 he made the lighter-coloured mug. Thinking of home and of his wife, Maud, he inscribed the base of the mug with: 'God bless and protect Bill, Jim, Ronnie, Eddie, Kenny, and my dear Maud. Changi Xmas 1944'.

Jim survived the war and was recovered from Changi in September 1945. These simple, unglazed mugs are now a reminder of his experience as a prisoner of war – his words and prayer forever captured by fire.

These mugs were made in Changi by Private Jim Blondahl of the 2/18th Battalion, and are his lasting mementos of captivity.
REL24462 / REL24461

THE BROOM-MAKERS OF CHANGI
FREDERICK ROCHE

After capitulation no equipment of any sort was supplied by the Japanese; it was necessary to rely solely on the army stores left by the British administration. Some eight or nine months later most articles were wearing out, including brooms, so local ingenuity was called on to supply the lack.

Several small groups commenced manufacture – in the true Latin sense of the word … The Royal Australian Artillery (RAA) Broom Factory started production on 27 November 1942 with the object of supplying the needs of several large barrack buildings occupied by the three AIF artillery regiments – the 2/10th and 2/15th Field Regiments and the 4th Anti-Tank Regiment. The staff being all good gunners, the artillery term 'search and sweep' was adopted as a rather apt motto. All products were branded with 'Ubique' – the first word on the artillery badge.

The timber which formed the doors of the buildings in the Selarang area was found to be particularly suitable for broom heads, so Selarang buildings rapidly became doorless. For bass brooms, suitable for use in drains and yards, split bamboo was used, while the centre rib of the coconut-palm leaf formed an excellent substitute in making brooms of the millet type. Later on, the supply of mature bamboo running out, palm-leaf ribs were used for all hard brooms, the very tips of the ribs being made up into scrubbing brushes.

In all these types the material was locked securely in the head of the broom by means of a tapered dowel driven in from the back and held by a nailed-over cover. The supply of light nails soon ran out, but this difficulty was overcome by making them out of the strands of steel wire and cable; heads were hammered on and the points cut with old army wire cutters. These cutters were rigged on a bench to act as a wire cutting machine. This was operated by a foot treadle and return-spring, and fitted with a gauge for cutting nails of various sizes.

Soft brooms for indoor use were made from beaten-out coconut fibre … held in place by wire which was also used for making the staples used in this type. The inexhaustible supply of barbed wire, unwound, provided this necessary article. Squeegees were another article which proved most useful in cleaning concrete surfaces. They were made from old truck tubes.

Production increased month by month as other units called on the RAA Broom Factory to supply their needs. Brooms by this time were all standardised and cut to pattern.

As time passed, timber and palm fronds became more and more difficult to obtain. Authorities, though very pleased to get brooms, were not so keen on providing the necessary men and materials. Barter was resorted to. Many a piece of timber changed hands in exchange for a broom.

This machine cut nails for reparing boots and making brooms. Murray Griffin, 1944.
ART26456

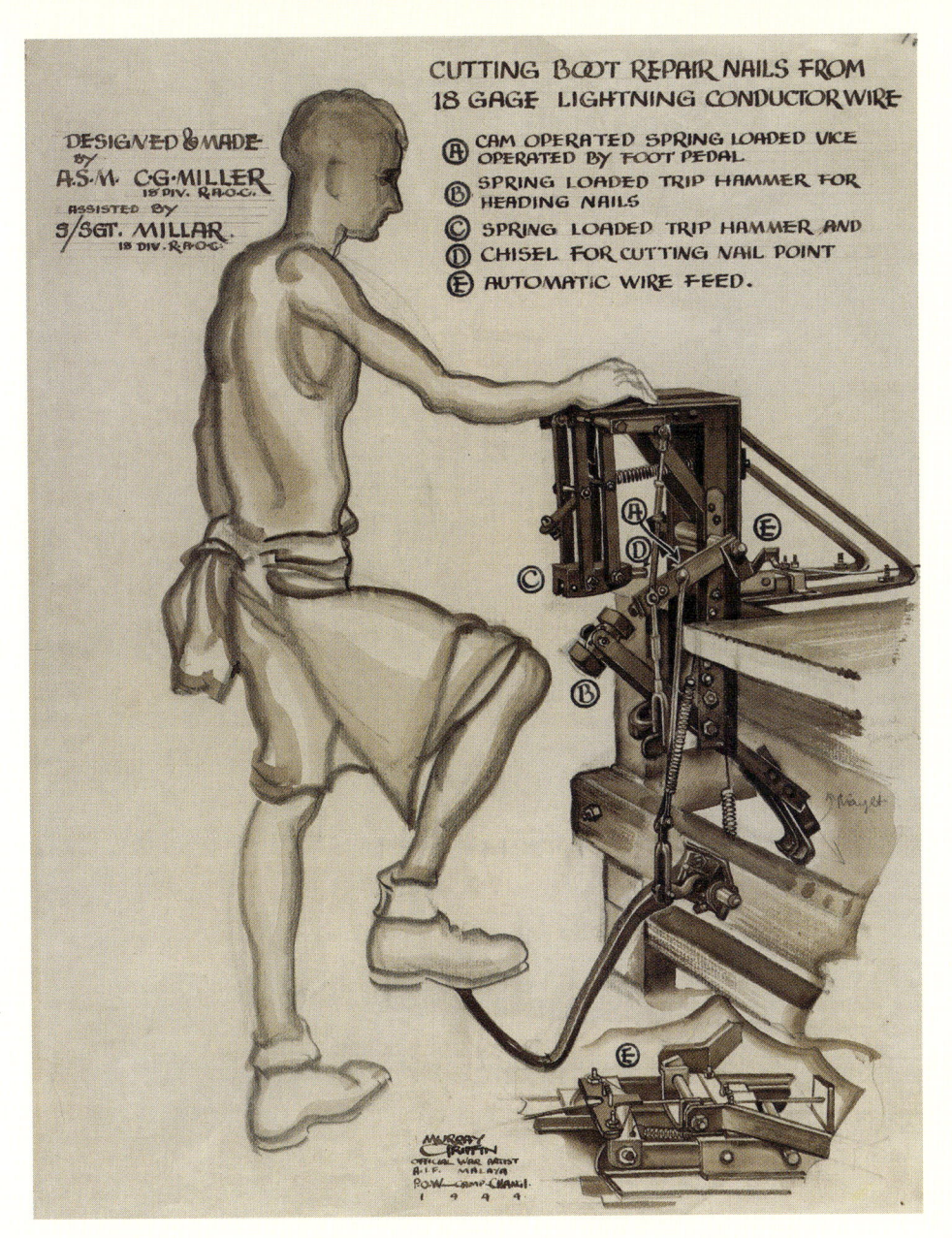

The Detention Barracks staff suggested that, as they had the labour available to strip palm fronds, they would supply large quantities if the factory would keep them in brooms. This scheme worked admirably.

Various sidelines were developed. Chalk made by a process of precipitation from white clay was in demand by orderly rooms, lectures and educational classes. Glue was made from fish scales … Tropical darning needles of hard copper wire – rust-less however wet the monsoon – were made … In fact, the factory came to be regarded almost as a universal provider.

215

CHANGI INDUSTRIES

Some of the requests were laughable. A head came round the door one day: 'Got any coconut shells?'

'What for?'

Back came the reply: 'Tits for the Concert Party.'

Some sweet young thing required uplift! Another day the order was for artists' paintbrushes, so a lanky gunner with a good crop of nice straight hair had to sacrifice a few locks in the good cause!

At a later date the reconditioning of toothbrushes was undertaken and a use found at last for the Scottish sporran – the white hair making very good tooth and shaving brushes.

However, sporrans were very difficult to obtain, Scots men, for some unaccountable reason, showing a marked reluctance to have this article of their national dress put to such a useful, if lowly service.

The ubiquitous coconut, as usual, supplied the answer – the beaten out fibre making a serviceable toothbrush without stirring up national hatred.

A species of ornamental aloe, akin to hemp, growing in Selarang gardens provided a beautiful white fibre which was made up into soft shaving brushes …

On moving to the gaol the British and the RAA broom factories were combined [to

This set of miniature brooms with presentation box was presented by members of the Changi Broom Factory to Lieutenant Colonel Galleghan. The lid of the box is inscribed with the motto and branding of the factory: Search and sweep/Changi Broom Factory/Ubique Brand.

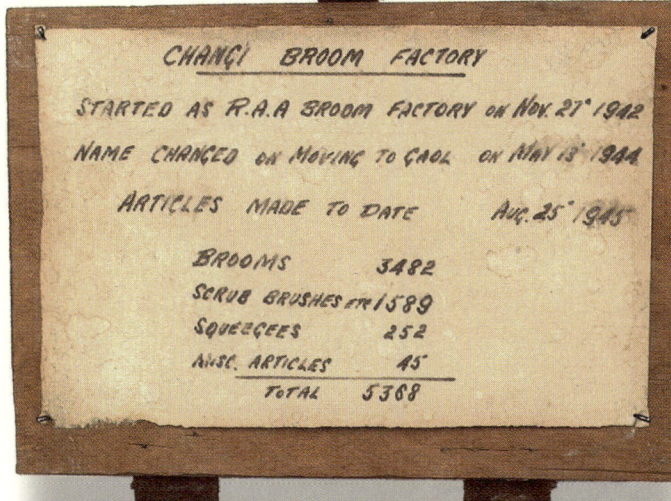

THE BROOM-MAKERS OF CHANGI

CHANGI BROOM FACTORY

STARTED AS R.A.A BROOM FACTORY ON NOV. 27" 1942

NAME CHANGED ON MOVING TO GAOL ON MAY 13" 1944

ARTICLES MADE TO DATE   AUG. 25" 1945

BROOMS	3482
SCRUB BRUSHES ETC	1589
SQUEEGEES	252
MISC. ARTICLES	45
TOTAL	5368

217

CHANGI INDUSTRIES

form the] Changi Broom Factory. However, the identity of the RAA Broom Factory was not entirely lost, as its products continued to be marked with its brand and motto.

The combined factories have since worked in complete harmony, supplying the needs for the entire camp, some 11 000 men making any type of brush called for – the latest being paste brushes for the bookbinders and tiny spiral brushes for the typewriter repair shop.

There is no doubt that the freedom from any serious epidemic which has so characterised Changi prisoner-of-war camp has been due in no small measure to the efficiency of the hygiene services made possible by the broom-makers of Changi.

Signed F.C. Roche, 9 September 1944.

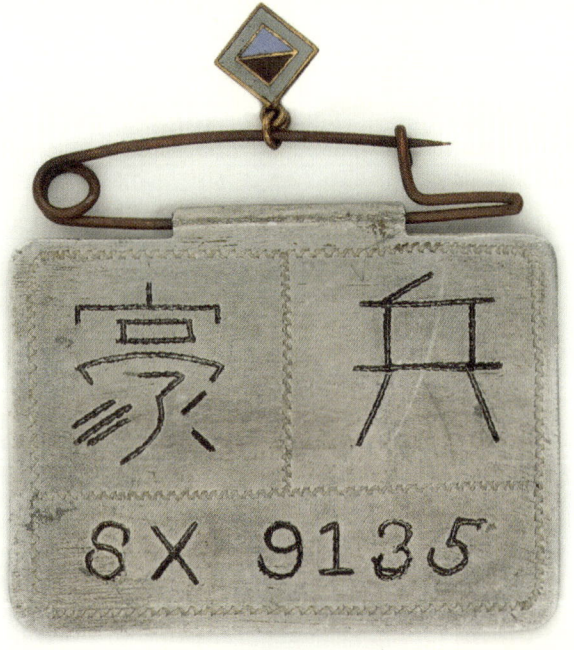

Changi's broom-makers go about their work. Murray Griffin, 1943.
ART26505

This prisoner-of-war identity disc belonged to Private John McMahon. McMahon worked at the SA Brush Company before enlisting in the AIF, and his skills were employed at the Changi Broom Factory. McMahon was seriously ill when the war finished, but survived and eventually returned to his former job at the SA Brush Company.
REL37856

ARTIFICIAL-LIMB-MAKING

ARTHUR PURDON AND S. LAD

Among the many industries set up in Changi (Selarang) Barracks by the prisoners of war is one that has been praised by the many limbless soldiers and highly commended by the more fortunate – artificial-limb-making.

Many men … had limbs amputated through the consistent contact with disease. All these men had to be catered for. Through the weary and monotonous months that followed the capitulation and the days that came after the return of working parties from Thailand and Burma there was always a prevalent possibility that a complex of uselessness would spin itself around those who had met with the misfortune [of amputation]. Something had to be done to overcome the obvious handicap and the self-consciousness that came after.

The advent of the AIF Artificial Limb Factory at Changi made it possible for many limbless to overcome that handicap, enabling them to move about and work with a maximum of freedom and balance. Much practice obtained in movement and manipulation of legs and arms during prisoner-of-war days, with limbs that were as near to perfect as possible under the prevailing conditions, would make it a simple matter to perfect when the tailor-made article was forthcoming on return to home countries. In many cases, civil occupations could be resumed with little or no inconvenience.

At No. 2 Convalescent Depot, Changi, sporting competitions embracing tennis, cricket and basketball were arranged with much success, and it was found that in a very short time one could become quite proficient with the 'homemade' limbs.

… Warrant Officer A.H.M. Purdon of the 2/30th Battalion, who had had previous experience in limb-making, was instructed to select a staff with the object of opening a factory.

The factory site was allotted in the coolie lines at the rear of the Convalescent Depot building.

…

A free hand was promised to Purdon and his staff, with no interference whatsoever. The venture did not progress as well as expected. Promises were never fulfilled, and on the whole it was a very disappointing beginning. However, the obstacles were soon overcome and the small band of technicians settled down to production. The medical authorities gave all the assistance they could, but to cooperate with the engineers and ordnance was difficult – they controlled the whole of the materials and plant in the camp, none of which could be obtained without first surmounting the miles of red tape that had followed the army from Australia. But one must see their side also. Demands from all quarters … made it necessary that a line of demarcation be drawn, and certain formalities gone through, to make sure that the goods in any requisition submitted to the stores were to be used in an essential industry or job, and would not be wasted. Materials were at a premium.

An indication as to the improvised materials and tools used in the manufacture of the artificial limbs can be gauged from the following lists:

Material available	Used as follows:
Panels of our trucks and cars which were destroyed or denied the enemy.	Construction of artificial limbs, upper and lower amputations.
Aluminium, electric fan blades, stew pans and pie dishes.	As above; advantage being lightness, but had to be reinforced where working parts were fitted.
High-tension copper wire, eight and 14 standard wire gauge (SWG).	Flattened to make baskets or moulds which were used in place of plaster of Paris. Rivets for joining panels and fitting plates together.
Ironwork from camp folding stretchers.	Hinges, knee and ankle joints, foot-raising apparatus inside knee joint.
Reinforcing steel fabric (matting).	Axles (ankle joint), reds for foot-raising apparatus. Heavy rivets hinge construction.
Fire hose.	Corsets for lower amputations. Body belts and shoulder straps. Sewing thread.
Rubber trees.	Making models and moulds for upper and lower amputations and feet.
Motor tyres.	Crutch rubbers, cushions, heels and soles for boots.

Under instruction from the Commander Royal Engineers, Private Combs of the AAOC constructed four draw knives, which under prevailing conditions proved an excellent job and showed what the Australian tradesman could do when put to the test. The only fuel available for the forging was rubber wood, which is unsuitable for the making of charcoal. The temper of the tools was even and, when sharpened, held the edge.

The engineers constructed two chains and calabashes for holding the timber while being worked.

The balance of the kit was donated by well-wishers among the troops and purchased by members of the staff from any personnel who had anything handy for use in the factory. Pliers, spanners, hacksaw frames, files, and an odd blade or two could always be had from the 'souvenir hunter' for an ounce or two of Java 'weed'…

Punches and cold chisels were made in the factory out of gudgeon pins, brake rods and various parts of dismantled motor vehicles. A drilling machine was constructed out of parts of three-breast drills and the ironwork of an ambulance stretcher, and fitted to a four-by-two-inch post. A jig-saw was built and driven by a $1/6$-horsepower refrigerator motor and would cut hardwood of up to three inches' thickness.

Files were mostly worn out and hard to procure. Sergeant J. Wilde of the RAOC made a set of eight files and a set of stocks and dies of $1/4$ inch which were of excellent quality and stood up to the work.

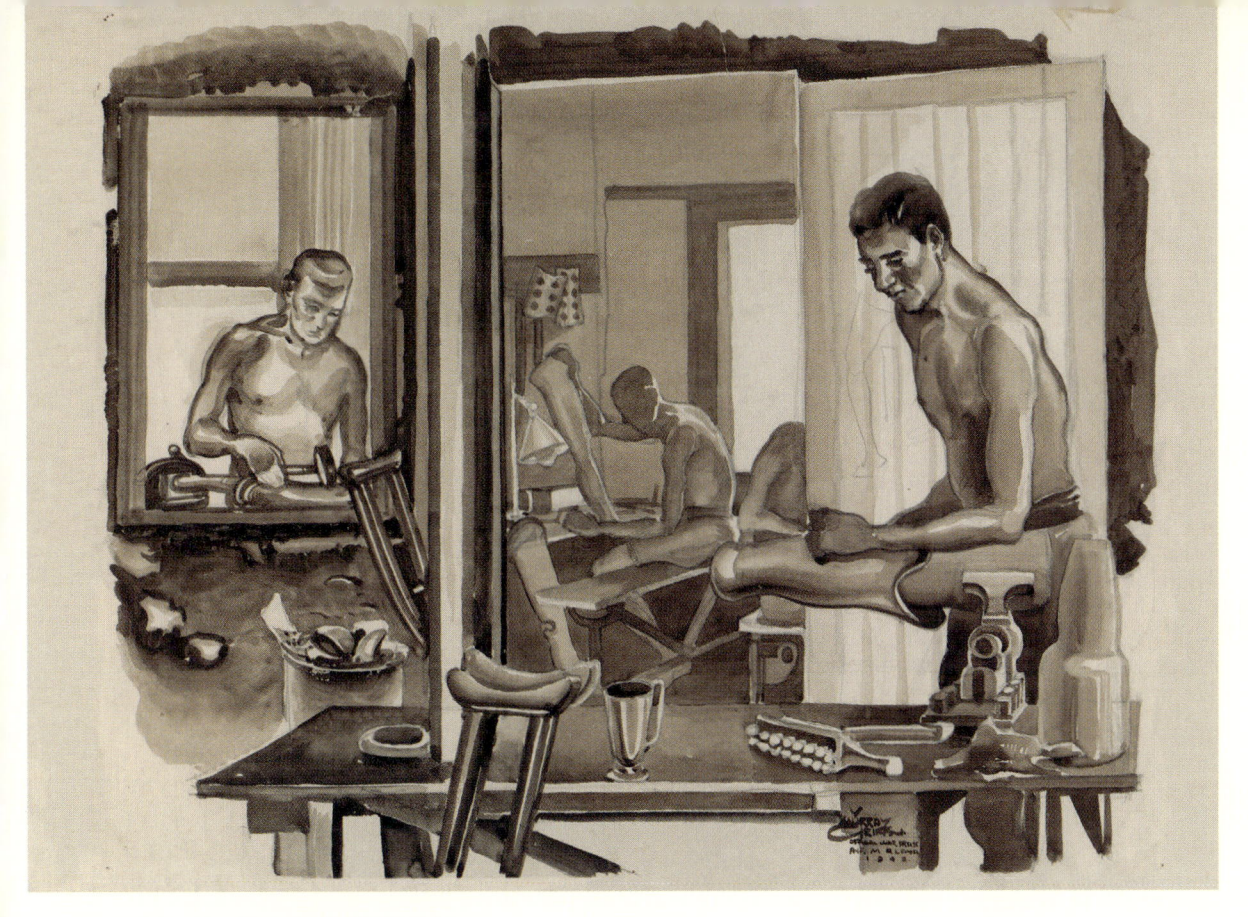

Workers in Changi's Artificial Limb Factory. Murray Griffin, 1943.
ART26503

Although articles made in the factory were never claimed to be finished ones … everything possible was done for the comfort of the wearer. There were a few faults that could not be overcome:

1. The weight of the lower limbs, at about 6¼ pounds, and upper limbs, at eight pounds, were excessive to the extent of about one pound.
2. The design of hinges to produce the desired functions had stops, pins and projecting pieces which would be destroying agents to one's clothing.
3. Springs and moving parts were noisy, in that there was no method of lubrication, giving the limb a metallic sound when in motion.
4. Bearings were just plain holes drilled through parts with a pin or bolt acting as a journal.

Many hours were spent studying the patient and thinking out ways and means of how to fit the limb so that the maximum benefit would be gained. For a time, it was one big game of trial and error. A comfortable fit would be obtained, and after the patient had worn the limb for a period, due to the

1. METAL CAGE SHAPED ON LIMB

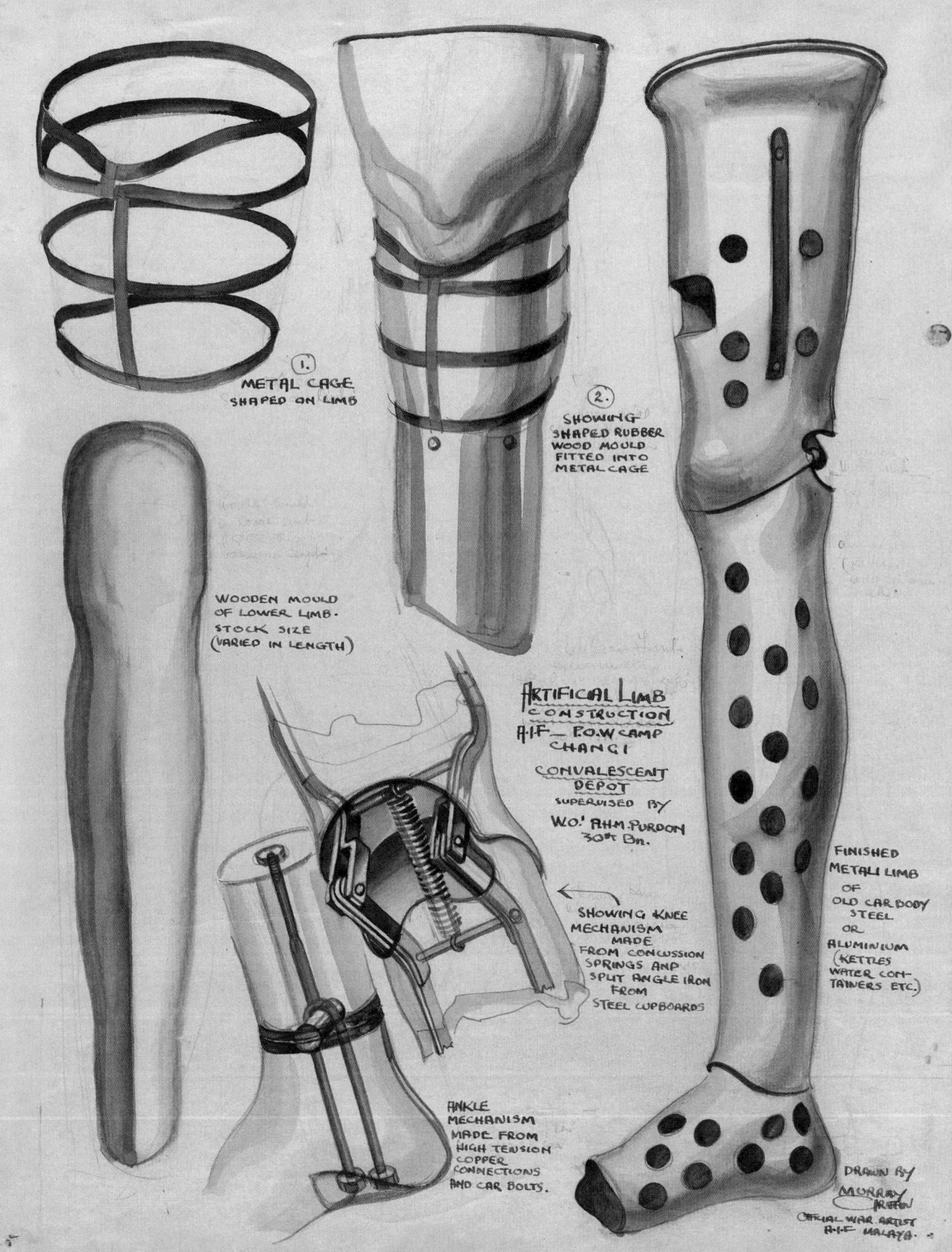

2. SHOWING SHAPED RUBBER WOOD MOULD FITTED INTO METAL CAGE

WOODEN MOULD OF LOWER LIMB. STOCK SIZE (VARIED IN LENGTH)

ARTIFICAL LIMB CONSTRUCTION
A.I.F. P.O.W CAMP CHANGI
CONVALESCENT DEPOT
SUPERVISED BY W.O.¹ A.H.M. PURDON 30ᵗʰ Bn.

SHOWING KNEE MECHANISM MADE FROM CONCUSSION SPRINGS AND SPLIT ANGLE IRON FROM STEEL CUPBOARDS

ANKLE MECHANISM MADE FROM HIGH TENSION COPPER CONNECTIONS AND CAR BOLTS.

FINISHED METAL LIMB OF OLD CAR BODY STEEL OR ALUMINIUM (KETTLES, WATER CONTAINERS ETC.)

DRAWN BY MURRAY GRIFFIN
OFFICIAL WAR ARTIST A.I.F. MALAYA

ARTIFICIAL-LIMB-MAKING

wasting of the tissues of the stump, the artificial limb would have to be remade.

The only footwear available were boots and a few South African Red Cross issues, and these normally would be much too heavy to attach to an artificial limb. When it was discovered that the limb was too heavy, the foot was cut off and a peg fitted.

Feet were first made of spruce from the rails of a billiard table that was used in the Gordon Highlanders NAAFI canteen …

The patients … in some cases were a problem. All had been through the terrors of battle, and making the best of poor hospital conditions in a prison camp on a deficient rice diet is hardly the place to build up strength after losing a limb. Others were overconfident. The latter were allowed the use of the limb for only one hour a day, and then [it was] taken from them. This method was used to allow the stump to harden up gradually. A few hours' practice over a few days and the patient was able to move almost naturally and without the aid of a stick or crutch

…

Too much cannot be given the small band of workers under Purdon who worked day and night in an effort to fit the many needy men. Corporal Webber did an excellent job in the carving of moulds. Sergeant Fanning was a fine tradesman and the most important man in the factory, doing the difficult work of fitting the lower amputations. Private Melrose proved an energetic and conscientious wood carver and assembler. Corporal Gould (a limbless himself), technically inclined, did wonderful work in any capacity. Later, Lance Corporal L. Campbell (2/10th Field Coy), another limbless, did splendid work on the mechanical and woodwork side. Purdon's task was a most arduous one, and his retentive memory of technical knowledge learned years previously can be thanked for the progress of the industry in Changi among prisoners of war.

The limbless will remember the early days in Changi when movement was a hardship, and later [when] the manufacture of artificial limbs raised morale and enabled them to take their place in activity alongside the fit men. Prospects of fitting employment at a later date … will be the least of the worries of others who have become so expert in the use of their limbs made from the proverbial scrap heap.

Drawing on his pre-war experience, Warrant Officer Arthur Purdon produced these designs for artificial limbs, as illustrated by Murray Griffin. The moveable joint, which allowed the artificial limb to move more naturally, became known as the Purdon joint.
ART26502

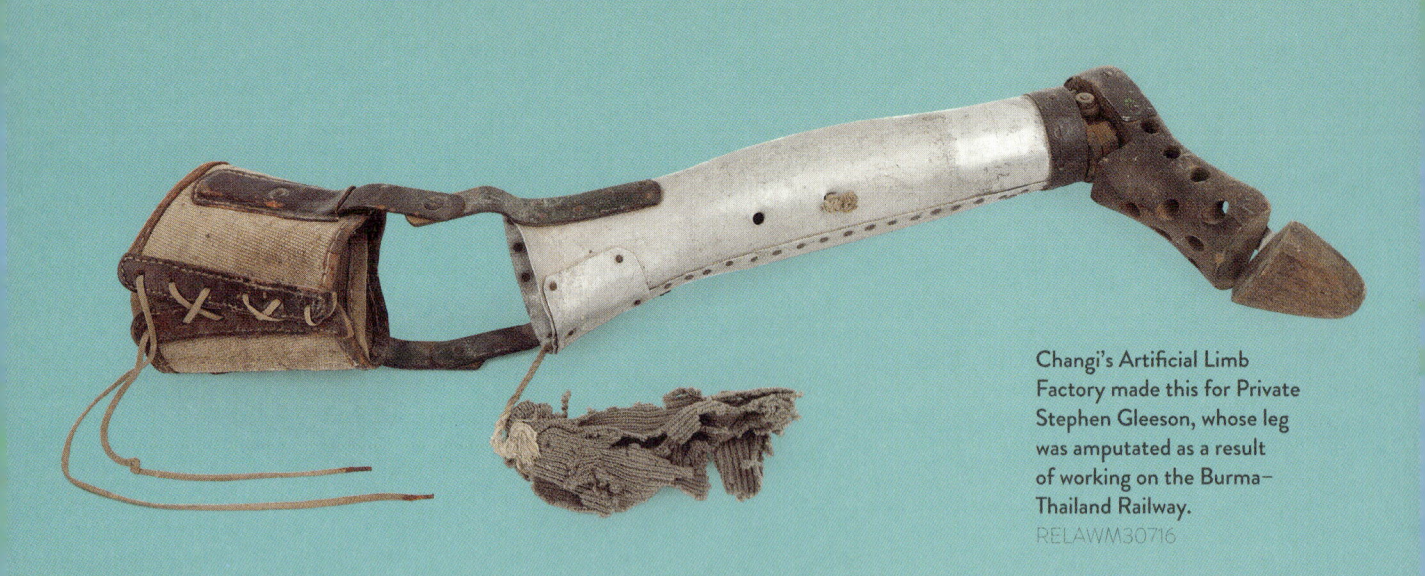

Changi's Artificial Limb Factory made this for Private Stephen Gleeson, whose leg was amputated as a result of working on the Burma–Thailand Railway.
RELAWM30716

Private Gleeson's artificial leg: a pioneering medical innovation

Kerry Neale
Australian War Memorial

A TRUCKER FROM the town of Boulder, Western Australia, Private Stephen Gleeson of the 2/4th Machine Gun Battalion was in Singapore for less than a month before the capitulation. After more than a year at Changi, Gleeson embarked with H Force in May 1943 to work on the Burma–Thailand Railway.

At some point after he left for Thailand, Gleeson's right leg was amputated below the knee. While working on the railway in the jungle, many prisoners got cuts or abrasions on their legs due to the lack of proper clothing and footwear, and these sores often became septic. This may have been what happened to Gleeson.

This leg was made for Gleeson in Changi by Warrant Officer Arthur Purdon of the 2/30th Battalion. Purdon was working as a health inspector when he enlisted in the Second AIF on 17 January 1941. During his captivity Purdon established a factory to make for his fellow prisoners artificial limbs from aluminium and other waste metal taken from Japanese dumps. As part of this work he invented the Purdon joint, which allowed the limbs to move in a similar fashion to a normal leg.

While the limbs may have been made from waste material, they were essential in providing much-needed support and a sense of freedom to men who were already battling difficult conditions in captivity.

Health and survival

THE VITAMIN CENTRE

ROBERT MORTON

Until a few years ago, very few people outside the medical profession had heard of vitamins. Even today people regard them suspiciously, as something new-fangled that patent food manufacturers say is contained in their products, and which will magically transform a thin, anaemic office worker into a veritable Don Athaldo [a famous Australian strongman/bodybuilder of the era who promoted a range of health elixirs]. How often do we hear people of the older generation say that in their day there were no such things as vitamins, and that they lived quite well on good, plain food … In Australia, where there is plenty of good food, people can safely forget about vitamins because there is an abundant supply of everyday food, and [cases of] sickness and death caused by their absence are unknown.

In the East, however, and more particularly in the prison camp, vitamins assumed a real significance, because the poor food supplied to us could not keep men in good health without being supplemented by vitamins from some extraneous source. The main or practically the only food supplied by the Japanese was rice … Rice, when it comes from the plant, contains quite enough vitamin B to enable the body to digest it, but to make it keep it is nearly always milled (for example, the outside layer, which incidentally contains the bulk of the vitamin, is removed, leaving the white polished rice of commerce). A diet consisting of this polished rice alone will not prevent that 'scourge of the East' – beriberi – which is caused by an insufficient supply of vitamin B1 in the food, and it was not long before a lot of men in the camp had this disease. One of the chief foods containing this essential vitamin B1 is yeast, and so in April 1942 at Selarang the Yeast Centre was established to supply ever-increasing demands for this vitamin.

This yeast, which is the same as that used in breweries, is a small living cell. Our hosts supplied some brewers' yeast from the Singapore brewery with which to start our culture and we carried on from this for nearly two years. The food on which yeast grows is potatoes, flour and sugar, and this had to be deducted from the general camp rations. The potatoes were boiled and mashed, the flour and sugar added, and some yeast seed placed in this mixture. Yeast cells multiply rapidly, and after about 36 hours the brew was ready for drinking – and quite a popular drink it was, too, judging by the number of people always hanging about trying to get 'one on the house'. In fact, yeast was the nearest thing to the 'dinkum brew' in the camp; one of the other things always present with yeast is alcohol, and I venture to say many a teetotaller enjoyed his yeast for reasons quite unsuspected by him. Before the yeast was distributed the number of cells it contained was always counted by microscope. A good yeast contains about 100 000 cells per cubic millimetre, which will be better understood by the average reader as about 30 billion in a tumblerful. Our hosts discontinued supplying flour to the camp late in 1942, and the yeast had then to be fed on rice polishings instead. This yeast was not quite as good, but we continued making it right up till January 1944, when over 100 gallons a day were being made for the AIF alone. The brewing room looked quite like a brewery, with eight or ten 54-gallon barrels lining the wall, and men who knew said the smell was identical … thirty to forty thousand gallons of yeast were made for the AIF in 20 months.

Early in 1943 medical officers were very concerned about a number of diseases breaking out, caused in their opinion by the lack of vitamin B2 in the food. This vitamin is largely contained in green vegetables and meat, and our supply of these articles, if any, was always most meagre. It was reasoned out that grass, being a green, should contain the same vitamin, and so began a process to extract the vitamin from it. At first the grass was merely boiled and the water drained off and drunk, but the heat partially destroyed the vitamin, so a process was evolved to extract it cold. The ordnance people made a machine for the purpose which, although it might have made Heath Robinson turn in his grave, served excellently. The best grass was found to be guinea or couch, with paspalum next, and a good last lalang, but grass was so scarce in the camp and so much was being used that before long we were glad to use any obtainable. Men were sent out in a trailer to gather bags of grass and bring it to the factory.

The machine for treating the grass was driven by an electric motor and consisted of a large lawnmower and two rollers. The grass was first put through the mower, which cut it into small lengths, and was then fed into the rollers – all by hand, of course. It had to be put through the rollers three or four times to break up the cells of the grass in which the vitamin is found. When the grass was crushed fine enough it was then rammed into large percolators of about 25 gallons' capacity, similar to

Murray Griffin's drawing of the main yeast distribution centre at Selarang.
ART26506

HEALTH AND SURVIVAL

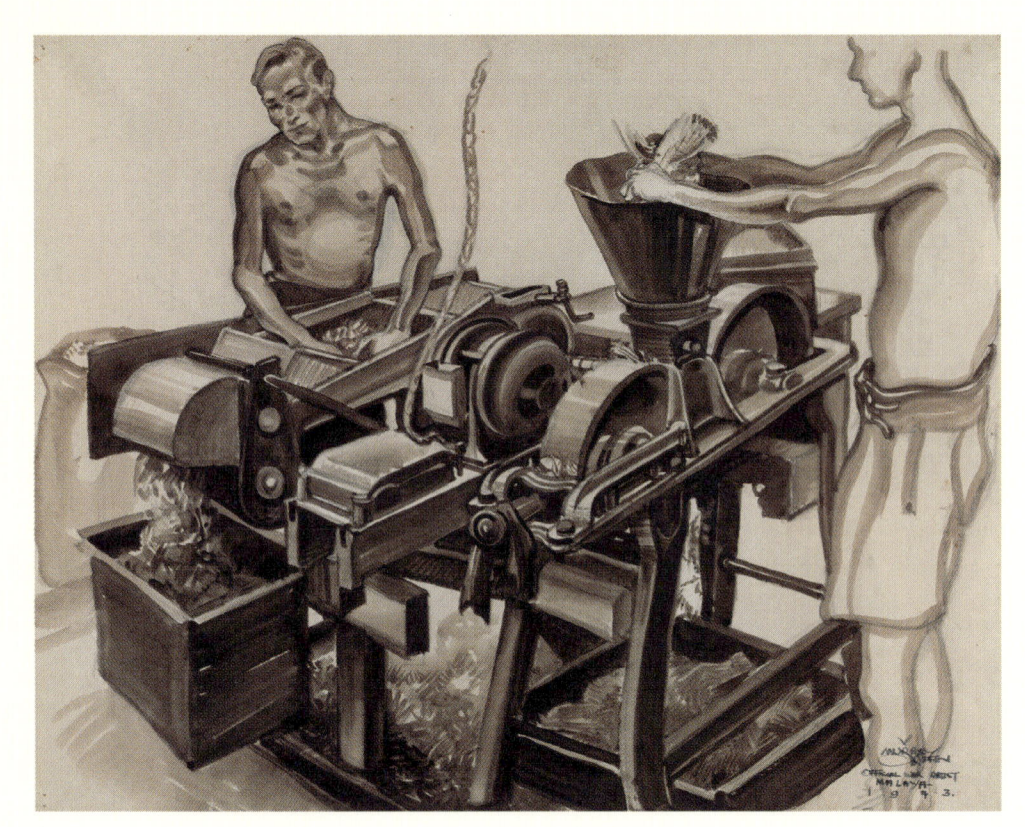

LEFT **Two members of the Vitamin Centre crush and soak grass. The B2 vitamins obtained from the grass extract helped prevent beriberi. Murray Griffin, 1943.**
ART24471

RIGHT **A rice-polishings extractor. Drawing by Murray Griffin.**
ART26454

the type a chemist uses, and the right amount of water added to the top. The water slowly seeped through the crushed grass, dissolving out the vitamin from the broken grass cells as it went, and when it ran out from the bottom of the percolator was ready for drinking. It was not nearly as pleasant to drink as yeast; in fact, some of the descriptions of its taste I have heard would never pass the censor … but to a camp so deficient in medical supplies of any kind it was a godsend. In October 1944, 80 gallons a day of grass extract were being made, and in the 18 months previous I would estimate that some 15 to 20 gallons were made. This was made from about 200 tons of grass or 15 000 sacks full. These figures will give some indication of the work involved in the collection and crushing of the grass.

Grass must be used fresh and cannot be stored against a rainy day. Leaves of certain plants contain the same vitamin as grass and these, if dried and powdered, can be extracted in percolation in the same way … and have the advantage of being able to be stored for months. They had on the other hand a serious disadvantage, and that was their vile taste. So leaf extract was only used when the grass-cutting machine broke down or to supplement the grass extract

THE VITAMIN CENTRE

1943 the Japanese, either through shortage of rice or kindness of heart, started to replace part of the rice ration with soya beans … one of the best foods in the world from a nutritional point of view. There was great rejoicing in the camp until the hygiene officer discovered that most of the beans were leaving the body just as they had entered it, being too hard to be digested. Some Dutchmen in the camp then came to the rescue and showed us how to make tempeh from the beans … There is a fungus named rhizopus found in hibiscus flowers, which abound in Singapore, and this fungus when grown on the beans softens them and makes them digestible. Before the fungus can grow on them the husks have to be removed from the beans. This is done by soaking the beans in water and then passing them between two loose rollers. After the husks are removed the fungus seed is mixed through the beans which are then spread about one inch thick on trays. After about 36 hours the beans are covered with a grey furry fungus like that which grows on a piece of old cheese, and have become a solid mass now ready for cooking. It is excellent fried, baked, or boiled; in fact, almost anything can be done with it. Medical officers were convinced that making tempeh from the beans was the best way to get the most value from them, and demonstrations were held at the Vitamin Centre to instruct the cooks how

Grass must be used fresh and cannot be stored

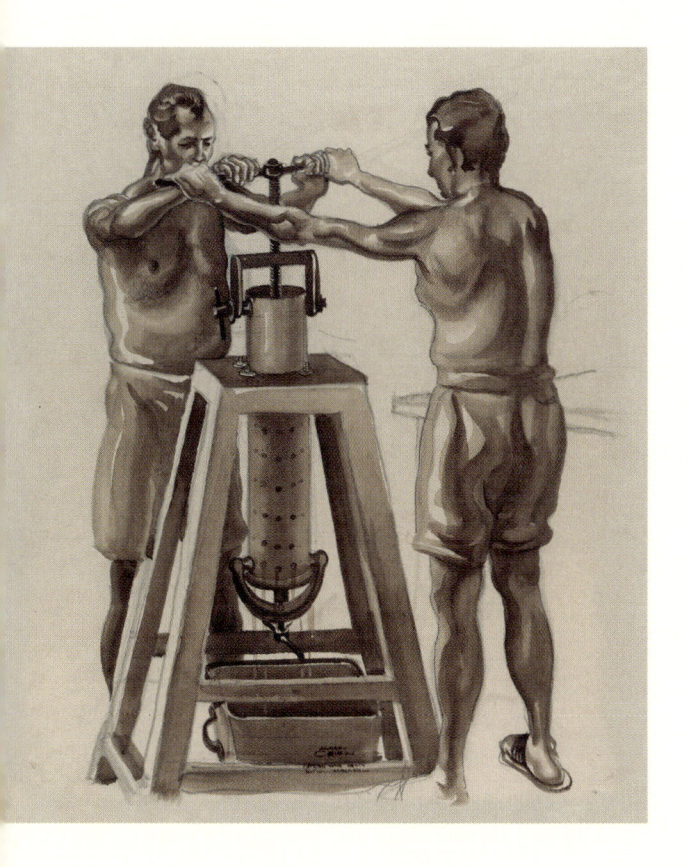

when demand exceeded possible production. The leaves used most were Straits rhododendron [and] Malaya passionfruit … The leaves were brought to the factory, where they were dried either in the sun or in a charcoal drying room. They were then powdered up finely by a homemade ball mill. This mill consisted of a 40-gallon steel drum containing old nuts and bolts, and was turned by an electric motor. When it operated the din could be heard miles away. The leaves thus reduced to a fairly fine powder were stored for use when required.

Another branch of the Vitamin Centre was the tempeh department. In the latter part of

HEALTH AND SURVIVAL

to prepare this Javanese dish. Personally, when fried I thought tempeh most tasty – something between mushrooms and pork!

Another branch of the work done in the Vitamin Centre was the making of rice polishings extract. Rice polishings are that part of the rice which is removed by milling, just as bran and pollard are removed from wheat. Most of the vitamin B1 in rice is removed with polishings, consequently these rice polishings are very rich in vitamins. They were used medicinally right through, but anything more than two to three ounces acts like a super-dose of Epsom salts. Sometimes the medical officers wished to administer much more than two ounces, hence the need for making an extract. To make the extract, the rice polishings were soaked in slightly acidic water overnight and next morning were wrapped in canvas and placed in the extracting press. This was a hollow steel cylinder into which a plunger was screwed. This squeezed the extract containing the vitamin out of the polishings. Men could drink up to a pint of this extract – equivalent to about ¾ pound of original polishings – without any ill-effect.

There was one more department in the Vitamin Centre which, although not connected in any way with vitamins, deserves mention. This was the distillery. Alcohol for use in the operating theatre and skin wards of the hospital was terribly scarce and suitably necessary. Quite a lot was made by fermenting old peelings, skins and sugar and distilling off the alcohol. When sugar rose to a price of $10 per pound and the peelings and skins were being used in stews the source of raw material was gone until, fortunately

ABOVE **This grass-cutting machine was built in Changi from bits and pieces and was run on electricity. The grass was collected and then cut, crushed and soaked for 24 hours. This soup would then be issued as a B2 vitamin supplement.**
ART26507

LEFT **This Aspinall photograph shows a group preparing rations. Men would receive a serve of rice and a serve of grass soup.**
P02569.138

– depending on how you look at it – our hosts sent into the camp a shipment of rice too bad to eat. With a fungus called Samsu, which the Chinese use for making rice wine or toddy, this bad rice was turned first into sugar, then alcohol. For obvious reasons this manufacture of alcohol was not generally known among the troops, and no doubt many would be surprised to know that the spirit which made them smart when applied to their tinea was made in the camp from rice too bad for them to eat.

How very fortunate the camp was in having at its disposal chemists, botanists, and engineers who were able by their knowledge and ingenuity not only to keep men tolerably healthy but also to save many lives.

HYGIENE
CARL GUNTHER

On arrival at the main prisoner-of-war camp it was found that the sewerage system had been put out of action by bombing, and that the whole area had been grossly fouled. Millions of flies were present. In addition, the water mains were out of action, and the only sources of supply were some large storage tanks and a few native washing-places at the outlets of subsoil anti-malarial drains. The first three tasks, undertaken at once, were to arrange for chlorinating all drinking water, to dig pit-latrines, and to clean up the area.

It was not possible, however, to destroy the infected flies before they could do any damage, and a widespread dysentery epidemic broke out. This outbreak coincided with the arrival of the Australian General Hospitals; these were not sited in the AIF area at Selarang, but were grouped with the British hospital at Roberts Barracks. The Australian hospital site was heavily fouled, and was without water or any form of sanitation. Large working parties quickly remedied these defects, and then the hygiene control of the whole hospital area was handed over to the British. The hospitals were overcrowded with dysentery patients from the day of their arrival.

Meanwhile, the problem of providing safe latrines for the AIF area was a difficult one, as there were no materials for fly-proofing and for making anti-larval aprons. The first move was to dig large groups of pits, 20 feet long by two-feet-six-inches wide, and 20 feet deep, distant some three to four hundred yards from buildings. These proved inconvenient and unsatisfactory.

Gradually, from various sources, a supply of 16-inch earth-augers was acquired. The AIF area was divided into sections, and each section was placed under the supervision of a trained NCO from the 2/5th Field Hygiene Section.

Boreholes proved to be most satisfactory in the soil of this area. The plan finally evolved was to dig 15 boreholes, 16 to 20 feet deep, per 100 men; five per 100 were opened for ten days, then sealed with pugged clay for 20 days. This procedure ensured that the flies which emerged from their pupa-cases from about the 12th day were trapped – they were found, dead, when the holes were re-opened … They were not offensive, and could safely and conveniently be sited close to living quarters. Overloading beyond the five per cent allowance caused trouble. Wooden covers with hinged lids were used on the boreholes; these were made at first by the RAE workshops, but later the hygiene staff took over all such construction work also. After the move to Changi Gaol, the IJA guards complained that the dropping of borehole lids was annoying them – it was never ascertained whether the real reason for this annoyance was that it disturbed their sleep or whether it was because the sounds so strongly resembled explosions – and a new type of cover had to be devised: Mark II, rubber-cushioned, was not successful, but Mark III, with pivoted sliding lid, was quite noiseless. The triple-rotation borehole system was also used after the transfer of the main camp to Changi Gaol.

When the camp was finally connected to the main Singapore water supply, and when it was established that enough water would be available to supply the sewers, the sewerage system was repaired with an astonishing variety of improvised materials. By the end of 1943 almost the whole of the AIF area was connected to the septic tanks; these were, of course, grossly overloaded, but an efficient service was nevertheless maintained. Where inside closets were insufficient, separate closets and 'family six-holers' made of metal from barrack lockers welded up by the RAE workshops were installed outside; these were either let into the inspection-chambers or tapped into the sewer-lines. Screens for latrines were plaited from coconut-palm fronds.

Owing to the frequent failures in the water supply [caused by] the inefficiency of the Japanese administration, it was necessary to maintain emergency boreholes all the time.

…

Refuse disposal was by burial in deep pits, digestion in Otway pits [septic tanks], or incineration, according to the type of refuse and the facilities available. A system of composting refuse to provide manure for the vegetable gardens was developed; manure was also provided by safely decomposed sludge from the septic tanks and by urine collected in buckets. Fly controllers on the hygiene staff patrolled all kitchens, latrine areas, refuse pits, compost heaps and gardens twice a week, and kept fly-breeding at a minimum.

After the first big fly-borne dysentery epidemic, [a result of] the fouled state of the area when the troops moved in, only sporadic cases of fly-borne dysentery occurred; there were a number of local epidemics of

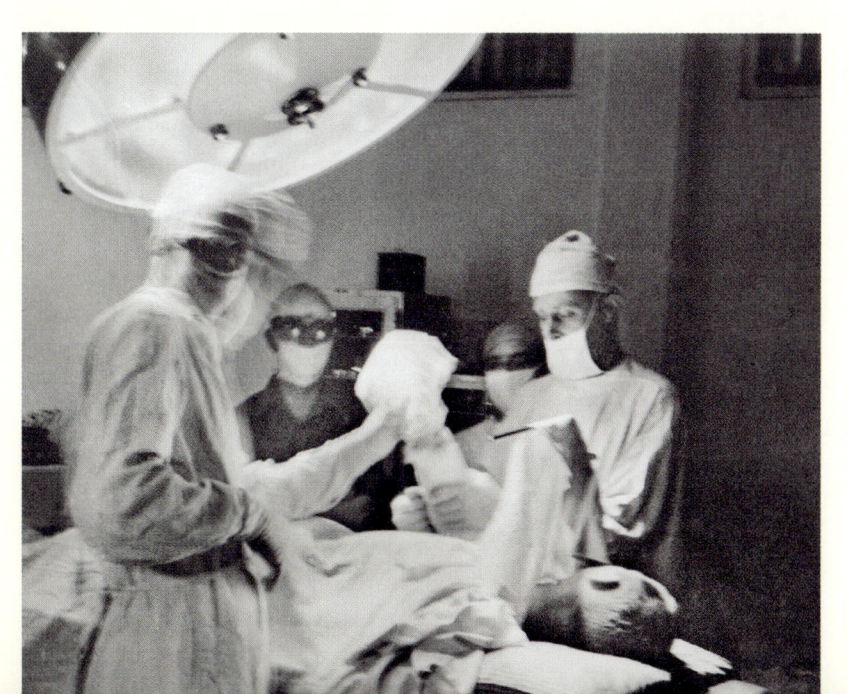

Lieutenant Colonel (Dr) Charles Osborn of the 13th Australian General Hospital with three of his staff, operating on a patient in Roberts Hospital. Photograph by Major John Rosson.
P04485.051

233

The latrines at Changi had closed lids designed to stop flies spreading disease. These photographs were taken secretly by Kennedy Burnside in 1942.

HYGIENE

This first-aid box was passed to Captain Willem van Beek of the Royal Dutch East Indies Army, who was a camp commander of the Burma section of the Burma–Thailand Railway. It had belonged to an unidentified Australian soldier in A Force. Inside the lid of the box the soldier had recorded the names of places he had visited with the AIF, from his enlistment in Martin Place, Sydney, to the final entry, 'Thailand' – possibly indicating that the owner died there. These names indicate he was with a unit of the 22nd Brigade. Captain van Beek – whom the Australian prisoners called 'Johnny' – returned to the Netherlands after the war. The box was later donated to the Australian War Memorial by van Beek's children, who felt that, although the box was their father's for a time, its place was in Australia.
REL33302

considerable severity, but all of these were traced to the presence of dysentery carriers among food-handlers. So many carriers were present among the troops that it was difficult to prevent this happening at times, especially as it was hard to persuade laymen that some of the minor hygiene regulations were not merely put out because of red tape and fussiness. In every instance these epidemics were under control within 24 hours of the first cases being reported.

…

Successful disease control depends to a great extent on the intelligent and willing cooperation of each individual concerned. No amount of work, however well organised and carried out, can produce successful results alone. The fact that the AIF had consistently the best results of any group among the camps on Singapore Island not only depended on the work done by the hygiene staffs but was also a tribute to the 'hygiene-mindedness' and essential discipline of the Australian troops.

SKIN DISEASE AMONG PRISONERS OF WAR IN MALAYA

BURNETT CLARKE

Skin diseases among the prisoners of war in Malaya were some of the major conditions with which the authorities had to contend, as so many factors had to be considered. It could be stated that after the third month of captivity – that is, late May or early June 1942 – approximately one-fifth of hospital patients were suffering from incapacitating skin lesions, while about half of the remainder had some form of skin trouble.

The problems had to be dealt with from many angles: the cause, the treatment and the economic effects. Our hosts insisted that we should maintain our own camps and also supply so many 'bodies' for work parties, so that shortage of manpower was an [issue].

Many diseases of the skin with which our medical officers were unfamiliar made their appearance. It has been stated that some of these diseases were not described in [our] medical books, and that they were due to those new and unexpected conditions into which we were unfortunately thrust so suddenly. Furthermore, the difficulties of treatment were increased as we were dependent upon our hosts for medical supplies, and it did appear to us that the Japanese had no time for the sick; this later became apparent when they sought the back door to consult our AMC officers. In this latter eventuality many amusing and even embarrassing situations occurred, two of which may be mentioned. One of the camp guards suffering from scabies of the buttock and genitals approached an officer for 'Medicine, make OK.' He was vigorously rubbing his groin, and when asked by the officer, 'Itchy?' looked astonished and went to great trouble to explain that he had two testicles. [The Japanese word *ichi* means 'one'.]

Very few medical officers of the AMC wore the Red Cross armband after the camp was established; it was almost invariably worn by non-medical officers and padres. On an occasion several 'Jays' in a truck saw an officer with a Red Cross armband … he said he belonged to the hospital, whereupon he was invited to get into the motor truck, taken to a lonely spot in the scrub, shown acute venereal disease and asked to treat it. The officer concerned was a padre. It is believed that he had to walk home.

There were many causes of skin troubles; among the chief were the constant humidity, which caused sweating, meaning the skin was inclined to become soggy and the other layers rubbed off easily. This exposed surface easily became infected, particularly with tinea and other germs … Again, our hosts were by no means liberal with soap, water and firewood, and as a result personal hygiene and washing of clothes were big problems and full of difficulties. Probably the greatest cause of skin troubles was due to food and vitamin deficiency, and possibly also to toxic or poisonous substances in certain foodstuffs. Again, the general health of the men had become so undermined that they lost their natural immunity, and became even seriously ill from infections which at home would not be even noticed.

Upon entering the prison camp our hosts placed us on a coolie diet, the main item of which was about 16 ounces of milled rice per man per day. The result was the early appearance of beriberi, to be followed about four weeks later by most distressing skin trouble, particularly around the genitals. The condition was known locally as 'rice balls' or 'Changi balls' – the medical term was scrotal dermatitis.

The main sign of this disease was a red, swollen scrotum, [the redness] often extending to the penis, into both groins, and back to the anus. The walk was most characteristic: legs wide apart, body bent forward and the slow gait, called by the men the 'Changi walk'. In the early stages of this complaint the itch was intolerable and the constant scratching with the hands whether in or out of the pocket was referred to as the 'Malayan salute'. Very few prisoners escaped this disease; more serious cases became completely bedridden. Some men who were on IJA working parties were brought to hospital in an appalling condition. This disease was almost invariably associated with other lesions, such as splitting of the corners of the mouth, swollen sore lips, and swollen red tongue with part of the membrane ulcerated.

The mucous lining of the mouth and throat was often in the same state. A great many developed eye troubles, sometimes so serious as to involve the eyesight; some men even went blind.

In a small percentage of scrotal dermatitis [cases] diphtheria infection took place in the raw areas and made the condition more serious – some deaths did occur. In a great many, there was also tinea or Dhobie itch present in addition to other complaints.

It did respond to Marmite given in daily doses

It was soon recognised by the characteristic appearance that we were dealing with a serious vitamin deficiency disease, and that it did respond to Marmite [which was high in Vitamin B] given in daily doses. Of course, treatment of the local condition was also necessary and in fact was most difficult at first owing to water shortage and consequent lack of bathing. Another big factor was that in an attempt to relieve the itch many strong caustic lotions had been used and these had caused 'chemical dermatitis' to supervene on the deficiency disease. Medical supplies were at this time very low, and in response to one appeal we were presented with a truckload of old clothes to wash up and turn into dressings. This condition was also present in the same proportion among the Timor, Java and other parties that arrived in Changi. Curiously enough, it was rarely seen amongst those of 'up-country' parties, or among those unfortunates who were incarcerated in prisons under Japanese management.

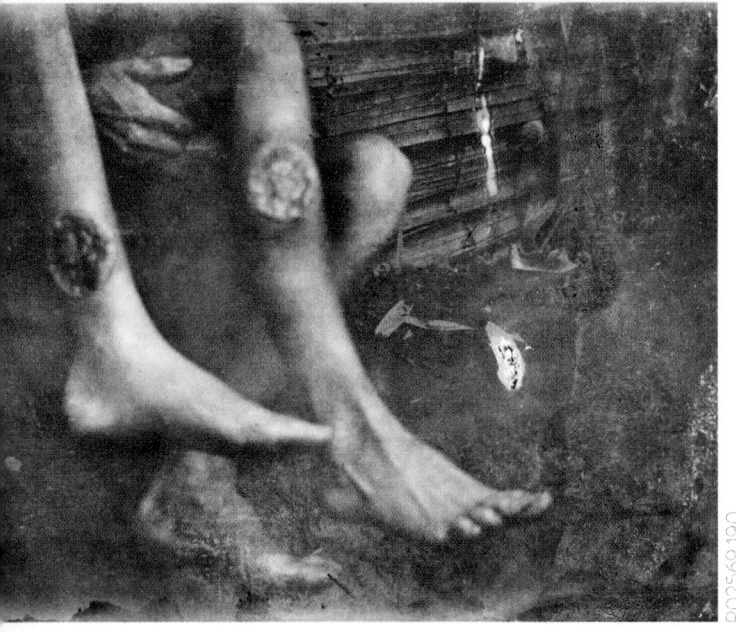

While with F Force in Thailand, George Aspinall took these photographs showing tropical ulcers on the legs of prisoners.

When the Red Cross ship arrived in October 1942 with food and medical supplies scrotal dermatitis completely disappeared, and except in a few instances was not seen again until July 1944, when the Japanese segregated the whole camp around the Changi Gaol and food supplies were limited to rice, green leaves and 'modern girls' [the name given to small dried fish, described as 'two-faced and no guts'] – the latter about twice per week. If meat was in the diet, the condition was not so severe, but the prisoners went months without meat, and on the few occasions that it was supplied to us the issue was about two or three ounces, including bone and fat, per man.

Many were the remedies tried out for this complaint, and local industry played its part. The [Vitamin Centre] produced many gallons of 'grass juice' – it was known by less-complimentary names … We believed it supplied some riboflavin [vitamin B2].

The [Vitamin Centre] 'under official patronage' was able to produce up to 30 ounces of 90 per cent pure alcohol per week from cookhouse refuse, bad fruit, banana skins and such-like debris.

An attempt to manufacture ersatz Marmite proved partly successful, but was abandoned owing to the high cost and inability to obtain the necessary raw material.

Whenever conditions changed for the better and cooler weather appeared this condition disappeared, only to return when we reverted to a poor regime. This was especially apparent in July 1944, when we were concentrated in the Changi Gaol area. At this time, however, the proportion of officers was greater than Other Ranks involved.

Painful feet, locally known as 'happy feet', affected hundreds of men. The curious feature of this was that while walking about there was no trouble, but immediately on rest, and particularly at night, pain was so bad that they could not sleep and preferred to get up and walk about.

Memories of Changi must recall scabies. It is extremely doubtful if any man from high-ranking officer to lowly private escaped. Sometimes the seniors bluffed themselves that it was a psychological itch or prickly heat, but finally gave in. For men whose health was undermined by malaria, poor food and the 'too-long-in-the-tropics' syndrome, and thus had lost their resistance to infection, scabies played havoc. The infected areas resulted in multiple ulcers of various sizes and abscess formation of huge proportions, especially in the buttock. They eventually healed, leaving behind pigmented scars with a tissue-paper-thin covering. As scabies was no respecter of personnel or of the area attacked, many awkward questions may be asked when we return to our civil life.

Control of scabies was most difficult, the chief reasons being: that sulphur was our only available drug and the purity of the rock sulphur supplied would not conform to Australian standards; and that opportunities for fumigation of clothes and bedding were few and far between, and as fast as one epidemic was under control our hosts would return to us men from outlying parties or from one of their gaols. These latter were so heavily infected that a fresh epidemic broke out. Things reached a stage where we began to feel lonely if scabies and bugs deserted us.

Tropical ulcers were one of our most serious diseases. As has been mentioned before, many factors like disease and semi-starvation undermined the constitution, rendering the man an easy victim to fresh troubles. These ulcers appeared mostly on the legs and feet; they varied in size and were extremely painful. Many men had amputations performed to save their lives and many will remain permanent invalids, while all will carry scars. Very few of even the small ulcers healed up under 100 days; many are still laid low after more than one year. The human wrecks that returned from the Burma–Thailand parties in December 1943 bore evidence of what our men were forced to suffer by their hosts. It all tended to confirm our view that [the Japanese] had no time for the sick man, as in their own country, at any rate, they had adequate replacements.

> **We began to feel lonely if scabies or bugs deserted us**

Many men suffered from a condition resembling, in many respects, pellagra. Some became acutely ill when certain foodstuff was served up. The epidemic of March and April 1944 – sore mouths, skinned tongues and lips, skin rashes on limbs and bodies, many [sufferers] of which were seriously ill and

HEALTH AND SURVIVAL

some [of which] died – will always be remembered by the sufferers and those who had to look after them in hospital. The subsequent curious discoloration of the skin involved traces of all colours. The brilliant red faded and left them spotted, black, red, brown and white all intermingled over the whole body. The skin was of the texture of a baby, reacted violently to sunlight and was easily ulcerated. Many men will return home with curiously spotted skins.

Owing to the lack of clothing, shirts were rarely worn: the usual daily dress was headgear of a variety of patterns, shorts in variable stages of repair and disrepair, and footwear varying from wooden clogs and sandshoes to a few good army-issue boots. In the majority of normal men the skin gradually tanned a dirty brown colour which withstood the sun, but this tan would not hold; after a few days in the shade, or if wearing a shirt, the brown left and precautions against sunburn had to be taken on resuming outdoor life.

The common everyday skin troubles were always with us as well as these deficiency diseases, but caused less concern as they did not necessarily put a man on the very sick list unless some sickness like malaria or beriberi were also present.

Tinea in its many varieties was always to be seen; some types would attack the flat surfaces of the body and spread over huge areas so that one was liable to consider that a map had been drawn on his chest or back. This complaint caused little or no inconvenience and was not always reported for economic

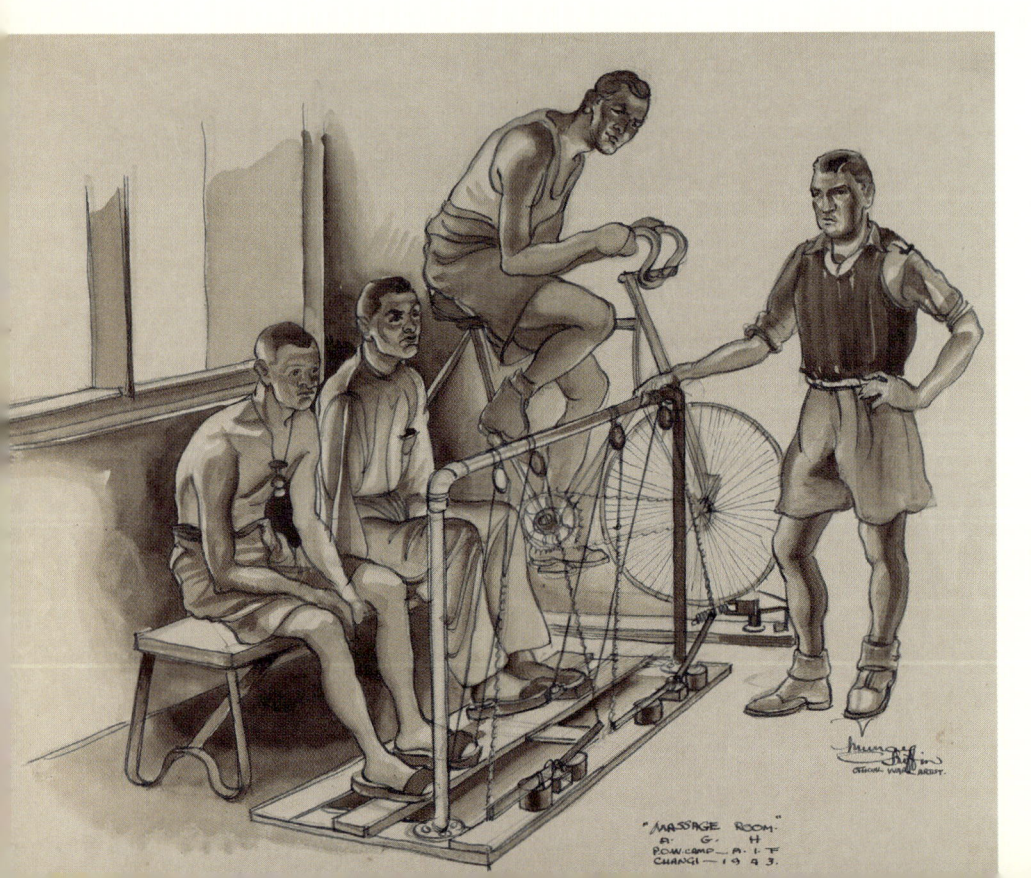

The massage (physiotherapy) room of the hospital. This machine, powered by bicycle, was made to exercise the feet of beriberi patients. Murray Griffin, 1943.
ART26504

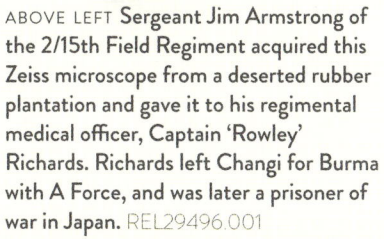

ABOVE LEFT Sergeant Jim Armstrong of the 2/15th Field Regiment acquired this Zeiss microscope from a deserted rubber plantation and gave it to his regimental medical officer, Captain 'Rowley' Richards. Richards left Changi for Burma with A Force, and was later a prisoner of war in Japan. REL29496.001

ABOVE RIGHT This medical box belonged to Major Alan Hazelton of the 2/10th Field Ambulance. Captured at Singapore, Hazelton became the senior medical officer in D Force on the Burma–Thailand Railway and at Nakhom Pathom camp in Thailand. REL/21924

BELOW This eye-instrument kit from HMAS *Perth* came into the possession of Major Hazelton. He was made the eye specialist owing to his training in ophthalmology at Royal Prince Alfred Hospital in Sydney. REL/21926

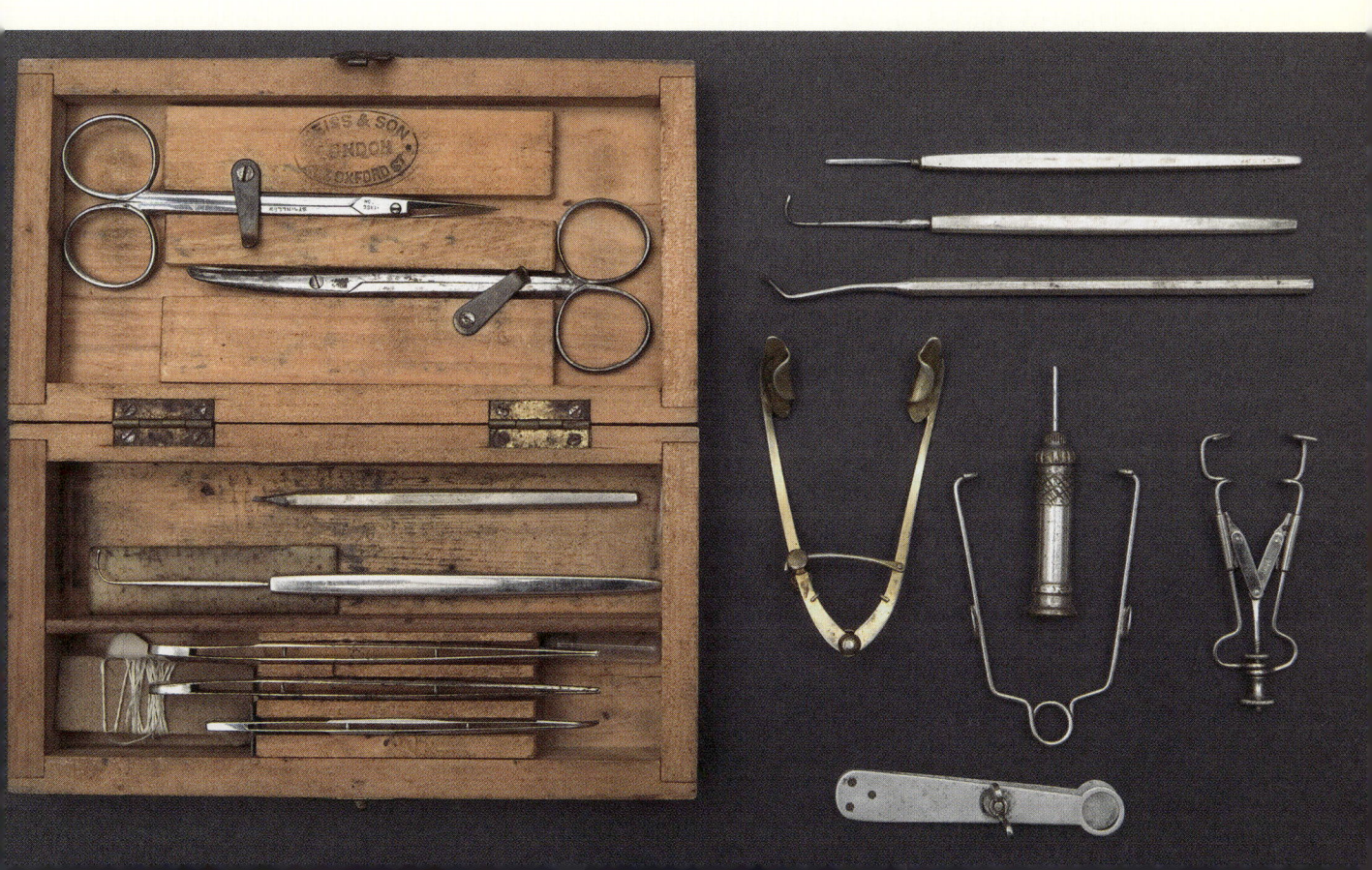

Sheets and uniforms hang on washing lines outside Roberts Hospital.

reasons ... Tinea in the folds – groins or armpits, feet or hands – soon forced its victim to seek relief, while tinea of the face was so unsightly that they would probably report for fear of subsequent disfigurement.

From the economic point of view, sickness was a serious matter. The IJA discriminated between Red Cross cardholders and others. The genuine cardholders were paid all the time, whether sick or fit, while the non-cardholders ... were paid only while at work, so that the majority of men delayed as long as possible before reporting sick. This method of non-payment to the sick may have got at a few bludgers, but it certainly penalised many genuine cases.

From the IJA monthly and fortnightly payments to all troops camp office deducted certain amounts of money in order to build up and increase our rations, so that from another point of view it was considered advisable to keep men fit.

Many were the protests of men upon being sent to hospital. There were no luxuries, no comforts, like cigarettes, to be handed around, and thus these men were deprived of obtaining their own amenities at canteens. Certainly, from camp funds the AIF received five cents per day while they were in hospital or sick, but for cigarettes at $1.80 for 20, or coconuts at $1 each, five cents was of small value. In early 1944 something seemed to go wrong with the currency: prices rose daily to more and more astronomical heights and supplies dwindled. Newspapers were cut for cigarette papers and it may be stated that many of us consider that the *New York Times* made the best cigarette papers.

However, any paper was used, and this had a deleterious effect on the lips, tongue and mouth. With the presence of deficiency disease ever ready to manifest itself, the type of tobacco plus the paper caused a considerable number of conditions rendering the mouth and throat very red and sore. One most interesting feature was the curious scarlet colour of the mucous lining the lips, tongue and cheeks.

A new type of skin disease referred to as tropical pemphigus appeared in the latter half of 1944. Curious blisters occurred on the face and trunk. Fortunately, it responded easily to ultra violet light. In the hospital area we were able to construct several of these [UV] lamps from remnants of search lights, motor car headlamps and other 'junk'. There was no means of scientific measuring of the light output, but results proved its value.

In addition to these special diseases, there was ever present the ordinary common diseases which are so frequently seen in private life ... Fortunately, there was very little trouble from lice, crabs and other friendly living creatures, if one is prepared to exclude scabies from this category.

Skin disease was so widespread among the prisoners that if in our future civil life any man should deny having had some lesion or other it may be implied that he is using a 'terminological inexactitude'.

28 August 1944

THE PATHOLOGICAL DEPARTMENT

UNKNOWN AUTHOR

Following the capitulation both the 10th and 13th AGH – by order of the IJA – proceeded to Selarang with their patients and whatever equipment they could take with them. In this move the problem of transport was almost insuperable. The IJA would not allow sufficient transport to convey the sick and wounded from the Cathay Building in Singapore where the 10th AGH was located. Owing to this policy each department had to jettison much of their valuable equipment. In the case of the 10th AGH whatever pathological equipment was deemed necessary had to be carried almost entirely by hand.

The 13th AGH, situated at Katong, was more fortunate, as it was almost halfway to the site designated by the IJA as the prisoner-of-war area and was also more fortunate as regards transport. Further, it had a more leisurely move in comparison to the 10th AGH during the last days of the action when [the 13th] left its war station in Johore for the hospital where they were ultimately made prisoners of war. The 10th AGH had to retire from its position under heavy shell-fire back to the Cathay, during which move it lost a quantity of valuable equipment … A few hours later Staff Sergeant Greenwood with Warrant Officer Mayberry and other members of the staff of the hospital made a dash back to the vacated site and rescued a small amount of very precious stain.

From this beginning Major R.B. Maynard, pathologist to the 10th AGH, and Major G.F.S. Davies, pathologist to the 13th AGH, and their staff … formed the Pathological Department …

The 13th AGH, moving independently, arrived at Selarang on 21 February, and the 10th AGH on the following day. The location was the Barracks Square … As the patients had to be served and, worse still, as an outbreak of dysentery had occurred, it meant that the department had to commence work at once.

Within 12 hours of arrival the staff was at work, having taken up a position on the verandah of what was the Officers' Mess of the Gordon Highlanders. At this time there were no amenities such as water, light and fuel. Every drop of water had to be carried by hand over a distance of several hundred yards, and the most stringent measures taken for its purification.

With dysentery and malaria figures on the increase, [pathology work] meant long and tedious hours of work under the most difficult conditions imaginable …

Australian medical officers working in the laboratory at Selarang Barracks, c. 1942. These photographs were taken secretly by Kennedy Burnside.

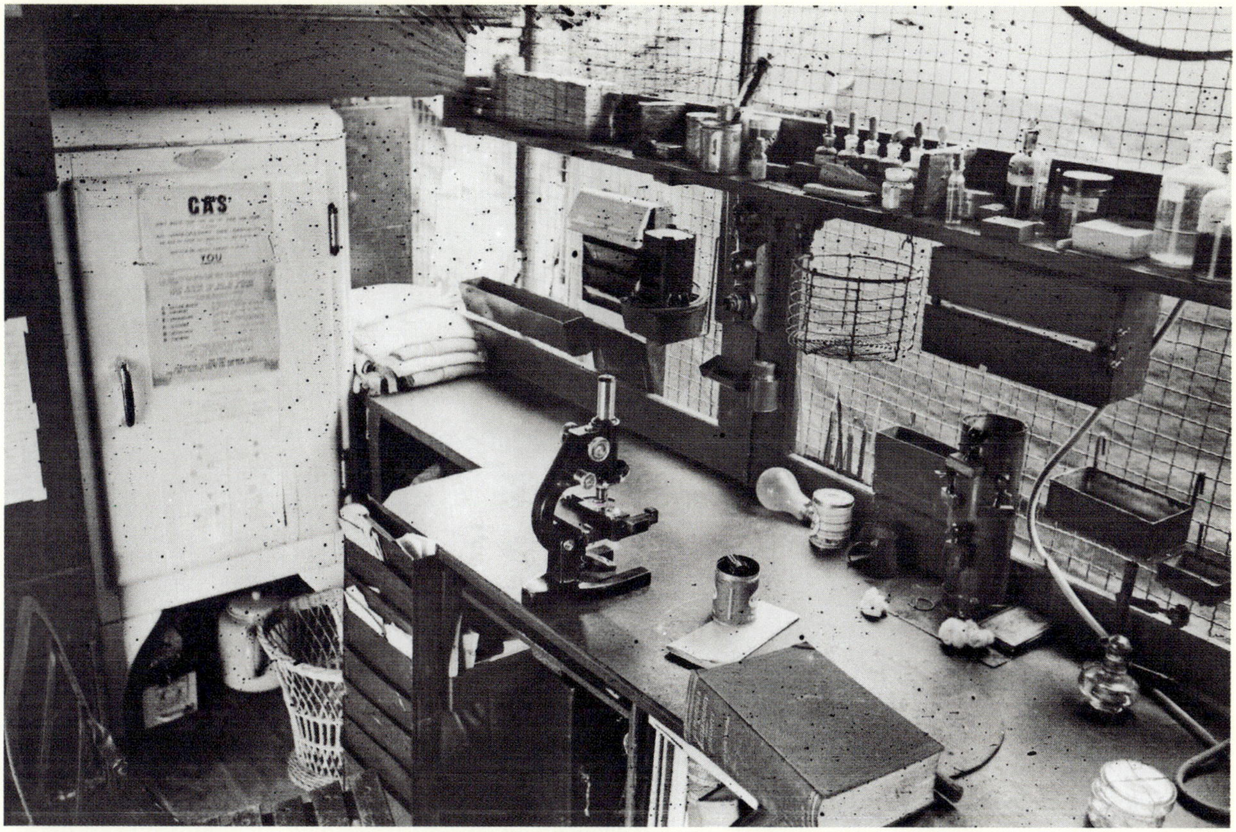

P03821.006

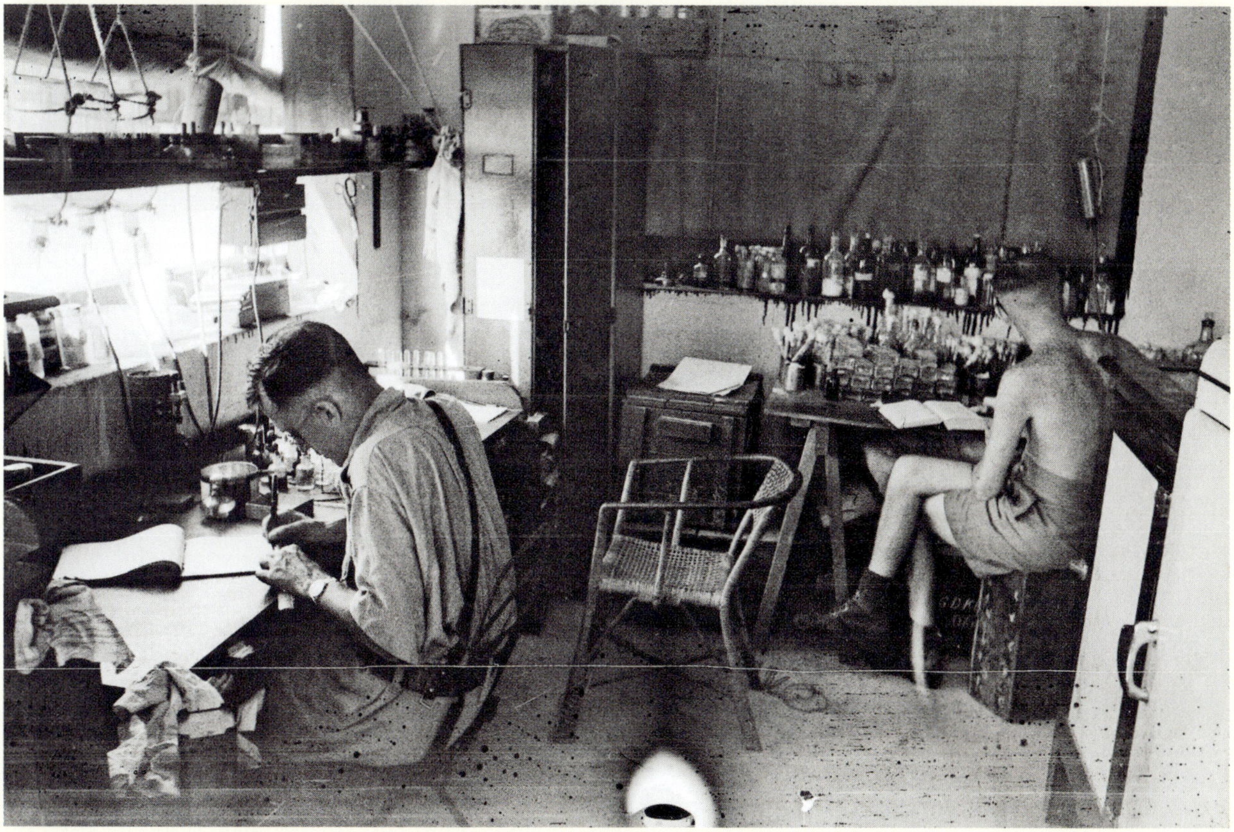

P03821.045

Sterilising equipment and medium-making in the pathology lab. Murray Griffin, 1943.
ART26485

At first only microscope work was possible and only certain types of that were feasible. On 8 March the department moved with the rest of the hospital to Roberts Barracks, and there formed a department to service the Australian wing of Roberts Hospital, which was part of the General Hospital set up to service the entire camp.

Repeated requests to the IJA for equipment and stocks of chemicals received negligible attention, so the meagre stocks had to be eked out. The shockingly overcrowded condition in which the troops were living soon made the presence of virulent disease a real and urgent matter. As each new infection struck the camp the department was called upon to identify it and materially assist in the war waged against it.

From the hospital's very inception improvisation was the order of the day. Very little research work could be undertaken owing to the lack of material necessary to carry it out. Bacteriological work necessitates clean surroundings and, if possible, still air – a sheer impossibility when it is considered that the laboratory was situated on an open verandah.

All culture work had to be carried out in an improvised glass-fronted box, in the side of which were two holes just sufficient for the hands to go through. Despite the fact that their effects are so deadly, disease germs or organisms are extremely delicate. To grow them many types of complicated bacterial foods are necessary and most of these have a meat basis. As meat was conspicuous by its absence from the menu, many were the subterfuges employed to obtain satisfactory growth.

Due to the deficiencies in the diet, blood conditions, some of them of extremely serious nature, manifested themselves. Extra work was necessitated for their investigation and it is hoped that the final report may be of scientific value even under civilian conditions. The work of the technical staff cannot be too highly commended for their unremitting care in the preparation of these media. The cooking and sterilisation of the media was effected over stoves which normally burned kerosene, but in Changi only heavy oil was obtainable, and the finished product always enveloped the entire surroundings in vile-smelling black soot. It became a matter for congratulation if the stove remained alight or even in one piece. On one memorable occasion, in an attempt to obtain the required heat, the stove excelled itself and burst, covering the technician in burning oil and severely injuring both his hands and arms.

Despite these and other similar difficulties, diphtheria and dysentery outbreaks were reasonably investigated. The IJA demand for medical services for working parties sent to Thailand and Burma as well as Borneo meant that Major Davies and Corporal McKinley had to go north with one of the parties, while the remainder of the staff stayed in Selarang.

There was no diminution of the work, and when the quality of the IJA rations deteriorated and the many attendant diseases appeared the department was hard put to keep pace with the demand. Still very little or no assistance was received from the IJA in the matter of equipment and chemicals.

On 15 June 1944 the department had to pack up once again and move, under IJA orders, to a site near the Changi Gaol ... Although these conditions were better than previously experienced they were still far from ideal for the work which had to be undertaken. As the health of the troops deteriorated due to the quality of the rations, the story of such deterioration was first told in the Pathological Department.

So through the long weeks and months and even years the department kept on with its work. Up to the middle of 1944 some 60 000 examinations of all types had been conducted in the camp, and at no time did the staff of the department exceed five. It must be remembered that even with the combined resources of the two Australian hospitals the total of the Australian-trained technicians was only two, and the consequent strain and excessive man-hours took its toll. Owing to sickness and consequent temporary loss in staff the department obtained the services of Quartermaster S.E. Lunt of the RAMC.

The typing of blood for troops who had left for overseas service in the British and Dutch forces without first being blood-grouped numbered several hundred. The department also carefully kept track of blood donors.

In the middle of 1944 it was decided after conference that a large stock of double-distilled saline for intravenous use was advisable, as the IJA had given repeated warnings of the possibility of air raids. Once again, improvisation was necessary. By using made-up hot plates and various bits and pieces ... the stock of saline was produced at the rate of a tablespoonful to the hour. In addition to specialised work an average of 100 examinations were made daily.

The hidden camera of Kennedy Burnside

Lenore Heath
Australian War Memorial

MAJOR KENNEDY BURNSIDE was one of a number of prisoners who secretly photographed life in Changi. A graduate in medicine from Melbourne University, Burnside commanded the 2nd Australian Mobile Bacteriological Laboratory in Malaya, using an army truck as a pathology laboratory for the study of tropical diseases. His unit later joined the 2/13th Australian General Hospital in Singapore. Following surrender to the Japanese the pathology truck was driven into Selarang Barracks Square. Equipment was transferred to a barracks building and a lab set up to carry out basic clinical pathology, diagnosis and administration. Burnside also continued his research into the control and treatment of malaria.

Burnside hid his Leica 35-millimetre camera and Bell & Howell eight-millimetre movie camera in the camp, and kept a typed diary. In mid-1943 concerns about Japanese discipline and a possible move led to the burial of Australian records and Burnside's cameras, film and diaries in 15-inch brass shell cases salvaged from the British naval guns. Engineers took star sightings to record the hidden locations, while Burnside made coded references in his diary: 'Attended burial party in the afternoon ... Wonder when those dead will see the light again.'[1] He continued with a handwritten diary for the remainder of his imprisonment.

Following liberation, 12 of the 13 shell cases were recovered, and the diary, stills camera and negatives survived. Burnside obtained some film and took more photographs of the liberated camp.

The images taken in 1942 and 1943 include camp activities, conditions and portraits of prisoners. Some feature the ingenuity of the medical staff in operating a laboratory in a huge camp. The diaries are detailed commentaries on life in Changi, medical work and issues with health, nutrition and hygiene. Descriptions of lectures, discussion groups, study, reading and shows document attempts by prisoners to keep up morale. References were made to lifelong bonds forged with fellow prisoners during times of hardship: 'Friends have been one of the most important things, and of them the outstanding one is Tom. Nobody could wish for a truer, more understanding, or more tolerant friend than Tom. He is, and, I think will always be, my best friend.'[2] Tom was Thomas Mitchell, barrister, politician and champion snow skier.

Burnside's photographs and diaries paint a vivid picture of life in captivity. He retained a positive attitude, with expectations of survival and a return to his loved ones: 'I look forward to the future with confidence.'[3] That future included a long and distinguished medical career.

Kennedy Burnside (right) and an unidentified officer eating a meal in their quarters. Selarang Barracks, c. 1942.
P03821.038

LIVE TO EAT
UNKNOWN AUTHOR

It has been said that some people 'live to eat'. In the case of prisoners of war in Malaya it was, for a period of 30 months, a case of 'eat to live', and very little pleasure in it at that … Two sources of food were of vital importance: canteens and camp general gardens … The sources of supplies were: (1) food brought into the camp by ourselves at the time of capitulation; (2) issues made by the IJA; (3) the black market; (4) the Red Cross; (5) purchases from local *kampongs* and later from Chinese contractors through IJA channels; and (6) such miscellaneous items as snails, cats, leaves, poultry and the like.

At the time of capitulation the AIF was being rationed from a supply depot at Tanglin established by the AASC on 13 and 14 February 1942 from other depots which were fast being destroyed by enemy action. Something over 200 tons of tinned foods were in this depot, of which approximately 170 tons were all that we were able to remove to Changi. The balance was partially destroyed by Japanese soldiers bayonetting tins and some was left by us owing to lack of transport … It was from these foods – preserved meat, meat and vegetables, biscuits, bacon, cheese, butter, tea, sugar, milk, jam, flour, tinned fruit, tinned vegetables – that the AIF was fed until 25 February and then were used to supplement the IJA issues until 11 March. The issues were of necessity small as there were 14 500 mouths to feed, and a portion was set aside for the future use of the hospital. These initial reserves proved invaluable even two and a half years later for special patients, and despite the climate the tins kept in very good condition.

> **One delivery of rice [from the IJA] was 43 000 pounds short**

The jar to our epicurean standards can be well imagined from a perusal of the ration scale laid down, and supplementary sources of supply had to be considered. The ration scale as set out was, more or less, supplied by the IJA – usually less, owing to the fixation by the IJA of 'standard' weights for bags and sacks of rice, sugar, and salt irrespective of the weight of the contents. I recall one occasion when one delivery of rice was 43 000 pounds short and the IJA refused to make it up. Similarly, vegetables and meat were usually under the scale. Supplemental sources were the Camp Messing Fund (CMF), the Red Cross, the black market, local purchases and other miscellaneous methods. [At a later date the Japanese introduced a ration scale that varied depending on whether a prisoner was undertaking heavy duties, light duties or no duties. Even so, the thiamine/non-fat calorie ratio, the measurement for vitamin B in the diet, was below the accepted minimum of 0.3.][1]

LEFT **Loading a cart with cooked rice for distribution to units, Selarang Barracks, 1942.**
P01344.009

BELOW **A trailer party transporting supplies, secretly photographed by John Rosson.**
P04485.053

HEALTH AND SURVIVAL

The CMF was established from deductions from officers' pay, pay of Red Cross cardholders, and IJA pay to Other Ranks, in addition to canteen profits. From this fund were purchased additional foods considered necessary to maintain health and provide extra diet for special hospital patients. The first issues from this source were made on 14 September 1942, when both pay and purchasing facilities were made available by the IJA. This issue was half an ounce of rice polishings per man, but later included many other items. From the commencement of the scheme until March 1944 over $154 000 had been expended in purchasing food for general consumption exclusive of hospital patients and convalescents. Up to this date the following items had been purchased: 81 300 pounds rice polishings; 137 400 pounds *towgay* [bean sprouts]; 266 000 pounds dried herrings; 18 300 pounds red palm oil; 52 000 pounds peanuts; 37 900 pounds *ikan belais* (dried fish) – known to us as dried whitebait; 56 300 pounds sweet potatoes; 3000 pounds soya beans; 42 000 pounds black beans; and a few miscellaneous items.

After 20 March 1944 the scheme was merged with the general mixed camp fund and continued to purchase such items as red palm oil, soya beans and *towgay*, although the price of the latter items had increased approximately 1200 per cent. A large variety of goods was purchased for the hospital. From June 1942 to May 1943 these included: 13 000 pounds bananas; 12 500 pounds rice polishings; 75 900 eggs (mainly duck); 1074 pounds *chekkurmanis* (a local leaf vegetable rich in vitamin A); 1750 coconuts; 244 tins meat and vegetables; 70 pounds onions; 299 tins preserved meat (12 ounces); 2400 pounds papaya; 400 pounds *ikan belais*; 1500 pounds maize flour; 300 pounds fresh fish; 574 tins sardines (15 ounces), 1300 pounds *towgay*; 1000 pounds sweet potatoes; 90 pounds dates; 1800 pounds peanuts; 5000 pounds fresh pineapple; 275 pounds raisins; 472 pounds soya beans; 700 pounds Chinese oranges; and, in small quantities, biscuits, *buah duku* (small fruit), Polymalt (a local attempt at Ovaltine), dripping, vegemite, barley, limes, tapioca flour, coconut oil and red palm oil.

…

In addition to the above, numerous individuals supplemented their diet in a diversity of ways. Snails were a morsel of food for some, amongst whom were a number of our medical fraternity. It was during our first six months that we made our acquaintance with 'jungle stew', made from a type of wild mint growing outside the camp; many kitchens sent parties out early in the morning to collect this weed and so was concocted a weak and unpalatable soup. The original residents of Changi area, I am sure, never dreamed of the use to which their nicely trimmed hibiscus hedges would be put … Towards the end of 1943 and early 1944 the camp population of cats and dogs, which had increased since our arrival, came in for some homicidal attention and a price was placed on dog and cat meat … Poultry, in

A trailer party, with guard.
Murray Griffin, 1944.
ART25100

the form of day-old chicks and ducks, became procurable through the canteen services at 22 cents during late 1942. They were susceptible to various ailments, and in some cases mortality was high. In all, over 17 000 birds were purchased by the combined Australian, British and Dutch ... The other great disadvantage was the problem of feeding. Any reduction from the daily diet in order to feed the birds was looked at askance by many who were considering the plunge ... many officers

"Hey! You can't bring that animal down here!"
"Can't I, by Jingo? — She's an honorary Colonel!"

This George Sprod cartoon pokes fun at an officer and his duck, an 'honorary Colonel'. While prisoners could own poultry in the camp, only officers, with their higher rates of pay, were in a position likely to be able to purchase extra food for feed.
3DRL/5040.002

were paying 75 cents and $1 per 100 snails for bird food. The IJA ordered the establishment of a piggery, which flourished for a time and provided a certain amount of meat for the hospital until early 1944, when it was possible to make issues from killings to the camp as a whole; on these occasions, every month or so until May 1944, the IJA deducted the amount of pork eaten from the amount of fish or meat due. As five grams of rice per man per day had been used in feeding the pigs this proposition left a good deal to be desired.

During March–August 1942 the AIF procured 1693 pounds of fish, which was issued to the hospital … [see 'Fishing from behind scratch', p. 326].

One of the most profitable sources of additional food was the unit or house garden. These were small plots dug up within the early part of incarceration around the various houses and huts in which we lived. These gardens were of tremendous value to unit kitchens, particularly in providing greens, which were, as a rule, non-existent on IJA rations … [see 'The Changi Garden Party', p. 290].

Hunger brought in its train the local black market. This market was operated by troops who climbed through the barbed wire at night, facing all the risks of such action, returning with tinned food purchased from the natives and selling such foods in the camp … [see 'The black market', p. 94].

It can be safely said that the food we ate as prisoners was, in the main, quite foreign to our normal diet. The principal item was polished white rice, and the quality was frequently very poor. A proportion of the ration was ground in the camp to assist the cooks by providing a coarse flour. The ration varied from ten to 17 ounces per head at various times. During the first 18 months of imprisonment we received a meagre ration of 0.176 ounces per head … During the first eight months of imprisonment we also received … 0.176 ounces of Canadian wheaten flour per man per day from our old stocks. Condensed milk at 0.528 ounces per man was issued until the end of April 1942, and that was the last we saw of milk until the one Red Cross issue was made in October 1942.

Meat and fish were forever causing us surprise and concern in view of their changing and doubtful quality and quantity. We were issued with Australian frozen meat until November 1942 at a varied scale of 1.3 ounces per man per day (including bone and fat). This was issued twice weekly … It was during this period that the IJA brought to the camp 28 head of local cattle. A poorer lot it is impossible to imagine. Their dead weight averaged 400 pounds and the meat was 'high' [pungent]. They were killed at Changi Pier, a distance of 1.5 miles from the AIF camp, and the ration for the whole AIF was collected at dawn on a handcart drawn by eight men. Meat of a different type made its appearance in January 1944 after a completely meatless period of 12 months. It consisted partly of boxed, frozen, boneless meat in 22-pound blocks and was quite pleasant, particularly so after our long

Small plots of gardens outside officers' quarters in Changi Gaol. Such gardens were an important source of additional food. Murray Griffin, 1945.
ART26462

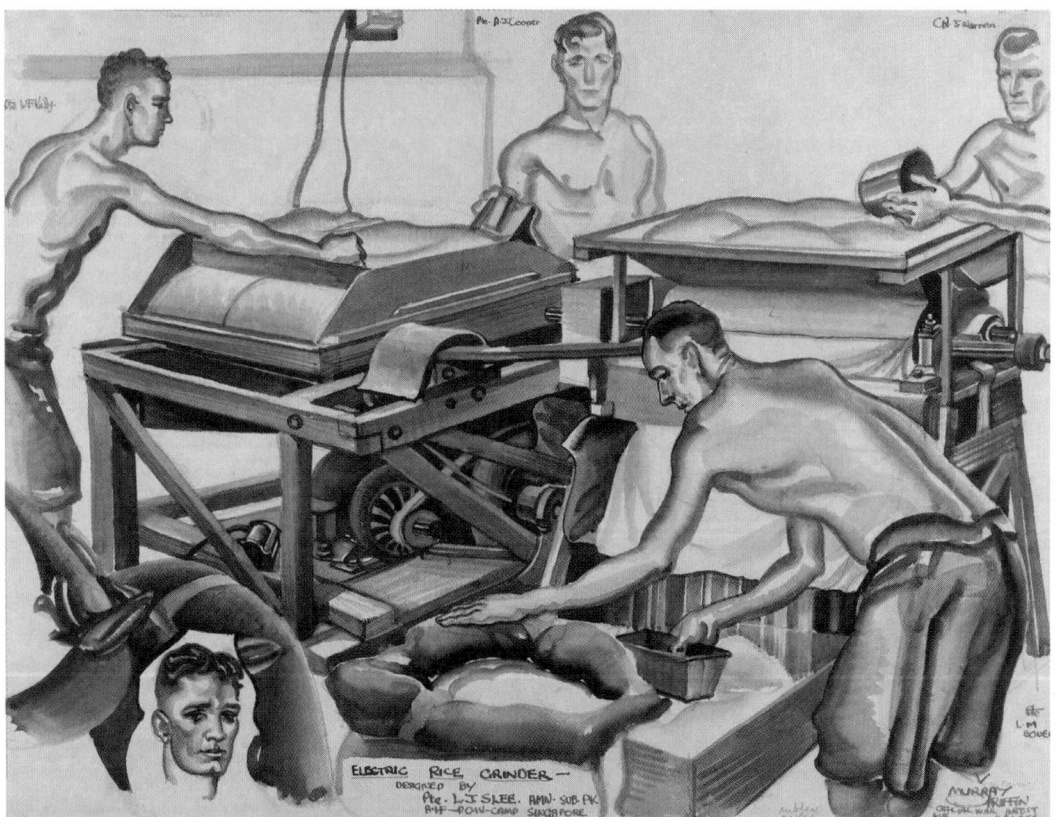

This electric rice grinder was designed by Private L.J. Slee (inset) and built from scrap. Murray Griffin, 1943–44.
ART25089

meat fast. Interspersed with these deliveries were deliveries of frozen, locally killed meat of poor quality and condition. The IJA insisted upon the return to them of meat and bones despite our request that they may be used for garden fertilisation. Fresh pork from the camp piggery was also consumed from November 1943 to May 1944 at a scale of 0.13 ounces per man per day.

...

It was in respect of dried and fresh fish that our greatest epicurean shock came. Any object living normally in the sea and being of a length of one inch or over constituted a fish, and our views of 'fresh' fish were governed by the question: 'Was it so bad as to be impossible to get it past the nostril to the mouth without feeling ill?'

Fish comprised a portion of our diet from January to December 1943 and from June 1944, although fish did take the place of meat on other occasions [see 'Fishing from behind scratch', p. 326] ... An example of the IJA attitude occurred when we complained about the large quantities of shark ... which was unfit to eat. The day following the complaint they produced fish about ¾ inch long and when we remarked on their size were told: 'Ah, yes, but it is fresh. You cannot complain that we bring bad fish.' Dried fish were frequently alive with maggots, and particularly bad in this respect were the dried herrings purchased locally towards the end of 1942. Their condition led to a complaint by one unit and they were ordered to 'wash and eat' them, discreetly omitting whether that meant the fish or the maggots, or both.

Vegetables were of numerous varieties, including sweet potatoes, tapioca root, and *keladi* or taro root. The green and red leaf vegetables comprised sweet potato top, Chinese spinach, *kangkong* [water spinach], amaranth, *bayam* [leaf amaranth], mustard leaf, and dried seaweed. A few miscellaneous items made appearances in small quantities such as *brinjals*, snake gourd, melon, ginger root, lady's fingers [okra], and long beans ... At times the issue would be under 100 pounds for approximately 10 000 persons, and being of perishable nature they would not be kept. At the end of 1943 and during 1944 the IJA delivered bananas, green papaya and pineapple in lieu of vegetables. These were often of very bad quality. Wastage was great despite the cooking and eating of bananas in their skins.

Until the disappearance of flour in October 1942 the AIF Field Bakery made bread for such units as required it and as were willing to allocate a portion of their rice ration to be turned into rice flour to mix with the wheaten flour. The Japanese Camp Commandant, Lieutenant Okasaki, had his bread baked by the AIF Field Bakery while it operated. It was necessary for the bakery to manufacture its yeast from such of our ration as available, such as sweet potato or pineapple, after having had a starter of brewers' yeast ...

There was an issue of oil for cooking purposes. This was, for short time, ghee ...

HEALTH AND SURVIVAL

TOP LEFT This small piece of hard dried fish belonged to Hugh King Ashby of the Straits Settlements Volunteer Force. From Westmorland, England, Ashby had been a scientist with the Colonial Service in Malaya before the war. As a prisoner of war Ashby would occasionally shave off a small piece of fish with which to brew tea on special occasions. After the war Ashby refused to talk about his time as a prisoner, but after visiting the Australian War Memorial in the 1980s he found a new desire to tell his story, and began his memoirs. He died in 1987, memoirs uncompleted, having requested that the few possessions remaining from his time as a prisoner of war be donated to the Memorial.
REL31501

MIDDLE AND BOTTOM LEFT An unusual souvenir, this dried squid was issued in Changi and later brought home by a former prisoner.
REL/18206

In this photo, taken shortly after liberation, AIF cooks are depicted in front of the cookhouse with some of the homemade utensils.
116541

Two men inspect the ration bucket, making sure no grain of rice goes to waste. Photograph by George Aspinall.
P02569.140

HEALTH AND SURVIVAL

The second and final issue of George Sprod's *Smoke-oh* magazine in February 1945 marked three years in Changi.
3DRL/5040.002

later substituted by coconut oil and red palm oil ... a few tins of lard came to hand, which we immediately set aside for medical use in preparing ointments ...

Our tea, sugar, and salt were normal, tea being army pack whilst sugar and salt arrived in sacks of various sizes. Soap, of which there was a small issue of three grams per man per day – from which hospital and other requirements had to be taken – was of local manufacture and very poor quality.

Among the other novel items of diet consumed was 'vitameal' or fertiliser. We had five issues totalling $3^{1}/_{2}$ pounds per man during the first few months. No doubt the IJA thought it contained good food value but it is believed that it was a garden fertiliser (held by a Singapore chemical company). However, we ate it, didn't like it, but were thankful for the small biscuits made with it.

...

A problem which consistently faced the camp was that of reserves ... From the whole camp's point of view a reserve ... was required of rice, sugar, salt, oil, and tea ...

The first occasion on which we were forced to use reserves was during the Selarang Barracks Square incident in September 1942 ... Fortunately, the AIF could at that stage have fed itself for three weeks comfortably and a little longer by rationing. When parties left the camp for distant destinations they were able to take extra food for the journey and to assist them on arrival ...

FOOD

UNKNOWN AUTHOR

The constant cry of all prisoners in the hands of the Japanese: 'Give us food.' If they were Australians, they bellowed, 'We want bullock!' Thus, with one faction demanding cakes and puddings and the other vast mountains of rice and hot curries, the workhouses of Changi led an extremely harassed life. Incessant petitions were made to sack all the cooks and send them out on the drome – they were too fat anyway – and get someone with some imagination, and successors to the vacated post found it not the gluttonous sinecure they had expected, and were soon sacked themselves. But, throughout, prisoners refused to believe that it was impossible to make cottage pie or Spanish cream out of rice and hedge leaves; and consequently their savagely alert criticisms made all of Changi's chefs very wary and very enterprising indeed. The results they eventually achieved can only be described as miraculous.

Consider the materials available. There was rice of a not very good quality, liberally sprinkled with an interesting collection of nuts, bolts, gramophone needles, and odd bits of steel: there was 'fresh' fish (which was bad), and dried fish (which was inedible). Finally, there were vegetables which even the natives refused to eat! There were, on the other hand, no eggs or butter or meat or flour – except on the few extremely rare occasions when the Japanese felt generous after a victory, or the Red Cross managed to send a consignment of parcels. Assuredly, there were not the ingredients with which ordinary masterpieces are achieved.

The first meals to be cooked in the earliest days of captivity were deplorable. A grey, glutinous mess: nauseating, though tasteless, the rice looked like boiled glue, and the change from civilised food to this uncouth diet affected everyone disastrously. Bladders worked with frantic speed; bowels ceased to function at all. A doctor, on being informed of the condition of a desperate Australian who had now been constipated for 19 days, replied that that meant nothing: he'd been constipated for three weeks himself.

Stews very quickly settled down into three types: thick stew containing sweet potatoes and greens; gas-cape stew containing such greens as Ceylon spinach ... and finally jungle stew made out of hibiscus leaves. This sad state of affairs persisted until the day of the release, more and more green leaves of every conceivable kind being used. Ornamental plants, such as amaranth, which look so pretty in public gardens, were devoured year in and year out. Not only that, but huge beds of them were planted, scientifically cultivated and carefully cropped.

HEALTH AND SURVIVAL

They were prolific, very unpleasant, set the teeth quite black and were allegedly good for one.

It is not surprising, therefore, that after a few months the era of 'doovers' began. A doover was anything made out of rice which had the saving grace of not looking like rice. Thus, rissoles of every shape and size, small tarts and large pies all came under the one genus of doovers. (The English, regarding this Gallicism as a trifle extravagant, coyly referred to them as 'efforts'.) This genus was then classified into many species – sweet, fish, cup and pastry – Changi cooking had arrived!

Pastry made out of minced boiled rice, filled with tapioca root, flavoured with *blachang* and finally fried in palm oil – that was the thing to which prisoners looked most forward of their scanty evening meal – and yet, what was it really? Tapioca is called by the natives '*ubi kayu*', which means 'wooden potato'; they

Making rice cakes. Murray Griffin, 1943.
ART25071

This kitchen in Selarang enabled chefs to cook rice in bulk for the hospital. Murray Griffin, 1943.
ART26482

regard it with the utmost contempt. *Blachang* is a sundried paste made out of fish offal, has an unbelievable, evil smell, and is quite inedible for most human beings. Palm oil is used for the manufacture of soap, was tried as a fuel in Japanese planes and engines without much success and was then issued to prisoners as cooking fat. It tastes like axle grease. These, then, were the luxuries of the prisoners of the Japanese.

Since the rations issued were so distressingly light, most men found it necessary to build them up. Accordingly, they ate a large variety of extremely unusual dishes. These included cats, dogs, snails, snakes, sparrows, wild-passionfruit leaves, numerous fungi, and frogs. The Dutchmen, of course, with their usual capacity for going too far – added rats, cockroaches and flying ants. For many, a regular Sunday midday meal of dog became a recognised institution. Snail suppers provided an excellent means of entertainment in a camp where hospitality had become almost out of the question. King cobras and pythons – once regarded with shudders of revulsion – were now welcomed with open arms, smitten firmly at the base of the skull and immediately thrust into the stew pot. So long as there were things that walked or crawled, Changi was determined not to starve.

By the end of their second year of imprisonment, most men had become quite accustomed to the Asiatic dried fish. No one can dry fish quite so unpleasantly as the Asiatics: little fish euphemistically known as whitebait and a kind of small herring were most common types – their presence anywhere being signalled by massed formations of deliriously excited flies. They were not nice. For many months prisoners could hardly bear their smell – let alone their taste – but eventually, worn down by the time and acute hunger, they succumbed. The day was to come when they looked forward to these nasty little pieces of salted filth with the keenest anticipation.

'Fresh fish' – the Japanese are a colourfully imaginative race – were also issued to prison camps. Although these covered everything from infant sprats to man-eating sharks and huge stingrays, consignments of them nevertheless had always three things in common: they never weighed as much as the Japanese said they weighed; there were never enough of them anyway; and they were invariably very, very bad.

The other food, about which details must be given, was 'pap' … This elegant breakfast dish is made by boiling ten gallons of rice with 40 gallons of water, and by continuing to add water as fast as it boils away. Next pour in some palm-oil and some more water and boil for hours until the whole mixture looks like an enraged custard and no longer resembles rice at all. Finally, sweeten the entire 50 gallons with two pounds of sugar. The dish is ready for consumption by the thousands of men who must then work on it until lunchtime, six hours later. On the march to their various tasks, it was usual for a halt to be called about halfway out for a massed passing of water. It was the custom then to remark with a sigh, 'Well, there goes breakfast.'

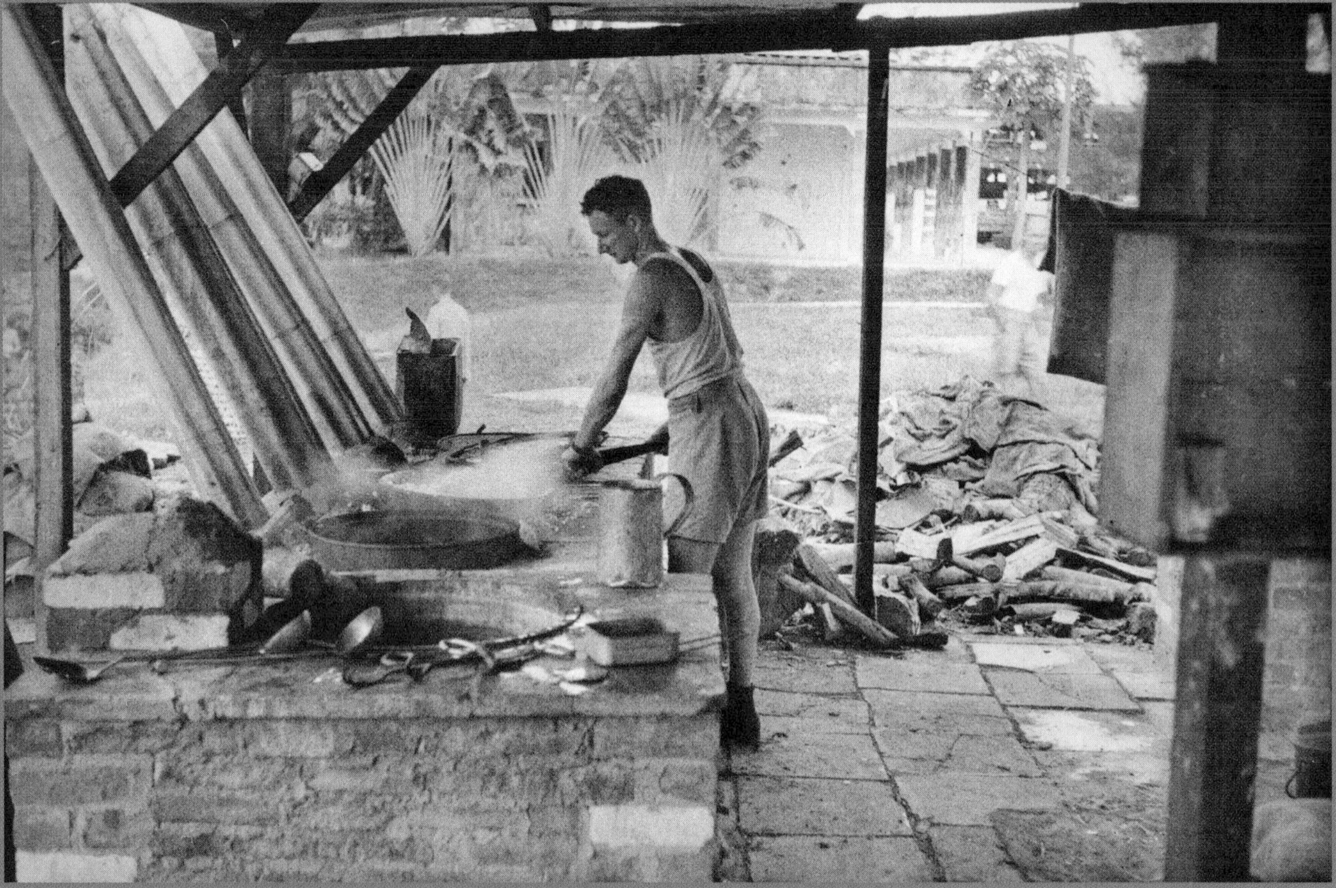

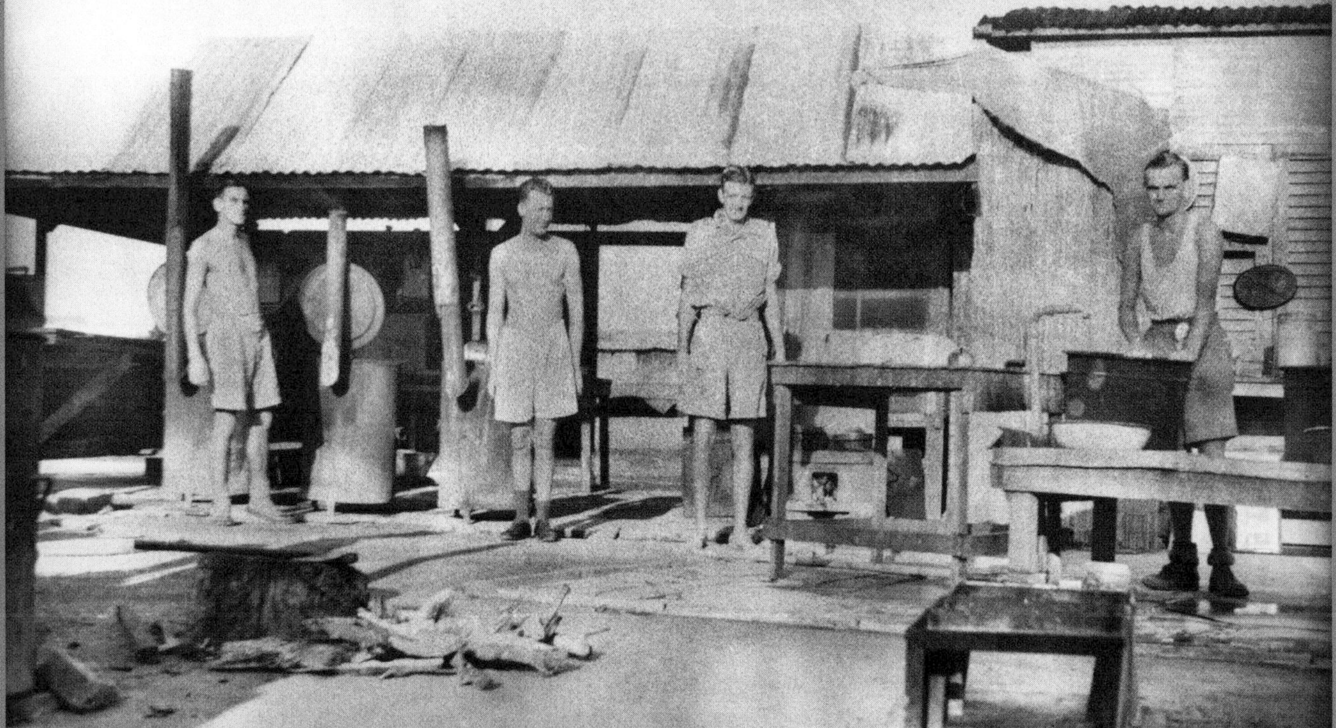

LEFT **These photographs of the cookhouse near Roberts Hospital were taken by Major John Rosson, who kept the negatives hidden throughout his captivity.**

Hauling firewood for the cookhouse.
P00761.007

Some idea of the inadequacy of the cooking utensils supplied by the Japanese can be gained from the fact that the gaol cookhouse, designed to cater for 200, had frequently to feed 6000 men. This scale can be regarded as the normal one: it meant that hundreds of trays, pails and containers had to be made, all out of the inevitable steel cupboard; that ovens had to be constructed; and that cooking had to be done in never-ending shifts. And yet, in spite of all this, the cookhouse managed on Christmas (by dint of months of saving and scraping and magnificent organisation) to produce for the day's meals 52 000 doovers, 500 gallons of stew, 700 gallons of pap, 2000 gallons of rice and 3000 gallons of tea.

Nothing the Japanese could do could ever throw out of gear for long the way of life which their prisoners had evolved for themselves in Changi. The story of cooking for those three and a half years is one of making not enough go around, or transforming filth into something which looked attractive and tasted reasonable, and of working with one-tenth the equipment that was needed. It was, in fact, the old story of no sympathy and a lot of obstructionism being overcome by endless resource.

Living with the legacy: the long-term health effects of captivity

Kate Ariotti
Australian War Memorial

AROUND 14 000 AUSTRALIANS emerged from prison camps throughout Asia at the cessation of hostilities with the Japanese in August 1945. Though emaciated and exhausted, these men and women were considered the lucky ones. The Japanese placed little value on the lives of prisoners of war, and some 8000 of their comrades – along with thousands of other Allied servicemen, servicewomen and civilians – had not survived their imprisonment. However, those Australians who returned home after three and a half years of captivity could not know at the time how their experiences would continue to affect their health and wellbeing until long after the war.

Nearly every prisoner suffered from ill-health at some point during captivity. Insufficient food rations caused nutritional illnesses such as beriberi, dermatitis and impaired vision, while forced labour under arduous conditions weakened immune systems and meant that relatively minor scrapes, cuts and other injuries could quickly become life-threatening. Overcrowding and limited sanitation infrastructure in many of the camps led to outbreaks of dysentery, while diseases endemic to the areas in which prisoners were held, such as malaria and cholera, swept through the prisoner population. Even parasitic infections such as hookworm, lice and scabies had flourished. In many cases prisoners suffered from multiple diseases at the same time.[1] Prisoner-of-war camp doctor Captain Ian Duncan recalled after the war that the widespread prevalence of these potentially fatal diseases in the camps meant that they soon came to be seen as 'the norm'.[2] Treating the sick was made difficult by a lack of medical supplies and equipment. Doctors were renowned for their ability to improvise, but despite their best efforts the majority of prisoners who died in captivity did so from disease.

At the time of their release, medical and military authorities thought it best not to proffer special treatment or concessions to the former prisoners. This was decided largely to minimise any sense of private difference or public comparison between servicemen and servicewomen who had experienced captivity and those who had remained on the battlefront. To an extent, the former prisoners were themselves complicit in this. Many downplayed health concerns at demobilisation medical checks in order to get home more quickly, while others refused to talk about their experiences with anyone other than fellow ex-prisoners.[3] This was a silence they would not be pushed to break, for families had been advised not to press returned prisoners to discuss their time in captivity.[4] In the immediate aftermath of the war, when the practice of psychology was still in its infancy, it was popularly believed that the less they spoke of their ordeal the quicker they – and their families and friends – could move on.

However, many former prisoners were struggling as they attempted to restart their civilian lives. In 1947, at the instigation of a group of ex-prison-camp doctors, the Repatriation Commission embarked on a survey of ten per cent of the ex-prisoner population to determine how they were faring. The results demonstrated that many were suffering from the repercussions of their time in captivity. Vision defects, recurrent bouts of the tropical diseases they had contracted, and ongoing stomach conditions were common, while many also reported difficulty sleeping or concentrating at work, as well as feelings of irritation, depression and malaise. As was common at the time, these reported behavioural and emotional problems were attributed to physical health concerns rather than psychological issues.[5] Nevertheless, the results of this survey prompted the Repatriation Commission to conduct a wider study a few years later, and it confirmed these initial findings.[6]

In the decades that followed, other groups explored the impact of imprisonment on the health of former prisoners. One study in the 1960s demonstrated that mortality rates among ex-prisoners were significantly higher than those in the non-prisoner population for the 15-year period following the war.[7] Younger ex-prisoners, in particular, recorded 'excessive mortality' rates from accidents and suicides.[8] Medical examinations of former prisoners by various groups in the 1980s showed that, some 40 years after their release from captivity, many still exhibited the effects of malnutrition and tropical disease. Reflecting rising interest in the impact of trauma on the mind, these later studies also placed much emphasis on the mental and emotional legacy of captivity. As did previous surveys, the 1980s studies found a high incidence of psychological issues among surviving former prisoners of the Japanese. Rather than ascribing such problems to physical illness, medical specialists drew on advances in mental health since the Second World War to link the prevalence of flashbacks, nightmares, depression and anxiety among the ex-prisoner population to ongoing post-traumatic stress disorder, a phenomenon that was slowly becoming recognised and appreciated as specific to survivors of particularly stressful or traumatic events.[9]

The evidence produced by these separate studies made it clear that captivity had adversely affected the quality of life and indeed the life-span of former prisoners of war. This was first officially recognised in 1974 when the government granted free medical care to all returned prisoners, and in 1990 the successor to the Repatriation Commission, the Department of Veterans' Affairs, published an information booklet about prisoners of war and their specific health concerns for dissemination to doctors across the country. In 2001, in recognition of the specific difficulties they had endured, all surviving former prisoners of the Japanese – or their widows – received a one-off payment of $25 000.[10]

Although those men and women who returned were indeed fortunate to survive their captivity, the conditions and nature of their imprisonment exacted a devastating toll on their health. As a result, many carried the physical and psychological scars of captivity well into the postwar period.

An example of a medical record written on a bamboo file from Thailand. The patient, Corporal Sam Moreau of the 8th Division Provost Company, later returned to Changi and survived the war.
RELAWM20253.001

SWAMPS, FUN AND FEVER
RODNEY MATTHEWS

In Malaya in 1930 tigers, crocodiles, buffaloes, and snakes killed a few dozen people. In Malaya in 1930 a tiny animal, scores of times smaller than a pinpoint, killed many hundreds of people and kept many thousands away from work. Tigers propel themselves to their prey, but nature, so rich in ways and means, has provided air-transport for the little parasite, and has even ordained that it need not concern itself one iota with its transport. The mosquito comes along, picks it up, carries it away and dumps in its new abode. All the parasite has to suffer is the inconvenience of a slight change of temperature and some internal rearrangement. But a B-29 with a belly full of bombs is of less consequence than the tiny *Anopheles* mosquito with a cargo of *Plasmodia*: the malarial parasite that kills more people each year than any other organism known. It kills 1 000 000 people in India alone each year …[1]

More 8th Division AIF troops died of disease in Asia between 1941 and 1945 than died of wounds received at the hands of Japanese soldiers, or from shells and bombs. Malaria killed some, but the most important aspect was the debilitating effect of malarial infection with its relapses. It paved the way for other diseases. It weakened us. It lowered our resistance. It kept up a continuous heavy stream of patients into hospital.

When the fighting ceased on Singapore Island on 15 February 1942 we were flung as prisoners of war into compounds on the eastern tip of the island, which before the fighting was one of the most heavily malaria-protected areas in the Far East. European civilians were interned, leading to serious dislocation of all disease-control measures.

It is little wonder that shortly after we were concentrated at Changi new malaria cases were coming in. This meant that breeding of carrier *Anopheles* mosquitoes must be taking place within a short distance of the camp. This was grim indeed. Here we were: prisoners of the Japanese, diet extremely ill-balanced, suffering with bacillary dysentery and now malaria. Medical conferences with our captors took place. We pointed out the urgent need of activity combatting breeding. It was absolutely imperative that we carry out surveys outside the camp boundaries to ascertain where *Anopheles* mosquitoes were breeding and to determine the species [and collect the] data necessary for effective counter-measures.

…

SWAMPS, FUN AND FEVER

With our squads organised, we were ready to start work. The Japanese insisted that an escort – one Japanese or Korean soldier – accompany each squad. The surveyors and oilers covered the area within a mile or so from the camp boundary. While bearing our main job well in mind we were not slow in turning to good use any fruit or vegetables we came across in our journeying. We filled our haversacks with these things, but the difficulty was to get them past the Japanese guards at the gate as we returned to camp. So, with the cognisance of the escort, we slipped the bags of stuff over the boundary fence at a quiet spot, then marched on around the road and so into camp past the guards, to whom we gave a smart 'eyes-right'. Generally speaking, the escort did not interfere with us helping ourselves to a few bananas or pineapples, coconuts, tapioca roots or sweet potatoes. We did not overdo the foraging because we benefited only at the expense of the Chinese or Malay gardener. Often, the escort would call over the gardener and give him two or three dollars. Maybe the lad knew we were both short of cash and hungry …

…

Perhaps our most interesting days – as well as our days of greatest discomfort – were Thursdays. We surveyed the mangrove swamps on Thursdays, searching out *Anopheles sundaicus*. As we squelched our black and oozy way through the swamp in conditions of extreme humidity, our few articles of clothing – hat, shorts, socks and boots – were soaking. Sweat literally streamed down our heads, faces, necks and bodies. Our legs and bare upper bodies were slashed by knife-edged grasses growing up to seven or eight feet at swamp margins. Ragged branches of mangroves scratched us, but the ultimate curses and aggravations were streams of large, very aggressive, very irascible red ants that leapt upon us as we fought our disgruntled way through the mangroves. For downright irascibility, for unreasoning, bling bad-temper, these wretched creatures can surely have no equal … Once these insects launched their attack they gripped with hot, biting jaws and, fume and froth as we would, the beasts would stick like so many little burning knives thrust into our sweaty, smarting, irritable beings. The realisation that, after all, we were lords of the earth would gradually be borne in upon us, and instead of flinging ourselves around like demented hens, muttering terrible imprecations, we would straightway take ourselves beyond range of further attack, and set to work plucking out these searing mandibles one by one.

…

These ants do not only frequent mangrove swamps; they are found inland, too, invading other trees. This reminds us of a north-country lad from the 18th Division mentioning to us that he would never again see Dorothy Lamour in her sarong, leaning against a coconut palm under a tropic sky, without wondering 'if some of them roody red ahnts will coom doon and bite on the boom'.

…

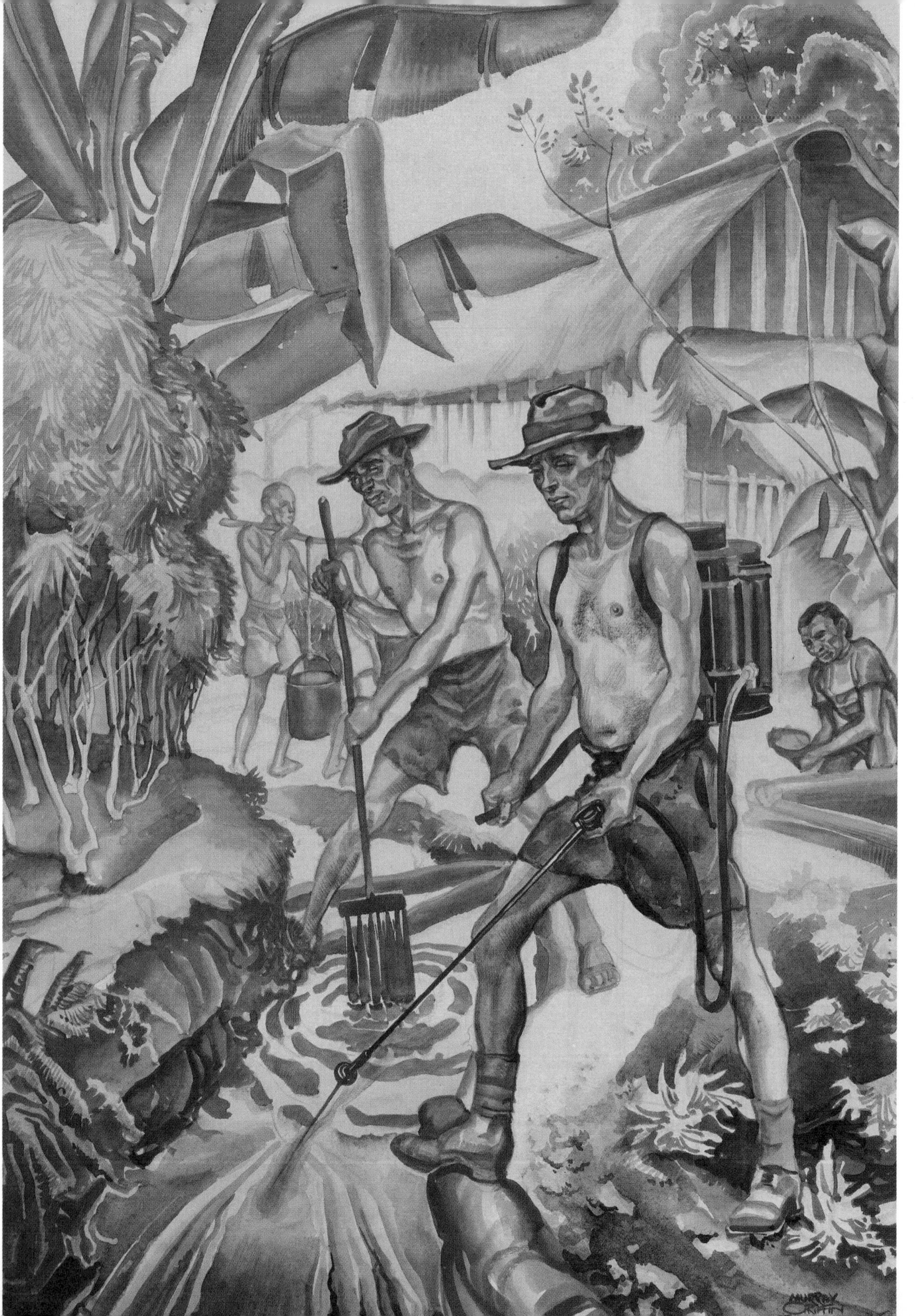

SWAMPS, FUN AND FEVER

Another important part of the work of the anti-malarial squad was draining swamps, covering manageable seepages and digging drains from others. One large sandpit some half-mile or so from camp gave us considerable work and variety. Along one side of the pit – 80 yards long – clear water was flowing freely from the ground: an *Anopheles maculatus*' breeding paradise. Removing boots and socks for wading in the disturbed, pink, muddy water, we wielded mattocks and shovels and dug a ditch of graded depth out into the gutter at the roadside. Small logs, bamboos, bushes and grasses were laid longitudinally in the ditch and covered with mud and clay, thus taking the seepage water down beyond range of sunlight and mosquitoes. We returned to camp spotted heavily with small lumps of yellow mud, pink mud, and brown mud.

...

Some weeks after the commencement of our surveying and oiling and draining we noticed with pleasure an appreciable decline in the numbers of malaria cases being admitted to hospital. This work was continued – with one or two unfortunate and costly interruptions brought about by the issue of Japanese orders forbidding it for reasons unknown to us – until the end, with results highly satisfactory to the medical authorities. And the work provided us, the squad, with all we wanted – a chance to get outside the wire, a bit of extra food, some fun, the consciousness that, after all, the work was for the benefit to the camp as a whole and ourselves as individuals, and – joy of joys – something fresh to grumble about each day.

23 August 1945

Men of the anti-malarial squad spraying oil on stagnant water to kill mosquito larvae. With little quantities of quinine to treat malaria, the disease posed a major problem. Murray Griffin, 1944.
ART25086

271

THE MOSQUITO SQUAD
'OR THE ANTI-MALARIAL SQUAD, MOSQUITO FLEET, OR WHATEVER OTHER NAME WE RECEIVE'
THOMAS MITCHELL

Prevention may be better than cure, according to the old adage, but cure is more popular than prevention. To everyone – our own crowd, the British, the Dutch, the Yanks, the Ities, and the Nips – we are just a plain nuisance. That is, until there is an outbreak of malaria, then everyone is after us.

…

But we are used to it.

We are split into three divisions: the surveyors, the maintenance party, and the oilers. The surveyors are the eyes of the whole outfit, and they have a strenuous life … They have to patrol the whole area at least as far as half a mile from camp – the maximum distance an average malarial mosquito can fly. Every inch of the ground must be crossed and re-crossed in a meticulous search for mosquito breeding places. A good surveyor covers all the ground but never by the same route twice … On finding a likely breeding place, the surveyor scoops up some of the water in a small white plate. He slowly and carefully examines the larvae to see if any are of the *Anopheles* genus. The larvae are a stage of development between the egg and adult and look like minute fragments of very thin grass. A mosquito larva breathes mainly through a kind of periscope near its tail. An ordinary nuisance mosquito has a long periscope and as a result hangs at an angle to the surface of the water. An *Anopheles* has a short periscope and accordingly floats parallel to the surface.

On detecting an *Anopheles* larva, the surveyor gingerly guides it into a wide-mouthed collecting bottle. This is well corked and, on return to camp, is taken to the laboratory. There are 49 species of *Anopheles* in Malaya, but only six, with a possible seventh, carry malaria to human beings. The microscope is focused and the hitherto minute larva is seen to be a segmented and very hairy monster. It is on these hairs that the verdict hangs … the surveyor has to ask himself, 'Are the inner and outer anterior clypeal hairs unbranched or with only a few short branches, *or*, are the inner anterior clypeal hairs with many conspicuous side branches, outer with long branches, brush-like?' … And so on until the larva has been definitely classified as harmful or not. If the former, the fact is immediately reported to Lieutenant Colonel Strahan, who records the finding and the species on a graph the up and down lines of which in various coloured chalks correlate this information with the malaria case incidence.

The second of our gangs is maintenance, and consists of a group of hearties armed with shovels, *changkols*, spades, scythes, axes, sickles,

Kennedy Burnside took this portrait of his friend Captain Tom Mitchell. As well as working for the Bacteriological Laboratory studying tropical diseases in Changi, Mitchell, a champion skier, also formed the 'Changi Ski Club', which held regular meetings.
P03821.073.

HEALTH AND SURVIVAL

and odds and ends of tools scrounged from goodness knows where, and concerning whose origin it is best not to enquire too closely. Their job is to keep in order all anti-malarial drains, to clean out the rubbish from the drains, and to cut such grass or vegetation as might trail in the water and form a shelter to which the larvae can [attach] with their minute but capable tail-hooks. In between times the maintenance gang builds earth bunds, digs anti-erosion drains, or thrashes about hip-deep in glutinous black mangrove mud.

The oilers are a small, dirty but cheerful squad. Their weapons are two knapsack sprays that seem to put more oil over the carriers than the water. Their raison d'être is to cover the water with a thin film of oil and thus suffocate the larvae by blocking their breathing periscopes. Good malaria oil spreads thinly and quickly in a series of concentric rainbow circles, but the heavy stuff the Nips give us is lethargic in its action. To help spread it we have a couple of chaps with brooms who sweep the water after the oilers …

The party is made up of a pair of men carrying sprayers, two men carrying brooms, two men carrying a spare drum of oil on a stick between them, two men to give them a rest, and a couple of officers …

This ID tag belonged to Corporal William Middleton of the 2/30th Battalion. Middleton was in such poor condition on the voyage home from Singapore that he did not expect to survive repatriation, and gave his prisoner-of-war ID tag to a New Zealand nurse for safekeeping. Middleton did recover, and his departed ID tag eventually made its way to the Australian War Memorial collection.
REL31368

DENTAL

UNKNOWN AUTHOR

Most men, at the beginning of their captivity, took one look at the diet of slops and glue and decided that inevitably – and quite soon – all their teeth must fall out. 'This', they said, 'is uncivilised: it is unhygienic – and is most unfortunate,' and without further ado they resigned themselves to a toothless middle age.

Strangely enough, they were wrong – teeth remained surprisingly firm, and there was not more than the usual amount of trouble caused by decay: there was, however, considerably less than the usual amount of dental supplies with which to treat that trouble when it did occur. After a few months there were none.

…

Therefore – as always – prisoners were thrown on their own resources: they accepted the situation cheerfully and promptly overcame it. No man can say that his teeth were neglected in Changi unless it was he himself who neglected them.

Lacking amalgam [for fillings], a great drive was instituted for donations of silver. Everything from golf trophies for going round 18 holes in an incredibly small number of strokes to cigarette cases for non-existent cigarettes came rolling in: Changi smiles soon glittered with this amazing by-product of savage tournaments and sentimental presents.

A very strange fact of the war now became apparent: an extraordinary number of people, it seemed, either had no teeth at all or, if they had any, kept them all on the one jaw, the other being merely a long vacant strip of virgin gum … [apparently] all these unfortunate gentlemen had, during the battle, been blown into the sea or down deep holes or out of trees or hundreds of feet into the air. When they landed or emerged … they were amazed, they announced gaily, to find themselves totally without teeth. Yes, it was odd. No, they had no idea where their teeth had gone. Probably, they thought, they had swallowed them. There was nothing to do but try to make them some more.

This was all very well – the demand was there, and a large vociferous demand at that – but the means for producing a supply simply did not exist. There were no teeth, no dental rubber, no casting materials and no vulcanizing equipment – life for the dental department had become very difficult, [and] their solution of the problem was magnificent.

Certainly, famous cement manufacturers never dreamed that one day a dentist would say, 'Open up please,' and insert a handful of this superior produce mixed with red clay into the unwilling mouth of a patient. But this was done, and even though experienced builders were horrified, and the cast was a little slow setting and the patient had an excruciatingly unpleasant roof to his mouth for weeks to come – the result was very satisfactory. From

HEALTH AND SURVIVAL

A Murray Griffin drawing of the Dental Centre at Changi, 1943.
ART26467

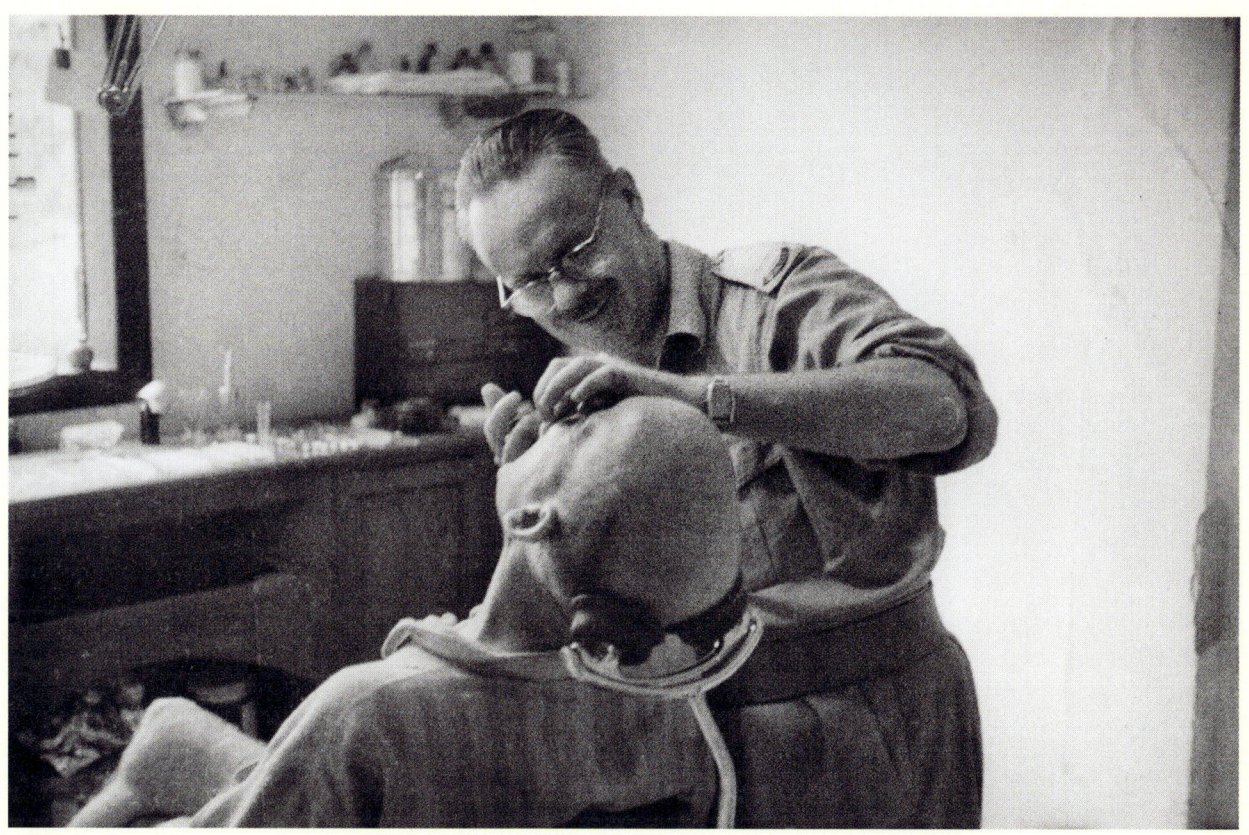

DENTAL

A toothbrush manufactured by Changi's Broom Factory. The handle is made of bamboo and the brush of coconut fibre.
RELAWM33851

A Changi dentist at work on a patient, secretly photographed by Major John Rosson.
P04485.024.

these casts perfectly fitting dentures (horrible word) were made.

To make the denture, however, required three things: first, some teeth; second, some substitute for dental rubber; and third, a means of vulcanising.

Teeth were easy: plenty of men were dying, and those who died did not go to Abraham's bosom with their plate in their mouth – false teeth belonging to these unfortunate men were removed from the denture, ground down to the right size for a new set and attached to it. The result was quite decorative and very efficient.

Having solved this problem, dental mechanics now attacked the more difficult one of making the actual denture. After months of experimenting they succeeded – the finished article was produced by fusing latex out of the local rubber trees with sulphur from the medical stores. This fusion was made possible only when certain vital chemicals had been derived by laboriously grinding down old broken dentures: it was then processed with an oil obtained – once again, after much research – from crude rubber. This finished material was quite revolutionary and equally as good as the commercial article.

The last problem, of course, was vulcanising. Innumerable experiments with steam, wood, fuel, dieseline and oil drums were made, but either the correct pressure and temperature could not be reached or, when it was reached, it could not be maintained. Nevertheless, the vulcanising was done and, finally, when the mass move to the gaol took place the whole problem was solved by the use of electrical hotplates.

Some idea of the tireless research that went on in the dental department can be gained when one realises that beehives were ruthlessly robbed for wax, crashed planes were stripped for the synthetic resin on the cockpit, mosquito cream was stolen for lamps and the cellophane off cigarettes sent by the Red Cross was thriftily collected to be used as a finish for the inside of dentures. To the mechanics and dentists of Changi we owe a great deal.

Work and work parties

SINGAPORE WORKING PARTY

CHARLES TRACEY

Six weeks after they had reached Changi the Japanese demanded that 1500 Australians should come immediately into Singapore city to work. To come immediately, Headquarters pointed out, was impossible; preparations must be made. The Japanese … allowed the party two days' grace to prepare themselves. When asked how long they would be away the Japanese stated blandly, 'A fortnight at most,' and consequently the men marched out with their toothbrushes in their pockets and very little else, happy in the knowledge that they would soon be back. They were to return eight months later.

…

[The men] maintained a steady pace, halting only to fill water-bottles, and to take frequent surreptitious advantage of the generosity of the Chinese, who offered coffee and bread in a lavishly unmercenary spirit which was most unlike them.

Eventually, after a number of wrong turnings and delays, the party arrived at Adam Park, which was one of the better-class residential areas of Singapore. To the right of the road was a partially burnt-out hutted British supply camp; to the left stretched Adam Park Estate, well laid out with private roads leading to large homes set among what had been well-kept gardens, shade trees and a profusion of flowering shrubs.

The bodies of unburied British soldiers lay everywhere.

The Japanese had buried their own dead and had marked the graves with simple white posts, but had apparently not seen fit to [conduct a] service for their enemies.

Abandoned and broken equipment lay everywhere, while both sides of the road were lined with vehicles of every description, both military and civil. Practically every vehicle had been holed with shrapnel and many were burnt out. Armoured cars, carriers, lorries and trucks were mingled carelessly with sporty MGs and expensive sedans. Bonnets raised, exposing motors to the elements, doors agape, sun-roofs open, tyres twisted and torn, passengers incinerated, presented a picture of needless waste and carnage.

The houses were in very little better shape. Shell-holes through roofs and walls had allowed the drenching tropical rains to wreak havoc on furniture and fittings … Clothing and food had seemed to be the main object of the looters, who after taking what they wanted had set about smashing up the homes of their late masters …

Sixty men were now allotted to homes that had once housed small families and, as only one day was allowed for settling in, the camp immediately became a hive of industry.

In no time water and light services were restored, the sewerage system functioned, roofs were patched and rooms were cleaned up and made habitable. The hutted camp, while not possessing the convenience of the houses, was quickly put in order and in a very short time was quite comfortable. By dint of constant scrounging each man soon had a cot of some kind erected and the cookhouses were turning out meals. The day of improvisation had arrived.

A carpenter's shop was established and before long boasted a bench, two vices, an anvil, a forge and a good assortment of tools. An electric rice grinder was made from parts taken from abandoned cars, a serviceable handcart for carrying rations was created out of a cut-down chassis, petrol drums became ovens, grass-cutters were produced from sheet iron, and tyres and cut-down packing-case nails were all that were needed to establish a boot-maker's shop …

A yeast centre was established which produced enough yeast to supply each man with three ounces a day, thus overcoming to some extent that shortage of vitamins which existed and which our doctors assured us would cause our almost immediate death.

The paint shop turned out signs, re-branded kit-bags and, with the help of the carpenter, made and branded crosses for the graves of the war dead as fast as they were buried.

Slowly, the camp lost its abandoned appearance: lawns and gardens were restored to something like their erstwhile neatness and before long the foundations of the burnt-out huts were all that remained as evidence of the enemy's activity during the siege.

The Japanese guards were all drawn from Engineer and Pioneer Units, and plans were made for the erection of a memorial shrine overlooking the Singapore Golf Course. The work entailed building some miles of road through the course, the erection of three bridges over the McRitchie Reservoir, several cuttings and the shrine itself.

…

Various working parties were allotted to these tasks and were mixed up only whenever the Japanese made one of their ordinary administrative errors. One large party went daily to a quarry to obtain the stone for the road surface; another drove trucks between the quarry and the golf links, and a third was engaged in digging out the foundations of the road and man-handling the earth in small Chinese wicker baskets. Still others were employed felling and dressing timber for the bridges, while the remainder cleared the site for the shrine itself.

As most of the sentries were also employed on manual labour the guarding of the prisoners was very lax. However, it soon became apparent that the possibility of escape was negligible …

…

At 9 am the troops would parade and the various Japanese guards would take them over and move off to their particular tasks. All went smoothly until the arrival of one Corporal Sano, who would try to run the parade himself. His entire lack of English did not help matters and, as he usually had only a vague idea of the arrangements, parades invariably became completely disorganised. Parties of the wrong size would be sent off to the wrong jobs, and trucks provided for the transport of workers at the more distant jobs would be sent off empty. Sano would then fly into a rage, shout himself hoarse and, throwing up his hands in despair, slap the faces of whoever was nearest him.

Little was known of the character of the Japanese at this time, and at first Sano caused a great deal of perturbation. Tales of his inconsistencies are many. For no apparent reason he would fly into an ungovernable temper, actually raving and frothing at the mouth; five minutes later he would be in the best of spirits, handing out cigarettes to lads whose faces he had recently been slapping.

On occasions he would arrive at Camp HQ during a conference and rave furiously in Japanese, banging the table with his sheathed sword. Then suddenly he would break off to enquire if enough sugar was available to make some afternoon tea or, again, to draw attention to a rather pretty butterfly that caught his eye.

On one occasion Corporal Sano decided that there were far too many men in hospital and that he would hold a sick parade himself. The offer of one of our doctors as an advisor was scornfully refused: Sano explained that he was quite capable of making his own diagnosis, as his brother was studying medicine in Tokyo. The parade was duly held and it quickly became apparent that any man with a bandage was passed, without question, as unfit, while a man suffering with an internal complaint was immediately marked fit. To balance things out a number of healthy men were promptly put through the parade wearing the most impressive bandages, the net result being that, if anything, fewer men than ever were fit for work the next day. No more medical parades of this nature were held.

Then one day Sano arrived at Camp HQ with information that he was returning to Japan: would the Australian Camp Commander please give him a letter of recommendation mentioning particularly his good work while he had been corporal of the guard? He was promptly given a most ambiguous letter and sent off delighted, after showering gifts of cigarettes upon everyone he met. They seemed a race beyond the comprehension of normal men.

When the work was about half-completed the Japanese abruptly packed up and left, taking with them all the tools the Australians had not had time to sell to the natives. Before they left, however, [the Japanese] gave away all the furniture from their house, cleared out all their rations and even smashed all the telephone and wireless sets so that the incoming unit would have to start off from scratch. This lack of co-operation between the

LEFT **Prisoners of war on a work party with a Japanese guard in Singapore, March 1942. The photograph was taken by a Japanese guard for Sergeant Shimizu, who was in command of the work party. Pictured are (left to right) Private Ronald Holberton from 8th Division Ammunition Sub Park; Ahmed, an Indian forced labourer; Sergeant Shimizu; and Warrant Officer Class 2 Sydney Barber, also of 8th Division Ammunition Sub Park.** P00078.001

BELOW **A work party with their Japanese guard, c. March 1942.** P0011.001

various Japanese units was most marked and, to prisoners, quite delightful to see on every occasion when changes between these 'guards' were made.

Thus it happened that two days after the departure of the guards the Japanese authorities in Singapore became slowly aware of the apparent large numbers of prisoners who were in the town and who showed no sign at all of being employed on any particular job. The *kenpeitai*, the Japanese military police, were called in, and after some hours they rounded up hundreds of these sightseers and returned them under guard to their various camps.

What had happened was that many Australians, in their customary casual manner, had decided that the change of guard provided an excellent opportunity to have a good look at the town: they had simply set off with that object in view. Many hailed buses and private cars and some of the really hard cases obtained lifts from Japanese army transport.

Their only punishment was a few days' confinement on a tennis court without food or water. On being questioned some said that they had just walked round having a look at bomb damage; others went to the pictures, while all admitted to having good meals. A shortage of cash had proved no obstacle as the Chinese shop-keepers were only too willing to advance a few meals in the hope of being repaid after the war.

The new guards proved to be far more efficient than their predecessors and did a great deal to improve the conditions of both the work and camp. A canteen was established which, despite the low working pay of ten cents per day, was able to sell at reasonable prices Javanese tobacco, bread rolls, dates, and tinned fish.

Working conditions were fair for all but those employed on the bridge construction jobs. These lads had to work all day up to their waists in water and were not well treated by the engineers in charge of the job. When they were working it was with the greatest difficulty that the Japanese were restrained from hitting men with the first thing that came to their hands …

…

At this time an order was published to the effect that it would be useless for the British to request the handing over of men caught outside the camp wire for punishment by their own officers. The offence was regarded as a serious one and would be treated as such by the guards, who intended to apply their own ideas of correction which were very odd and barbaric. Despite constant warnings, however, it was only a matter of a few days before three men were apprehended doing some 'shopping' at a *kampong* some distance from the camp.

The camp commander, an Australian colonel, was sent for and required to show cause why these men should not be shot. The guards gave evidence that the prisoners had been caught red-handed and that the food had been paid for by the Japanese themselves and brought back as evidence. In [the men's] defence the colonel pointed out various aspects of the case and put in a plea for leniency. He was told by the Japanese officer to point out the gravity of offence to the prisoners and to tell them they could go. As the crestfallen lads were leaving the room the officer called them back and gave the 'evidence' that the guards had paid for. Little wonder that, for the next few days, a great deal of shopping was done.

At this stage the Japanese decided that the Australians would move to Bukit Timah. Five lorries arrived almost immediately and the guards were amazed to see the old camp removed lock, stock and barrel. As they watched roofs come down and plumbing torn up they shrugged startled oriental shoulders, puffed stolidly at their cigarettes and made obvious mental notes that all prisoners of war were mad but that Australians were the maddest of them all … When the party finally marched out only a few walls remained to mark where the old camp had been.

The whole process of building a camp had to be gone through again. Seven houses were made available, and those not in houses were accommodated in tents. The new guards proved far more sympathetic than the Adam Park ones, and no reasonable request was refused. One Japanese who acted as interpreter, disrespectfully known as 'Hank the Yank', had lived in the USA for 17 years and had been most unwillingly caught in the draft while on a visit to Japan. Having a clear understanding of the Western mind, he was sympathetic to many requests that otherwise would not have been understood by our captors and did everything in his power for the prisoners, expressing the sentiment that perhaps one good turn would later deserve another, and turning a blind eye to almost all their outrageous offences against the regulations of his own army.

Adjoining the camp was a Fogden Brisbane [a company which was dissolved in the 1950s] factory with a large junkyard attached. Despite orders that this yard was out of bounds the temptation proved too great and a deal of raiding by Australians resulted. The local Chinese would buy anything. Each night they would line the wire behind the camp and settle down to an hour's bargaining. One Sikh nightwatchman was no match for the number of enterprising prisoners of war who found this an easy method of augmenting their poor working pay. Cement brought $10 per bag … one night's record amounted to seven tons, all carted away from under the nose of the watchman without a sound. No comment was made by the Japanese when they noticed that the kitchens developed concrete floors and that good cement drains took off the surface water …

The new task was the erection of a shrine on the summit of Bukit Badok and the construction of a road, as straight as an arrow, to the summit … the shrine was to be dedicated to the dead of both sides in the Malayan campaign, and the ultimate result was a single

> **The shrine was to be dedicated to the dead of both sides**

A Japanese postcard showing Australian and British prisoners of war 'servicing a bridge' at the war memorial built at Bukit Timah, Singapore.
Garth O'Connell collection

plain column of wood for the Japanese dead (fatally riddled with the white ants inserted in its base by the Australians who erected it) and a large cross set in a garden plot to the memory of the British fallen.

In addition to the parties employed on the actual site a number were employed in the quarry obtaining the stone for the foundations. Others formed a ration party, to supply five camps daily with the rations obtained in Singapore by the simple process of sending in a truck with a Japanese NCO in charge with a bag of cash to do daily purchasing at the markets. As time went on the relationship with the Japanese camp commander improved and he was prevailed on to make transport available for all sorts of purposes.

Each Monday a truck went to Singapore for canteen supplies; on Tuesdays to Johore Baru for rice-polishings (cooked with the food as a prophylactic for beriberi); on Thursdays any required distance north of the island for pineapples; and on Saturdays to the Malayan breweries for yeast.

With the completion of the shrine a holiday was declared. The day dawned bright and fine and at 9 o'clock all the senior British and Japanese officers were assembled on the summit. After the Japanese had held their own ceremony the party moved round to the cross.

Speeches were made by both sides and at the conclusion a bugler played the Last Post and Reveille, with all the British standing rigidly to attention and saluting. As the last notes of the bugle died away Colonel Tamura, the Japanese commander, placed a wreath at the base of the memorial.

With the conclusion of the more serious side of the ceremony both sides mingled quite freely round the two centres of attraction – the boxing and wrestling rings. The Japanese made a start with a display of wrestling … and drew a large crowd. However, as soon as the boxing started the wrestling was deserted by British and Japanese alike … At the conclusion of the sports the Japanese distributed bottles of sake, beer and soft drinks to both winners and losers, and to all the officials responsible for the tournament. The remainder of the day was devoted to a cricket match in the camp.

These same Japanese engineers were later to murder men in their thousands in Thailand and Burma. Their apparent generosity was the result of three factors – the huge and seemingly inexhaustible fruits of their victory, the fact that it cost them nothing, and their own overweening desire (inspired by that sense of inferiority so often to be seen in them) to impress the white man and show him that they were as civilized as he. The flush of victory wore off and, the loot of the large city exhausted, they were seen to reveal themselves as they really were – devils incarnate.

At this time the transport company was having petrol trouble. Apart from driving and servicing 45 captured British trucks it was responsible for the issue of petrol to the Japanese-driven and -maintained vehicles.

It was a common practice for a Japanese driver to fill up in the morning with 20 gallons of petrol and come back to the filling-up point an hour later out of gas. This practice was faithfully followed by the prisoner-of-war drivers. It was a common sight to see a truck pull up on a quiet road and the driver descend, raise the bonnet of his truck and tinker with the motor. Scarcely had the truck come to rest before a Chinese would appear with a tin and a length of rubber piping, quickly syphon out ten gallons and, handing over his $50, vanish. Down would come the bonnet and the truck would proceed on its way.

The transport officer soon became worried and eventually reported to the Japanese commander that the system in vogue – recording the amount used by the prisoners and not the amount used by the Japanese – was most unsatisfactory. He was told in reply that it was not a matter to worry about. 'If you have 2000 gallons to start the day and the prisoner-drivers used 500 and at the end of the day you have only 500 gallons left, then it is obvious that the Japanese trucks must have used the difference – 1000 gallons.'

Business under these conditions became extremely brisk and the drivers rapidly became sufficiently affluent to 'stake' not only themselves but also their friends with ample pocket-money.

On one occasion an enterprising syndicate came into possession of a 65-gallon drum of petrol, but they could not find the means of getting it past the guardhouse at the entrance of the camp. At last a scheme was hit on: for some days small quantities of tar were brought back to camp from the road-construction party until enough was collected to smear the outside of the drum and give it the appearance of a tar barrel. Then it was rolled gaily down to

Signalman Edward Fox of the 8th Division Signals found this 'Britannia' badge of the Royal Norfolk Regiment at Adam Park camp. Fox was later sent to Japan and kept the badge with him. When he returned home he took it to a jeweller to turn into a brooch, adding a boomerang inscribed with 'Singapore 1942'.
REL/12930

the road under the very noses of the guards. On being questioned they gave the explanation in fluent Japanese: 'Workee roadu,' adding with a confident wave of the hand in the general direction of the worksite, 'Chinee come, take all men work roadu.' … some minutes later a decrepit lorry in charge of a Chinese coolie arrived, loaded the drum on the truck and $350 changed hands. The party returned to its billet well satisfied with the morning's work.

These conditions could not last. Finally, a native watchman from the Fogden Brisbane yard gave a warning that a trap was being set that night to catch the people responsible for the rapid shrinkage of stores. Despite the warning, some of the more adventurous souls decided that a little risk could not be allowed to interfere with legitimate business and decided to carry on. Accordingly, at about midnight all hell broke loose. The main gates had been left invitingly open and a large number of Sikhs, armed with sticks, had been placed at vantage points in the yard. On being attacked by these Sikhs the culprits had retaliated with great enthusiasm, and as a result there were many casualties on both sides – most of all among the Sikhs.

Japanese guards had then appeared, and six prisoners were taken. The Australian commanding officer was at once called to HQ, where he had to face a tribunal of five wrathful Japanese officers who talked executions and shootings for some hours. The outcome of the court was that the Australian prisoners would never learn to cooperate (as they should) with the Imperial Japanese Army (which was quite true), and it would be much better if the whole camp were to return to Changi.

As all the tasks had been completed the Japanese were extremely glad of the excuse to rid themselves of an expensive encumbrance, and so after eight months of strange experiences the party returned to the fold, there to remain until it was sent off to Thailand with the ill-fated F Force, from which so many were destined not to return …

From Changi to an uncertain fate

Lachlan Grant
Australian War Memorial

A CONSTANT AT CHANGI was the departure and return of working parties, leading to fluctuations in the overall population of the camp. These movements also stripped Changi of the fittest, most capable and skilled men.

From May 1942 the Japanese began sending working parties to various destinations overseas, and by rail up the Malayan peninsula to Thailand. Travel, whether by foot, rail or ship, was the most dangerous period in a prisoner's life. Conditions on long marches, railway journeys and ocean voyages were horrendous.

The table below shows the destinations and sizes of the working parties that departed Changi. At war's end, Australian prisoners of the Japanese were scattered throughout the region: in New Britain, Ambon, Java, Sumatra, Borneo, the Philippines, Malaya, Thailand, Burma, French-Indochina, Hainan, Manchuria and Korea.

Departure date	Workforce	Size of force	Destination
14 May 1942	A Force	6000	Burma/Thailand
8 July 1942	B Force	1500	Borneo
8 July 1942	Special Party	400	Formosa
16 August 1942	Japan B Party/Senior Officers' Party	1000	Japan via Formosa and Korea
28 November 1942	C Force	557	Japan
14–18 March 1943	D Force	5000	Thailand
28 March 1943	E Force	1000	Borneo
18–30 April 1943	F Force	7000	Thailand
25 April 1943	G Force	1500	Japan
5–17 May 1943	H Force	3270	Thailand
15 May 1943	J Force	900	Japan
25 June 1943	K Force	230	Thailand
24 August 1943	L Force	115	Thailand

THE CHANGI GARDEN PARTY

H. HUTCHANCE

One morning in the first week of October 1942 the Japanese informed Camp Command that a garden was to be laid out, the produce of which would be used by the prisoners. A squad of 400 men was called for, soon to be increased to 1000 and later to 1500, and an area of 70 acres adjacent to the camp was nominated. They had been detailed for the Garden Party. The ground was undulating and quite thickly wooded with rubber trees, a tangled undergrowth and coconut palms.

Clearing was strenuous work. Timber was felled by an energetic group which later became the regular forestry party, and this, together with the stumps, was used in insatiable camp kitchens. By December these erstwhile wooded slopes had emerged as a purposeful market garden.

When the work began there were excellent opportunities for the troops to lose themselves for the day. It was an easy matter to wander into a secluded *kampong* and there exercise that lust for trade which is the hallmark of the Australian prisoner. However, Japanese supervision was shortly to be tightened. One day the officer of the guard told the prisoners that he was putting 120 Korean sentries in the garden – not for intimidation, but to encourage work. The company of sentries duly arrived, slipped off their shirts and, in the face of astonished prisoners, commenced work. During rest periods they handed out cigarettes and smiled amiably. The next week they were less enthusiastic and by the week after that they carried sticks with which they struck the men for not carrying out ridiculous orders. Later the company was withdrawn, leaving only one Korean to each area. Thereafter, for the prisoners, one of the chief virtues of the gardens was the scarcity of the enemy, a place where one could 'get away from the blasted Nips'.

In November of the same year the Japanese ordered the formation of the Central Garden Control and a permanent body of officers and men, experienced in gardening, who would be responsible for the garden. This group was also to take orders directly from the Japanese in garden policy. Thus, on 9 November a combined British and Australian Garden Central unit (consisting of 16 officers and about 50 men) was established. Despite various changes in its membership, this group remained in existence until the imprisonment was over. To them success of the gardens is primarily due.

To maintain a big market garden, hacked from tropical jungle and deprived of all save the most rudimentary tools, is no mean undertaking. The Japanese had called for 'agricultural experts', and indeed these were forthcoming, but here were problems beyond the experience of the most learned botanists. The soil was arid and sour, and water ran in only a trickling stream; there was no compost, no manure, no fertiliser, no lime, no nursery, no seed-bed. Moreover, the crops were of a type whose behaviour no civilised gardener would demean himself to study. Like the rest of Changi industry, the gardens were built on trial and error, enterprise and hard work. That by July 1945 an area of [70] acres produced 58 000 pounds of vegetables for one month alone is an eloquent testimonial of their success. Of the total amount of green food consumed by the camp in the month prior to its release, 75 per cent was produced by the prisoners themselves.

Prisoners of war tend the gardens at Selarang. Murray Griffin, 1943.
ART26483

… An abandoned Chinese house was converted into a nursery, and with seeds obtained from the Japanese the first sowings were made … Anti-erosion measures were commenced: drains were constructed, wells were dug and primitive hand pumps fitted. Reticulation reservoirs, made from the bodies of disused motor trucks, were dotted about the area so that limited watering could be carried out. Meanwhile, the arduous task of bed-making was proceeding, and soon the garden emerged, ordered and businesslike.

Of the roots, it was tapioca which saved the day

The equipment at the gardener's disposal consisted of a broad-bladed hoe, an implement common to the Chinese of Malaya. The chief tool was the *changkol*, used for every conceivable purpose – digging holes, felling trees, tilling ground …

The Assam fork, a formidable weapon of primitive design resembling a spiked hoe, was used as a variant of the *changkol*. Ordinary light rakes of inferior design were the only other implements provided for the tillage of this expansive garden.

The Japanese, with a generosity which soon deserted them, produced a fairly large quantity of fertiliser; this was stowed away and used sparingly. The most useful manure was supplied by the camp piggery under the direction of Major the Lord de Ramsay. Of his pigs General Arimura remarked, 'They are better off than anybody on Singapore Island' – a poor advertisement for co-prosperity, but a truism none the less.

Cuttings and seedlings were mostly produced from the small gardens already existing in camp, but the Japanese allowed a few trips to be made to Singapore and Johore to procure *keladi* suckers, tapioca sticks and pineapples.

Squads of men digging, or leaning on the handles of their implements, timed their maximum labours for the arrival of the supervising officer. When he came, they lashed themselves into a fury of activity, only to subside into a tropical indolence when he had passed. In the distance the white canopy of the interpreter's tent looked inviting. From it, at regular intervals, rang out the pleasant notes of the stop-work bell – the rim of a motor wheel struck with a bar of iron.

The order of battle was as follows: first, the reclamation parties felling the timber; followed by teams of men with ropes banking the stumps into heaps to be heaved onto the waiting trailer. Behind the reclaimers came the *changkol* gangs, digging the soil for the first time, and the Assam forks grubbing for roots. Thereafter the ground was pegged and lined for paths and roads and the beds were made. On the heels of the bed-makers were the fertilisers, who spread the manure and raked it in. Finally, the planters arrived [and] spiked holes, planted the seedlings and covered them with a coconut husk for protection against the sun.

…

THE CHANGI GARDEN PARTY

It is never easy to get prisoners of war to work. Where work is to be done for the enemy a policy of camouflaged inactivity is encouraged, and the Australian prisoner is a master of passive resistance. Soon, however, the troops found it impossible to distinguish between work for the enemy and work for the camp. Both require from him unwelcome effort, and the niceties of principle take no weight from a *changkol*. The Central Garden Control, realising this, was at pains to explain that work in the gardens was work for the camp, and that someday the gardens would be a vital factor in the saving of lives. As the Japanese supply of food decreased these words gained force, so that by the end of the imprisonment a gardener was an energetic and conscientious worker.

During the earlier period the uncertain future discouraged labour, and many small parties attached themselves to shaded retreats for extended lunchtime rests. One such party was discovered by the Japanese in command of the garden. They were playing Bridge, a game which never appealed strongly to the captors of the 8th Division. In a rage the Japanese ordered all players out into the sun. Here he stood them to attention for three hours. Alas! It was impossible to explain that, at the moment of his entry the north-south pair was playing a grand slam vulnerable, doubled and redoubled.

Eventually, the health of the troops working in the garden improved. The work was classified as 'light' duty until with the food restrictions of 1945 it became 'heavy' duty. However, it was always policy to send semi-fit men to the garden, and many complaints, such as skin diseases and partial blindness from vitamin deficiency, responded [there] after [hospital] treatment had failed. The open-air work and the extra meal of garden produce provided for lunch were the chief contributing factors. Hours of work varied how the prisoners progressed. At the outset the men were on the job at 9.30 am and were dismissed at 4.45 pm, with an hour's lunch and two pauses, one during the morning and the other in the afternoon. Wednesday and Sunday afternoons were free. Later the rest on Sunday was abolished and on 15 August 1945 (Japan's Capitulation Day) the rest on Wednesday was abolished also.

In common with other occupations in Changi, the gardeners complained of being constantly transferred from one job to another. A gardener today would find himself a woodchopper tomorrow, then a grass-cutter, then a labourer on the aerodrome or a digger of boreholes, only to return as a gardener a week later. With such diversity, it was too much to expect of the men to maintain enthusiasm. Of course, command was criticised. Any state of affairs which is disagreeable is assumed to be directly caused by the whims or incompetence of those at the head of affairs …

The crops to which all these labours were directed bore no resemblance to an Australian market garden. Firstly, the equatorial climate [prohibited] all vegetables most dear to Australian palates; cauliflowers, cabbages, peas, carrots, parsnips, marrows and pumpkins … Secondly, the soil was of a type so arid and so uncongenial that even tropical vegetables would not grow without constant attention.

The more hardy grower was red amaranth, a bitter-tasting decorative border plant common to most Australian botanical gardens. To eat it at all one must be hungry; to enjoy it one must be insensible to flavour. It is a wretched vegetable. Sweet potatoes were also grown, not so much for their roots, which take many months to mature, but for their leaves. By prison standards these are quite pleasant if boiled and fried in oil – then taste is not offensive since they have none.

Of the roots, it was tapioca which saved the day. Like all other crops in Singapore it may be planted at any time, as there are no seasons on the island. It flourishes in poor soil with the minimum of attention. From cuttings planted in rigid soil it grows into a picturesque tree varying between five and 12 feet high …

ABOVE The gardens at Selarang, photographed by George Aspinall.
P02569.127

LEFT Showing the garden party at work, this 1944 drawing by Murray Griffin depicts two prisoners carrying a basket of Ceylon spinach.
ART26499

To crop tapioca the tree is pulled from the ground and the tuberous roots collected. When boiled these are not unlike an inferior potato and may be used for a great variety of cooking, all of which were fully exploited by the prison cooks.

Ceylon spinach was another staple crop. It is a fleshy leafed creeper with a red stem, a rapid grower, and may be eaten either raw or cooked. The prisoners considered it a luxury: the natives, on the other hand, found it inedible …

It was not until the move to the gaol had been accomplished that a new vegetable appeared, more prolific, more popular than all the rest. The internees, who had developed an excellent garden within and without the gaol walls, had specialised in *bayam*. The prisoner of war continued with it and *bayam* became the chief crop.

Bayam requires good soil, with plenty of compost or manure. Indeed, if the soil be poor the *bayam* makes a strange protest; the seedlings grow smaller day by day until, after several weeks, the plant appears in miniature, about one inch in height. With rich earth, however, its growth is remarkable … and in 30 days after planting it may be cropped. Under good conditions, *bayam* yielded at the rate of 2½ to three tons to the acre if cropped 32 days after planting and in the subsequent six weeks a further 3½ to four tons … *Bayam* was the ideal medium for the high-pressure gardener at the gaol. Here it was eaten twice daily by everybody in camp …

Once the move to the gaol had been ordered, the Japanese also stated that within the next three months practically the whole of the existing garden area would have to be abandoned. By July 1944 only 15 of the original acres, so laboriously and so assiduously worked, remained … The abandonment was a bitter blow. To start a new undertaking afresh after 27 months' imprisonment requires great stamina and determination. In the gardens, no less than in all other Changi activities, this was not found wanting.

The loss of the old garden was offset by the acquisition of the fine garden [found] in and adjacent to the gaol. This comprised about one acre within the walls and about three acres surrounding them, all of which had been established by the civilian internees. It had been intensely cultivated with a supply of artificial manner [fertiliser: manure nitrogen evaluation routine] ingeniously obtained or manufactured. One such was bonemeal, made from meat offal received by the internees during the period in which meat was supplied to augment the rice ration.

This area, though good, was insufficient for so large a camp. The Japanese accordingly made available a strip of 45 acres of coastal land running north from Tanah Nerah Besan Road, which was about half a mile distant from the camp. Formerly, this had been under rubber, but the timber had already been used for camp firewood. What remained consisted of poor laterite slopes, with patches of more promising soil flanking two malarial drains …

At once, a gang of 400 men were set to work … [and] it was not long before good results were being shown. By this time further supplies of artificial manner were forthcoming and it was decided to concentrate on the better-looking areas convenient to a water supply for greens, and to place the whole of what remained under tapioca.

Grass parties were instituted. Men armed with sickles reaped the spiky lalang grass and piled the hay on trailers. This was turned over with other grass, dug into the sub-soil and

Men attend the garden area inside the walls of Changi Gaol. Note the stack of firewood in the background. Murray Griffin, 1945.
ART25053

again into the topsoil. Seaweed from nearby beaches was also collected and with ash and any available vegetable matter was dug into the soil. Thereafter, with continuous watering and raking, the garden produced surprisingly good results.

The chief fertiliser, however, was urine, a substance in which the camp was unusually productive. An elaborate organisation was set up in the gaol for its collection and gradually arrangements were made for its distribution to all gardens. For this purpose tanks were built on trailers, each with a capacity for 250 gallons. These were hauled out each morning by the men working on this particular garden. The normal procedure was to dilute the urine with water in the proportion 1:2 and apply it in watering cans. Although this practice completely destroyed any of the aesthetics of gardening, it was an invaluable adjustment to the soil … supplying nitrogen and breaking down the compost already dug into the earth. Urine rapidly became a precious fluid. The moment it arrived in a receptacle – a specially constructed tin of enamel bath – it became camp property. To appropriate any of it for use in a private garden was a punishable offence … The output from the camp amounted to some 2500 gallons each day, the quantity varying with changes in temperature. Gardeners were thus doubly enthusiastic when they sensed the arrival of a cold snap.

When the entire reclamation of the Tanah Nerah area was completed, a further 25 acres of the poorest soil were made available along Wing Loon Road, and later 25 additional acres at what became known as 'the valley'.

Once again the maintenance gang commenced its essential operations. They built new drains, constructed 'bands' to prevent soil erosion and installed the water reticulation systems. Starting with nothing except a few lift and force pumps, tools and equipment were gradually stolen, made or improvised and lengths of piping were exhumed from unauthorised places. In addition they set up a workshop and forge where cropping knives and a great variety of implements were made. Even axes were forged and finished off out of any old steel discovered abandoned about the area.

With each increase in the area under cultivation the supply of labour became more difficult. However, when work on the aerodrome was completed a much larger labour force was at once available. It was realised that food in the period immediately prior to the release would be extremely scarce. The Japanese had already stated that, on the Allied invasion of Malaya, the supply of vegetables from outside sources would cease immediately. Gardening, therefore, was rightly regarded as a vital occupation. Under the competent direction of the by now highly experienced garden staff, the output from the 120 acres under cultivation was still further increased until it represented 65 per cent of the vegetables consumed in camp.

> **The chief fertiliser, however, was urine**

Production rose as follows:

March: 39 tons
April: 42 tons
May: 52 tons
June: 44 tons
July: 53 tons
August: 58 tons

The maximum production prior to the move to the gaol had been approximately 34 tons in July 1943. The total output for the entire garden scheme reached the total of 850 tons.

Prisoners cutting lalang grass. Murray Griffin, 1945.
ART25091

In the later stages the garden performed another function in that it enabled a large number of men to eat the Japanese 'heavy-duty' ration. This advantage was fully exploited. Any man fit enough to walk to the gardens was sent out and thus had the benefit of a little extra food at a time when rice was almost measured by the grain. In this way 1500 were employed. Naturally, general efficiency was low, and even on the extra rations everyone lost weight and daily grew weaker.

The value of the gardens was universally recognised and the result achieved was yet another instance of the faculties for improvisation and surmounting of difficulties so characteristic of the Australian temperament.

New life for Captain Dahl's guitar

Chris Goddard
Australian War Memorial

IN 1941 AN UNIDENTIFIED private in the Australian Army Service Corps bought this guitar from a shop in Malaya. It was played in the Changi concert parties by Captain Edward Dahl (84th Light Aid Detachment) before both men were sent to Thetkaw Camp on the Burma railway and the private traded it to Dahl for food. The tropical humidity played havoc with both the guitar and its strings, and by the time Dahl completed the march to Kanburi Camp in February 1945 the guitar's body, already held together with wire, disintegrated in Dahl's arms. Only the fingerboard and tuning heads survived.

With the help of Sergeant Crowther of the Royal Northumberland Fusiliers, who scrounged nails and wood from Japanese stores, Dahl built a new guitar body from tea chests, with the curved corners carved from solid chunks of camp firewood. The body was stained with a mixture of Condy's Crystals, brown boot polish and petrol. Strings were made by wrapping signal wire cores with thin copper wire stolen from radio transmitters, but the wrapping required some 7000 hand-turned revolutions to produce a viable string. A scrounged wind-up gramophone motor later provided a set of 10:1 ratio gears which, mounted to a frame, finally enabled tightly wound and bound strings to be efficiently produced. Nonetheless, the difficulty in making strings meant the guitar was adapted to take only five, rather than six strings. The inside of the three-ply wooden body still bears black stencilled markings from the tea-chests, and one of the original hand-wound strings (the bottom E) remains.

The guitar is accompanied by a protective carrying bag also made by Dahl. This was cut from a brown cotton military valise, the components sewn together using thread pulled from canvas and handmade needles. A carrying strap was adapted from a 1941 webbing equipment strap.

Such artful and inventive improvisation ensured this guitar remained central to the concert parties that Dahl organised and played in until the war's end.

Captain Edward Dahl's guitar is a rare survivor from both Changi and the Burma–Thailand Railway.
RELAWM24605.001

THE AIF FORESTRY COMPANY

E.J. ORAINES

Shortly after the arrival of the AIF at Selarang, it became apparent that firewood was going to be a problem.

The first few days seemed to be taken up in a search conducted by all units for any material that would burn. The most popular firewood appeared to be doors, window shutters and frames in the buildings which were prisoner-of-war billets. Naturally, such sources of firewood had to be protected, if only to preserve the buildings themselves for shelter.

… Division HQ sent instructions to the commanding officer of the Australian Army Ordnance Corps (AAOC) that he was to send a fatigue party to search the camp area for all available firewood and make a fuel dump which could be drawn upon by the bakery and laundry units once they were established.

A party of men of the AAOC, with myself in charge, went to a nearby *padang* and began to saw into lengths of coconut-palm trunks that had been erected in the form of tripods all over the playing fields as obstructions for enemy aircraft. The sawn trunks were then carried to a dump by a chain of men for a distance of about half a mile. This method had to be employed as no trailers were in operation at this time.

This work went on for a short time until … [HQ] decided that, owing to the acute firewood shortage, an organised system to overcome this problem would have to be devised. As a result the AAOC was to be responsible for the supply of fuel to the AIF …

I was informed that I was to be officer in charge of firewood supplies to the camp and that I was to get something organised immediately.

The first problem was where to find a source of supply that would provide a minimum of 16½ tons of firewood a day, sufficient to issue at the rate of 2½ pounds per man per day.

It was found that the trunk of the coconut palm, of which quite a lot were lying about the area, was not suitable as firewood. I then considered the mangrove growing in the swamps in the vicinity of the camp. But the extractions could only be done at low tides, and as the mangrove was of small growth it would have been impossible to obtain the required amount daily. Considerations of health were also a big factor against this idea. As few indigenous trees grew on this part of the island, the only material left to consider was the rubber tree, which was planted extensively all over the island … [It] made good firewood and, as there was no objection to the felling of such trees, our source of supply was assured.

The next problem was the question of tools, which would have to be provided by ourselves as no help could be expected from any other quarter. A search of the camp area resulted

301

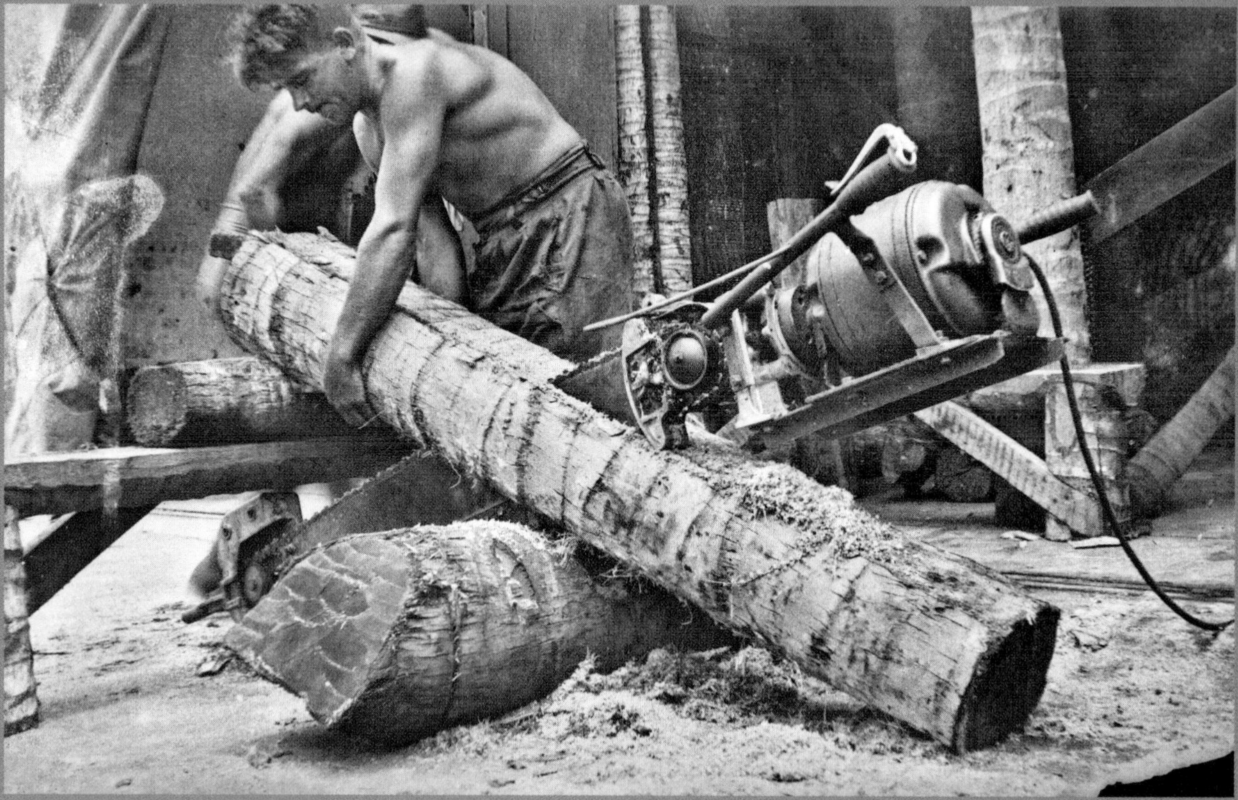

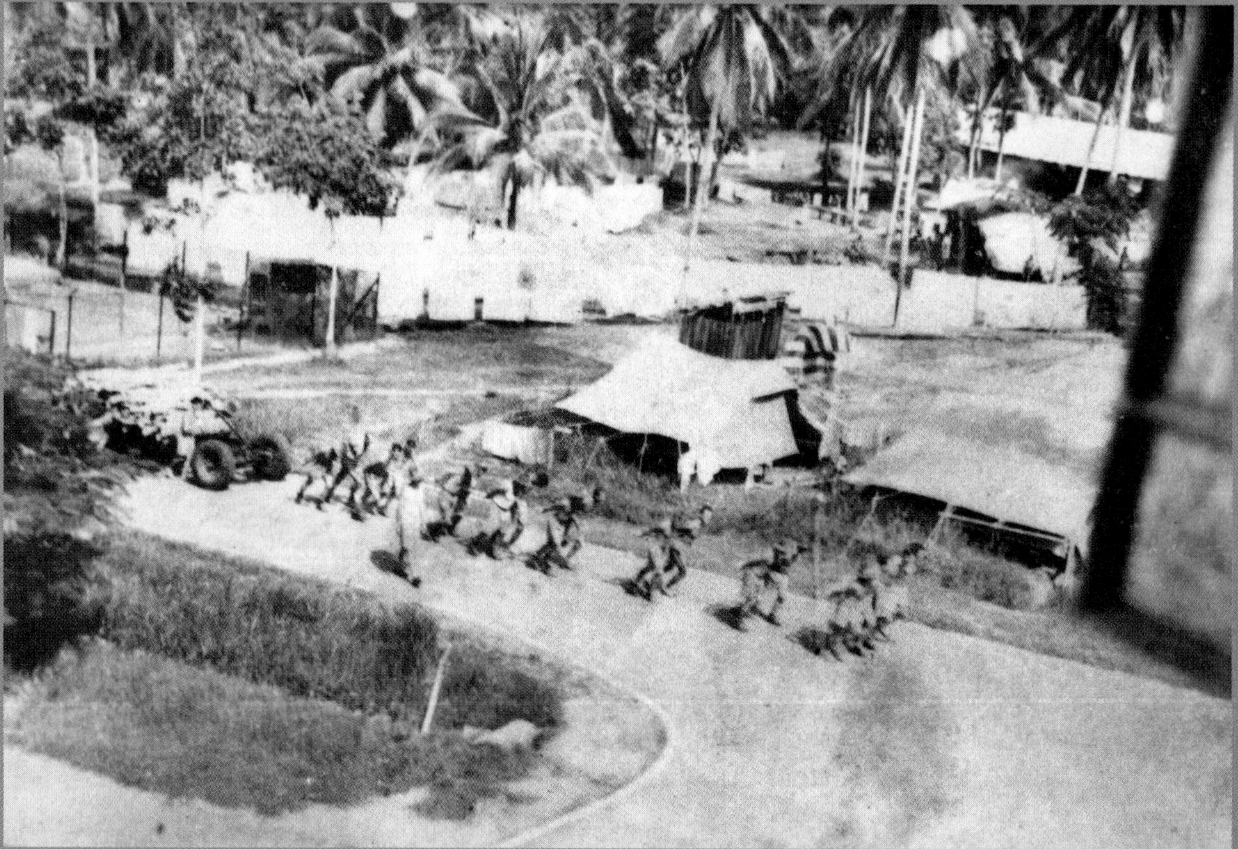

TOP LEFT **A prisoner uses an electric saw, photographed by George Aspinall.**

BOTTOM LEFT **Secretly taken from a window in Selarang Barracks, this photograph shows a trailer party hauling a load of firewood.**

ABOVE **Members of the Forestry Company strip logs near Roberts Barracks. Secretly photographed by Major John Rosson.**

Cutting firewood in
Changi. Murray Griffin,
c. 1942–43.
ART24476

in six crosscut saws and eight axes being obtained which made it now possible for the AIF firewood party to make itself useful.

I was given a party of 50 men ... and work commenced about the 25 February 1942. At the request of Major Maxwell, who wanted to begin a camp vegetable garden, the firewood party commenced to clear a valley situated within the camp boundary, thus serving the dual purpose of clearing the garden area as well as providing fuel for the camp.

... The majority of the men were not used to such work, which was very arduous, and the production of fuel was far behind the requirements. To overcome this difficulty I asked permission of HQ to call for volunteers for this work. This was done and very soon a party of 65 men, mostly experienced axemen and crosscut-sawmen were gathered together.

Transport problems were overcome with the advent of the trailer ... which could be drawn along by 15 or 20 men according to the weight of the chassis. The importance of these trailers and their value to the camp as a method of transport cannot be exaggerated. Without them it would have been impossible to supply the camp with the quantities of fuel required.

So now, having an unlimited supply of firewood, the men and the tools to hew it, and trailers for transportation, it was not long before an efficient system was in operation. Axemen would fell and trim the trees, sawmen would cut the timber into two-foot lengths, the sawn timber was loaded onto trailers and hauled to a depot where the blocks were split. The split wood was then weighed and stacked ready for issue to the various units, who would arrange to collect their quota each day.

In this manner the first 800 tons of firewood were delivered, but, owing to greater demands from the camp, the issuing of split wood had to be abandoned, and from then on firewood was issued in five-foot lengths and the unit cookhouse personnel were told to cut it to suit their own requirements. The number of men employed on this job was then 55 in the field (felling, trimming and sawing), 90 hauling trailers and 15 at the fuel depot splitting, weighing, stacking and issuing the firewood: in all a total of 160.

The British prisoners ... were much impressed

It was not long before every unit was in possession of a trailer ... Instead of obtaining supplies at the fuel depot in the camp all units were instructed to send their own trailers to the cutting area twice a week and load and haul their own firewood to their unit lines.

The British prisoners, of whom there were about 30 000, were split up into three areas in close proximity to the AIF area and were much impressed by the skill, method and organisation of the AIF wood-cutting party. At their request, a demonstration of tree felling, axemanship and crosscut-saw work was carried out ... the three British areas then organised woodcutting parties on similar lines to the AIF.

The early days of prisoner-of-war camp life were not all that could be desired: food was at a minimum, and the spirit of the men to say the least rather lethargic. Not knowing how much a man could work on rice and 'grass stew', I began by placing two men to one axe (working at short intervals alternately) and four men to each crosscut saw. The men hauling trailers were relieved frequently and the whole team was spelled ten minutes every hour. Once the men became hardened to the work it was found that, despite the food and the conditions [and] provided the hours were not overlong, they could carry out quite a good day's work without any apparent physical disability.

…

The wood party's 65 men were drawn from several units (2/4th Machine Gun Battalion, 2/26th Battalion, and the AAOC) and used to assemble at the fuel depot each day. Owing to the variation in quantity and quality of food issued from their own cookhouses, which caused quite a lot of discontent, I applied to HQ to have these men formed into one unit for the duration of the camp. This was done, and the Forestry Company came into existence; we were quartered and fed with the AAOC for some months until being allotted quarters of our own, where we set up our own administration.

Owing to the movement of the parties going to Singapore, Thailand, and Borneo, the strength of the prisoner-of-war camp was very much reduced and the Forestry Company's strength varied accordingly. The first seven months passed with the work going very smoothly. To enable the unit to work outside the boundaries of the camp a flag was issued by the IJA which was an authority for free passage in and out through the wire. Very little supervision by IJA guards was experienced – actually, the only soldiers seen were occasional bicycle patrols who, on seeing the flag, did not interfere.

The morale and comradeship … set a very high standard

In August 1942 one of the British areas … found that it had no more trees to cut … and asked AIF HQ would the AIF Forestry Company help them out. An arrangement was made whereby the AIF company would supply the British with firewood, provided the latter would supplement the AIF party to the extent of 80 men and the necessary officers. This was done, and a combined team of AIF–East Surreys–Manchesters–Leicesters–RAF, [along with] marines and seamen from HMS *Repulse* and HMS *Prince of Wales*, was soon working together in complete harmony. This arrangement carried on until, owing to both British and AIF units requesting further cutting areas, the IJA decided that only one central wood-cutting area would be allowed.

An organisation was then set up by the British Command, forming the British and AIF forestry companies into one group which consisted of approximately 850 men

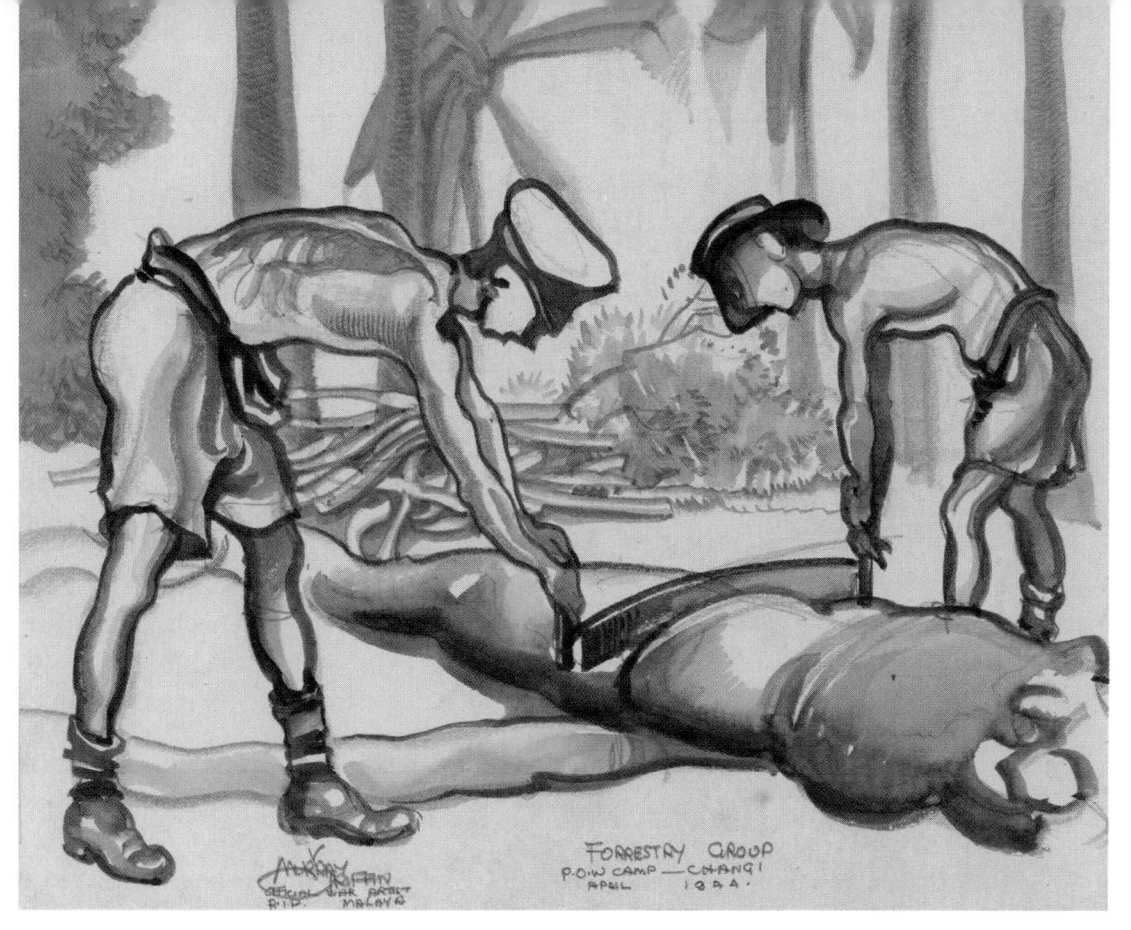

Members of the forestry group sawing logs outside the camp. Murray Griffin, 1944.
ART25098

A member of the forestry group. Murray Griffin, 1944.
ART26517

to supply the entire camp (strength 28 000) with firewood. This meant that the camp would require, including reserves, about 60 tons of fuel to be felled, trimmed, sawn, hauled, weighed and delivered each day. Of this quantity the [men of the] AIF unit, because of their greater skill and better physique, produced about 50 per cent. The AIF Forestry Company at its maximum strength of 153 represented every unit of the 8th Division, and the morale and comradeship of this unit set a very high standard to the camp as a whole. Their work has been commended on several occasions …

…

A sports meeting was held on Christmas Day 1942 and the Forestry Company contributed by conducting a wood-chopping and crosscut-saw competition. These events proved the most popular of the day, and some axemanship and sawing was witnessed by quite a big audience. In the latter the British personnel were the most interested and were greatly impressed by the skill of Corporal Anning, who won the open underhand woodchop (12-inch log of green rubber tree) in the excellent time of 55 seconds, and the vigour of Privates A.G. Walters and J.J. Tierney in winning the open crosscut-saw event by sawing through a ten-inch log of green rubber tree in the remarkable time of $10^{1}/_{5}$ seconds.

During the new year an open boxing tournament was conducted and many entries came from the British and AIF forestry companies, and as I was selected to act as one of the judges, it made our representation complete.

Apart from the Forestry Company's job of supplying firewood to the camp, it also provided timber for the seating of our AIF concert hall, goal posts for basketball courts, staging for group concert platforms, wood for moulds for the Artificial Limb Factory, and wood for the manufacture of clogs by the Convalescent Depot patients. The unit also provided its own axe helves and *changkol* and shovel handles.

I have only the highest praise for the officers, NCOs and men who have worked with the AIF Forestry Company and helped to clear hundreds of acres of ground for vegetable gardens, as well as providing thousands of tons of firewood.

Their work has been of the highest value and was most essential at all times.
18 August 1944

WHEN NOT WORKING, prisoners did their best to take their minds off their predicament. Much has been made of the theatre productions performed by the Changi Concert Party, but less has been said about sporting activities and other informal games and entertainment. Serious organised sport does not match the stereotype of emaciated prisoners of war, but a variety of sport – including all the major football codes – was played in Changi and even in some of the worst camps on the Burma–Thailand Railway. For participants, the playing field could provide a sense of freedom; for the spectators it boosted morale and brought a sense of normality to their lives, breaking up the monotony of camp life and taking their minds – albeit fleetingly – off the arduous work details.[1]

Organised by Corporal Wilfred 'Chicken' Smallhorn, who won the 1933 Brownlow Medal with Fitzroy for best and fairest in the Victorian Football League, the first match of the inaugural Changi Australian Football League season took place in August 1942. The seven teams were named after Victorian league clubs, and they played

Sport, games and gambling

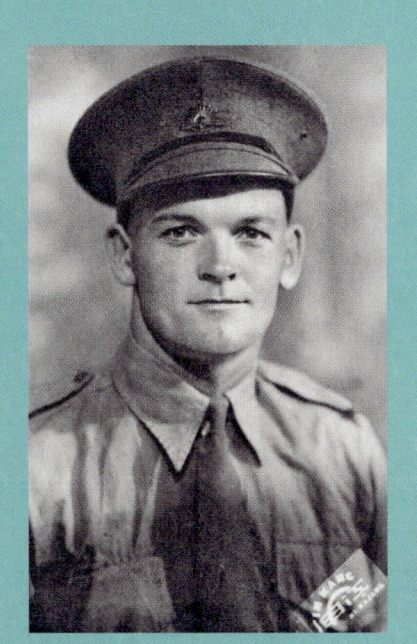

Lachlan Grant
Australian War Memorial

Corporal Chitty (left) of the 2/2nd Motor Ambulance Convoy was awarded the 'Changi Brownlow' (centre and above) in 1943.
P04441.001; REL32808

309

three matches a week. In the grand final, Richmond upset the heavily backed Carlton 10–9–69 to 6–8–44, and the spectacle proved so popular that it was decided the league would continue. Eventually, however, the game was banned because of mounting injuries and a shortage of medical supplies. The last match in Changi took place on 24 January 1943 between Victoria – wearing the traditional 'Big V' – and 'The Rest'.[2]

Captaining the Victorian team was Corporal Leslie 'Peter' Chitty, who was awarded the 1943 Changi Brownlow Medal as the season's best and fairest. Chitty survived the war, and was later awarded the British Empire Medal for his outstanding conduct and devotion to fellow prisoners on the Burma–Thailand Railway.

Cricket was also very popular in Changi, and the Australian vs England 'Ashes' rivalry allowed tensions existing between groups of soldiers since the fall of Singapore to be played out on the sporting field in a more controlled, ordered fashion. The first of the Changi tests took place on 26 April 1942. The Australian team held the only test player in Changi, Captain Ben Barnett of the 8th Division Signals, in its ranks, and was almost unbeatable, so when England broke through for their maiden victory in September it sparked wild celebrations among the British troops.[3] The final test match in Changi was played on Christmas Day 1944, shortly before the Japanese banned sport the following January.

As well as field sports, basketball, golf and boxing were also popular pastimes. On the first Tuesday of November prisoners also replicated Melbourne Cup racing meets. In some places prisoners playing the roles of the thoroughbreds carried smaller men as jockeys. In other places frogs were used as a substitute for horses. The frogs, each painted differently for identification, were let go from under a box in the centre of a circle, and the first out of the circle was the winner.

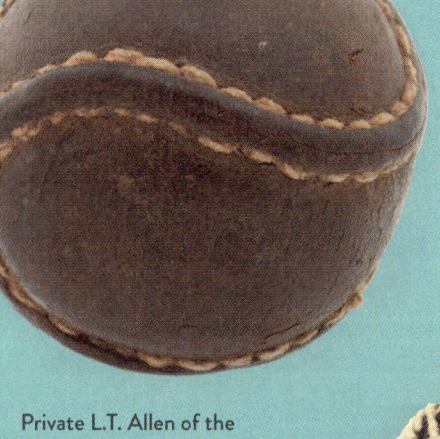

Private L.T. Allen of the 105th Australian General Transport made this cricket ball (above) from the leather of an army boot. It was used in one of the Australia–England test matches. Another example of a handmade cricket ball (right) was souvenired by Ernest Henry, a civilian internee in Changi Gaol.
REL/11924 / REL19909.001

310

The event was detailed in the diary of Sergeant John Nevell of the 2/10th Field Regiment:

> The frog racing is getting underway here ... The kitchen was nearly turned over this morning when the favourite got out of his stable, but was found under the wood supply to the great delight of his backers. The excitement is terrific and it really is something to see two frogs pull up on the finishing line, while another takes a mighty bound over them to win ... Some of the bookmakers were doing the same job at home. They really enjoy themselves. Forget where they are for a while and so do most of us ... One owner was put out for life by the Stipendary Stewards because he tied a bent pin to the back leg of his frog so that every time it squatted it sat on the point and jumped again.[4]

ABOVE The Melbourne Cup trophy awarded to the frog 'Triggerman', owned by Captain William Dixon of the Australian Army Service Corps, from the meet at Adam Park Camp in Singapore.
REL AWM31985

RIGHT The race judge's badge belonging to Driver Edward Davis of the 2/3rd Motor Ambulance Convoy.
REL30164

These playing cards were handmade from the backs of cigarette packets by Major B. Hunt of the 2/13th AGH. The Joker is marked with J. Joker's gravestone and 'The jolly Joker died in Thailand'. *Jacks*: Hearts carries a tray of food; Spades is an emaciated prisoner with a bowl, spoon, cigarette and patched shorts; Clubs carries a log of wood; and Diamonds is chopping wood. *Queens*: Hearts is a girl in a photo frame; Spades is a *Queen* magazine cover; Clubs is a pin-up girl; and Diamonds is a postcard addressed to 'Mrs POW Australia'. *Kings*: Hearts is a naval officer; Spades is a cook; Clubs a Japanese guard; and Diamonds a military policeman; *Aces*: Hearts shows the sentry post at Gaol Corner; Spades shows Changi Gaol; Clubs shows Changi Gaol in 1945; and Diamonds the entrance to the gaol.
REL/04536.001

As Nevell reveals, much of the pomp and ceremony of the real cup meet was followed, including the gambling. In fact, gambling was of great concern to AIF Command. Within weeks of entering the camp, organised gambling and the issuing of IOUs, which more than often related to gambling debts, were banned.[5] Regardless, men lost items of clothing and possibly even food or water rations in waging bets. In July 1942 one prisoner wrote in his diary that 'some men won twenty or thirty thousand dollars and could live very well'.[6]

2ND ECHELON

UNKNOWN AUTHOR

During normal times – that is, during times when each unit of the army is performing its normal functions, whether it be in peace or war – there are comparatively few members of the force who know what the functions of 2nd Echelon are. Indeed, there are many who have not even heard of it at all.

This state of affairs changed almost overnight when the 8th Division in Malaya became prisoners of war. It was natural that everyone was anxious to know: What had become of their missing friend or relative? … The answer was, 'Go to 2nd Echelon. They will tell you!' So, in a very short time the unit was well known by almost every prisoner of war in the camp.

It is often referred to as the Records Office, but the keeping of records is only part of the functions of 2nd Echelon. There are several departments, such as medical, casualty, and personal effects and registry sections, in addition to the records section. The latter is, however, the biggest and represents the bulk of the activities …

Records was kept fairly busy because of the fact that the force was allowed to administer itself and the camp was more in the nature of a training camp, with notable differences such as food and barbed wire.

During action we lost all our records … [but] on 16 February 1942 we were able to get back to Stephens Road, Singapore, where our office was last located, and collect a good deal of the records left there. The house wherein we were quartered … had been thoroughly ransacked and our stuff was scattered all over the landscape. Fortunately, the basic records – the personal history sheets of all personnel – were in good order.

These were brought to Changi and we were able to build up a working organisation on this foundation … The number who marched out to Changi from Singapore approximated 15 000. Then started a hectic time for the 2nd Echelon staff. The IJA was yelling for rolls of all prisoners of war. Our own people needed strength returns for ration purposes; units were demanding information so that they could supply information and returns demanded from them. During all this we were receiving all manner of reports relating to the whereabouts or deaths of personnel who were scattered all over the Malaya peninsula and surrounding islands. All of these had to be investigated and recorded. In addition we were compiling rolls of casualties in the hope that the IJA would get them home immediately – vain hope! The first complete roll of all known casualties was handed to the IJA early in March 1942. Prisoner-of-war rolls had been given them earlier. As men were turning up all the time and fresh casualties were being reported, we supplied supplementary rolls twice per month. We were under the impression that this was being sent home …

In August 1945 members of 2nd Echelon recovered records that had been hidden and buried in water tanks. On the left is Lieutenant Alexander Kenneth Marshall, the officer in charge of 2nd Echelon Malaya. In recognition of the significance of his work in Changi, Marshall was awarded a Member of the Order of the British Empire in 1947.

Working conditions during this period were terrible. We were continually being moved from building to building. Space was very limited, we had no light, and frequently were almost washed out during heavy rains. However, strained though our tempers were, we were so busy that time simply flew, and this fact was truly a blessing. We had no time to sympathise with ourselves, or each other.

Although we were recording a sad and sorry tale, there was a certain amount of excitement and interest attached to it. The office was organised in much the same manner as it was previous to capitulation. Clerks had the same unit records to keep as previously and even if they did not know each soldier in those units personally they had, through months of keeping track of each man, acquired a personal interest in each one. When any one of these turned up in camp, or was reported to be in Sumatra or elsewhere, the excitement was equal to that experienced when an old friend has been met after a period of absence. When a report of death came in, the feeling of sorrow was just as intense.

Looking back over the records compiled during those early days one wonders how in the name of goodness such information reached us. But on recollection one remembers notes passed to us by a stray Chinaman or Malay, written by one of our lads weeks previously giving names of chaps who were in a Chinese or Malay camp miles away in the jungle. Tales of great hardship, cruelty and heroism were passed to us by these underground routes.

In March 1942 the IJA started to take parties of prisoners to Singapore for work on various jobs … on the wharves, building shrines, memorials, and temples … until by September the same year more than 7000 AIF and many more British were out on those jobs. On a few occasions burial parties were allowed to visit certain areas to locate and bury the naked bodies of fallen men. These parties did good work, and forwarded their reports to 2nd Echelon, giving the identifications where possible, dates of burials and map references. All very useful, but the identifications were often very mistaken. Fortunately, we were well aware of their difficulties and the traps into which they were likely to fall. Identity discs were useless after they had been in the open for a few weeks. They rotted very quickly in this wet and hot climate. Soldiers wore each other's clothes and steel helmets, so the markings on these articles were misleading. Pay books were missing from most of the bodies, and the bodies themselves were unrecognisable. The parties were not 'awake' to all these traps and, consequently, identifications were often wrong. We were very cautious about accepting these reports and posted all the casualties reported by these parties as 'missing' or 'missing – believed killed in action'. The case of a certain lieutenant occurred early in our prisoner-of-war days and served as the best possible lesson to us [as to] how careful we must be in accepting identifications.

A British burial party came across a number of AIF bodies and buried them, forwarding their report in due course to 2nd Echelon. Now, these chaps did an excellent job of work, giving very full details …

The officer in charge of the burial party supplied us with all the particulars necessary to establish a positive identification – number, rank, name, identification disc, pay book number, but no pay book. He gave us other details which further strengthened identification, [but] this lieutenant was in Changi Camp and alive. We wrote to the party commander and asked for any other information which he may have and which may help us to identify the body. I suppose he thought us mad … in his mind, there was no doubt whatever that he had done a good job of work. Imagine his surprise when he subsequently learned that his lieutenant was alive and well.

…

Our work went on, month after weary month. Our great satisfaction lay in the fact that we were doing an essential work – and for ourselves – whereas most prisoners

ABOVE A Church of England chaplain officiates at the funeral of an ex-prisoner-of-war in the Changi cemetery. The man had died in the days following liberation.
117660

LEFT A burial cortège carrying a coffin swathed in the Union Jack passes through the hospital area in Changi. Murray Griffin, 1945.
ART26480

were thoroughly miserable doing nothing, or working for the IJA.

Just as we had the hard work done and had our records of casualties in good shape, along came the grim stories from Burma and Thailand. These were far worse than any of the fighting period experiences. The casualties were five times greater, and from Records' point of view the collection of vital information was five times more difficult. In fact, until the final count, when are all assembled, it will be impossible to get a true picture of the sad experience.

THE WORK OF THE AUSTRALIAN CHAPLAINS' DEPARTMENT

UNKNOWN AUTHOR

That long trek, two days after capitulation, through country unknown in the darkness which hid every thing of beauty which might have made such a march interesting … landed at Selarang, a body of men feeling rather like a boxer who, expecting to deliver the knock-out blow, finds himself just coming-to in the dressing room.

The spirit seemed one of disappointment and unreality: it all seemed so outside our expectations and almost beyond possibility that British troops should have in so short a time have had to capitulate. Tiredness and hunger combined to supply the ground for the most despondent gloom to settle, and it was in this atmosphere that the Australian Army Chaplains' Department had to find and offer suitable inspiration.

Such inspiration had to be more than soothing; it had to be virile and positive. A caption or motto for the period seemed to be found in a verse of a Psalm [blessing those] 'Who going through the vale of misery use it for a well', and the task of the chaplains seemed to be to encourage men to see even in this calamity something from which could be wrested a positive good which, by its virility and purposefulness, would banish the sting and bitterness of captivity.

This was the tone set at the first services held in the new area, and it was the purpose of the department throughout the capitulation period not merely to keep our chins up, not merely to show that 'we can take it', but [to show] that we can use it, and come out of it better than we went in, with lessons learned which would make us better citizens in the life which lay ahead – as we hoped then – in the near future.

On that first Sunday, with many of the chaplains still on duty in the hospital to which they had been sent, services were held in every AIF area. These were well attended, and it seemed that there was a response to the suggestion made above, that we should rise above the circumstances and build a citizenship worthy of our race to be used in the afterwar period.

…

Services normally were in the open air, and continued to be well attended. At one centre more than 100 men each Sunday morning attended Communion in the open, and these services breathed an atmosphere of reality and sincerity which will make them long-remembered …

Gradually, however, it was realised that our stay would be longer than at first we in our wild hopes and dreams had imagined, and the need for more permanent locations for services was realised. The AAOC got busy with a small chapel made by the troops, and while that unit was in that location it was of immense value. A more permanent structure was built

An early Roman Catholic chapel, Changi. Murray Griffin, 1942.
ART25061

by the sappers on a piece of ground opposite Headquarters. This proved to be a centre of beauty as well as of usefulness. It was on a green sward which reminded one somewhat of an English green, though the foliage and house in the near vicinity were tropical rather than English. By hard work and the passing of time a garden was developed round it and it brought in the somewhat barren atmosphere of the camp an oasis of freshness and beauty which was appreciated by all – and there were many passers-by and worshippers alike. It was dedicated to the name of Andrew on Whitsunday 1942 – this happened also to be Empire Day – and it fulfilled a role which must have gladdened the heart of those responsible for its building.

One of the earliest tasks which chaplains had to undertake was the burial of men who came out with our hospital units after wounds received in war. The first of these was on the first Sunday in camp. The location was given to

Chapel of St Andrew and St Luke, one of the denominational chapels built by prisoners in Changi. Murray Griffin, March 1945.
ART26460

the chaplain concerned and on arrival he found an area of fairly dense jungle growth with a space sufficient for one or at most two graves … It must be confessed that for many months the cemetery was not a place of inspiration; nothing much more was done for it than to clear sufficient space as it was needed, but later a Cemetery Party was permanently employed and their work resulted in a lovely spot, quiet and peaceful, a fit resting place for men who have offered their lives to their country's cause.

It was here that the first Armistice Day memorial service was held on 11 November. Many of the troops had gone to working parties in the city and others to what became to be known as 'overseas' parties, but some 1000 paraded under the AIF commanding officer at that spot and remembered comrades of two wars in a very simple, yet impressive, service.

… Nearly 3000 troops assembled in front of the Convalescent Depot on Anzac Day 1942… at break of dawn. Looking down on the assembly from the platform it was not difficult to imagine the original day. Across the lawn there were figures of troops making

THE WORK OF THE AUSTRALIAN CHAPLAINS' DEPARTMENT

their way to their places, quietly and, in the darkness, shadowy. Beyond them one could see the waters of the straits, and above in the distant east the grey lines of the approaching dawn. Suddenly, a call to attention, and across the parade marched some 500 men of that old war with their ribbons bearing witness to that fact. A few hymns, prayers, and a short address – the light all the time gradually becoming brighter – and then the final blowing of the trumpets, and a silence …

During this time confirmation classes had been conducted throughout the camp, and in August the Bishop of Singapore, accompanied by his own Malay chaplain and escorted by a Nipponese officer, came out and administered the rite of confirmation to some 180 men, English and AIF, in a chapel in the Indian lines which had formerly been a Mosque. It was most impressive, but what followed was even more so. An English welfare officer admitted to the Order of Deacon at St Andrew's Cathedral during the last few days of that bombardment of the city was ordained to the priesthood in the presence of English, AIF, and Malay clergy, with an officer of their Japanese enemies, all of whom knelt at the Communion rails. It was symbolic of what Christianity really meant, when properly understood – the fellowship of all men, of all nations in common loyalty to the one person. Unfortunately, such symbols are rare, and the subsequent history of the camp and certain news which reached us on that very day took away from the joy of that fellowship.

Possibly some of the most impressive services were those held on Christmas Eve … In some cases preceded by carol services and then Christmas music later in the night, Communion services were held at midnight. The response was amazing, hundreds attending each service. It is not too much to say that these services set a tone and called forth a spirit which made that Christmas worthy of comparison with others spent in the happier days of peace. It seemed that the men, having little of the material accompaniments of that usually festive season, had sought the inner and deeper significance of the day, and were caught by the spirit of the Christ …

One Chaplain interested himself in the training of future Scoutmasters, and a troop was held for many months … In the realm of sport and other recreational exercises the chaplains have taken a keen interest, arranging lectures and giving them, associating themselves with the official educational program as well as privately coaching men in subjects needed for future examinations.

…

The normal and primary work of the chaplains – by making contact with men in their lines, and by participation in their work by days spent in the garden groups and with the aerodrome party – has been going on the whole time. The hospitals have been visited and detention barracks serviced.

One other avenue of service which originated within the Chaplains' Department has been the work of the Changi Union.

321

The chapel seen here in 1945 was packed up and sent to the Australian War Memorial. Reassembled in 1988, it is now the Changi Chapel National Prisoner of War Memorial, located in the grounds of the Royal Military College at Duntroon, Canberra.

THE WORK OF THE AUSTRALIAN CHAPLAINS' DEPARTMENT

Originally, it was intended to hold a series of addresses at the St Andrew's Chapel, but this was enlarged by the invitation of YMCA representatives and other interested laymen to organise a wider series at the Convalescent Depot. Although at the time the camp was not numerically strong, yet the series was attended by crowded audiences and the questions each night showed a keen interest. From this grew a further series of study circles and later another series of meetings and a more permanent organisation. The Changi Union has since developed an employment bureau to assist men in preparing for the future, and an immigration bureau to give information and to assist men thinking of Australia as their future home. The work of the union has been one of the features of the camp life.

… From an early date working parties were organised for Singapore and later for 'overseas' parties. As far as possible chaplains of the AIF were sent with all these parties or, when impossible, arrangements were made for English chaplains accompanying the parties to attend to AIF personnel. The reports of their work have been gratifying – it was often under hard conditions – especially in the north.

Here it was that the AIF suffered the loss of two chaplains. Ross Dean and Geoff Vellacott travelled with troops [and] Ross was struck down on the journey. Geoff continued doing good work [until he too was struck down with illness] and their memory lives with us … Many of our chaplains are scattered all over the lands of the Pacific, but we hear of them from time to time from men who return through our hospitals; the news is always good and the reports of their work bring gladness.

[This] is not a full account. In the nature of things it must leave much out. The work of the chaplain is not overly dramatic or exciting. Perhaps the best part of it is never known. One is often asked, 'What has been the impact of the work of the chaplains upon the life of this camp?' The question is not one which can be answered. Statistics of services, of communicants, of classes, and of hospital visitations could be given, and they would be impressive … It is clear that much more could have been done. Chaplains are human beings subject to error of judgement, to failure to grasp every opportunity, [along] with the faults of other men: but the work during this period has been well maintained … and has made its contribution to the upholding of the spirit of men … what is more important: it has been directed to the development of such quality of manhood as will be permanently directed to the bringing in of the kingdom of God in the life to which we all look forward after the war is over. The forces which play upon the character of man, checking his tendencies to forget his true manhood and become merely an intellectual animal, have found great opportunity in our incarceration to attack men with great vigour. The work of the chaplains is directed to bringing men back to the realisation that they are sons of God as

323

WORK AND WORK PARTIES

well as sons of the soil. The impact of such work must be impossible of exact determination – only the men concerned fully realise it … It has been a great opportunity: it has been a hard job, continuous, tiring and exacting, calling for the full concentration of all one's faculties without aid of those things usually at a padre's disposal, but it has been gloriously worth while. The writer of this article would not have missed the experience for anything. It will remain a treasured memory, its influence to be a contribution to the re-building of life in Australia on our return.

ABOVE **Carved from teak, this memorial tablet once decorated the Chapel of the Good Shepherd at Changi.**
RELAWM27489

This imitation stained-glass window by Murray Griffin adorned the Chapel of St Andrew and St Luke.
RELAWM27488

> Went to the dawn service and it was one of the most impressive services that I have been fortunate enough to attend.
> *Sergeant Lennon, Anzac Day, 25 April 1942*

Anzac Day in Changi

Lachlan Grant
Australian War Memorial

Sergeant John Leslie Lennon was a veteran of the First World War, having enlisted in the First AIF in January 1916, aged 21. He lied about his age in order to enlist for the Second AIF in June 1940, claiming to be 38 when in fact he was 45. The day of Singapore's capitulation was Lennon's 47th birthday. By this time he had survived not only the battle of Passchendaele in October 1917, where he was wounded and gassed, but also the fighting in Malaya and Singapore. He also endured three and a half years as a prisoner of war, returning home safely in 1945 as a 50-year-old sergeant.

Lennon was one of more than 500 'old diggers' in Changi for that first Anzac Day in captivity. The 8th Division War Diary estimated that 200 of these men were original Anzacs who had fought on Gallipoli. In total, more than 2000 men attended the dawn service. A parade followed, led by the piped band of the Gordon Highlanders.[1]

The following year many of the men present in 1942 had since departed on work parties to Burma, Thailand or Borneo. For members of D Force, Anzac Day 1943 marked their arrival at Hellfire Pass on the Burma–Thailand Railway. On Anzac Day 1944 word spread through Changi that the camp was soon to relocate to the gaol. Regardless of the happenings or circumstance, Anzac Day was always marked by the prisoners of war.

Officers lay floral wreaths by a cross marked 'In remembrance' at the cemetery between Roberts Barracks and Selarang Barracks on Anzac Day, 1942.
P04485.035

FISHING FROM BEHIND SCRATCH
JACK BENNETT

Shortly after the Japanese concentrated at Changi the prisoners … decided that due to the lack of suitable foods a scheme should be put into operation with a view to obtaining fresh fish for our seriously wounded and sick personnel. My first contact with the scheme was an intimation that I had been appointed Director of Fishing, AIF – such an important-sounding title that it almost scared me.

No nets, lines, hooks, boats or other material normally used in fishing were available, and requests made to the Japanese and subsequently repeated for some of these items, of which there could have been no shortage, brought forth absolutely nothing. Our hosts expressly forbade us to build a boat, raft or any structure that would float. Apart from a small quantity of small hooks and a few lines which we were able to purchase sometime after we commenced operations, we were unable to get any fishing gear whatever.

However, I selected a small party of men from 2nd Company AASC, mostly Queenslanders, including some who had fishing experience off the Queensland coast and in the Great Barrier Reef. Despite the total absence of tangible assets, the working partners (there were no sleeping ones) in this venture provided excellent capital in the form of determination plus stacks of Australian initiative and bushcraft.

Reconnaissance revealed that our operations were limited to a short length of Tanah Merah beach, from which one looks out over the South China Sea. However, the beach above high tide and the adjacent area were still mined with anti-tank and anti-personnel mines …

Lieutenant Alan Dobbie of the Royal Australian Engineers, who knew the minefield, picked a track through it for us. This track was marked by tying pieces of rag on sticks and coconut palms … In the water we found barbed wire and beach obstacles while concrete pill-boxes were along the beach front – we could not help remarking, however, how helpful similar defences would have been if located on the part of Singapore Island where a few weeks before the AIF had stood the onslaught of the Japanese attack and landing.

It was evident that under the best circumstances there was not much scope for successful fishing, and less under the conditions that were forced on us. But the need for fish was urgent and it was decided that after clearing the wire and obstacles from the water we would erect a fish trap, and that while the fish trap was being erected we would endeavour to maintain a supply of fish to the Australian General Hospital by exploiting a big lagoon in a coconut grove near the beach.

The abandoned Malay *kampongs* in the coconut grove yielded a limited amount of old wire netting, poles and timber. By joining lengths of wire netting and interweaving small saplings a rough net was constructed. We then stripped off and carried this net into the lagoon, the party being distributed along the length of the net, each man placing the toes of one foot in the bottom line of the mesh to hold it under the water while the top of the net was held above our heads. Often chaps would bump into a submerged snag or walk into a deep hole and disappear to the slimy bottom. However, with this contraption we made several sweepings of the lagoon daily and succeeded in catching quite a quantity of good fish which was taken back to the camp and delivered to the hospital …

Australian prisoners preparing fish. From the Aspinall collection.
P02569.135

After getting a reasonable catch from the pool, the days were occupied collecting material from the abandoned *kampongs* as well as the prisoner-of-war camp for the building of a fish trap into the sea. The party worked like Trojans, scrounging materials and man-handling them considerable distances over tracks to the beach.

The type of trap decided upon was made up of a main fence, about 12 feet high and 180 yards in length, running out from the shore into the sea; at the seaward end two wings, each of about 15 yards, were built out from the main fence. At the point of junction of the main fence and the wings was a mesh reception box on a wooden framework, which in turn was kept in position by a frame of steel rails scrounged from a narrow gauge railway. The trap was raised and lowered by pulleys and, owing to the lack of raft or a boat, the trap could be cleared at low tide only.

The boys went to it with a will and worked long hours. The sea-bed proved rather treacherous, having a thick, slimy bottom, plentiful in snags. Spiked fish were also encountered. From one thing or another legs and bodies came in for a considerable amount of rough treatment. To drive long poles into the mud bottom it was necessary for one man to stand on the shoulders of another, and the chap underneath often sank so deep into the slime that the services of a couple of his cobbers were required to pull him out of the evil-smelling muck. At the end of the day's work it was a difficult matter getting bodies cleaned, as we soon learned in our first days of imprisonment that soap, like most of the other commonplace commodities which were formerly accepted as a matter of fact, was now a luxury item … While we were erecting the trap our engineers were taking up the minefield; occasionally a mine would explode but, apart from a shower of sand, no damage was done.

The trap was completed and the catches were reasonably satisfactory … In the lagoon we carried out limited operations with the wire-netting devices with a view to supplementing, when necessary, the catches from the sea trap, thus leaving a supply of fish in the lagoon for breeding and also to serve as some sort of reserve supply should the yields from our fish trap fall off unduly.

The powers that be decreed about the middle of March 1942 that this lagoon was no longer available for fishing by the AIF but was to be set aside for angling by British officers. Naturally, we were both disappointed and annoyed. However, a couple of months later the lagoon disappeared as a result of some Tamils opening the cocks which drained the water out into the sea … to quickly obtain what fish were left …

With the passing of war clouds over the island, Malays and Tamils commenced to return to their *kampongs* along the beach and in the coconut groves. With their return, poaching of the trap commenced … it was obvious that the trap should be picquetted, and endeavours were made to get the Japanese to agree to some of the fishing party being quartered in the pillbox or unoccupied hut – but to no avail.

There were periods when the flags issued by the Japanese for use as authority to proceed out of camp perimeter were insufficient to permit daily visits to the beach, while on other occasions Japanese regulations dealing with cholera forbade us going. It was during these periods of absence that Malays, Tamils and others became very conversant with the working of the trap. Despite our 'working the tides', visiting the beach before dawn, and remaining there as late in the evening as the Japanese or Sikh guards would permit, we could not overcome this poaching problem … we combated the menace and some of our methods met with limited success, but it was impossible to beat the intruders who had boats and access to the trap at night when we had to return to the camp. The Japanese said that they had 'warned off' the natives about poaching, but if this was done it had little – if any – effect.

Big organised net-fishing parties operating under Japanese authorities then made an appearance along the beach and scores of boats fished in the deeper waters. This meant more competition. The next trouble was raids on the trap by Malays and others who cut out and stole long lengths of wire netting. Storms and heavy seas also played havoc at times.

Despite these difficulties the stalwarts who made up the Fishing Party cheerfully persevered. Often up before dawn and down to the beach for some hours, not getting back to camp for the first meal of the day … Rations are very light and poor but [there is] never a complaint about the job. After the meal, back again to the beach to effect repairs, picquet the trap and later clear it at low tide and deliver the fish to the hospital. Each day they walked miles and did plenty of work … Despite the aching voids caused by hard work and poor rations, it would have been difficult to obtain a happier or harder-working lot of chaps. The senior NCOs were Sergeant K.K. 'Katie' Smith, a farmer from Queensland, and the most expert fisherman, Lance Corporal L.T. 'Darcy' Smith, also from Queensland. Darcy had a great reputation as a fisherman/cook on the Barrier Reef and we all agreed that after our stay with the Nipponese was finished the party would have a reunion on the Reef, each man bringing an agreed quantity of beer and tucker, and Darcy would do the rest.

…

The benefits accruing to our hospital patients as a result of fish supplied by the party caused our British friends to become interested, and it was decided that the British formations would put similar schemes into operation. We furnished them with details of our trap and gave them the benefit of our experience and sited some places for the erection of traps in the area.

Private 'Jock' Campbell smoking fish in an improvised smoker made from a metal locker. Note Campbell's prosthetic leg. While the nearly rotten fish depicted here had been issued as rations by the Japanese, fresh fish was also provided to the hospital by the AIF Fishing Party. Murray Griffin, 1943. ART25075.

Eventually, we were able to purchase a small quantity of fish hooks and lines and started set-line fishing. For a while the set-lines were quite successful, but the opposition soon made their observations and the result was the disappearance of 50 out of 60 hooks and much line, all within 24 hours.

One morning we found a stubborn-looking visitor on our beach in the form of a 500-pound TNT mine; apparently it had broken from its moorings in the minefield across the entrance to Johore Straits and Keppel Harbour. A bomb disposal officer judged it to be in a dangerous condition. The Japanese promised to explode it by machine-gun fire but showed no inclination to give effect to the promise, and so the mine kept us company until we ceased our activities at the beach some time later.

> **The AIF Fishing Party caught ... almost 2000 pounds of fish**

It was evident, due to the lack of co-operation by the Japanese in making reasonable facilities available ... that the effort required to catch the ever-decreasing quantities of fish would be out of all proportion. Accordingly, we inspected the foreshore of the Johore Straits adjacent to Loyang Submarine Base. This area was then closed to all natives and the prospects of good yields were reasonably bright. Arrangements were made to dismantle the traps at the Tanah Merah beach and move the material to Loyang ... but just as we were about to make the move the Japanese navy took over the Loyang base – that, of course, meant our exclusion from the area, and so the activities of the AIF Fishing Party were brought to a close.

The party started from behind scratch and met with plenty of interference in the race for fish. While it may not sound much, the AIF Fishing Party caught and delivered to the Australian General Hospital almost 2000 pounds of fish over a period when such food was urgently required for seriously wounded and ill patients. Medical officers stated it was of considerable value to many and helped some 'around the corner', particularly those who had limbs amputated and were struggling against the Grim Reaper without the assistance of the nourishing foods that normally would have been available to them. Because of that we felt that the effort was worth while.

...

This uncoloured account of the AIF Fishing Party would be incomplete without reference to the undermentioned chaps who made it a successful venture. The working of long hours, endurance and fatigue, the discomfort of bites and stings from marine creatures, and absolute honesty despite the temptation arising from handling an appetising form of good food when they themselves were poorly fed are but a few of the things that one can say of these good sons of Australia:

Sergeant K.K. Smith
Lance Corporal L.T. Smith
Private E.B. Praske (died in Thailand)
Private W.P. Wright (died in Thailand)
Private E.A. Coates
Private G.H. Singleton (died in Thailand)
Private A.A. Richards
Private W.H. Bernard
Private J.A. Britton (died in Thailand)
Private H.R. Short

J.W. Bennett
20 September 1944

THE AERODROME AT CHANGI POINT

STAN ARNEIL

There is an aerodrome at Changi Point, an attractive drome, too, built in the shape of a cross with the main strips 300 metres wide by 2000 long, with one green arm pushing its coconut-bordered edges right into the lazy tropical sea and with friendly, red-roofed buildings sitting on a hill and gazing down.

It is a pleasant drome, well drained, with evenly sloped banks bordering the strips, a solid sea wall and long, smooth roads winding around and about the whole of the area. It is pleasant to ride along these roads, where the coconuts give way to glimpses of green grass and sparkling blue water, but it is rather a shock to stop beside either of the two cemeteries. They, too, are well kept, and beneath those simple mounds lie dozens of men who at some time worked on the Changi drome.

In September 1943, after some slight verbal sparring between the Japanese and Camp Headquarters, 800 men began work … In order not to offend the Australian military conscience, Camp HQ was solemnly assured that the men were to be used only to level off a sports field …

The first month's work was quite a change from the usual camp duties. Caterpillar tractors were used to push acres of palms flat to the ground and thousands of ripe nuts were carried into camp to augment the rations.

The harvest did not last very long; every tree which fell to the ground had to be cut into sections and carried to the edges of the perimeter. Men recently out of hospital or lately convalescent were not well enough to stand the strain of heavy lifting and, continually falling sick, forced the fitter men to work every day without the benefit of an occasional holiday.

To ease the situation the Japanese blandly agreed to accept two types of labourers: one for light-duty jobs and the other for heavy work. It was a great theoretical improvement, but as the Japanese overseers took not the slightest interest in light- or heavy-duty personnel and handed out log-carrying jobs and grass-clearing tasks with no discrimination at all, the idea was quickly abandoned.

Shelter on the job was non-existent, and during the frequent storms men stood in the rain, like horses, with shoulders hunched to the weather, wrapping their ragged shirts and long-since unserviceable capes, if any, around them. After each wet day a percentage of men would automatically suffer relapses of malaria, but no decrease in the numbers of workers was allowed for such a trifling complaint.

By the end of January 1944 the strain of the constant work was so great that convalescent personnel from the remnants of the lately returned F and H Forces began to work on the drome, which was then beginning to take on the outlines of a landing field.

George's Sprod's cover for *Smoke-oh*, 1945. The magazine ran for two issues only and was discontinued when Sprod was drafted for a party building Japanese defences.
3DRL/5040.002

Light, two-foot gauge railways crept across the cleared sections of ground and men shifted hundreds of tons of earth daily by filling skips of one cubic yard capacity and pushing them to a dumping point where the soil was levelled out. The work was constant and was made a great deal harder by the crude tools issued to the workers: shovels and *changkols* with straight wooden handles and blades fashioned from petrol tins or galvanised iron made the work a great deal harder than it should have been.

The prisoners worked in hats and ragged shorts; the luckier men wore old boots or makeshift clogs hewn from rubber trees.

These scanty clothes were less decent than those worn by the coolies, and afforded little protection from the hot sun which beat down upon the area and reflected from the bare ground with such fierce intensity that scores of men were placed in hospital suffering with strained and affected eyes.

The daily loss of salt from constantly perspiring bodies could not be replaced by the meagre ration ($1/2$ ounce per man daily) provided by the Japanese, and men lost weight rapidly and began to take on a 'burnt-out' appearance with accompanying lassitude and lack of energy. Repeated requests to the IJA authorities for more salt were curtly refused; instead, a few grams of rice, enough to give each man less than a pint of thin gruel, were issued to the workers.

This stop-gap was turned to good account only by the Australian ingenuity of the tea boilers attached to each party. These men, who were always selected for their 'scrounging' abilities, began the practice of gathering 'pig weed' and tender grasses which were boiled with the rice in sea water. The resultant gruel was salty enough to make up for some of the salt deficiency in the camp rations.

Conditions altered slightly when two-thirds of the men were transferred from all-day work to six-hour shifts, the first shift finishing at 2 pm and the second at 8 pm. This meant that troops working on an afternoon shift were able to sleep late in the morning but by the same token did not eat their evening meal until 9.30 pm. No official rest periods were allowed during these shifts and the men drank a cup of black, unsweetened tea and swallowed their miserable gruel when time and the Japanese permitted.

The altered working hours were welcomed for other reasons than those which could be classed as legitimate and official: the black-market facilities on the drome were increased in proportion to the increase in total working hours, and the changing parties of men on the job gave the Japanese overseers less time to watch for these determined traders.

From the first hour of the early shift until the troops were assembled to march home through the sunset, ragged prisoners contacted Indians, Malays, and Chinese in the thick mangrove swamps and coconut plantations surrounding the drome. The Japanese threatened awful punishments, and stern orders were issued from Camp HQ warning offenders of the results of these practices, but the trading stopped not one whit.

…

Up-to-date machinery, left undestroyed in Malaya, now made its appearance on the work site. The light railways were replaced by heavy metre gauge, and tracks and caterpillar tractors towing four- and ten-yard-capacity skips moaned across the growing drome. Modern electric shovels and a great steam navvy kept half-a-dozen diesel locomotives pushing long lines of skips heaped with soil to the swamp edges. As each train stopped at a dumping point the ragged workers attacked it with their crude shovels, and within 15 minutes the empty train would be puffing back to the refilling point, leaving the prisoner, sweating and gasping, sitting on the line until the next unloading.

The prisoners followed the psychology that the best method of obtaining rest was to unload trains more quickly than the electric shovels could fill them. They preferred a short, 15-minute burst of labour twice per hour rather than a slow, continuous unloading of train after train.

This system was usually quite successful, but many of the Japanese taskmasters resented the sight of men at rest and forced them to remain on their feet, packing the sleepers with earth, levelling off non-existent bumps in the ground or shifting the railway line.

The prisoners always retaliated with such maddeningly deliberate 'go slow' tactics that at times a Japanese, goaded beyond all endurance, would grasp a stick and rush among the troops, foaming at the mouth and hitting all and sundry. Many incidents of this kind occurred; on occasions the officer or warrant officer in charge of the party also suffered a few blows. To take any punishment with stoical calm prevented these incidents from developing into serious trouble.

From the beginning of the work the prisoners had comforted themselves ... that the war would be over long before the drome was complete, but in June 1944 they watched three fighter aircraft land on the northern arm and the first stage of the work was over.

The work progressed more rapidly from that time. Miles of dispersal roads dotted with large aeroplane shelters were built around the perimeter, the edges of the four arms of the drome were sloped and grassed and a substantial sea wall was commenced at the edge of the eastern arm. More men were sent from camp, and Australian, English and Dutch prisoners together with hundreds of Tamils, Indians and Chinese coolies covered the area from Ferry Point to Changi Gaol.

> **The prisoners always retaliated with ... 'go slow' tactics**

Pilots flying over the extent of the drome were amazed at daily changes taking place, and within a short time light bombers were using the field. It was a busy, changing scene, but the one thing that did not alter at any stage was the complete unconquerable spirit of the Australians.

Always hoping for a cessation of hostilities, they were still able to smile when the first 12 months' work was completed. They were laughing as they worked into the month of December, and on Christmas Day the Japanese were confounded to see the prisoners singing as they toiled, jeering at one another for even suggesting that by that time they should have been free. They chaffed the Japanese all that day and marched back to camp with the snap of a Guards Brigade, roaring in the moonlight the marching songs they had sung in Australia ...

Changi today

Emma Campbell
Australian War Memorial

MOST VISITORS TO SINGAPORE today know Changi as an international aviation hub rather than for its prisoner-of-war connections. But the modern airport that processes tens of millions of travellers each year sits on the foundations of the original aerodrome, built with prisoner-of-war labour in 1944.

The Changi area of Singapore remains the centre of remembrance and a place of deep significance for Australians and Britons seeking to connect with the story of prisoners of war. But it bears little resemblance to its appearance during the Japanese occupation – the inclusion of the airport, which sprawls across 1300 hectares of the Changi peninsula, is just one of the changes.

After the war Changi Gaol was seen as a 'monument and a memorial' to those who suffered or died as prisoners under the Japanese. When the news broke in 2003 that it was to be demolished so that a more modern prison could be built in its place, senior Australian politicians tactfully lobbied the Singapore government to preserve at least some parts of this transnational heritage site. The original entrance gate and a section of the outer wall were subsequently retained.

Changi still has one of the main concentrations of military facilities on the island – used by the Singapore Armed Forces – but much of the original garrison has been demolished or built over. The Selarang Barracks that housed Australian prisoners of war were torn down in 1986, and there is no public access to the rebuilt site. A memorial plaque at the entrance to the barracks tells its history.

In 1942 and 1943 British prisoner of war Stanley Warren painted five large murals of scenes from the New Testament on the walls of a hospital chapel set up in the Roberts Barracks of the Changi compound. These barracks have also been demolished, but the building with the murals remains – although access is limited due to its status as a military site.

The Changi airport now covers what was once the Changi prisoner-of-war cemetery, created in 1942 with sections each for the British and Australian war dead. The bodies were exhumed after the war and moved to the Kranji War Cemetery in the island's north.

The main prisoner-of-war site for visitors is the Changi Museum, about a kilometre from the gaol. It houses displays of letters, photographs, drawings and personal artefacts belonging to prisoners of war. It also features the Changi Chapel, a replica of one built by prisoners in the gaol in 1944–45. Replicas have also been made of Warren's Changi murals.

The Changi of today may be disheartening for those hoping to be able to see more of its prisoner-of-war past. But the modern Singaporean government does recognise the area as a site of historical importance, and continues to welcome tourists and families of former prisoners of war.

THE PEACE COMES TO X PARTY
UNKNOWN AUTHOR

Realising the extreme peril of their situation, now that the invasion of Malaya [by Allied forces in 1945] seemed imminent and Japanese atrocities inevitable, Australians working in X parties [work parties deployed to build defensive fortifications] began to discuss seriously possible lines of action to be adopted. It was insane simply to lie down and be shot.

In all these cases, there were three possibilities: to take what was coming; to attempt escape; or to put up a fight. In his heart every man began secretly to make his decision. Meanwhile, it was essential that accurate information be obtained about the war situation. It was impossible to make plans without any knowledge of what was happening in the outside world …

…

Slowly the news filtered through, until by 15 August everyone knew. The miraculous had happened – now there was no need to make decisions: it was no longer necessary to sweat about the future. A few more days would see it over.

And so, for three more interminable days, during which the Japanese guards knew nothing and their prisoners knew all, work continued. Tunnels were still dug, weapon pits were still prepared and guards still raved: silly work, irritating work, but the men stood it all with a grim pleasure because they knew, and their guards did not …

Finally, on one of the evening roll calls, an English interpreter came rushing into the camp. Instructions had at last come through that all prisoners of war were to return to Changi …

And so that night, as the guards sat miserably in their hut, terrified that they were going to be attacked, nervously fingering their rifles, hundreds of riotous and sleepless prisoners of war sat talking endlessly in theirs. A huge fire blazed in the centre of the long wooden building, and on it dozens of billies boiled, innumerable brews of tea. As the fire grew low a fresh section of the hut would be torn down, and once again the flames would leap into the air.

… there across the way cowered the guards in their hut, terrified.

'Poor bastards,' said one large Australian. 'I'll take 'em a cup of tea.' There was a murmur of assent and quickly he made his way across the dark parade ground toward the Japanese … fearing poison and other frightful things the guard commander promptly refused. The Australian pressed him to accept, and once again the guard commander refused. It was too much … 'Curra,' bellowed the enraged prisoner of war. 'Drink this bloody tea.' Without a word the Imperial Japanese Army took the proffered cups and drank the tea. The war was over.

AS DAWN BROKE over Singapore Island on 20 August 1945 Captain Frederick Stahl raised this improvised Australian flag over Camp X3 at Bukit Panjang, a work camp near the centre of the island. The flag's pole was Stahl's cane walking stick attached to the gable of his hut. It was the first Australian flag to have flown over Singapore since the island fell in 1942.

Two weeks earlier news had filtered through that an atomic bomb had been dropped on Japan. Sensing the end of hostilities, Stahl was determined that an Australian flag would be flown as soon as peace was declared. He enlisted the service of Sergeant Darcy Smith, a former tailor from Gympie, Queensland, to make the flag, and then appealed for materials. A Union Jack that had been used for burials was donated and blue material was stolen from the Japanese stores. Stars were made from Red Cross handkerchiefs, and sewing thread was gained by unravelling Japanese socks.

The contraband was hidden under the prisoners' beds and lookouts were posted while Smith sewed the materials together. The flag

The moment of freedom: Captain Stahl's flag

Craig Blanch
Australian War Memorial

ABOVE **Many prisoners kept small autograph books to record the names and addresses of friends and contacts so they could keep in touch after the war. This booklet was made from cigarette packets by Corporal Mick Kildey.**
PAIU2002/122.05

LEFT **Captain Frederick Stahl's homemade flag, with the inscription on the Federation Star.**
RELAWM31805

was completed on the day of the dropping of the second atomic bomb. On the evening of 19 August a Japanese guard confirmed to Stahl that the war was indeed over and the flag flew at *Reveille* the next morning.

That afternoon he carried the flag as they marched out to Changi Camp. When he arrived he was summoned by Lieutenant Colonel Galleghan, who requested the flag be flown beside the Union Jack over Changi Gaol. Stahl's flag remained flying until after the official Japanese surrender.

On the flag's return Stahl found an inscription on the Federation Star: 'Dear Stahl. Good luck. A very game action to fly this flag. F.G. Galleghan LT Col comd A.I.F (P.W) Malaya 20 August 1945'.

Thoughts of home: liberation and repatriation

LACHLAN GRANT

News on the night of 10 August 1945 that Japan was willing to surrender began filtering through Changi Gaol the following morning. On 15 August, the day of the official announcement that Japan had accepted the terms of the Potsdam Declaration, work parties around Singapore and Johore in southern Malaya began returning to Changi. The first party to return was the group of 97 prisoners of war held by the *kenpeitai* at Outram Road. To the men in Changi they appeared 'a sorry picture after their brutal treatment'.[1]

Prisoners reacted differently to the news; since the Japanese were still in charge and British forces had not yet returned, they continued to exist in a state of limbo. Eventually, the Japanese admitted what many of the prisoners by then knew: that the war was over. Some prisoners had by this time taken it upon themselves to wander off into Singapore. One recalled that he went to a street stall in town and ordered a gargantuan meal, and as he ate generous locals kept bringing more and more food to his table as a gift.[2]

After days of the men watching vacant skies for Allied planes bringing relief, and subsequently feeling deflated, radios broadcast on the evening of 29 August that a food drop would occur over the Changi aerodrome the following day. Around midday the next day a lone four-engine B-24 Liberator from Ceylon flew over the camp and dropped six British soldiers by parachute. They comprised two officers, two medical officers and two medical orderlies. Later that day three more B-24s flew over the camp and began dropping tons of supplies by parachute. Knowing the war was over and now so close to going home, the ex-prisoners agonised over their homecoming and dreamed of better days. As Stan Arneil wrote in his diary: 'Thoughts of home, that is where we excel; men sit alone or in groups talking or just thinking of home.' Arneil himself thought of nights on Sydney Harbour, and days in the Blue Mountains or on the beach with a cold beer.[3]

Following the formal surrender ceremony aboard USS *Missouri* in Tokyo Bay on 2 September, local surrender ceremonies

Murray Griffin's *Looking Towards Home*, 1942, depicts three prisoners atop the water tower at Selarang. The water tower and the roof of the barracks – vantage points used for many artworks and photographs – were later ruled out of bounds.
ART24470

began taking place across Asia and the Pacific. Although the men in Changi were now technically free, they were still awaiting the arrival of large numbers of Allied troops. On 5 September Singapore was finally liberated by soldiers of the 5th Indian Division from Admiral Lord Louis Mountbatten's South East Asia Command. They arrived in Changi the following day. With liberation came frustration, and one British soldier wrote: 'We are still prisoners, but not of the Japanese; we are prisoners of the RAPWI' (the Repatriation of Allied Prisoners of War and Internees, the body assigned to organise the recovery and return home of the prisoners).[4]

Some prisoners were soon being airlifted back to Australia, but most had to wait a few more weeks. Biding their time, they caught up on old news from newspapers newly delivered, they went on 'French leave' into Singapore, they ate, they drank, or they went to the cinema. On 22 September the moment they had all been waiting for finally arrived as they boarded trucks bound for the harbour, where ships waited for their journey home to Australia.[5] As the trucks made their way through Singapore thousands of local Chinese lined the roadside giving the 'V for victory' sign and cheering for joy.[6]

As they boarded ships, the former prisoners took with them diaries, papers, drawings, artworks, photographic negatives, items and mementos – all records of their time in Changi. However small, these were cherished reminders of their survival, of their war.

It is to those men and women, who were so dedicated to keeping this record, that the Australian War Memorial dedicates this book in the year of the 70th anniversary of the end of the Second World War. Special mention must be made of C. David Griffin and his colleagues in the AIF Education Centre in Changi who worked so tirelessly to bring the original collection of essays together. As the editor of this volume, I feel indebted to Griffin and to all the authors, artists, photographers and craftsman whose work is presented here. Seventy years on, this volume stands as a record of their work, and of their own individual experiences of Changi.

Acknowledgments

The production of this work would not have been completed without the assistance and support of many people. Firstly, I thank Edward Griffin and the Griffin family, Mark Sprod, Alexander Downer, Keith Bettany, and Sheila Allan for their support and permissions. At the Australian War Memorial I acknowledge the support of my colleagues in the Military History Section: Kate Ariotti, Steven Bullard, Peter Burness, Emma Campbell, Ashley Ekins, Meleah Hampton, Karl James, Michael Kelly, Aaron Pegram, Juliet Schyvens, Haruki Yoshida, and editors Christina Zissis, Robert Nichols and Andrew McDonald. I also appreciate the support and work of many people across the Australian War Memorial. They include Anne Bennie, Rebecca Britt, Shane Casey, Eleni Holloway, Meagan Nihill, Ricky Phillips, Craig Tibbitts, Robyn Van-Dyk and all of the staff in the Research Centre. Kevin Donnellan and the team in multimedia have done a terrific job producing the images for this book, as have the Memorial's photographers, Kerry Alchin and Fiona Silsby. I am also grateful to all of the contributors – those aforementioned as well as Craig Blanch, Chris Goddard, Vick Gwyn, Lenore Heath, Warwick Heywood, Garth O'Connell, Kerry Neale, Jane Peek and Lucy Robertson – each of whom has shared here with readers just one small part of their immense knowledge of the Memorial's vast collections. Instrumental in making this project possible was Mark Small, a great supporter of publishing and the showcasing of research at the Memorial. Particular praise must be given to Christina Zissis, who worked tirelessly in editing the manuscript. At NewSouth, many thanks to Elspeth Menzies for her enthusiastic support and in sharing the vision for this book, and to the NewSouth editors Heather Cam and John Mapps. To my greatest supporter, Amanda Kate Wescombe, words cannot express my gratitude for your encouragement and enthusiasm.

Notes

LETTERS FROM THE PAST

1. John Nevell, diary, July 1942, Australian War Memorial: PR00257.
2. For an account of the campaign see Karl Hack and Kevin Blackburn, *Did Singapore Have to Fall? Churchill and the Impregnable Fortress*, RoutledgeCurzon, London, 2004.
3. James Roxburgh, diary, 16 February 1942, AWM, PR94/117.
4. Alan Warren, *Singapore 1942: Britain's Greatest Defeat*, Talisman, Melbourne, 2002, pp. 303–304.
5. Lionel Wigmore, *The Japanese Thrust*, AWM, Canberra, 1957, p. 642.
6. Kevin Blackburn and Karl Hack, *Forgotten Captives in Japanese Occupied Asia*, RoutledgeCurzon, London, 2008, pp. 16–17
7. Fred Stringer cited in Hank Nelson, *POW: Australians Under Nippon*, ABC, Sydney, 1985, p. 68.
8. Stan Arneil, *One Man's War*, Pan Macmillan, Sydney, 2003 [1980], p. 30
9. Stephen Garton, *The Cost of War: Australians Return*, Oxford University Press, Melbourne, 1996, pp. 211-12
10. Russell Braddon, *The Naked Island*, Penguin, Melbourne, 1993[1952], pp. 239–40.
11. 'Miscellaneous records in the original dealings with the activities of the Australian Army Education Services – 8th Australian Division during period of captivity – Changi, Singapore Camp 1942–1945', AWM: AWM54 554/11/33.
12. C. David Griffin, *Changi Days: The Prisoner as Poet*, Kangaroo Press, East Roseville, New South Wales, pp. 23–24.
13. 'Suggest publication by Australian War Memorial', 19 October 1944, 8th Division War Diary, AWM: AWM52 1/5/19.
14. Michael McKernan, *Here is Their Spirit: A History of the Australian War Memorial 1917–1990*, University of Queensland Press with the Australian War Memorial, St Lucia, Queensland, 1991, pp. 172–74.
15. Griffin, *Changi Days*, p. 31.
16. Joan Beaumont, 'Prisoners of war in Australian national memory', in Bob Moore and Barbara Hately-Broad (eds), *Prisoners of War, Prisoners of Peace: Captivity, Homecoming and Memory in World War II*, Berg Publishers, Oxford, UK, 2005, pp. 189–91.
17. Stephen Garton, 'Changi as television: myth, memory, narrative and history', *Journal of Australian Studies* 73, 2002, pp. 84–85; Robin Gerster, *Big-noting: The Heroic Theme in Australian War Writing*, Melbourne University Press, Melbourne, 1987, p. 225.
18. Nevell, diary, July 1942.

CHANGI LIFE AND SOCIETY

1. Kevin Blackburn and Karl Hack, *War Memory and the Making of Modern Malaysia and Singapore*, NUS Press, Singapore, 2012, pp. 140-41 and 180; Lachlan Grant, *Australian Soldiers in Asia-Pacific in World War II*, NewSouth, Sydney, 2014, pp. 151–52; William Miggins, diary, 23 February and 25 April 1942, AWM: PR00373; Nevell, diary, July 1942.
2. Recollections of Brigadier Sir Frederick Galleghan, AWM: S01329.
3. Interview, Lionel Wigmore and Galleghan, 1 February 1950, p. 3, AWM: AWM73, part 1.
4. Frederick Galleghan service record, National Archives of Australia, Canberra: B883, NX70416; Galleghan recollections, AWM: S01329.
5. Galleghan recollections, AWM: S01329.
6. Garth Pratten, *Australian Battalion Commanders in the Second World War*, Cambridge University Press, Melbourne, 2009, pp. 139–42.
7. Report by Brigadier Frederick Galleghan, p. 3, AWM: AWM54, 554/11/4 part 1.
8. 'Black Jack Galleghan', *People*, 30 December 1953, p. 10.
9. E.E. Dunlop, *The War Diaries of Weary Dunlop: Java and the Burma–Thailand Railway 1942–1945*, Penguin, Ringwood, Victoria, 1990 [1986], p. 167; Letter, Dunlop to Galleghan, 19 January 1943, AWM: 3RDL/2313, part 2.
10. Arneil, *Black Jack: The Life and Times of Brigadier Sir Frederick Galleghan*, Macmillan, Melbourne, 1983, p. 122.
11. 'Hero of Changi dies', *Canberra Times*, 21 April 1971, p. 11.
12. Lieutenant Colonel F.G. Galleghan to AIF troops, 9 September 1945, AWM: AWM54, 554/11/17.
13. 'Total number of adults interned up to 25th September 1942', private

343

record collection of Freddy Bloom, Imperial War Museum (IWM) documents 66/254/1.
14 Helen Beck, 'Internment (From a Woman's Personal Viewpoint)', private record collection of Lieutenant Colonel Stahle, AWM: PR89/59.

GEORGE ASPINALL'S SECRET CAMERA

1 Oral histories undertaken by Tim Bowden and later published in his book of George Aspinall's photography, *Changi Photographer*, ABC, Sydney, 1984.

BUYING AND SELLING

1 R.P.W. Havers, *Reassessing the Japanese Prisoner of War Experience: The Changi POW Camp, Singapore, 1942–45*, London, RoutledgeCurzon, 2003, p. 60.
2 8th Division War Diary, 3 June 1945, AWM: AWM52 1/5/19; AIF Routine Orders.

MURRAY GRIFFIN

1 John Reid, *Australian Artists at War: Compiled From the Australian War Memorial Collection*, vol. 2, Sun Books, Melbourne, 1977, p. 8.
2 'War scenes glamourised', *Sydney Morning Herald*, 4 December 1946, p. 10.
3 Alan McCulloch, 'Murray Griffin's art', *Argus*, 24 October, 1946, p. 7.
4 'Singapore and after: war paintings by Murray Griffin', *Kalgoorlie Miner*, 17 July, 1947, p. 1.
5 *Courier-Mail*, 8 June 1946.
6 *Advertiser*, 21 January 1947.
7 *News* (Adelaide), 9 January 1947.

THE HIDDEN RADIO

1 www.iwm.org.uk/history/civilian-internees-in-the-far-east#; accessed 14 July 2014.

CHANGI'S FLUCTUATING POPULATION

1 Blackburn and Hack, *Forgotten Captives*, pp. 16-17; Havers, *Reassessing*, p. 182.

THE HIDDEN CAMERA OF KENNEDY BURNSIDE

1 Kennedy Burnside, diary, 8 August 1943, AWM: 3DRL/7665.
2 Burnside, diary, 30 July 1943.
3 Kennedy B. Burnside, 'The end of World War Two, as seen by Major K.B. Burnside, RAAMC, AIF, Malaya: Japanese prisoner of war, 1942–45', p. 31, 4 September 1945.

LIVE TO EAT

1 Lieutenant Hodge, 'Ration Scale', AWM: 3DRL/0369; Allan Walker, *Middle East and Far East*, AWM, Canberra, 1953.

LIVING WITH THE LEGACY

1 For more on the medical issues and diseases faced by prisoners in Japanese hands, see the accounts of captive doctors, including: Rowley Richards, *A Doctor's War*, HarperCollins, Sydney, 2005; Leslie Poidevin, *Samurais and Circumcisions*, Burnside, South Australia, self-published, 1985; and Dunlop, *The War Diaries of Weary Dunlop*.
2 Duncan quote in Nelson, *POW*, p. 216.
3 Rosalind Hearder, *Keep the Men Alive: Australian POW Doctors in Japanese Captivity*, Allen & Unwin, Sydney, 2009, p. 192.
4 Hearder, *Keep the Men Alive*, p. 185.
5 Stephen Garton, *The Cost of War: Australians Return*, Oxford University Press, Melbourne, 1996, p. 221.
6 Garton, *The Cost of War*, p. 223.
7. Michael McKernan, *This War Never Ends: The Pain of Separation and Return*, University of Queensland Press, St Lucia, Queensland, 2001, p. 163.

8 Garton, *The Cost of War*, pp. 223–24.
9 Garton, *The Cost of War*, p. 226.
10 Australians held captive by the Germans during the Second World War did not receive a similar payment until 2007. For more on the legacy of captivity in Germany see Peter Monteath, *POW: Australian Prisoners of War in Hitler's Reich*, Macmillan, Sydney, 2011, pp. 417–30.

SWAMPS, FUN AND FEVER

1 These figures are confirmed in Sandhya Polu, *Infectious Disease in India 1892–1940: Policy-Making and the Perception of Risk*, PalgraveMacMillan, Basingstoke, UK, 2012, p. 82.

SPORT, GAMES AND GAMBLING

1 For further reading on sport in captivity see Kevin Blackburn, *The Sportsmen of Changi*, NewSouth, Sydney, 2012.
2 Blackburn, *The Sportsmen of Changi*, pp. 146–55.
3 Blackburn, *The Sportsmen of Changi*, pp. 123–44.
4 Nevell, diary, 8 November 1942.
5 8th Division War Diary, 10 March 1942.
6 Nevell, diary, July 1942.

ANZAC DAY IN CHANGI

1 John Lennon, diary, 25 April 1942, AWM: PR00875; 8th Division War Diary, 25 April 1942.

THOUGHTS OF HOME

1 David Nelson, *The Story of Changi, Singapore*, Changi Publication Co., Singapore, 1974, p. 181.
2 Interview, Wigmore and Galleghan, pp. 635–37.
3 Stan Arneil, diary, 29–30 August 1945, AWM: PR88/076.
4 Nelson, *The Story of Changi*, p. 185.
5 Interview, Wigmore and Galleghan, pp. 635–37; Havers, *Reassessing*, pp. 161–65.
6 *Salt*, vol. 11, no. 5, November 1945.

Further reading

Adams-Smith, Patsy, *Prisoners of War: From Gallipoli to Korea*, Penguin, Melbourne, 1992.

Arneil, Stan, *Black Jack: The Life and Times of Brigadier Sir Frederick Galleghan*, Melbourne, 1983.

Arneil, Stan, *One Man's War*, Pan Macillan, Sydney, 2003 [1980].

Beaumont, Joan, 'Contested transnational heritage: the demolition of Changi prison, Singapore', *International Journal of Heritage Studies*, 15:4, 2009, pp. 298–316.

Beaumont, Joan, Grant, Lachlan and Pegram, Aaron (eds), *Beyond Surrender: Australians Prisoners of War 1915–53*, Melbourne University Press, Melbourne, 2015.

Blackburn, Kevin, *The Sportsmen of Changi*, NewSouth, Sydney, 2012.

Blackburn, Kevin, and Hack, Karl (eds), *Forgotten Captives in Japanese Occupied Asia*, Routlege, London, 2008.

Blackburn, Kevin, and Hack, Karl, *War Memory and the Making of Modern Malaysia and Singapore*, NUS press, Singapore, 2012.

Bowden, Tim, *The Changi Camera*, Hachette, Sydney, 2012.

Braddon, Russell, *The Naked Island*, Penguin, Melbourne, 1993 [1952].

Brune, Peter, *Descent into Hell: The Fall of Singapore – Pudu and Changi – The Thai–Burma Railway*, Allen & Unwin, Sydney, 2014.

Dunlop, E.E., *The War Diaries of Weary Dunlop: Java and the Burma–Thailand Railway 1942–1945*, Penguin, Ringwood, Victoria, 1990 [1986].

Garton, Stephen, *The Cost of War: Australians Return*, Oxford University Press, Melbourne, 1996.

Garton, Stephen, 'Changi as television: myth, memory, narrative and history', *Journal of Australian Studies*, 73, 2002.

Gerster, Robin, *Big-noting: The Heroic Theme in Australian War Writing*, Melbourne University Press, Melbourne, 1987.

Grant, Lachlan, *Australian Soldiers in Asia-Pacific in World War II*, NewSouth, Sydney, 2014.

Griffin, C. David, *Changi Days: The Prisoner as Poet*, Kangaroo Press, Sydney, 2002.

Hack, Karl and Blackburn, Kevin, *Did Singapore Have to Fall? Churchill and the Impregnable Fortress*, RoutledgeCurzon, London, 2004.

Havers, R.P.W., *Reassessing the Japanese Prisoner of War Experience: The Changi POW Camp, Singapore, 1942–45*, RoutledgeCurzon, London, 2003.

Hearder, Rosalind, *Keep the Men Alive: Australian POW Doctors in Japanese Captivity*, Allen & Unwin, Sydney, 2009.

McCormack, Gavan, and Nelson, Hank, (eds), *The Burma–Thailand Railway: Memory and History*, Allen & Unwin, Sydney, 1993.

McKernan, Michael, *Here is Their Spirit: A History of the Australian War Memorial 1917–1990*, University of Queensland Press, St Lucia, Queensland, 1991.

McKernan, Michael, *This War Never Ends: The Pain of Separation and Return*, University of Queensland Press, St Lucia, Queensland, 2001.

Moore, Bob, and Hatley-Broad, Barbara (eds), *Prisoners of War, Prisoners of Peace: Captivity, Homecoming and Memory in World War II*, Berg, Oxford, UK, 2005.

Nelson, David, *The Story of Changi*, Changi Publication Co., Singapore, 1974.

Nelson, Hank, *POW: Australians Under Nippon*, ABC, Sydney, 1985.

Pratten, Garth, *Australian Battalion Commanders in the Second World War*, Cambridge University Press, Melbourne, 2009.

Richards, Rowley, *A Doctor's War*, HarperCollins, Sydney, 2005.

Twomey, Christina, *Australia's Forgotten Prisoners: Civilians Interned by the Japanese in World War Two*, Cambridge University Press, Melbourne, 2007.

Walker, Alan, *Middle East and Far East*, AWM, Canberra, 1953.

Warren, Alan, *Singapore 1942: Britain's Greatest Defeat*, Talisman, Melbourne, 2002.

Waterford, Van, *Prisoners of the Japanese in World War II*, McFarland & Company, London, 1994.

Wigmore, Lionel, *The Japanese Thrust*, AWM, Canberra, 1957.

Index

2/4th Anti-Tank Regiment AIF 13
2/5th Field Hygiene Section 232
2/10th Australian General Hospital 36, 244
  see also Roberts Hospital medical organisation 36
2/13th Australian General Hospital 36, 244
  see also Roberts Hospital
2/15th Field Regiment, flag of 160
2/29th Battalion AIF 13, 172–73
2/30th Battalion AIF 13, 15, 52–53, 78, 274
2nd Battalion Gordon Highlanders 35, 164
2nd Convalescent Depot 156, 159, 165, 206, 210, 219
  see also convalescence arrangements
2nd Echelon 50, 313–17, 314
5th Indian Division liberation of Changi camp 342
8th Division AIF
  in Singapore 13
  preparation for imprisonment 33–35
  prisoners from 15
  soldiers' essays 16–19
  surrender to Japanese 30
  war diary entries 20, 21
22nd Brigade AIF 13–15, 235,
27th Brigade AIF 13–15

A Force in Burma 50, 235, 241, 289
Abbott, Harold, *Reunion at Changi* 12

accommodation at Changi 164–73
Active Service, Christmas annual 21
Adam Park working party camp 280–82
'Advance Australia Fair' 136
aerodrome construction at Changi Point 332–35
Ahmed (Indian labourer) 283
AIF
  see Australian Imperial Force
AIF Artificial Limb Factory 156, 219–24, *221, 224*
AIF Bookbindery 109, *110, 111*
AIF Concert Party 26, 134–53
  Griffin illustrations *136, 137, 140, 141, 144–45*
  importance of 47
  performers 144–45
  re-formation of 47
  Sprod drawing *135*
  Smoke-oh drawing *139*
AIF Education Centre
  convalescing troops make use of 156, 158
  classes run by *112, 113*
  education scheme 47–48
  essays compiled by 19, 342
  Griffin illustration *114*
  lecture series 116
  library maintained by 104
  political discussions 115–16
  Sprod drawing *108*
AIF Field Bakery 257
AIF Forestry Company 301–308, *302, 303, 307*
AIF Garden Scheme 210
AIF Seedling Nursery 205–11, *209*

AIF Theatre *140, 141*
alcohol production 230–31
Alexandra Hospital massacre 30
  see also Sook Ching massacre
Allan, Sheila 161
Allen, Private L.T. 310
Allied forces
  see also Australian Imperial Force; British Army; Indian troops
  Japanese surrender to 28, 340–41
Ambon, Australian prisoners of war on 16, 289
amputees 156–60, 210, 219–24, 239, 331
Anning, Corporal 308
Anopheles mosquito 268–69, 272
Anzac Book, The 21
Anzac Day services 320–21, *325, 325*
Arimura, General 60, 63, 292
Ariotti, Kate 9, 266–67
Armistice Day memorial services 320
Armstrong, Sergeant Jim 241
Arneil, Stan 6, 18, 332–35, 341
artificial limb construction 219–24, *221, 224*
As You Were series 21
Ashby, Hugh King 258
Aspinall, George 88–89
Aspinall photographs
  Changi prisoner-of-war camp 39, *44–45*
  F Force 57, *58*, 88, 238
  firewood collection *302–303*
  leg ulcers 238
  naval guns 34

preparing fish *327*
preparing rations *230, 259*
Selarang Barracks *166*
vegetable gardens *295*
attap huts 66, 168–69, *169*, 177–80
augurs, latrines drilled with 38
Austen-Hofer, Eunice 161
Australia, lack of books about 107–109
Australia–Netherlands Indies Society 118
Australian Army Chaplains Department
  see chaplains, work of
Australian Army Ordnance Corps, firewood collected by 301–308
Australian Changi quilt 161–63, *162, 163*
Australian flag 339–40, *339*
Australian Imperial Force *see also* 'AIF...'; *names of units*; Selarang Barracks Square incident
  daily prisoner-of-war parades 24–25, *26*, 48
  defence of Singapore 13
  Headquarters at Changi 37
  losses in Malaysian peninsula 15
  moneys collected by 90
  Tanglin supply depot 250
Australian Red Cross
  see also Red Cross
  quilts made for 161
Australian War Memorial 27, 79
autograph book *339*
Autumn Crocus 138

346

INDEX

Bale, Sergeant Wilfred 160
Balsillie, Andrew John 'Jack' 78–79
banknotes issued by Japanese Army 92–93
barbed-wire fences, erecting 38
Barber, Warrant Officer Sydney 283
Barnett, Captain Ben 310
Barracks Square incident
see Selarang Barracks Square incident
Barton, Private William 114
bayam, as food 257, 296,
Beadman, Walter 6, 124–33
Beatty, Eric 144
Beck, Helen 64–65
Beek, Captain Willem van 235
Bennett, Jack 6, 326–31
beriberi 42, 72, 102, 226, 237, *240*
Bernard, Private W.H. 331
Birdwood Camp 165, 168
Bishop of Singapore 321
blachang 102, 262–63
black market
as source of food 250, 255
operation of 94–8
prisoner-of-war economy and 102
razors and watches 101
risks involved in 43
Blanch, Craig 9, 339–40
Blondahl, Private James (Jim) 213
blood grouping 247
Bloom, Freddy 65
Boardman, Jack 154
Bob Mutton's Hut 165
boiler room radio set 124–25
book binding
see AIF Bookbindery
books in Changi Library 103–10
borehole latrines 232–33, *235*
Bostey, Major 54
'Boulevarde des Invalides' 69
Bowden, Tim 89
Braddon, Russell 19
Brightfield, Fred 144
British Army
Changi accommodation 35
drops supplies after surrender 341
firewood collecting parties 305–308
prisoners from 15
Britton, Private J.A. 331

broom and brush manufacture 214–18, *218*, 277
broom radio set 124, *130*, *131*
Bryant-Smith, Sergeant Stanley, razor used by *100–101*
Bucknell, Rex 6, 156–60
Buffaloes, membership certificates *118*, *119*
Bukit Badok shrine 285–86
Bukit Timah
Japanese war memorial at 59
petrol pipeline 100
Singapore work camp moved to 285, *286*
Burma 16, 50
Burma–Thailand Railway 16, 23, 53, 120, 239
Burnside, Kennedy 248, *249*
Burnside photographs
concert party production *26*
latrine construction *234*
medical laboratory *245*
prisoner-of-war accommodation *166–67*
prisoner-of-war parade *40–41*
Selarang Barracks *24–25*, *26*, *39–41*, *165–66*
Captain Thomas Mitchell *273*

Callaghan, Major General Cecil 35, 51
Camp ... see Changi Gaol; Changi prisoner-of-war camp
Campbell, Emma 9, 336
Campbell, Lance Corporal L. 223
Campbell, Private 'Jock' *330*
canteens 51, 90, 250, 284
casualties
Australian, in Malaysian peninsula 15
burial of *316*, *317*, 319–20
lists prepared by prisoners of war 50
records of, provided to IJA 313
catering 261–65
see also food in Changi
cattle killed for food 255
cemetery, construction of 320
Central Garden Control 290, 293
Ceylon spinach 206, *294*, *295*
chalk production 215
Chalmers, Hector 6, 80–87

Changi Airport, cemetery covered by 336
Changi Australian Football League 309
Changi beach, Chinese massacred at 32, 41
Changi Broom Factory 216
Changi Brownlow Medal 309
Changi Chapel National Prisoner of War Memorial 322
Changi Chapel replica 336
Changi Gaol
accommodation in *170*, *171*, *172–73*
Christmas in 182–83
food in *183*, 238
gardens cropped on move to 211
latrine lids changed in 232–33
library set up in 107
logistics of move to 168–69
picture of *70–71*
prisoner-of-war camp moved to 66–71
radios discovered at 124
Sprod drawings *174*, *180*
vegetable gardening 211, 256, 296–8, *297*
women interned in 64
workshop operations in 190, 194
Changi library 103–10, *106*
Changi Memorial Book proposal 18, 20–21
Changi Museum 336
Changi, naval guns at *34*
Changi Photographer, The 89
Changi Point aerodrome 63, 332–35
Changi prisoner-of-war camp
see also Changi Gaol; medical conditions and treatment; Roberts Hospital; Selarang Barracks
accommodation at 35–36, 164–73
aerial photographs 39, *40–41*
as staging camp 61
barbed-wire fence 38
Camp Messing Fund 250–52
camp potter 212
Christmas in 181–83
industries in 185–224
literary competition flyer 19–20
location of 33

maps of 2, *22–23*
population of 174
post-war history of 336
reaction to Japanese surrender 77, 341
Changi Union 323
Changi village, black-market transactions in 94
Chapel of St Andrew and St Luke *320*, *322*
chaplains, work of 318–25
Chinese residents of Singapore
aid provided to prisoners of war by 35
burial parties for 38–41
food taken from 269
massacred by IJA 32
trading with prisoners of war 43, 99
Chitty, Corporal Leslie 'Peter' *310*, 309
cholera attacks 43, 61
Christmas
cards 181–82
dinners 181, 265
in Changi Gaol 181–83
pantomimes *136–37*, 142
religious services 321
sports day meetings 308, 310
working parties on 335
churches and chapels, construction of 54, 165–66, 318–19, *319*
Churchill, Winston 77
cigarette box made from aircraft parts *183*
cigarette papers 243
civilian internees, female 64–65
Clarke, Burnett 6, 236–43
Coates, Private E.A. 331
Combs, Private 220
Concert Party
see AIF Concert Party
convalescent arrangements
artificial limbs 219–24
move to Gordons' Mess 165
No. 2 Convalescent Depot 156–60
vegetable gardening 210
cooking at Changi
see food in Changi
cooking pots, repair of 186
cribbage board *194*
cricket matches 287, 310
Crowther, Sergeant 300

D Force, departure of 59
Dahl, Captain Edward 300

347

Davies, Major G.F.S. 244, 247
Davis, Driver Edward 311
de Grey, Slim 137–38, *144*
de Ramsay, Major the Lord 292
Dean, Ross 323
deck golf game *159*
dental care 275–78, *276*
dentures, manufacture of 275–77
Department of Veterans' Affairs 267
Detention Barracks prisoners supply broom materials 215
Dick Whittington *137*, 142
diet
   see food in Changi
diphtheria outbreaks 237, 246
disabled troops
   see convalescence arrangements
discipline
   see military discipline
distillery 230–31
Dixon, Captain William, winning frog owned by 311
Dobbie, Lieutenant Alan 326
dogs, as food 263
door handle souvenir *68*
door sign *179*
'doovers' 262
Downer, Alexander 'Alick' 6, 19, 115–19
dried squid *258*
Duncan, Captain Ian 266
Dunlop, Lieutenant Colonel Edward 'Weary,' clashes with Galleghan 52–3
Dutch prisoners of war 61, 118
dysentery attacks
   civilian internees 64–65
   investigation of 247
   result from poor hygiene 43–45, 232–34

Education Centre
   see AIF Education Centre
Edwards, Private M., postcard sent by *51*
Elliman, Corporal S.K. *169*
entertainment in Changi 63
   see also AIF Concert Party; sporting events and games
Exile magazine 110
eye-instrument kit *241*

F Force
   departure of *57*, 58

photos of *89*
return of 53, 61
rush to join 60
false teeth 275–77
Fanning, Sergeant 223
field bakery *257*
Field, Jack, door sign *179*
field kitchens
   see food in Changi
firewood collection and use 301–308, *302*, *303*, *304*, *307*
first aid box *235*
fish, as food 255, *257*, *258*, 263, 326–31, *327*, *330*
food in Changi
   see also rice; vegetable gardening
   AIF cooks *259*
   bayam *257*, *295*, *296*
   beef issue 255
   blachang 102, 262–63
   black market in 18, 21, 43, 94–98, 101, 102, 250, 255
   catering for 261–65
   Ceylon spinach 206, 295
   cooking arrangements 42–43, *259*, *262*, *264*, *265*
   dogs as 263
   field bakery *257*
   field kitchens 37
   fish 255, *257*, *258*, 263, 326–31, *327*, *330*
   importance of 41–42
   medical conditions resulting from 237
   men receiving rations *230*
   'pap' (cereal) 263
   prior to Japanese surrender 72
   reserves of food 260
   salt deficiency in 334
   sources of 250–60
   vegetables in diet *257*
   vitamins absent from 226, 237
foot pain 239
football matches 309–10
fountain pen market 101
Fox, Signalman Edward, Royal Norfolk Regiment badge *288*
frog racing cup 310–11, *311*
Fukuye, Major General Shimpei 65, 86

Galleghan, Lieutenant Colonel Frederick 'Black Jack'
   announces death of escapees 86

   as Commanding Officer 51, 52–53
   emphasises discipline 28
   initial refusal to sign Non-Escape Declaration 58–59
   miniature brooms presented to 216–18
   orders signing of Non-Escape Declaration 87
   pictures and photos *53*
   requests Australian flag be flown 339
   supports Garden Scheme 210
gambling, money changing hands due to 312
Garden Scheme
   see AIF Garden Scheme
garden working parties 290–99
gates, mottoes on *48*
Geoghegan, Jack 146
Gleeson, Private Steven 224
glue production 215
Goddard, Chris 9, 184, 300
golf, played by convalescents 157, *159*
Good, Judy 161
Gould, Corporal 223
Grant, Lachlan
   as contributor 9
   background to book 13–28
   on Anzac Day services 325
   on Changi population 174
   on Japanese surrender 341
   on long-term effects of captivity 289
   on prisoner-of-war economy 102
   on Sook Ching massacres 32
   on sporting events and games 309–12
grass soup factories 54, 227, *228*, *231*
grease production 198
Green Circle Library 105
Greener, Captain Leslie 19, 109
Greenwood, Staff Sergeant 244
Griffin, Sergeant (Charles) David
   as contributor 6–7
   essays compiled by 19–20, 342
   flyer from *19–20*
   on books for POWs 103–10
   on Changi POW camp 30–77
Griffin, V. Murray 121

   as war artist 20, 120–23
   illustrating the essays 27
Griffin, V. Murray illustrations
   25-pounders in Action at Gemas, 15 January *123*
   AIF Concert Party *136*, *137*, *140–41*
   AIF Education Centre *114*
   AIF Seedling Nursery *209*
   artificial limb production *221*, *222*
   Bob Mutton's Hut *165*
   book binding *111*
   broom and brush production *218*
   burial cortège *316*
   Changi Gaol *70–71*
   Changi Library *106*
   Chapel of St Andrew and St Luke *320*
   collecting firewood *304*, *307*
   cooking in Changi Gaol *183*
   cutting lalang grass *299*
   deck golf *159*
   Dental Centre *276*
   electric rice grinder *256*
   Galleghan portrait *53*
   grass soup factories *228*
   gun emplacements *123*
   halt for midday rice *207*
   Hospital Ward, Thailand Railway *121*
   imitation stained-glass window *324*
   Looking Towards Home *341*
   massage room of hospital *240*
   move to Selarang Barracks Square *178*
   nail-making machine *215*
   pathology lab equipment *246*
   Percival portrait *122*
   pottery-making *212*
   rice cake production *262*
   rice-polishings extractor *229*
   Roman Catholic chapel *319*
   rubber production *201*, *204*
   sandal-making *202*
   Selarang AIF area *46*
   Selarang Barracks kitchen *262*
   smoking fish *330*
   soap manufacture *197*
   spinning thread from hemp twine *192*
   spraying for mosquitos *270*
   thread manufacture *193*
   trailer *67*
   vegetable gardening *256*, *291*,

INDEX

294, *297*
view from Barracks Square *49*
working party *253*
yeast production *227*
Gunther, Major Carl E.M. 7, 37–38, 81
Gwyn, Vick 9, 89

handcarts 67, 281
see also trailers
'Hank the Yank' (guard) 285
'happy feet' 137, 239
'Hardacre Avenue' 81
Harrison, Private William 114
Harvey, Frazer *145*
Haskell, Arnold *108*
Hay Fever 138
Hazelton, Major Alan *241*
health in Changi
see food in Changi; hygiene and sanitation; medical conditions and treatment
Heath, Lenore 9, 248
Henry, Ernest 310
Heywood, Warwick 9, 120–23
Highland Chief 160
Hill, Colonel 190
Hill, Noel 7, 189–93
Hindley, Gunner Peter, souvenir key *68*
Hodgkin, Ernest, door sign *179*
Holberton, Private Ronald *283*
Holloway, Eleni 9–10, 213
Holmes, Colonel E.B. 52, *53*, 80, 86
Hospital Ward, Thailand Railway 120, *121*
housing 164–73
Hunt, Major B., playing cards made by *312*
Hutchance, H. 7, 290–99
huts 66, 168–9, *169*, 177–80
hygiene and sanitation 232–35
see also medical conditions and treatment

identity tags 217, *274*
I'll Take You 142
imitation stained-glass window *324*
'immigration bureau' 117–18
Imperial Japanese Army
banknotes issued by *92*, *93*, *96*
huts built by 168
lack of co-operation between units 282–84
Non-Escape Declaration 58–59, 80
payments made by 90–93, 243
prisoner-of-war communications limited by 50–51
prisoners make tea for 337
punishments for absentees 284–85
records provided to 313
Singapore occupied by 13–15, 30–31
surrender ceremonies 341–42
treatment of prisoners of war 35, 61–63, 143
war memorial built to 281
working parties controlled by 41
Indian residents of Singapore 99, 328–29
Indian troops 32, 342
industries in Changi 185–224
instruments
see musical instruments used in Changi

James, Karl 10, 52–53
Japan
see also Imperial Japanese Army
makes compensation payments 267
prisoner-of-war camps in 16
surrender to Allied powers 28, 77, 340–41
Japanese flag souvenir *96*
Japanese postcard *286*
'Japanese quilt' *65*, 65
Johnson's Baby Powder *184*, 184
Johore 13,
defences on 72, 143
Straits of 38, 105, 164
Jungle Warfare war annual 21

Kappe, Lieutenant Colonel 60
Kemp, John 7, 196–99
key to Cell Block G *68*
Kildy, Corporal Mick, autograph book made by *340*
Kranji War Cemetery 336
'Kremlin Club' 116

Lad, S. 7, 219–23
ladle constructed in Changi *187*
latex sandals
see shoe production and repair
latrine construction 38, 232–33, *234*
'Lavender Street' 69
leaf extract 228–29
lecture series 116–18
Lee, Ronald 191
leg amputees, parade of 158–59
Lennon, Sergeant John Leslie 325
literary competition flyer *19–20*
Little, Corporal John *88*
Looking Towards Home 338
Loxton, Helen 161

Mack, Val *145*
Maddern, (Norman) Peterson 'Peter' 7, 205–11
mail communications with Changi 51, *51*
malarial infections 268–71
Malay Peninsula 13, 72
Malayan residents of Singapore
fish poached by 328–29
trading by prisoners of war with 43, 99
maps
AIF area at Changi *22–23*
Changi prisoner-of-war camp *2*
Marmite, ersatz manufacture and use of 237–38
Marshall, Lieutenant Alexander Kenneth 314
massage room of hospital *240*
Mathers, Doug *144*
Matthews, Patrick
as contributor 7, 124–33
radios built by *128*, *129*
sentencing of 128
Matthews, Rodney 7, 268–71
Maxwell, Major 305
Mayberry, Warrant Officer 244
Maynard, Major R.B. 244
McCubbin, Louis 122
McGowan, Private John, cigarette box gift *183*
McIntyre, Vera 161
McKinley, Corporal 247
McMahon, Private John, identity disk 217
McPherson, Signalman William, cribbage board made for *194*
meat issues 255–57
medical conditions and treatment
see also dysentery attacks; hygiene and sanitation
cholera attacks 43, 61
deaths 268
diphtheria outbreaks 237, 246
during Barracks Square incident 86
health in Changi 225–79
in Changi Gaol 69
long-term effects of imprisonment 266–67
medical kit *241*
medical record *267*
pathological department 244–47
skin diseases 236–43
Meike, Eric, door sign *179*
Melrose, Private 223
memorial tablet *324*
microscope *241*
Middleton, Corporal William, identity tag *274*
military discipline
emphasis on 28, 48
Galleghan on 52
in Changi Gaol 69
milk of magnesia production 198
Miller, A.S.M. 190
Miller, P.G. 7, 194–95
Mitchell, Thomas 7–8, 248, 272–74, *273*
model parliament 117
model ship *114*
Moffett, Robert N. 8, 200–202
Montevideo Maru, prisoner-of-war casualties from 16
Moreau, Corporal Sam *267*
mortality rates among former prisoners of war 267
Morton, Robert 8, 226–31
mosquitoes, as malaria carriers 268–74
'Mount Gunther' 86
mugs made in Changi 213
Muira, Lieutenant 72
Mulvany, Ethel 161
musical instruments used in Changi 47, 154, *154–55*, 300
Mutton, Bob *165*

naval guns at Changi 34
Neale, Kerry 10, 224
Nevell, Sergeant John 27–28, 311–12
New Testament murals 336

349

Newey, Lieutenant Colonel 69
Newsom, Anthony 19
No. 2 Convalescent Depot
   see 2nd Convalescent Depot
Non-Escape Declaration,
   refusal to sign 58–59, 80–87

O'Connell, Garth 10, 78–79
officers
   see also military discipline
   accommodation for 164
   as prisoners of war 31–33
   commanding working parties 38
   higher ranking prisoners of war sent to Japan 51
   Non-Escape Declaration signed by 87
   paid more for work than Other Ranks 91, 92–93
   tending vegetable gardens 205
   trading banned by 102
Officers' Mess, library in 105
Okasaki, Lieutenant 38, 257
Old Ford Factory museum 79
One Man's War 18
Oraines, E.J. 8, 301–308
Ordnance Workshop, repair shop started in 189
Osborne, Lieutenant Colonel Charles 233
Outram Road Gaol 99

P Party 99
'Panzer Division' (leg amputees) 156–60
'pap' (cereal) 263
paper manufacture 198–99
parades, daily 24–25, 40–41, 48
Pathological Department 244–47
payment for work 51, 90–93
Peart, Doug 144
Peek, Jane 10, 154–55
pellagra-like conditions 239–40
Percival, Lieutenant General Arthur
   Griffin portrait of 120, *122*
   surrenders to Japan 15, 30, 78–79
petrol theft 287–88
piano for Concert Party 154–55, *155*
Piddington the magician 142
piggery 255, 257, 292

playing cards *312*
population of Changi 174, 289
postcard from Changi *51*
potash solution, manufacture of 196–97
potteries in Changi 212
poultry raising 252–55, *254*
POW WOW magazine 65
Praske, Private E.B. 331
prisoners of war
   see also Changi Gaol; Changi prisoner-of-war camp; food in Changi; medical conditions and treatment; working parties
   accommodation for *166*
   after German surrender 72–77
   books for 103–10
   captured at fall of Singapore 14–15
   Changi as staging camp for 50, 61
   eager to join working party 59–60
   economy of 102
   'exchange for wool' rumour 48–50
   experience on return home 27–28
   number of deaths of 174
   numbers of 16, 174
   politics among 115–19
   radios used by 124–33
Purdon, Warrant Officer Arthur H.M. 8, 219–24

radio broadcasts 54
radios, hidden in Changi 77, 124–33
razor manufacture and sale 100–101, *100–101*, *191*, 192
Records Office (2nd Echelon) 313–17, *314*
red amaranth 294
red ants 269
Red Cross
   armbands worn by non-medical officers 236
   boots issued by 203
   certificate holders paid more 92–93, 243
   Christmas supplies from 182
   food supplied by 250, 255
   IJA attitude to 51
   medical supplies from 238
   representatives of 161
Redfearn, Norah 161

refuse disposal 233
   see also hygiene and sanitation
religion in Changi 318–25
repair shop operations 189–95
Repatriation Commission
   survey of former prisoners of war 266–67
Repatriation of Allied Prisoners of War and Internees 266–67, 341
reserves of food 83, 250, 260
Reunion at Changi 12
Reveille magazine 78–79
rhizopus fungus 229–30
rice
   cakes made from 262
   issues of *251*, 255
   polishings from 229, 230
   shortage in supply of 250
   vitamins lost from 226
Richards, Captain 'Rowley' 241
Richards, Private A.A. 331
Rivett, Rohan 19
Roberts Barracks
   see Roberts Hospital
Roberts, Corporal 109
Roberts Hospital 37, 233
   cookhouse 262, 264, 265
   during Barracks Square incident 81
   dysentery patients 43–45
   goods purchased for 252
   housing for 36, 165
   murals in hospital chapel 336
   pathological department 246
   play staged at *143*
   sanitation problems 232
   tents surrounding 54–55
   washing lines 241–42
Robertson, Lucy 10, 64–65
Robinson piano 154–55, *155*
Roche, Frederick C. 8, 214–18
Rosson, Major John, photos taken by
   accommodation 54–55
   AIF Forestry Company 303
   cookhouse 264
   dental treatment 277
   surgical operation 233
   theatrical show *143*
   transporting supplies 37, *251*
Roxburgh, James 15
Royal Antediluvian Order of Buffaloes 118–19
Royal Australian Artillery Broom Factory 214–18

Royal Engineers
   buildings repaired by 107, 164–65, 168
   draw knives designed by 220
   huts moved by 177–80
   old welding workshop 186
Royal Norfolk Regiment badge *288*
rubber production 54, 200–202, *201*, 204
rubber trees, used as firewood 301–305
Russell, Tom 191

quilts
   see Australian Changi Quilt

Saito, Major General 63–65, 124, 142
saline production 247
Samsu fungus 231
Sandakan prisoner-of-war camp 16
sandal-making
   see shoe production and repair
sanitation
   see hygiene and sanitation
Sano, Corporal 282
scabies 239
Scoutmaster training 321
scrotal dermatitis 237–38
Searle, Ronald 110
seedling nursery 205–11, *209*
Selarang Barracks
   11th Indian Division moves to 165
   accommodation at 164, *167*
   aerial photograph *40–41*
   AIF camp sited at 35–37
   bomb damage to *56*
   demolished in 1986 336
   evening parades 24–25, *26*, 48
   gardens at 295
   medical laboratory 245, *246*
   photographs of 24–25
   view from *49*
   water tower at *39*
Selarang Barracks Square incident 80–87
   Griffin illustration *178*
   photos taken during *82–83*, *84*, *85*
   prisoners refuse to sign Non-Escape Declaration 59
Services Party 115
sewerage system 232–33

A NewSouth book
Published by
NewSouth Publishing
University of New South Wales Press Ltd
University of New South Wales
Sydney NSW 2052
AUSTRALIA
newsouthpublishing.com
First published 2015
10 9 8 7 6 5 4 3 2 1

This book is copyright. Apart from any fair dealing for the purpose of private study, research, criticism or review, as permitted under the Copyright Act 1968, no part may be reproduced by any process without written permission. Inquiries should be addressed to the publisher.

The Australian War Memorial asserts ownership of copyright of all material appearing in this publication, except for that held by the original authors or creators, as stated.

Every reasonable endeavour has been made to contact relevant copyright holders. Where this has not been possible, the copyright holders are invited to contact the publisher.

National Library of Australia
Cataloguing-in-Publication entry
Title: The Changi book/edited by Lachlan Grant.
ISBN: 9781742231617 (hardback)
9781742247373 (ebook: pdf)
Notes: Includes bibliographical references and index.
Subjects: Changi POW Camp (Changi, Singapore)
Prisoners of war—Singapore—Changi—Biography.
Prisoners of war—Australia—Biography.
World War, 1939-1945—Personal narratives, Australian.
World War, 1939-1945—Prisoners and prisons, Japanese.
Other Creators/Contributors: Grant, Lachlan, editor.

Dewey Number: 940.547252

DESIGN Di Quick

FRONT COVER *Reunion at Changi* by Harold Abbott, 1945, ART23949.

BACK COVER This cigarette box made from Japanese aircraft parts was a 1944 Christmas gift to Private John McGowan of the 2/9th Field Ambulance. REL/17494

PAGE 1 The slouch hat is one of the great icons of the Australian soldier. This hat belonged to Gunner John Wilkinson of the 18th Anti-Tank Battery, who passed through Changi en route to the Burma–Thailand Railway. The hat clearly demonstrates the wear and tear on the clothing of prisoners. The only item of its type in the collection, it is displayed in the Second World War Galleries. REL/12431

PRINTER Everbest

This book is printed on paper using fibre supplied from plantation or sustainably managed forests.